Gentlemen, Gypsies and Jesters

The Wonderful World
of Wandering Cricket

Gentlemen, Gypsies and Jesters

The Wonderful World
of Wandering Cricket

Anthony Gibson
& Stephen Chalke

foreword by John Barclay

FAIRFIELD BOOKS

Fairfield Books
17 George's Road, Bath BA1 6EY
tel 01225-335813

First published 2013

ISBN: 978 0 9568511 4 7

Printed and bound in Great Britain by
CPI Group (UK) Ltd, Croydon, CR0 4YY

About this book

This book is the brainchild of Simon Dyson, a driving force in the *Chance to Shine* project. Never before has there been a full-length book about the world of wandering cricket. Why, he asked, didn't we write one and use it to raise money for *Chance to Shine*? Two birds killed with one stone. He would find a few benefactors to pay the production costs, and that way all the funds from sales could go straight to the charity.

Generous donors were soon on board; our thanks to them are recorded on page 314. And Simon is such an infectiously enthusiastic fellow that he had little difficulty in persuading Anthony Gibson and me to take on the writing and editing and to see it all through to publication. The original idea was that we would profile a cross-section of 40 clubs in a book of something like 200 pages. But somehow the project has grown ... and grown – until we have finished up with 320 pages, featuring 77 full-length entries, a further 37 short ones and a section on the related world of old boys' cricket.

We decided to include not just the grand historical clubs, *I Zingari*, *Free Foresters and Incogniti*, and the county-based sides, *Gloucestershire Gipsies*, *Sussex Martlets* and *Yorkshire Gentlemen*, but also a few of the many sides which have sprung up in more recent times, such as Tim Rice's *Heartaches* and Marcus Berkmann's *Rain Men*. In geographical terms there is a bias towards the south of England, as this has always been the heartland of wandering cricket, but we have ensured that our selection has several clubs from the north as well as two from Wales and a round-up of wandering cricket in Scotland.

It is not a definitive encyclopaedia, it cannot be, and indeed the eagle-eyed will spot that the book contains two clubs who now have their own grounds – and four who have recently gone out of existence. Should we include Lord's Taverners and Old England? Yes, we decided. And MCC? With an annual fixture list of several hundred games, almost none of them at their home ground, it could be argued that they are the greatest wandering club of all, but in the end we thought they did not quite fit the mould.

If any club is disappointed not to have been included, we can only apologise. Our aim has been to feature all the grander, ancient clubs, as well as some of the more colourful and more interesting of the modern ones. But there has inevitably been an element of chance in the way in which some have made the final cut. Sometimes the sheer enthusiasm of the club to take part has made the difference.

The 77 included clubs have either submitted their own copy or told their stories to Anthony Gibson or me. I have written the shorter entries, and Steve Pittard, with help from Nick Syrett, has rounded up the old boy sides. So the book contains a range of approaches – historical, humorous, sometimes pessimistic, often celebratory – and that is part of its charm. There are, however, recurrent themes, and I have drawn these together in an introduction. As well as the cricket, the book provides a delightful slice of English social history, and with this in mind we have arranged the clubs in order of the date of their foundation.

It has been a fascinating book to put together. I hope it now gives great pleasure and raises a lot of money for *Chance to Shine* – so that future generations will gain as much joy from this game of ours as the many contributors to this book have experienced.

Stephen Chalke

Chance to Shine

The Cricket Foundation's Project
to bring competitive cricket to state schools

1959

Ronald Groves (Master of Dulwich College): "... and so Simon, what are you interested in?"

Simon Dyson (aged 11): "... oh, cricket and the *Goon Show*, sir."

This simple answer changed my life, and as a result I was moved from a 'school' for homeless children in Reedham, clutching my 11-plus certificate and a cricket bat, to a private school boarding house in the leafy suburbs of SE21. Thanks to the government's direct grant scheme I spent seven subsidised years at Dulwich College; and so through cricket (and Spike Milligan *et al*) I was given my personal chance to shine.

When I retired from corporate life and started to work in the charitable sector, I suppose it was no surprise that I sought out cricket as a place where I thought I could help other youngsters change their lives.

Chance to Shine (C2S) is simply the best venture in which I have ever been involved. As Mervyn King, who was a critical influence when the Cricket Foundation started the project, is often heard to say: "It is not what millions of youngsters can do for cricket, it is what cricket can do for young people." Quite simply, giving children in state schools an opportunity to play cricket provides rare, well-organised, extra-curricular activity which develops valuable attitudes and values, not to mention self-esteem. Everyone buying this book knows just how special cricket is as a game; the chance to learn team skills and come to terms with individual responsibility is the special gift of cricket.

Before C2S started in 2005, fewer than 10 per cent of state schools played any form of meaningful cricket. Seven years on, C2S is the single biggest school sports initiative in the UK. In that time over 1.8 million children have been 'educated through cricket' in almost 30 per cent (6,500) of our state schools. The programme is inclusive and crosses social, ethnic and gender divides. Nearly half of the children (46 per cent) are girls, and six of the England Women's cricket team are employed as coaching ambassadors.

£15 pays for a child to benefit from C2S for a year, and for every £1 donated the charity spends 85p to benefit children directly, and 15p to raise the next £1.

Thank you for buying this book, and for making a positive contribution to the lives of thousands of young people through cricket.

Simon Dyson
Trustee, Cricket Foundation

Details of how to donate to *Chance to Shine* can be found at the foot of page 314.

A message
from the Chairman of Lord's Taverners

"It'll never work!"

We're a nation of pessimists, and that's what 'they' said when the Cricket Foundation announced its bold 10-year plan in 2005 to raise £50m to get competitive cricket back into state schools through the *Chance to Shine* programme.

But it did work, and it continues to work, with nearly two million kids being introduced to the great game, more every day. So how were the gainsayers defeated and why does it work?

For a start, it's a simple, relevant idea. 'Getting cricket back into state schools' does what it says on the tin. The best ideas are always simple. Look how well 'Help for Heroes' has done. And it's true in business too. Nike built a global brand on 'Just do it' and Heineken became the leading lager because it refreshed the parts the other beers couldn't reach. And like all these examples *Chance to Shine* was a 'campaign' too, a banner behind which good people could march, good people from disparate backgrounds, such as Sir Mervyn King, Duncan Fearnley, Mark Nicholas, Sir Tim Rice, Simon Dyson, Wasim Khan, and lots of others who make it work.

Of course the nuts and bolts of the programme had to be in place. It had to be good value. It had to be scalable. It had to be sustainable. It ticked all those boxes. And that's why big-time supporters piled in like Allianz, Brit Insurance, the ECB, Sport England and the Lord's Taverners. Because it's good and it works.

But backing up all these superlatives is the game of cricket itself. Football might be the biggest team sport these days, but cricket's the best, because it's a team game and an individual sport too, because you can play it from childhood to old age, because everyone can play it: girls, boys, men, women, both able-bodied and those with a disability.

So, shine on *Chance to Shine*, and if you love the game of cricket like I do, you'll love the book too!

Tom Rodwell
Chairman, Lord's Taverners

Contents

Clubs featured

Website

www.nomadiccricket.com

A website of nomadic cricket has been set up. Its first purpose is to promote sales of this book, but the intention is to extend the site so that it includes a directory of wandering clubs, each of which will provide and keep up to date its history and current details. The directory will include all the clubs in this book plus many others.

It is hoped that the website will become a forum for the nomadic cricket community, putting clubs and their members into closer contact with each other. It will also explain the ethos of wandering cricket and encourage newcomers to play it.

In time the website may be expanded to make easier the organisation of games, helping match managers to contact and recruit players.

In short, it intends to play an active part in strengthening the world of wandering cricket, thus providing 'more cricket for more people'.

The website is looking to be interactive so any feedback will always be welcome. The e-mail address for this is: hezza174@me.com

Illustrations

The etching of 'The Great Match', on page 230, appears by courtesy of the artist Norman Ackroyd.

The painting of Chelsea Arts Club CC at Keevil Manor, on page 262, appears by courtesy of the artist Liz Wright, Chelsea Arts Club.

The watercolour of the Journeymen at Kew Green, on page 270, appears by courtesy of the artist Susanna Kendall.

The photograph of cricket on Tilford Green on the front jacket of the book is reproduced with the kind permission of Getty Images.

The photograph of Lords and Commons cricketers, on page 34, is reproduced with the kind permission of Graham Morris.

The cartoon of Douglas Jardine in a Harlequins cap, on page 39, is reproduced with the kind permission of Getty Images.

The photograph of the Gentlemen of Staffordshire, on page 115, is reproduced with the kind permission of Milford Hall Cricket Club.

Other photographs and art work, together with club colours and crests, have been supplied by the clubs themselves. We thank them for their co-operation, which in some cases involved much research.

Names in captions are always listed left to right.

Foreword

As a boy, I played for a team called the Southdown Rams. Amongst our many rivals was a team in Surrey known as the Wapshot Hippos. We wore a smart green cap with a yellow ram's head on the front, while the Hippos sported a blue cap with a pink hippopotamus on it, so far as I can remember. This was my first taste, and an early one, of the wonderful world of wandering cricket. Little did I know that a whole multitude of clubs had sprung up over the years with funny and fancy names that epitomise the eccentricity and humour of an extraordinary game. Flycatchers, Woodpeckers and Frogs; Penguins, Butterflies and Grannies. Mostly they've grown from a small seed, perhaps as a memorial to someone or possibly founded by an enthusiastic cricketer who just couldn't get a game elsewhere and so established his own club to make sure of playing regularly. Each club has its own special and unique story to tell and this book will thus come as a revelation to those who have always wanted to know from where, for instance, 'The Badgers' and many others emerged.

You will find that not only is this a book of great interest but one also of great charm and with a spring in its step. It paints pictures throughout its pages which illustrate the impact and valuable contribution made by wandering cricket clubs offering, in the process, an imaginative alternative to the competitive nature of some club cricket. To my thinking, the two sit side by side in complete harmony and both serve to enrich the game and its history in their different ways.

Not only will this book give enormous pleasure to a great many cricketing people but it will also be looking to the future by providing opportunities for the young, through the *Chance to Shine* project, to experience a game much loved and admired by the clubs described in this book.

John Barclay

The early years of wandering cricket

from *A Few Short Runs* (1921) by Lord Harris

I had the good fortune to play with, or to know intimately, most of the founders of IZ, and a merrier crew it is impossible to conceive. Very good cricketers many of them, and keen to win, but so merry with it that they were indeed welcome at all the great cricketing country-houses, and on all the regimental grounds where a decent team could be mustered. I don't know that there is quite as much jollity about cricket nowadays – we are all so terribly in earnest – as I remember in the IZ and BB of my youth.

EW Swanton on wandering clubs

from *Barclay's World of Cricket* (1986)

The wide and diverse array of wandering clubs is an army that no man can number, for they neither acknowledge nor need any formal affiliation either to any other body or to one another. In each case the genesis is the same; a few kindred spirits meet and decide that they would like to band together to play cricket. From a common beginning the resultant clubs have taken widely different forms. Some have become large and prestigious, others purposely restricted to a limited company of friends. Some such clubs, once the playing days of the originators come to an end, quietly fade away. All in some degree are selective, the ambition being to form a happy, homogenous whole.

Aims and playing rules of The Journeymen Cricket Club

(not always observed – but they do try)

The aims of the club shall be:
  (a) to play good cricket with a good humour and a good grace in the hope that, whatever the result, both teams will go home happy;
  (b) to create an atmosphere in which players are valued for themselves and not just for their cricketing abilities;
  (c) to make every effort to secure a satisfactory level of involvement in the game for all those representing the club.

All members are expected to observe the following playing rules:
  (a) Batsmen, who know that they are out, will walk;
  (b) Bowlers and fielders will not appeal if they know the batsman not to be out;
  (c) Appeals will be lodged without intimidation or aggression;
  (d) There will be no questioning of umpiring decisions.

The memories of a Somerset Straggler

Patrick Lennard-Payne

Now, as an old man, I think of the long drives back from Instow or Sidmouth. The scents at midsummer. The Exe at Bridgetown and the supper after a match in which a knowing captain would always post his mid-off at the top of the slope to catch an attempted six. The long pole with the net attached to fish the ball from the clutches of the river.

Yes, those were days to be savoured. The ex-colonial officers from Africa or India returning to play during their leave. Lindsay Hassett making a speech in the Castle Hotel and one of that team asking to be made a member of the Stragglers. It was a wonderful period of long summers and warm evenings.

One who did not experience it cannot understand.

Setting out for a cricket match in Kent

from England, their England *by AG Macdonell (1933)*

At five minutes to 11 there was a respectable muster, six of the team having assembled. But at five minutes past, a disintegrating element was introduced by the arrival of Mr Harcourt with the news, which he announced with the air of a shipwrecked mariner who has, after twenty-five years of vigilance, seen a sail, that in the neighbourhood of Charing Cross the pubs opened at 11am. So that when Mr Hodge himself turned up at twenty-five minutes past 11, resplendent in a blazer of purple-and-yellow stripes, each stripe being at least two inches across, he was justly indignant at the slackness of the team.

'They've no sense of time,' he told Donald repeatedly. 'We're late as it is. The match is due to begin at half-past 11, and it's fifty miles from here. I should have been here myself two hours ago but I had my Sunday article to do. It really is too bad.'

When the team, now numbering nine men, had been extricated from the tavern and had been marshalled on the pavement, counted, recounted and the missing pair identified, it was pointed out by the casual youth, who had returned shining and pomaded from the barber, that the char-à-banc had not yet arrived.

Mr Hodge's indignation became positively alarming and he covered the twenty yards to the public telephone box almost as quickly as Mr Harcourt covered the forty yards back to the door of the pub.

. . . .

At 12.30 it was decided not to wait for the missing pair, and the nine cricketers started off. At 2.30, after halts at Catford, the White Hart at Sevenoaks, the Angel at Tunbridge Wells, and three smaller inns at tiny villages, the char-à-banc drew up triumphantly beside the cricket ground of the Kentish village of Fordenden.

Introduction

by Stephen Chalke

Gentlemen, gypsies and jesters: these are the three threads that run through this book. First, there are the gentlemen, the clubs created exclusively for people of a certain social standing, often in their early days playing their cricket on the estates of country houses. Then there are the gypsies, taking to the road with a spirit of adventure: wanderers, nomads, romany, zingari. Their bonds are not those of geography but of kinship – bands of brothers. And finally there are the jesters, representing the spirit of fun that pervades it all – with that added hint of theatre, which has been such a strong strand of wandering cricket throughout its history.

These three threads – social class, travelling and fun – get stirred together in this book in a quintessentially English way. Why else in a book on wandering cricket would you include an entry on the Hampshire Hogs who for almost fifty years have been in possession of a home ground at Warnford? The explanation, we are told, is that they have 'the ethos of a wandering club'. The Armadillos, who play all their fixtures at Sheffield Park in Sussex, have a website that makes exactly the same claim: 'Welcome to the Armadillos CC, a wandering club with a home ... a club whose ethos is firmly steeped in the traditions of wandering cricket.'

So, we find ourselves asking, if it is not necessary for a wandering club to wander, what on earth does it all mean?

We go back to the founding of I Zingari in 1845, to those early Victorian days of rough pitches and round-arm bowling, when the ancient public schools were beginning to realise the character-building virtues of team games and when for the first time young men were wanting to take their enjoyment of those games into their adult lives. A team of young gentlemen – Cambridge graduates – played a match at Harrow School, and in the after-glow of the day, over a sumptuous evening meal, they resolved to become a club with a fixture list, rules and colours – but no home ground. It was all set up in a spirit of fun, as befitted a group of men who also enjoyed amateur dramatics. Most significantly, however, they decided that on all occasions they would field a wholly amateur eleven, breaking with the common practice of hiring professionals to do their bowling. Some contemporaries thought the idea absurd – "You'll never win a match" – but, of course, they did, becoming one of the foremost teams in the land and establishing the template for many wandering clubs that followed.

In the late 1870s the Old Harrovian Arthur Haygarth compiled a list of 90 such gentlemen's teams, which we have reproduced on page 303, and it is clear that, following on from I Zingari, there was a great flowering of the idea of wandering cricket. Some of these teams survive to this day – Free Foresters, Quidnuncs, Harlequins, Incogniti, Butterflies – but most of them were ephemeral creations, about which we know little but the names: Desperadoes, Will-o'-the-Wisps, I Lazironi, Anythingarians, Unmitigated Duffers. They were groups of like-minded friends wanting to enjoy the fun of cricket, just like the modern clubs towards the end of this book: the Grannies, Weekenders, Heartaches, Boxbusters and Spasmodics.

Being of the right social class was undoubtedly an essential qualification for membership of most of these clubs. School, university, military service, these were the bonds that drew cricketers together, and a spirit of exclusiveness added to the special flavour of it all. It was said of Lord Harris, one of the supreme powers of late Victorian cricket, that he once chaired a Band of Brothers meeting at which a new member was proposed with a glowing recommendation. "Has anybody anything less favourable to say about him?" he asked, and the answer came: "Well, he is rather a snob." "That's settled then," Lord Harris responded. "He's in." As late as 1956 John Pretlove, fresh from Alleyn's School and Cambridge University and playing cricket for Kent as an amateur, was invited to apply for membership of the Band of Brothers, only to find out some time later that he had been rejected. "I'm sorry, John," he was told with some embarrassment, "but your father's in trade."

The world of country-house cricket had its heyday in the Edwardian Age, and that is reflected in the profusion of wandering clubs – eleven in this book – created between 1900 and 1910. That way of life, with its long summers of leisure, was never the same after the nightmare of the Great War, but it did survive in a reduced state in the '20s and '30s. Indeed, in 1923 the Gloucestershire Gipsies were formed with the condition that members of the club should be the sort of people who would be 'acceptable guests in the average country house'. Very little was left of that world after the ravages of the Second World War and the introduction of increased death duties by the post-war Labour Government.

Yet it is still part of the ethos of wandering clubs that they look to play their cricket in the best of settings – and are prepared to travel far to do so. From Paul Getty's Wormsley to the Duke of Norfolk's Arundel, from Lord Vestey's Stowell Park to the Earl of Carnarvon's Highclere Castle, there are grounds that preserve a little of that lost world of country-house cricket. Additionally, Oxford and Cambridge colleges will hire out their well-maintained grounds, especially in the long summer vacation. Then there is Devon where so many of these teams have traditionally toured each summer: the seaside Sidmouth club, alongside the tall Regency buildings; North Devon, with its thatched pavilion, on the estuary of the rivers Taw and Torridge; and the dramatic Valley of the Rocks ground at Lynton and Lynmouth. In August there are so many wandering club fixtures that some of these host clubs are taking the field every day of the week.

In recent years the wandering has become global, with clubs on the continent of Europe regularly entertaining nomadic visitors. It is a curious irony of modern life that, while cricketers find it harder to get away from work and family commitments to play as often as once they did, they are able to undertake longer and more adventurous tours. In the case of the Captain Scott XI they have created something of an extreme sport out of touring: playing cricket on all seven continents in a madcap venture immortalised in *Penguins Stopped Play*.

The life of a wandering cricketer is a lovely one if you don't mind the travelling. There is never a tea to prepare, a pitch to roll, a broken roof tile to mend, a plague of moles to defeat. But it is not all one-way: the hosts giving and the visitors taking. There is something about a wandering side that can be attractive to the club which entertains it – a spirit of fun, that is evidenced not only in the plentiful bar takings in the evening but also in the atmosphere on the field of play. It is a different cricket – a very different cricket – from that played on Saturdays in the league. Therein lies something of the nub of this book.

Our world has changed much since the days of Lord Harris. An Old Etonian, born in 1851, he took into cricket the values of his High Victorian upbringing: a stern belief in the established social order and a missionary desire to spread the virtues of his culture. 'Cricket,' he wrote to *The Times* at the age of 80. 'It is freer from anything sordid, anything dishonest, than any other game in the world. To play it keenly, generously, honestly, is a moral lesson in itself, and the classroom is God's air and sunshine. Foster it, my brothers, protect it from anything that will sully it, so that it will be in favour with all men.'

In his autobiography of 1921 he wrote of the role that wandering clubs played in this:

> It is by means of these great amateur clubs that the high standard of cricket is maintained, and enjoined on those whom they meet in the field. They are most valuable educationalists; they preserve tradition – that indefinable influence which counts for so much in the preservation of honoured and valued institutions; and therefore they deserve all support, both physical and financial.

But what is this 'high standard of cricket'? Was he writing of the quality of the batsmanship, or of the manner in which the game was played, or both? In the early part of the twentieth century there existed a class of men who had both the time and the financial means to play their cricket as amateurs, and some of them – Fry, Ranjitsinhji, Jessop – were the best and most entertaining cricketers in the land. To be called an amateur in the 21st century is no great compliment; it implies that one is an unqualified enthusiast, a dabbler who, by implication, is not good enough to earn money from the activity – and money is the measure of everything. Yet in those days an amateur stood high above a professional; he was a freer spirit with a wider vision of life. And he was a gentleman. It fell to him not just to score runs and take wickets but to look after the game and the spirit in which it was played.

There is a story of Charlie Parker, Gloucestershire's curmudgeonly slow left-armer, bowling to Ranjitsinhji and being repeatedly leg-glanced. In frustration he turned to his captain, an amateur: "Excuse me, sir, do you think we could move second slip across to stop that?" The captain stared witheringly at him: "Good God, man, are you trying to spoil the game?" Something of the same exchange took place in a wartime charity match in India when Dickie Dodds, a young army officer, later to open the batting for Essex, was bowling leg-breaks to the Indian batsman Mushtaq Ali. Two balls in a row were despatched to the same unmanned boundary, and Dodds asked his captain, the great Douglas Jardine, for a field change. "No," came the brisk reply, and another four followed. When finally a wicket fell, Jardine marched across to him. "Dodds," he barked. "Now listen to me. You and I are amateurs. It's only professionals who ask to have their field shifted when they're hit for four."

We laugh now at the quaintness and the absurdity of it. By the 1950s few of the amateurs in first-class cricket were properly amateur any more, either in their financial arrangements or in the way they approached the playing of the game. The amateur status had become an anachronism, and in 1963 first-class cricket became a wholly professional game. At the Labour Party Conference that year, Harold Wilson described Britain as 'a nation of gentlemen in a world of players', promising a new order – based not on the advantages of birth but on professional qualifications – to reverse our post-war decline. With a radically different agenda Margaret Thatcher had something of the same objective, promoting the self-made men of business rather than the old-style gentlemen.

Wandering cricket has always been at its strongest in the south of England, where until the late 1960s, unlike in the midlands and the north, there was no league cricket. In fact, the second object of the Club Cricket Conference, to which all the established clubs in the south-east belonged, was 'to foster amateur cricket on non-competitive lines', making it a condition of membership that, with very limited exceptions, 'no club shall be connected with any organised cricket league or other competition.' In such an environment the ethos of wandering cricket clubs was not difficult to sustain.

The years of post-war deprivation were over by the 1960s, and there were great changes taking place in our way of life. Many were the other attractions pulling people away from cricket; no longer was the leisureliness of the club game in accord with the prevailing zeitgeist. By 1966 the modernisers, spearheaded by Raman Subba Row in Surrey, were looking to bring fresh urgency and an extra edge of competitiveness to club cricket and, as a result, in 1968 a new Surrey Championship was established. It did not take long for league cricket to sweep its way across the south of England; then in the 1990s, as a result of Lord MacLaurin's *Raising the Standard* report, there was a further set of changes, increasing the competitiveness by streamlining the leagues into regional pyramids. Club cricket had to play its part in creating a successful national team.

Within a lifetime cricket, like much of the British economy, has been transformed – and the popular view is that both are stronger for the changes, better able to meet the demands of international competition.

And yet ... and yet ... Cricket below the first-class level is about so much more than fast-tracking the most talented, about more than creating the England teams of the future. It is also about friendship and fun, fresh air and fulfilment – all those invisible things you cannot find in the averages at the end of the season: the enjoyments that transcend the winning and the losing; the spirit of the game – once so ingrained in every cricketer, yet now needing to be set down in words in a preamble to the laws.

There are many wandering clubs in this book, and each has its own story. Some are on their last legs, struggling for players and fearful for their futures; others, finding ways to renew themselves, are in rude health. Some have great histories which they celebrate with pride; others are recent creations, their founders still taking the field. There are those whose cricket is not far short of first-class standard and those whose natural level is the village green. Yet what is common to their stories, as told in these pages, is a warmth of feeling.

It is a different cricket from that which is played in the leagues and, for many of those who play it, it is a more enjoyable cricket. Friendships and camaraderie are pivotal to it all, and that extends to a greater fellow-feeling between the two sides. They are not only playing cricket against but with each other.

It is a theme which recurs throughout this book. The Incogniti's aim is to play 'good cricket with a smile on our face'. The Wiltshire Queries' aim is that 'those who play against us should want to do so again the following season'. The Glamorgan Nomads speak of the 'joy of skills without arrogance, competition without rancour, partisanship without hostility'. The Arabs 'came into being to enjoy ourselves. If we succeeded in that, our opponents would naturally become our friends.' The Band of Brothers value 'friendship more than technical excellence', and Tim Rice writes that his Heartaches cricket has brought him more enduring friendships than his glittering career in the world of entertainment. 'There is nothing in my other life,' he says, 'with which I feel more satisfaction than that which I get from being part of a wandering cricket team.'

Tim Rice is a good example of a character who recurs repeatedly in this book: the cricketer of no great distinction who sets up his own team and plays happily for years alongside men of far greater ability. In some cases they have started the team because they cannot get a game at their local club – or, if they are picked, find themselves fielding at fine leg at both ends and batting at number eleven. This is not the way of wandering cricket where those with little cricketing skill can, if they bring character, be a rich part of the mix. In the words of one club founder in this book, a man who has organised more than 700 games and only ever hit one fifty, "I really have had the best career of any talentless cricketer."

Predominantly league cricket is over-limit cricket while wandering cricketers prefer to play a time game. In theory over-limit cricket should be more positive because there is no option for the team batting second to play out the draw. But in practice it frequently does not work out like that. An unadventurous conservatism creeps into the over-limit game, with the fielding-team captain rotating his bowlers to a formula, focusing more on the prevention of runs than on the taking of wickets. The time game has a subtler plot, a greater role for inspired captaincy, with victory easier to achieve when the contest is kept open. It is a type of cricket hard for the uninitiated to grasp, and increasingly – in whole swathes of club cricket – it is non-existent. Only in the world of wandering cricket does it still hold sway.

The geographically based clubs are a vital part of our national life. They maintain and reinvigorate their local communities, and through the top leagues they provide pathways into the higher levels of the game. The extra edge of competitiveness, which league cricket has brought, is in harmony with the culture of our times.

Perhaps wandering cricket is now no more than an anachronistic sideshow to the main event. The old-style country houses are few, and the days of leisure – when a man could slip away from work during the week or leave his wife and children on both days of the weekend – are gone. Gone, too, are the long evenings in the clubhouse when the two teams could drink round after round and, at the end of it all, drive happily home.

Yet, as this book shows, wandering cricket is not dead. Far from it. Some of the ancient clubs are struggling for survival, but others go from strength to strength – and, as the latter part of the book reveals, there are newer clubs emerging all the time, creating their own traditions. Some, like the Anythingarians and the Unmitigated Duffers, will die within a generation. Others may feature in another book such as this a hundred years from now, their founding fathers celebrated with the same respect that Free Foresters show William Bedford and I Zingari John Loraine Baldwin.

Nothing stays the same for long, certainly not this strange game of cricket which we all love. In the last forty years, at its highest level, it has become a harder game, the old etiquettes giving way to a professionalism that embraces practices that would once have been considered underhand, ungentlemanly, 'not cricket'. There is much money at stake, and the modern press thrives on the moments of controversy.

The former England wicket-keeper Keith Andrew, who in later life was Chief Executive of the National Cricket Association, looking after the 'recreational game', was a passionate believer that cricket needed to protect its soul:

> I wish we could put a greater warmth back into it. Being successful is one thing, but we want to enjoy our lives as well – and part of that enjoyment is friendship between sportsmen. If people are cheating, they don't respect one another, and the feeling for the game disappears. You don't go home at night feeling half so well.
>
> Cricket is a game. You play to win. You play to be top of the pile. But that's not *why* you play cricket.

Is this just old-fashioned tosh, of little relevance in the modern world? Or are there values in here that we would all be the better for re-asserting? Nobody wants to return to a world in which a cricket club could refuse a man membership because his father was in trade – or, worse, in the case of the great Frank Worrell, because he was black. But reading the entries in this book, feeling the warmth of it all and the sense of fun, it is clear that wandering cricket at its best has a vital role to play in preserving much of what is so special, what we all so love, about cricket.

Gentlemen, gypsies and jesters. The three strands are curiously entwined. The gentlemen – at their worst riddled with hypocrisy and snobbery, at their best upholding with great idealism the spirit of the game. The gypsies – living parasitically on the efforts of their hosts, yet bringing with them life and colour as the best of guests always do. The jesters – not so much striving to be the best but remembering always that sport for most of us is for fun, for recreation, for re-creation, the renewal of the human spirit.

As John Barclay so wisely says in his foreword, league cricket and wandering cricket can sit side by side in harmony. Each has its virtues, and our game will be the richer for the continued existence of both of them. For that to happen, though, it is necessary that the world of wandering cricket – the gentlemen, gypsies and jesters – has confidence in itself and finds its means of renewal.

It falls to each generation to look after what it has inherited, to refresh and renew it and to pass it on. If this book, by celebrating the many clubs herein, helps in that process, it will have done a service to cricket. It will have done an even greater service if, in raising money for *Chance to Shine*, it brings the youngsters in our schools to a love of the game.

I Zingari

Founded: 1845

by Anthony Gibson

I Zingari may not be quite the oldest wandering cricket club nor, because of the size of its fixture list, quite the most exclusive, but it is unquestionably the most historic, the most famous and the most influential: the club whose existence almost defines the concept. The founding fathers of IZ liked to claim, not least when they celebrated their first 50 years, that they had succeeded in their mission of taking cricket to the masses. That was, at the very least, an exaggeration, given that IZ played most of its matches in the parks of country houses, but it did come to stand for an entire cricketing genre, its example serving to inspire the creation of a host of other wandering clubs, and on that account at the very least it can justly claim to have changed the face of English cricket.

The circumstances surrounding the formation of IZ have passed into cricketing folklore. On 4 July 1845 John Loraine Baldwin drove a party of cricketers to Harrow in his horse-drawn omnibus to play the school. Several of the team had been at Cambridge together, and they shared a love of amateur dramatics as well as of amateur cricket. That evening Baldwin invited three of his fellow cricketers, Frederic and Spencer Ponsonby and RP Long, to join him for dinner at the Blenheim Hotel. After a good meal, and refreshed with plenty of excellent claret, the four of them agreed that what had made the day's cricket especially enjoyable was that it had been contested by two entirely amateur sides. There had been no professionals – 'given men', as they were known – to do the bowling and lower the tone. Why should this not always be the case, they wondered? Why not, indeed, form a club that would have no ground of its own, and which would play purely amateur cricket, bowling and all?

By this stage the evening was well advanced, and RP Long, who seems to have had a particular weakness for good claret, was slumped, barely conscious in his chair. "So what shall we call ourselves?" one of the company asked. Long stirred himself. "The Zingari, of course," he slurred, before relapsing into his slumbers.

So, I Zingari – Italian for The Gypsies or, at least, something very like it – it was and, having fixed on a name for their new club, the surviving diners got on with writing its rules, which are a famous mixture of the serious, the facetious and the just plain daft. But they certainly wasted no time, and by the end of the following day letters had been sent to William Bolland, to advise him of his Perpetual Presidency, and to 20 other of their cricketing friends to inform them of their election as members of the new club.

Exactly when the famous IZ colours were chosen isn't entirely clear, but they were certainly being worn by the middle of the 1846 season, and that they did have some gypsy provenance and that the black, red and gold did indeed signify 'out of darkness, through fire, into the light' is beyond question. A particularly fine display of the colours is always to be found at Canterbury Week, worn not only by IZ members but by the Old Stagers, a theatrical group formed by Bolland and co at Cambridge, and which supplied no fewer

The Founders
Sir Spencer Ponsonby Fane, JL Baldwin and Lord Bessborough

than 13 of the original Zingari. These days the Old Stagers are hosted by the Band of Brothers, but the black, red and gold stripes still fly proudly from the flagpole, and a volunteer can always be found – if sometimes with some difficulty – to give a rousing rendition of the IZ song at the conclusion of events.

That we know so much about the early years of IZ is thanks mainly to JL Baldwin, Annual Vice-President in Perpetuity, who effectively succeeded Bolland as IZ's top man when the latter died in 1863 (although not as Perpetual President, a position that Bolland will hold for all eternity, just as Baldwin will forever be Annual Vice-President). It was Baldwin, one suspects, who was responsible for IZ's motto – 'keep your promise – keep your temper – keep your wicket up' – and it was certainly he who kept the IZ scrapbooks which provide such a fascinating insight, not only into the doings of the club but into Victorian social history. His is the central figure, in the bath chair, in the famous painting which hangs in the Pavilion at Lord's, with the two Ponsonby brothers standing behind. He looks a rather supercilious cove, decked out in his IZ finery, but he loved the club with a passion, and it was he as much as anyone who made sure that IZ wasn't just a bunch of cricketing toffs with a liking for claret, theatricals and high jinks, but a cricketing force to be reckoned with.

In that first season of 1845, IZ played just two fixtures, against Newport Pagnell and against the Gentlemen of Suffolk at Campsey Ash. But they soon built up an impressive fixture list, taking in Dublin by 1851 and Scotland by 1852, and – in defiance of the Jeremiahs who suggested that, without professional bowlers, they would lose every game – winning plenty of them. It wasn't always easy to raise a side, of course, even in those more spacious days, and 'emergencies' had frequently to be pressed into service. Some early IZ members also seem to have had a tendency either to bunk off early from their matches – 'preferring their dinner to their duty' was the accusation – or not to turn up at all. For the match versus New Forest Rangers in 1876, only five Zingari appeared, and two of those turned out to be suffering from sprained ankles!

IZ's opponents were a mixture of the great public schools, the stronger club sides, the various county Gentlemen teams, invitational sides and the military. The standard of the cricket seems to have varied widely, but at its best it was very good indeed. IZ played their first first-class match against a Gentlemen of the South side featuring both WG and EM Grace in 1866, and from 1877 to 1890 the club played every year bar one in the Scarborough Festival, holding their own against a succession of strong Yorkshire sides, despite their lack of professional bowlers. They played the Australians twice (with the Demon Spofforth in the opposition ranks both times), in 1882 and 1884, and their, to date, final first-class game, celebrating the 80th birthday of Sir Spencer Ponsonby Fane (as he had now become), was a game at Lord's against the Gentlemen in 1904. Even in the absence of IZ regulars like FS Jackson, AC MacLaren and the Foster brothers, IZ won comfortably, Captain Teddy Wynyard scoring 147 in IZ's second innings and BJT Bosanquet, the inventor of the googly, taking 11 wickets.

Whilst IZ's avowed mission was to spread the gospel of cricket to every corner of the land, and whilst they did indeed take it to such outposts as Ireland, Scotland and Wales, they were unquestionably a patrician bunch, whose natural habitat was the park of a stately home. In 1866, when they went to play the Gentlemen of Norfolk at Sandringham, they contrived to recruit the future Edward VII to their ranks and, despite making a duck on debut, he remained a loyal IZ member and supporter for the rest of his life.

The First World War was, inevitably, something of a watershed in IZ history. It brought to an end the Golden Age of cricket, and of country-house cricket especially, and there were many who wondered whether the game in general, or IZ in particular, could ever be quite the same again. Recovery after the war was slow and the '20s was a difficult decade for the club. Too many of the match managers were long past their prime, and the players they enlisted tended to be of a similar vintage. As RL Arrowsmith wrote, in his history of the club, 'IZ became a by-word for producing sides of elderly non-benders who might draw a match but were unlikely to win it, and who were not much fun to play with, or against.'

IZ v Gentlemen of Norfolk, Sandringham, July 1866
standing: Hon T de Grey, HA Arkwright, Hon E Stanhope, CF Buller, Lord Skelmersdale,
Capt GH Grey   sitting: Lady Morton, HRH Edward Prince of Wales,
Lord Suffield, W Hart Dyke, HRH Alexandra Princess of Wales

There was some recovery in the standard of cricket in the '30s, as younger match managers were appointed, but, nonetheless, by the time Sir William Becher was asked by Ronnie Aird to take on the Secretaryship in 1951, the club was, in the words of one of Becher's successors, Richard Compton, 'tired and in vital need of rejuvenation'. Becher gave the club the boost it needed. He may have been autocratic in his methods, operating from his club, White's in Pall Mall, as a not always very benevolent dictator, but over more than 40 years, by insisting on the recruitment of good, younger cricketers, and on the highest standards of behaviour, he transformed the club from being almost a cricketing laughing stock, into once again one of the best club sides in the country.

Becher personified IZ: old-fashioned, slightly pompous, but utterly devoted to the game. As my father, Alan Gibson, wrote when he reviewed Arrowsmith and Hill's excellent *History of I Zingari* for *The Times* when it was first published in 1982: 'Since 1845 it has serenely gone on its various ways, its collective nose firmly stuck in the air. It is very Victorian, very aristocratic (the team lists over the years sparkle with peers, baronets and double-barrelled names), very amateur ... It is also very endearing, like great-grandmother's sampler.'

Whether this is quite so true as it once was may, however, be open to doubt. The club's current figurehead – 'Governor, 6th Wicket Down', as he is known in deference to Bolland's Perpetual Presidency – is Dennis Silk, a man of broad cricketing horizons with not a snobbish bone in his body. When Col Malcolm Havergill and Richard Compton between them took up the reins from Billy Becher they modernised the club and broadened the membership base. And the present Secretary – or 'A Secret' as his office is known in

*Ronnie Aird (MCC Secretary 1952-62), Lord Home
and Lavinia, Duchess of Norfolk*

*HMC Havergal, JCS Hardy, Lord Vestey,
DRW Silk – Governor 6th Wicket Down*

the IZ constitution – Harry Steel, is convincing when he says that the old snootiness is dying away and that what is coming to distinguish the club these days is the quality of the new players it can attract, even if potential recruits are still referred to as Si Benes (short for si benegesserit, which roughly translates as 'to see if they behave well') and are still, almost to a man, the product of the grander public schools. Fewer first-class cricketers are members than in the past, but a strong IZ side will usually feature a fair smattering of Oxbridge Blues and the standard is never lower than school/university first XI and often closer to minor county. Today's IZ win more than they lose, against strong and varied opposition, and draws are still a rarity, always provided the weather doesn't intervene.

Harry Steel

Interestingly, where there are distinct echoes of the club's Victorian roots is in the recent revival of country-house fixtures, against invitational sides at grounds like Sir Paul Getty's Wormsley, Arundel Castle and Norwood Park. And the club is once more making a conscious effort to fulfil something close to its original mission by taking what they call 'proper cricket' – no limited-over nonsense – to all corners of the land. Tours have made a come-back, too, whether full-on cricketing tours, to places like South Africa and India, or more relaxed 'half-play tours', taking in a spot of culture and sight-seeing along the way.

Of the old IZ rules, two are still as strictly observed as they ever were – that candidates for membership may not put themselves forward nor, if nominated, know the identities of their proposer and seconder; and, if an IZ is unable to play, that he should find his own replacement. The rule which laid down that if a Zingaro ever played against IZ for another side he should be expelled was dropped in 1970 and, whilst 'the rub' – 'of heads, hats, caps etc when a ball accidentally passes near a wicket' – remains officially proscribed, the custom is not always strictly observed. There is a fascinating collection of IZ memorabilia in the Cricket Museum at the County Ground, Taunton, much of it donated by Charles Clive-Ponsonby-Fane, Sir Spencer Ponsonby's great-grandson.

It would be silly to pretend that IZ isn't still a very grand cricket club, with the strongest possible links to the cricketing establishment at Lord's. To be elected an IZ remains one of the highest social honours that the game can offer. But is that necessarily a bad thing? I Zingari, and the many clubs which they have helped to inspire, not only bring colour to the scene, they also stand for and maintain some of cricket's most precious standards and traditions. Harry Steel summarises their mission as being "to play cricket around the British Isles in the right spirit and in the right way". It is an aspiration which IZ's founders shared, and which many of us would argue is every bit as valid today as it was when the club was founded, all those years ago.

Gentlemen of Worcestershire

Founded: 1848

by Phil Mackie

The origins of the Gentlemen of Worcestershire are intertwined with the formation of the county cricket club. The earliest surviving record dates back to 1848 at around the same time that the first efforts to form a county side were being made. Many of the same names appear in the Worcestershire side that played Shropshire in 1844 and the County XXII which lost to an All England XI two years later.

The Gents maintain a close relationship with Worcestershire, and many former first-class players have turned out for the club over the years. Matthew Rawnsley and Duncan Catterall are the current match managers who have worn both green caps in the past. The great Worcestershire cricketing families of the 19th and 20th centuries, among them the Lyttletons, Berkeleys, Foleys and Fosters, have featured in Gentlemen of Worcestershire teams.

In the early days the Gentlemen of Worcestershire undertook tours overseas, especially in Europe. The club was among the first to play in the Netherlands, Germany and Denmark. Its last 'international' fixture was played against the touring Fijians in 1982. The tour to Nazi Germany in 1937 had its share of controversy and incident, in part due to the atmosphere in Germany at that time. The Germans' approach on the field was also rather aggressive, though often directed at their own side. One famous tale, told by those who went on the tour, involves a young German fielder dropping a 'dolly' in the outfield, at which point the German captain strode over and punched him in the face. The story of the tour is the subject of a book, written by Dan Waddell, to be published in 2014.

The club still maintains fixtures against other great wandering sides like the Gloucestershire Gipsies, Cryptics, Free Foresters and the Warwickshire Imps. It plays an annual game against Cross Arrows on the Nursery Ground at Lord's and has recently renewed its annual fixture against the county, though nowadays this is played at New Road against the Worcestershire Academy XI. The Gents also play regular fixtures against the local public schools, Malvern, Bromsgrove and Kings Worcester. Although there hasn't been a game against Worcester Royal Grammar School for several years, many Old Elizabethans continue to turn out for the club. The link with Malvern College is particularly strong thanks to the work of GH Chesterton, who sadly passed away in 2012. He played first-class cricket for Worcestershire, taught at the college and was a stalwart of the club after the war.

Today, although many old boys from the local public schools still play, the sides are equally made up of players from clubs which feature in either the Birmingham or Worcestershire leagues. 'Home' fixtures are played at Ombersley, King's School Worcester, Malvern College, and Belbroughton CC.

Website: *www.gentlemenofworcs.play-cricket.com*

Gentlemen of Worcestershire at Amstelveen in Holland, August 1895

Gentlemen of Worcestershire versus the Warwickshire Imps, Harborne, July 2011
back: Mrs C Mills (scorer), T Mills, D Naughton, J Inglis, J Rose, O Moseley, H Patel
front: D Haggar, H Dimond, P Mackie (captain), D Collins, S Harris

Gentlemen of Cheshire

Founded: circa 1850 (though playing from 1805)

by Richard Grubb

The Gentlemen of Cheshire CC's very first game was against the Gentlemen of Shropshire in 1805. From that day to this, it has been and remains a true gentlemen's wandering cricket club.

That first game seems to have been a bit of a one-off, but from the 1820s the club played regular matches. From 1890 onwards, we were very fortunate to be able to play at Eaton Hall, the home of our Patron, the Duke of Westminster. The Dixon family from Chelford were our other main patrons, and we played regularly at the Chelford ground until it was commandeered in the Second World War for a munitions dump. From 1970 until the mid-1980s, we were back at Eaton Hall, but since then we have been made welcome at many of Cheshire's loveliest grounds by the clubs from which we draw our members. What we have always sought to offer is a high class of cricket, played in pleasant surroundings with a gentleman's attitude to the game: in essence, good cricket, good companionship and excellent hospitality.

Over the last 200 years, our fixture list has changed surprisingly little. We play our fellow county Gentlemen's sides from Shropshire, Staffordshire, Yorkshire and Worcestershire, as well as clubs as distinguished as the Free Foresters, Cryptics, Harrow Wanderers, Northern Nomads, Eton Ramblers and, from a slightly more recent era, AJ McAlpine's XI. This last fixture has been one of the highlights of our season for many years, played in the McAlpine's Cricket Week at one of the north-west's leading cricket grounds. The cricket has always been of the highest standard, as the McAlpine's team usually bristles with county cricketers, who have come for the week, not only for the cricket but for the excellent hospitality, including, not least, the many glasses of vintage port – a true gentleman's drink – served after lunch.

We have been privileged to have had many of Cheshire's leading players in our ranks: men such as Ken Cranston, who captained England in a Test match in the West Indies in 1947, Bobby Cooke, Dr Billy Bennett, Michael Groves, John Seward, Dudley Bailey and Bill Bromley-Davenport. These days we can still attract good cricketers from clubs across the county, especially those who may be looking for a break from the intensity of league cricket.

We celebrated our bicentenary with a tour of Barbados, organised by William Hobhouse. This proved to be a glorious success. It coincided with Bob Cooke's 60th birthday party, where everyone danced and drank the night away, and the Gentlemen of Cheshire gave a good account of themselves on the field of play as well. We were narrowly beaten by Windward CC, went down heavily against Cable and Wireless CC at Joel Garner's home ground, but then came back strongly to beat Dover CC in our final game.

Gentlemen of Cheshire at Giggleswick, 1996

Back in 1805, that first game against the Gentlemen of Shropshire was reputed to have been played for a purse of 50 guineas and a hogshead of beer, the losers to buy dinner at the Myrtle and Mermaid in Shrewsbury. The stakes weren't quite so high when the bicentenary game was played at Shrewsbury School in 2005, but it was a splendid day. On a glorious summer's day, in beautiful surroundings, the Gentlemen of Cheshire displayed the true spirit of gentlemanly cricket by offering our Shropshire opponents a generous declaration, which they duly took advantage of to win the match. But we were very grateful to them for their part in celebrating such an auspicious occasion in such grand style.

The Gentlemen of Cheshire may be over 200 years old but, as a club, we are very much looking to the future, by encouraging younger cricketers to play for us and so be able to experience for themselves the true meaning of the words 'gentlemen's cricket'. And being able to witness how much they enjoy it re-doubles our confidence that wandering cricket in general, and the Gentlemen of Cheshire in particular, have a bright future.

Lords and Commons

Founded: 1850

by Stephen Chalke

I Zingari was only five years old when it took on for the first time a team representing the Houses of Lords and Commons. They played at Vincent Square, Westminster, on 22 June 1850 and, according to IZ's report of the match, the parliamentarians were obliged to bat first because several of their number, kept up late the previous night by a division, were not present at the start. The game ended in a draw, and a return game was arranged for three weeks later at Lord's.

The social connections between the two teams were many – the Earl of Darnley in one side, his younger brother the Honourable Edward in the other – but IZ were much the better cricketers and, to even up the contest, the Lords and Commons elevens included professionals: in the first game, they were 'Houses of Lords and Commons, with Wisden'; in the second, they were 'The Houses of Parliament, with Diver and Royston (who was to bowl only)'. Between them the hired hands accounted for 23 of the 24 IZ wickets to fall, and the 24th was a run out. It was the same story in the two matches the following summer.

The next recorded game between the sides took place in 1857, when finally a bona fide Lords and Commons player, the 19-year-old Earl of Coventry, took a wicket. For this match they were batting 22 men against IZ's eleven. With a first-innings deficit of 79 runs, they held on for a draw, closing the day on 67 for 15. Two years later the young Earl, 'a hard slashing hitter and a slow lob bowler', was elected President of MCC.

For some years in the 1860s the Government played the Opposition at Lord's, matches in which the standard of the cricket was not high. At one point in the 1863 game the fielding was so bad that, to the mirth of the large and fashionable crowd, the Earl of Leicester's younger brother, playing for the Government, was able to complete an all-run ten. The publication *Scores and Biographies*, including the card of an 1873 game at Woolwich between Lords and Commons and the Royal Artillery, added the comment: 'This match is scarcely worthy of a place in these records, but it is inserted to demonstrate the efforts of our legislators in the cricket field.'

Gradually other fixtures entered the social calendar of the parliamentarians: Westminster School at Vincent Square, the Household Brigade at the Prince's ground in Chelsea, Harrow School, then Eton College and the Eton Ramblers. Such was the enthusiasm that by the 1890s there was talk for a while of a team undertaking a 90-day tour of the British Empire, playing matches in Australia, Ceylon and Canada. A manager and secretary were appointed and, we smile, expenses were arranged. But no record exists that the tour ever took place.

The First World War put a stop to their cricket, and no matches were played till 1922. Sir Rowland Blades, Conservative MP for Epsom, was the man responsible for the team's revival, and that year they resumed the fixture against Westminster School, also beginning the tradition of using its nets. Then in August at Lord's they took on a visiting Canadian XI, on which occasion they were led by the 71-year-old former England captain Lord Harris, who scored 15 and took two for 20. The previous summer Alec Douglas-Home, playing for the Eton 2nd XI, had bowled at Harris: "I remember being warned that it would be useless to appeal for lbw, because no umpire would dare to give him out. The caution was in fact irrelevant, as he played all the bowling with the middle of the bat and with easy timing."

In 1923 Blades booked The Oval for a Thursday match between House of Commons North and House of Commons South, though the southern bias in cricket-playing members led to the North side featuring MPs for Chatham, Ipswich, Battersea and – in the case of their opening batsman Clement Attlee – Limehouse.

From 1924 to 1939, driven by Blades' great enthusiasm, Lords and Commons cricket reached new heights. The I Zingari fixture was revived, school games were played against Westminster, Eton and Harrow, and they also took on, among others, the Metropolitan Police, the Civil Service, the Honourable Artillery Company and the Lords and Commons Staff, a game which was held each year at The Oval with a band playing in the intervals. The highlight of the summer, though, was the July fixture against MCC at Lord's. Now, unlike the games of the mid-Victorian era, Lords and Commons were a proper cricket side, able to call on such men as the former England captain Lord Tennyson, the Norfolk cricketer and MP Michael Falcon, the former Lancashire captain and MP for Manchester Exchange Peter Eckersley, and Lord Aberdare, the gifted all-round sportsman whose unbeaten 187 in a thrilling run chase in the 1938 Lord's match remains the most outstanding innings played in the history of Lords and Commons cricket. Rowland Blades, now Lord Ebbisham, remained at the heart of it all. Indeed, he was still playing at Lord's in 1939, at the age of 71, throwing up his high donkey drops for eight overs and taking four wickets for 68, three of them catches held in the deep by his son Bobby, who after the war would captain Surrey 2nd XI.

Seven of the Lords and Commons team, victorious against MCC at Lord's, 1938
left to right: Major Gwilym Lloyd-George, Michael Falcon, Waldron Smithers,
Lord Aberdare (captain), Peter Eckersley, Lord Ebbisham, Richard Grant-Ferris.

Politically in those inter-war years the team was Conservative almost to the man. Brian Johnston, playing for Eton against them in 1931, recalled being 'led to believe' that one of the team was a Labour MP: 'We thought that this was most unusual. At that stage of our education we just could not believe that someone in the Labour Party actually played cricket!'

By 1945 the world had changed. The newly elected Labour MP for Buckingham was Aidan Crawley, Old Harrovian, Oxford Blue and Kent cricketer, while the Prime Minister Clement Attlee, though not much of a player himself, was so keen on the game that he would instruct his party whips to provide whatever pairs were needed for the Conservatives in the Lords and Commons side to play without distraction. The records of this era have been lost, but it seems that by the 1950s, when Conservative numbers were greater, the fixture list was once more healthy – with regular matches against the Law Society, St Paul's School, the Stoics and the Civil Service Crusaders. However, the team cannot have been as strong as it was before the war, as it appears that only once during these years – in 1957, against Westminster School – was a victory recorded.

Among those to be found on the scoresheets are Lord Dunglass (later Alec Douglas-Home), Jim Prior (a Charterhouse contemporary of Peter May) and Keith Joseph (an opening bat who had been in the Harrow School 2nd XI). But perhaps inevitably the stalwarts were those whose political careers did not rise to such heights: Ian Orr-Ewing, Charles Mott-Radclyffe and Walter Bromley-Davenport.

Ian Orr-Ewing, Charles Mott-Radclyffe and Walter Bromley-Davenport pad up for pre-season nets at Vincent Square. Eric Bullus is in the background.

Then there was Eric Bullus, a Yorkshireman who was Conservative MP for Wembley North and whose passion for Lords and Commons cricket led to his compiling statistical records of each season and writing a brief history of the team. Such was his devotion to the side that he was said to be upset if ever a Labour team member lost his seat.

The fixture against the Civil Service Crusaders was abandoned in the early 1970s, as they had become too strong a side, but their place on the card was taken by another team of civil servants, the Mandarins, in an annual match at the Bank of England ground at Roehampton. It was this fixture in 1975 that produced the most memorable finish in the history of Lords and Commons cricket.

Lords and Commons v MCC, 1982
Ian Orr-Ewing, between Neil Durden-Smith and Charles Fry, is wearing the only surviving Lords & Commons blazer. It was made in 1924 for Rowland Blades

With one ball remaining, the final parliamentary pair were at the wicket: Michael Latham, MP for Melton, anxiously preparing to face a Mandarin fast bowler with a long run-up, and Lord Orr-Ewing at the non-striker's end, set to run like a hare the moment the ball was in the air. Latham duly missed, stumbled in setting off for the winning run and managed with an agonising crash to hit the top of his head on his partner's aluminium box. For several minutes he lay unconscious while Robin Butler, the Prime Minister's Principal Private Secretary, shouted for water. A red fire bucket appeared and, when Latham finally came round, a Mandarin fielder alertly broke the bowler's end wicket and appealed. "Not out," the umpire ruled. "Surely you can see that he's retired hurt."

Notable MPs who played for Lords and Commons in the '80s and '90s include John Redwood, Tom King, Robert Atkins, Nicholas Scott, Michael Mates and Peter Brooke. But inevitably, with a fixture list of 20 or more games, it is necessary to call on a wider circle of men. Sons and grandsons of peers and MPs are considered legitimate playing members, as are research staff and parliamentary candidates. The police used to be a good source for last-minute recruits, but now there are days when the guest players include not only researchers but friends of researchers – in fact, anybody with whites!

Sometimes, anxious to improve the strength of the team, they have called on Test cricketers: the West Indian Conrad Hunte in the '60s, Phil Edmonds in the '80s, the Sri Lankan Arjuna Ranatunga once and, on a recent tour of Israel, John Emburey. Set against that, when they toured India in 2012, they found their opponents, the Indian Parliamentarians, were led into the field by the former Indian captain Mohammad Azharuddin, now representing a constituency in Uttar Pradesh.

It is not easy to run a team whose members have so many other calls on their time. Rarely a game goes by when somebody does not have to arrive late or leave early. In one match two Liberal Democrats, Danny Alexander and Andrew George, were the opening bowlers, and both had to make premature retreats to reach their constituencies that night: Alexander by the last plane to Inverness, George by the last train to St Ives. A match scheduled for the day of, or immediately after, a government reshuffle has been known to play havoc with availabilities, too. Through it all the role of the secretary is vital, and following in the footsteps of Rowland Blades and Ian Orr-Ewing the team has been well served by Henry Bellingham and now by the ebullient enthusiasm of Matthew Hancock, elected to the Commons in 2010 at the age of only 31 and already a junior minister. He is assisted by Nigel Adams, a keen club cricketer in Yorkshire.

There are some lovely venues on their fixture card, not least Highclere Castle where they play the Earl of Carnarvon's XI, and Stowell Park, against the Gloucestershire Gipsies. But they have also played ACAS at the Civil Service ground in Chiswick, where on one occasion it was a struggle to get into the locked pavilion to find some stumps, and at the Fuller's ground near Kingston where the pitch is no billiard table but the beer comes free.

In 2011 their annual match against MCC returned to Lord's for the first time since 1939. It was, alas, a rain-ruined day, but there was time for 11 overs to be sent down by their opening bowlers: Joe Johnson, brother of Boris, and Danny Alexander, the first serving Cabinet Minister since the war to turn out for the club and taker of the one wicket to fall. They were captained by James Morris, a former Oxford University cricketer who is now MP for Halesowen, and included in their eleven Labour's Ed Balls, the Sports Minister Hugh Robertson, the never-say-die John Redwood and the MP for Reigate Crispin Blunt, a stalwart of the side and a good enough batsman to have scored a century.

Inevitably, among such high-powered men, a certain competitveness is never far from the surface. But they do not pretend to be great cricketers. They have far weightier matters to worry about. They play their cricket for relaxation and for fun, as they always have.

Nigel Adams, Ed Balls and Crispin Blunt, Lord's, 2011

Quidnuncs

Founded: 1851

by Anthony Gibson

The Quidnuncs of Cambridge are the senior of the two Oxbridge wandering clubs, founded in 1851, a year before the Harlequins, and serving very much as a model for that club's founding fathers. Yet despite that early start and – thanks to their links with the university – the strongest possible foundation, it wasn't many years before they faded from view. They played the Harlequins for the eighth time in 1870, but then not again until the 1970s.

It doesn't seem to have been the case that the club ceased entirely to exist in the interim. In 1897, a contemporary account refers to 'numerous teams of Quidnuncs, in residence and out of residence, play(ing) against the different public schools and various garrisons and regiments'; Gubby Allen certainly raised a Quidnunc side in 1924 to take on the Royal Artillery; and Percy Chapman famously wore his Quidnunc cap in the field when captaining England against Australia in 1926, much as Jardine was to do with his Harlequin cap two and six years later. But of regular fixtures, there appear to have been none, for the best part of a century.

It was a strange state of affairs, for one of the most prestigious cricket clubs in the land and one which was still appointing new members every year. Part of the explanation may have been its very exclusivity. The number of current undergraduates who could be Quidnunc members was limited to 25 at first, reduced subsequently to only 15. Even with the university 'old boys' who make up the balance of the membership, it didn't produce much of a pool from which to select teams, especially as most of the members of that pool would either be playing cricket for the university during term-time or in demand from their counties in the long vacation.

Be that as it may, the Quidnuncs certainly played plenty of cricket in the early years. Its three founders were all university cricketers: Robert King of Emmanuel College, and Frederick Whymper and Alfred Baillie of Trinity. Their motivation was straightforward enough: to create an amateur cricket side, which would allow the cream of university cricketers to enjoy the fellowship and competitiveness of university cricket not only whilst they were up, but more importantly – and hence the restriction on undergraduate membership – after they had gone down.

The only early fixtures of which any details survive are those against the Harlequins. The first match was at Oxford in 1853 (at Cowley, rather than the Parks). Perhaps as a sign of the problems which were to come, the Quidnuncs could muster only seven players and did well to lose by no more than eight wickets. They did manage to assemble almost a full team the following year, but still lost. In fact, of the eight matches between the two sides from 1853 to 1870, all but two were won by the Harlequins and they were both draws. This shouldn't necessarily be taken as symptomatic of the relative strength of the two sides. Cambridge cricket was every bit as strong as Oxford's in this era, and most of the early Quidnuncs sides were bolstered with their fair share of Blues. It seems to have been just one of those things, but it did mean that the Quids had to wait for the little matter of 122 years before they were able, at last, to savour the sweet taste of victory over their old rivals. ('Quids' seems to have been their original nickname, though 'Nuncs' came to be preferred later.)

Apart from those matches against the Harlequins, the Quidnuncs' early fixture lists seem mostly to have consisted of country-house games against the military, I Zingari and the MCC, and sporadic matches with Eton and Harrow. They seem to have been a convivial bunch. All resident Quidnunc members were expected to dine together once a term at the Red Lion Inn in Cambridge, and it became the tradition for the Quids to serve 'claret cup or Badminton' (a particularly lethal cocktail) at their matches.

But despite the popularity that this must have engendered, their fixtures became progressively fewer and further between, so that, from the last decades of the century onwards, they became only a very occasional wandering club. A letter appeared in *The Times* in 1920 from Neville Tufnell, a former Cambridge wicket-keeper who played one Test for England in South Africa in 1910, suggesting a meeting of Quids in London 'to put the club on a sounder footing', but it is not clear if anything came of it.

The one Quids match from this era of which we do have a detailed account was against the Royal Artillery at Woolwich in 1925. That the game was played at all seems largely to have been thanks to Gubby Allen, who had only recently come down from Cambridge covered in cricketing honours and glory. The Gunners were a strong side at the time, and Allen got word that one of their number had been less than complimentary about the quality of the opposition they were about to face, even going so far as to suggest that Gubby himself was "nothing like so good as he thinks he is".

Retribution was swift and conclusive. In one of the most remarkable all-round performances of all time, Gubby took all ten wickets, including the hat-trick, as the Gunners were bowled out for 106, followed that with 101 out of the Quidnuncs' 198, and then took seven more wickets to leave the Quids victors by an innings. But mark this: of the Quidnuncs side that took the field that day, only one other player, Basil Hill-Wood, had been to Cambridge and was therefore qualified to be a member. All the others were Gubby Allen's cricketing friends and acquaintances, roped in for the occasion. No wonder the Quids played so few matches.

It wasn't until 1961, 110 years on from their foundation, that the Quidnuncs were finally revived and restored to their former glory. Credit here belongs to three fine cricketers and determined organisers, Spencer Block, Billy Griffith and Michael Melluish, who put together a strong committee and officially re-formed the club, a development which didn't pass unnoticed by the *Sunday Telegraph*, which reported on 9 July:

> That exclusive Cambridge cricket club, the Quidnuncs, whose membership is limited to Blues and near-misses, is getting itself organised. Following a meeting at Lord's, the newly elected committee have decided to ask S.A. Block to become their first president.
>
> Mr. Block, a Malburian was a notable Athlete in the 1920s and '30s. He won blues at cricket, rugger and hockey, and was also a scratch golfer

and fine tennis player. Later he captained England at hockey, and played in a final trial at Twickenham. Legend has it that he dimmed his chances of becoming an international by turning out for this encounter without studs in his boots.

That seems an excellent qualification for the presidency, but since I was told it by a Quidnunc I am inclined to doubt its accuracy. The dictionary definition of quidnunc is 'a person given to gossip'.

In 1964, the re-formed club took on the University, captained by Mike Brearley, for the first time since 1868, Peter May (by now effectively retired from first-class cricket) scoring a century for the Nuncs, as they now referred to themselves. The following year, the Quidnuncs' side featured Henry Blofeld and Christopher Martin-Jenkins (who sadly missed out on a Blue), alongside Roy Kerslake, now President of Somerset CC.

Under the successive presidencies of Jack Davies, Freddie Brown and Hubert Doggart, the modern Nuncs have settled to a small, but sustainable fixture list of three regular games a season against the University, the Harlequins and the Free Foresters. In 2010, this was extended to four, as the inaugural T20 fixture was played against the Harlequins at Dulwich, bringing the club well and truly into the modern era.

They have been on tour as well, to South America, no less, in 1978, and the prestige of Quidnunc membership has been fully restored by the award of the dark blue and yellow club tie to newly elected members during the one-day match against Oxford at Lord's. And, in a pleasing echo of the conviviality of the early years, they now hold formal dinners every five years, a tradition struck at Simpson's-in-the-Strand in 1980 and, since 1990, carried on in the Long Room at Lord's.

When it comes to captains of England, the Quidnuncs can outdo even the Harlequins with, by my reckoning, ten, in Lyttleton, Steel, Chapman, Allen, Sheppard, May, Dexter, Lewis, Brearley and Atherton. But it was a cricketer of much less renown who achieved a feat as remarkable in its way as Gubby Allen's. In 1978, in a match against the Royal Navy, the Nuncs were set to score 202 in an hour plus 20 overs. David Hays, who opened the innings with Edward Craig, then proceeded to score 161 not out, in 78 minutes from 66 balls. But what was truly remarkable was that he moved from 100 to 150 in nine deliveries – the minimum possible – seven sixes and two fours. It is a record which can never be beaten and has yet to be matched at this level of cricket.

So, despite the long hiatus in their playing history, the Quidnuncs are once again firmly established as a small but glittering star in the firmament of wandering cricket. Only one mystery remains, and that is the name. As that *Sunday Telegraph* cutting suggests, a 'quidnunc' has come to mean someone inquisitive and eager for gossip, a bit of a nosy parker. But what I am sure Robert King and co had in mind was the literal translation – 'what now' – as a reference to what might follow university cricket. It is all of our good fortune that they found such a felicitous and, as it turned out, enduring answer to their implied question.

Harlequins

Founded: 1852

by Anthony Gibson

The Harlequins is one of the most venerable, distinguished and exclusive of English cricket's wandering clubs. It was at a dinner in the rooms of Charles Currer, a fellow of Merton College, in the spring of 1852 that the club had its genesis. Currer's guests that evening were two Old Harrovians in Edward Chandos Leigh and Edward Charles Leigh, and an Old Etonian, Joseph Chitty. All four were considerable cricketers, and although their precise motivation is unclear, because all the earliest records have been lost, the theory propounded by Alfred Cochrane in his *Records of Harlequin Cricket Club 1852-1926* – that they wanted to create a club which could serve as Oxford's answer to the Quidnuncs, founded at Cambridge a year or so previously – seems entirely reasonable.

In reporting on their first match, against the Quidnuncs in 1852, *Bell's Life* describes the Harlequins as 'a kind of University Zingari', which sums it up very well: a wandering club drawn from Oxford cricketers. But to play for the University was by no means an automatic passport to Harlequin membership. Right from the outset, the founding fathers set out to create a club which would represent the cream of Oxford cricket – "election to it was a means of marking the position of leading University cricketers," in Cochrane's

The Harlequins team who played the Quidnuncs at Lord's, June 1863
The two-day match started on Friday, following the Varsity match which was scheduled for the three previous days. Six of the Quidnuncs and five of the Harlequins played in the Varsity match.

words. Hence the rule – which still applies – that no more than 20 undergraduates could be members at any one time (graduates become 'honorary members') and, rather like I Zingari, you had to be the right sort of chap, as well as being a damn good cricketer, to become one of the elect. Not surprisingly, this degree of selectivity hasn't been to everyone's taste. Even in the very early days, the Oxford wicket-keeper, RT Reid, an Old Cheltonian who went on to be President of the MCC, declined election as a Harlequin on the grounds that the club was too dominated by Eton and Harrow. And although the public school influence is less than it was, there is still a very distinct cricketing and social cachet about being a Harlequin.

Ostentation has often gone hand in hand with exclusivity in the world of wandering cricket, and never more so than when the early Harlequins selected their kit. We will never know the identity of Cochrane's 'daring aesthete' who was responsible for the Harlequin uniform, but he earned the club a reputation for having the jazziest of jazz hats, which it has never entirely lost. The early Harlequins took to the field in blue trousers and crimson shirts with buff facings and collars! And although they'd abandoned their coloured clothing by the 1860s, they still had the blue, crimson and buff in a stripe down the side of their trousers for most of the rest of the century. Self-effacing, the Harlequins have never been.

However, it was Douglas Jardine who earned the Harlequins' colours their lasting notoriety, when he wore his multi-coloured, quartered Harlequin cap on tour to Australia, in what gave every indication of being an act of premeditated provocation, first in 1928/9 and then, to the Australians' redoubled fury, on the infamous 'bodyline' tour of 1932/3. As far as his hosts were concerned, that Harlequin cap became the defining symbol of English cricketing snobbishness – something in which any subsequent Harlequin might well be forgiven for taking a secret, slightly guilty pride.

A 1929 cartoon of Douglas Jardine wearing his Harlequin cap

Every wandering club of note has had its moving spirit; the Harlequins' was Charlie Marsham, who succeeded AH Faber as President in 1864, and served in that capacity for another 37 years. Forceful, impulsive and completely obsessed with Oxford cricket (to the extent of famously smashing his umbrella against the pavilion rails at Lord's when Oxford lost the 1870 Varsity match by two runs), he oversaw the slimming down of the Harlequins' fixture list from maybe ten or a dozen matches per season, mainly against the oldest and grandest public schools, to just three or four. Selectivity may again have had something to do with this. Cochrane speculates that, with sides having to be raised for so many fixtures, it was inevitable that non-Harlequins would be enlisted to make up the numbers, and equally inevitable that the cricketers concerned would aspire to be members. Fewer matches made for greater purity of the Harlequin ideal.

So, by about 1870, Harlequins' regular opponents had been whittled down to Harrow, Royal Artillery, and Royal Engineers, with the later addition of the Aldershot Command. They played the Quidnuncs regularly before they disappeared from view in the 1870s, and did twice play the University XI, in 1870 and '71, but then not again until 1926, by which time the August tour to Kent and Sussex had become an established feature of the fixture list. Cochrane suggests that, of the Harlequins' early fixtures, those against the Quidnuncs, the leading amateur club Southgate (personal fief of the Walker family) and the University would have been considered first class. So, undoubtedly, was the match played in 1924 against the touring South Africans, which was lost by six wickets, despite the best efforts of the likes of Douglas Jardine and Edward Bettington. Arguably, the Harlequins' finest hour in first-class cricket was also its last, when they played the touring West Indies at Eastbourne in 1928 and beat them by an innings, John Knott scoring an unbeaten 261 in the Harlequins' mammoth 676/8 declared, and Robertson-Glasgow taking six wickets.

Unsurprisingly, given the nature of the club, the quality of Harlequin cricket has always been high, and for many years, having played first-class cricket (probably for the University) has been a condition of membership. It can lay claim to no fewer than eight captains of either England or England/MCC touring sides: Harris, Foster, Fry, Leveson Gower, Warner, Jardine, Cowdrey and Smith. Scores of Harlequins have played test cricket, and not just for England. Both Pataudis were Harlequins, as was the great New Zealand left-hander Martin Donnelly, and the current membership list includes Clive van Ryneveld, who played 19 tests for South Africa, as well as rugby for England. Imran Khan turned out against Berkshire in 1980 at Stowe School, but the club's most recent internationals have been Jason Gallian and Jamie Dalrymple, who actually took his Harlequin cap with him on tour to Australia in 2007, but was dissuaded – thankfully for all concerned – from emulating Jardine and wearing it on the field of play.

In his chapter on Harlequin cricketers, Cochrane chooses CB Fry and the relatively unknown CJ Ottaway as the two best all-round athletes to have been members of the club, predictably in Fry's case, interestingly in Ottaway's. He would only play 37 first class matches before dying of a chill, caught during a night's dancing, at the age of just 27 in 1878, but he played four Varsity matches for Oxford, captained them in 1873, played football for England and in three FA Cup finals and was also a brilliant rackets player.

As with many other wandering clubs, a combination of social change and cricketing fashion has taken its toll of the Harlequins' fixture list. As the supply of parsons and teachers dried up in the 1970s and '80s, so it became harder and harder to raise sides of the requisite quality. The August tour disappeared in the early 1990s, only the golf at Rye surviving, and the fixture list these days is as spare as it was in Charlie Marsham's day. But there has certainly been no loss of quality. The annual match with the Quidnuncs in the glorious surroundings of Arundel is always fiercely contested, with the game against the University in the Parks not far behind.

By the normal standards of wandering clubs, Harlequin cricket is serious stuff. The club has never gone in for giving people games out of sentiment. The aim is always to field the strongest available side, and to play to win, if always in the proper spirit. This is a strong club, with a strong link to the University and they may even get to play a few more fixtures. "When I watch Arabs or IZ sides with eight Quins in their ranks, I do wonder whether we shouldn't have one or two more games," explains the club's Honorary Secretary, Bryan Hamblin, slightly wistfully. The trouble is that, with only around six new Harlequins being elected each year, and many of those either living abroad or busy making their way in the world, the club doesn't have a particularly large pool of cricketers to draw upon, if the expected high standard is to be maintained.

But however many fixtures they may or may not play, this is a wandering cricket club whose future is secure. As one Harlequin member put it to me: "It's a real honour to be elected; something that you cherish for the rest of your life." And if proof were needed of that, a dinner held at Merton in June 2012 to mark the club's 160th anniversary provided it, as over 100 Harlequins, many from overseas, gathered to celebrate one of the great Oxford sporting institutions. Snobbish, the Harlequins are not; proud of their history and conscious of their heritage, they most certainly are.

Peter Carroll, the epitome of a gentleman wandering cricketer.

A Harlequin, Arab, BB, Straggler of Asia and Free Forester, he has captained seven IZ Senior Superstars tours – to India, Malaysia, Argentina, Oman, Australia and Hong Kong – during the 2000s.

Here, at the age of 70, he is batting at The Parks during the Harlequins' 160th anniversary match.

41

Free Foresters

Founded: 1856

by Anthony Gibson

Apart from their obvious longevity – 157 years and counting – what sets the Free Foresters apart in the world of wandering cricket is the size of the club, and the level of cricket to which, throughout their history, they have aspired. Even today, when the cricketing and social tide has been running so strongly against the wanderers, the Foresters can still boast a membership of over 2,000 and sustain a fixture list of 80 matches a season. And if they no longer play any officially designated first-class cricket, they did so for a longer period – 1912 to 1968 – than any other club side, barring, of course, the MCC.

Rev William Bedford

The Foresters' founder was the Rev William Bedford, Rector of Sutton Coldfield. He may not have been a particularly talented cricketer, but he was desperately keen, so much so that he created a cricket ground in the extensive grounds of his rectory, and, in 1856, organised a match to inaugurate it. This was between a side called the Pilgrims of the Dee, raised by his friends, the Armisteads, from Cheshire, and Bedford's own scratch team, which just happened to consist of cricketers from either the Forest of Arden in Warwickshire or the Forest of Needwood in Staffordshire. Hence the 'foresters'; we will come to the 'free' in a moment.

It proved to be a close and exciting encounter, in which the Foresters (65 and 57) prevailed over the Pilgrims (38 and 66) by just 18 runs, and it was agreed to repeat the fixture the following year. By this time, an idea was forming in Bedford's head. According to the splendid *Annals of the Free Foresters*, which record every game they played up to 1895 and every aspect of the club's organisation, he was 'infected with a desire for the promotion of that which may justly be termed "the noble science", the game of games' and had a vision of creating 'an intimate family band of keen cricketers'.

The second match against the Pilgrims provided the opportunity to turn vision into reality. The Armisteads were as keen as Bedford to establish a strictly amateur club dedicated to top-class cricket, an enterprise whose feasibility had already been demonstrated by the success of I Zingari, and the Free Foresters Cricket Club was duly formed. Membership was restricted to what might loosely be described as the Midland counties (a condition which was dropped in 1892 and never applied to officers in the armed services) and, in keeping with Bedford's vision of a 'family' club, special 'Founders' Kin' membership status was (and still is) granted to the members of the three families – Bedfords, Armisteads and Garnetts – around whom the new club was built.

And the 'Free'? That was to signify that, unlike IZ, Free Foresters' members would not be thrown out of the club if they had the temerity to play against it for some other side. Hence, as well, the club's very neat anagramic motto 'United, but Untied'. The club colours chosen were crimson, green and white, something which became a source of both controversy, given that these were also the colours of the left-wing Chartists, and incident, when the wife of a Free Forester was arrested in the Vatican for having the colours in a ribbon on a dress, these being also shared with Garibaldi, who was just at that time annexing large chunks of the Papal lands.

The Rev William was evidently well connected in cricketing circles, for it didn't take long for his club to acquire the reputation of being one of the strongest in the land, with fixtures to match. As early as 1861, Free Foresters were taking on MCC at Lord's and a (professional) United England XI at Manchester, and beating them both. It is true that the Foresters had the advantage of fielding 16 in the latter fixture, but they soon showed that their success was no fluke, when they played the joint county champions, Surrey and Nottinghamshire, in 1863. Surrey were beaten, whilst the game against Notts – then at the height of their powers – ended in a thrilling tie when the Notts wicket-keeper was given out lbw by his own umpire, after he had taken his side to the brink of victory in a last-wicket stand of 63.

Any number of county and international cricketers played for the Free Foresters in the nineteenth century. One of them, the great Lionel Palairet, described it as 'one of the most difficult clubs in the world to get into', an accolade indeed from such a lordly cricketer. Yet in this era, and well on into the twentieth century, the Foresters were as well known for their excess off the field as their excellence on it. On the intervening night of a two-day fixture, even against tough opposition, they liked nothing better than to stay up half the night, drinking, dancing, playing billiards and, above all, singing. They would break into male-voice harmony at the slightest pretext, and their gallantry where the ladies were concerned knew no bounds.

Besides the *Annals*, the exploits of the early Foresters have also been lovingly recorded by Teddy Rutter, who played numberless games for them from the 1860s through to 1910, and served as the club's Secretary for 40 years. The fixture against the Royal Artillery at Shoeburyness seems to have been a particularly lively affair, even by Forester standards, judging by this account:

> So when the wine had run its usual number of times round the table, all adjourned to the smoking and billiard rooms, for in those days no smoking was allowed in the dining room. There was usually a festive pool in the billiard room. Then came gymnastics, in which the sofas in the smoking room were used as parallel bars, big chairs as vaulting horses, cock-fighting and other trials of after-dinner strength and skill, after which there was always a sing-song. There was quite a lot of talent in those days, both among the Foresters and their hosts. So these post-prandial concerts lasted well into the early morning. I well remember our old chief, General Fisher, saying after a final whisky and soda: 'Well, I think I shall go out for a stretch before bed-time'. It was then 4.30 am!

When they weren't whooping it up in the officers' mess, the early Foresters would be disporting themselves on the broad acres of England's great country houses, enjoying hospitality which was usually lavish, and sometimes slightly eccentric, as on the occasion when they played at Condover Hall, near Shrewsbury, as guests of Mr Reginald Cholmondeley, who kept a zoological gardens. His pride and joy was a large yellow bird, of which a Forester called Cecil Read fell foul.

For some reason, it took a violent fancy for sitting on Cecil Read's head. Poor old Cecil didn't like it a bit. But he had to put up with it though he didn't greatly enjoy his breakfast weighed down by this weird encumbrance and the uncertainties of its behaviour. It helped itself to anything it chose, but when it transgressed in any way the fairly liberal code of its regulations, it was attached to the toast rack as a punishment.

What great days they must have been!

The early Foresters' tours were no doubt similarly Bacchanalian, although the very first one, to Scotland in 1864, could hardly be counted an unqualified success. Bedford could find only five members prepared to make the trip, but set off regardless, confident that Foresters in the north would make up the numbers. In the event, just two turned out, leaving Bedford to lead out a depleted band of six team-mates as they took the field against Glasgow and, to cap it all, it poured with rain. This didn't prove to be an omen. The Foresters have since been on dozens of tours, not just to other parts of the UK, and Ireland, but as far afield as Australia, Canada, Egypt, Singapore, Hong Kong, Kenya, the USA, the British Army of the Rhine in Germany, and, most regularly, to the Netherlands, of which more anon.

Free Foresters at Seaton, 1924
back row: unknown; EJ Mordaunt; WW Meldon; Whitehead; RE Satterthwaite; unknown;
GHM Cartwright; J Fossett; unknown; R Satterthwaite; T Thompson
front row: EM Guy; RL Holdsworth; AEH Wright; AC Johnston;
LCH Palairet (captain); GC Elers; GLA Heslop; Dorman; EGF French; unknown

How many of the big games that the Foresters played in the nineteenth century would be rated as 'first class' now, we can have no way of knowing. But they certainly played first-class cricket from 1912 onwards, when the three-day games against Oxford and Cambridge that they had been playing since 1906 won recognition from the MCC. This may have been slightly anomalous, and could have owed something to Forester influence in high places, but it was entirely in keeping with the club's original intention, of playing matches against 'County, University, College, Schools, regimental XIs and with recognised clubs in desirable localities'.

Over 150 Free Foresters lost their lives in the First World War, their names recorded for posterity on the memorial in the pavilion at Lord's. When peace returned, recovery was swift, thanks not least to the efforts of the joint Secretaries, Eustace Mordaunt and Walter Druce, and by 1930, the fixture list had swelled to over 100 matches a season, including two in India and three in the Netherlands. The Dutch connection is a fascinating one. It had begun during the war, when Free Foresters were among the allied prisoners interned in Holland, which was a neutral state. They naturally set about organising some cricket and so inspired the natives that, when the war ended, they decided to form their own wandering club, the de Flamingos, modelled on the Foresters. The two sides have been exchanging visits ever since, and the Foresters still tour the Netherlands every other year. Up to 1983, this would include a match against the Dutch national side. More recently, it has been Netherlands A, sometimes reinforced by World Cup players, including on one occasion the current Dutch captain, Peter Borren, who arrived at the wicket when they were 50 for six and went on to score a match-winning century.

The 1930s was in many ways almost as golden an era for the Foresters as the pre-war days had been. The club could still attract amateur cricketers of the highest calibre, including umpteen Test players and a veritable galaxy of wandering cricket stars, including such ubiquitous nomads as Percy Chapman, Gubby Allen, 'Father' Marriott, Bryan Valentine, Douglas Jardine, 'Plum' Warner, 'Crusoe' Robertson-Glasgow and Hugh Bartlett. And if they didn't turn out very often, they didn't need to, thanks to a playing membership of over 700, every one of them, almost by definition, a top-class cricketer.

Nor did standards decline after the Second World War. By this time, the club was in the safe hands of Ken Stanley and Bobby Blades (later Lord Ebbisham). Between them, they organised 52 fixtures in 1946 – the first of them in the unlikely surroundings of Cairo – and by 1950 the club had been restored to its pre-war strength in terms of both fixtures and membership. In 1954, the team that took on Oxford University contained no fewer than four former England captains: Freddie Brown, Gubby Allen, Bob Wyatt and Nigel Howard, plus Errol Holmes who captained an MCC tour of Australia. And if most of them were past their best, they belied their years, Wyatt making 63 at the age of 53 and Allen, a year younger, taking three for 12, including the wicket of a future England captain Colin Cowdrey, who three years earlier had made the first of his 107 first-class centuries whilst playing for the Foresters against the University.

If the Free Foresters could be said to have had a distinct flavour during these years, then it would have been a military one. Officers in the armed forces had always been particularly welcome as members, even to the extent of having their own category of membership, and a succession of ex-army secretaries and presidents through the '50s and '60s did nothing to

Free Foresters at Kirkby Stephen, 2006
Photograph taken by John Ratledge (Cambridge University, Lancashire II and Cumberland)

weaken the services' influence. It would be fair to say that, by the 1970s, the Foresters had the reputation – especially among the school and university cricketers who played against them – of being a rather stuffy club, which looked backwards rather than forwards.

But it would also be fair to say that that has changed a lot in more recent years. The membership has become more inclusive, without the Foresters ever compromising on the high standards of behaviour they expect, both on and off the field. The current Match Secretary, James Dean, has made a particular point of encouraging younger players, who now have their own 'Academy' side, whose enthusiastic Patron was the late and much lamented Christopher Martin-Jenkins. They have taken on Ireland Under-19s and, for the last two years, have taken part in a quadrangular competition featuring both 50-over and two-day cricket with the Under-25s of Bedfordshire, Buckinghamshire and Hertfordshire, and have won both competitions, although not in the same year. It was also largely James' influence which has created a strong link between the Foresters and the Refugee Cricket Project, which grew out of him coaching Afghan asylum seekers in the indoor nets at The Oval.

The fixture list has changed. Most of the old service sides have disappeared, although the Foresters do still play the Army, Navy and Royal Air Force; and there aren't quite so many games against public schools as there used to be, even if the strongest of them, like Eton, Harrow and Millfield, do still feature. "We prefer declaration cricket," says James Dean, "but we're very lucky to have the fixtures we've got, and we'll play whatever form of the game our opponents prefer." In 2012, that meant playing two T20 matches against Cambridge, either side of lunch, as the University was looking for practice ahead of the T20 version of the Varsity match. This year, by contrast, they will play Oxford in a two-day game in the Parks.

The 'Western Series', in early July, remains one of the most cherished and long-established features of the fixture list, taking in usually four or five games, at Seaton, Sidmouth and Budleigh. And, as an indication of the quality of the cricket to which the Foresters still aspire, in 2011 it included a bruising encounter with a Somerset CCC Academy X1, featuring Jos Buttler, who dispatched the Foresters' bowlers to all parts, for 200 not out, the last 50 coming in just 12 balls.

No wandering cricket club, not even the Harlequins, Quidnuncs or I Zingari, can boast of more England players than the Free Foresters. The grand total stands at 88, of whom a remarkable 36 were captains, as well as many distinguished overseas cricketers, including Sir Frank Worrell, Keith Miller and Ian Craig. The Foresters have also played more international cricket than any other club, always excepting the MCC. Besides the Netherlands, they've taken on the national teams of the USA, Canda and Ireland, for whom Eoin Morgan made his debut in a match against the Foresters at Eton in 2003, and they would have played Nigeria in 2009, had the authorities not refused to issue visas to the Nigerian team. That record gives a strong clue as to what it is that sets this club apart. Even more than the strength of their fixture list, it is the quality of their cricket. Year in, year out, they have been the strongest of all the wandering clubs.

But there is more to the Foresters than that. In his history of the Free Foresters, published to mark the 150th anniversary in 2006, a former president of the club, Philip Whitcombe, writes about what has changed about the club since William Bedford's day, and what remains the same, and concludes that 'Fundamentally, there has been no change in the spirit in which cricket is played by the Free Foresters.'

It is a proud claim to be able to make, and one which I have no doubt would be heartily endorsed by all the many cricketers who have played for and against the Free Foresters down the years.

Oakhill in the lea of the Wicklow mountains, 2009

Band of Brothers

Founded: 1858

by Anthony Gibson

If one were choosing the most idiosyncratic of the older generation of wandering clubs – and the competition would be fierce – then, with all due respect to I Zingari, Kent's famous Band of Brothers would have a strong case for being selected. The membership of BB, as the club is universally known, are 'The Brethren' collectively, or 'Brother so and so', individually; the affairs of the club are managed in accordance with 'The Mystery', one of whose rules is 'that the sisters of Brethren be admissible as Brethren upon undertaking to marry any Brother on demand'; whilst the records of the club, which date back to its foundation, are held in 'The Books', which collectively now weigh more than a hundredweight.

All of these jealously guarded and fiercely maintained traditions are owed to the founders, the 'Original Brethren': the nine officers of the Royal East Kent Mounted Rifles who decided to form a society to carry on the high old time they were having under canvas during yeomanry training in Dover. They took their name from a popular song by the Christy Minstrels and chose as their colours black and 'Kentish grey', which is actually a shade of light blue. This was in early 1858 and it didn't take long for the Brothers' attention to turn to cricket, playing their first match on 12 August that year, against a side from Torry Hill, the estate of the Leigh-Pemberton family (four of whom were Original Brethren), and winning it comfortably.

In the early days, the Brethren seem to have adopted the same sort of sybaritic attitude to cricket as they took to life. According to Lord Harris, they were a 'boisterous crew', playing a few games a year as the spirit moved them, and not caring too much whether they won or lost, as long as they had a thunderingly good time and the ladies were suitably amused. But as the originals aged and dispersed so the activities of the club ebbed away, so that by the late 1870s, according to a contemporary report, 'The only symptoms of vitality displayed by the BB Club was the pitching of their tent on the St Lawrence Ground (for Canterbury cricket week) and the display of their colours by the fair sisters in the ballrooms.'

In fact, BB might have disappeared for ever had it not been for the intervention of one of the greatest figures in English cricket at that, or indeed of any other, time, Lord Harris. In the words of the club's *History*, 'From 1880 until his death in 1932 it is no exaggeration to say that he was BB.' Harris took his cricket seriously, he was passionate in his love for his native Kent (even though he was actually born in Trinidad) and he mixed fairness and kindness with single-minded despotism in the way that he led and managed his beloved BB. He was also a very good cricketer, who captained England on what proved to be their controversial tour of Australia in 1879, which meant that he could assemble other very good amateurs to play for his club – always provided that they were either Kentish Men or Men of Kent, of course. Harris himself would play for the club from 1867 to 1928, when he played his last game against the Buffs and took four wickets with his lobs. No individual can ever have given more to any club, on and off the field, than Lord Harris did to Band of Brothers.

The original Brethren
back: Edmund Pepys, Wykeham Leigh-Pemberton, Wyndham Knight, Harry Leigh-Pemberton
front: Sir Courtenay Honywood, Edward Leigh-Pemberton, Henry Denne, Loftus Leigh-Pemberton

The Edwardian era was BB's golden age, as it was for cricket more generally. By the turn of the century the fixture list had become relatively familiar and established, with matches against the Kent public schools, as well as clubs like Free Foresters and IZ, the Royal Artillery and other services sides, as well, of course, as the needle matches against West Kent. This was a fruitful period for county cricket in Kent as well as for BB, and virtually all of the talented amateurs who helped bring the championship to Kent in 1906 and again in '09 and '10 turned out as well for the club. They had become a formidable cricketing side, who recorded some massive totals in these years: 575/8 declared v the Royal Marines in 1911, for example, and 523 against Kent Club and Ground in 1902.

After the First World War, BB continued to go from strength to strength. In 1923, they came oh so close to beating the West Indies touring side, Learie Constantine and all, losing in the end by just three wickets, thanks mainly to some fierce hitting by Joe Small when all had seemed lost. Once again, a galaxy of Kentish amateurs turned out for the club, including that brilliant all-round sportsman, Bryan Valentine, who went on to captain the county after the Second World War, and Percy Chapman, the embodiment of the debonair amateur, who captained England when they won the Ashes in the Oval Test of 1926, and went on to be a hugely popular captain of Kent from 1931 to '36.

The biggest change since the Second World War has been the disappearance of the two-day fixtures that had previously formed the staple of the BB fixture list. There are fewer armed services sides as well, 'whilst the Town Clubs' interest in league cricket has reduced their affinity with wandering clubs', as the BB history gently puts it. But matches with more of the Kentish schools, and some London clubs, have come along to fill the gaps, and the games against the old enemies – Yellowhammers, IZ, Stragglers of Asia, the Bluemantles, etc – are as well supported as ever, many of them played at Torry Hill, where the Leigh-Pemberton family remain amongst the BB's greatest supporters. In the 2012 season, the club played 24 matches, including two against the BaBes, the BBs' junior branch, which was set up as long ago as 1903 and continues to provide a steady stream of good young cricketers for the senior club.

Proper declaration cricket is still very much the rule for BB cricket, with limited-overs games an occasional exception, when a full day may not be available or the weather intervenes. Whether Lord Harris would have approved of such a proceeding, one cannot be entirely sure, but at least the overs games are played in the proper BB spirit, of which he most certainly would approve.

Maybe the BBs don't attract quite so many big names from the county club as they once did, but the post-war roll call still includes Colin, Chris and Graham Cowdrey, Mark Benson, Richard Ellison, Matthew Fleming and the most recent of their England players, Ed Smith, and the standard of cricket is as high as ever. In 2006, BB scored 404/2 in chasing down Hurlingham Club's 402/3 declared, the highest number of runs ever scored in a single day in BB's history. The club has even broken new ground with its first overseas tour, to Paris in 2010, playing three matches and winning them all convincingly.

BB is a club which is as proud of its history and traditions as any in the country and, as its *History* concludes, what is perhaps most remarkable of all about the club is the way it has 'ridden the changes triumphantly and enters the 21st century with the same happy features which gave it birth in the middle of the 19th.'

It continues:

> Those whose playing career for BB now extends over many years can detect no difference in atmosphere and enthusiasm from the days when they first wore the honoured colours. No doubt if we could call in evidence the Brethren of the last century they would find equally little difference in these things. No man ever could or ever will turn BB sides into super-efficient cricketing machines. None in his senses would wish to do so. Keenness there is and ever will be, but the supreme virtue is the comradeship and the friendship rather than technical excellence and victory, and this remains today as strong as ever, and may perhaps contribute to making us welcome to our many friends and hosts.

They may have their quirks and their quaintness, but this is a very happy band of cricketing brothers, thoroughly comfortable in their own skin.

Website: *www.bandofbrotherscc.com*

Incogniti

Founded: 1861

by Anthony Gibson

There is something appropriately inscrutable about the Incogniti. Take the club's motto, for example: *Incognito Incognitis*, 'Unknown to the Unknown'. What were the founder members seeking to signify? That they were unknowns? Or, more probably, the complete opposite, that they were so well known that only a cricketing ignoramus would not have heard of them? On this, the club's voluminous, leather-bound records are silent. Even the wonderfully comprehensive history of the Incogs, written by Claire Whickman, offers no decisive explanation.

Most of the cricketers who turned out for Charlie Brune's scratch 'Incogniti' side against the XYZ club at Lord's on 25 May, 1861, had been at school together at Godolphin in West London; and the Hemming brothers, AWL and PL, who were so influential in the Incogs' early history, do seem to have had in mind providing a club for armed services personnel home on leave from foreign parts during the summer. But beyond that, there seems to have been nothing in particular – school, university, geography, profession and so on – that unites the Incogs, save only a love of cricket and a reasonable proficiency at playing it. I'm not sure if that adds to their inscrutability, but they are certainly not easy to pigeon-hole.

The early Incogs had all the hallmarks of a Victorian wandering cricket club. They don't seem actually to have played in their black, mauve and gold striped shirts, but they

The Incogs at Wolverhampton, 1865

certainly turned up in them and wore them around the ground. They were great ones for nicknames, as well: Crusher, Tosspot, the Colonel, and the Great Unknown (which was probably a euphemism for the club itself). My favourite is the Jabberwock, evidently not the greatest of fielders, as the Incogs records relate that, on one particularly wet afternoon (and the early cricketers often carried on under the most appalling conditions), 'The Jabberwock, who fielded in the great-coat of his grandfather's fat coachman, utterly failed to arrest the ball's progress.'

Charlie Brune on the field and the Hemming brothers off it gave the club the most solid of foundations, and both fixture list and membership grew rapidly. By the 1870s, they were playing over 40 mostly two-day games a season, many of them in the grounds of country houses. Membership reached 200 by 1881 and 900 twenty years later and included both celebrated and celebrity cricketers. Among the former were Ivo Bligh, who captained the English touring side to Australia in 1882 and to whom was presented the Ashes urn, Lionel Palairet, the beau ideal of Edwardian cricketing style, Reggie Schwarz and his googly-bowling mentor BJT Bosanquet; and, from a slightly later generation, Douglas Jardine, Arthur Gilligan, HDG Leveson Gower (England captains all of them), Teddy Wynyard, Jack MacBryan and the legendary founder and long-time headmaster of Millfield School, RJO 'Boss' Meyer.

Among the latter were two of the most popular authors ever to put pen to paper, Sir Arthur Conan Doyle, whose cricketing prowess is well known, and Pelham Grenville Wodehouse, who played only one game for the Incogs, in 1908, but who must have been a pretty decent cricketer, judging by his figures of five for 16, and who, of course, named his most famous character after the Warwickshire medium-pacer Percy Jeeves.

Touring has always been important to the Incogs. They first visited Devon in 1872, and have been going back ever since. There were also early expeditions to Wales (1883-96), Ireland (1886) and the Channel Islands (1896) and in 1913 the Incogs travelled to the USA, as guests of the Gentlemen of Philadelphia. A return visit to celebrate the peace was made in 1920, and since then the Incogs have played cricket all over the world, their most recent ventures being to South Africa and Western Australia.

The Incogs flourished between the wars, as the fixture list grew to include schools, the stronger club sides, Oxford and Cambridge colleges, other wandering clubs like the Sussex Martlets, as well as the regular tours. It was in 1929 that a man who would become an Incog legend, Oliver Battcock, first turned out for the club. A tall, cheerfully combative, apparently inexhaustible outswing bowler, who spent his winters playing

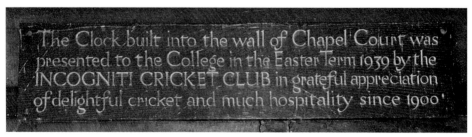

The plaque below Jesus College pavilion clock – legend has it that the clock sometimes goes backwards

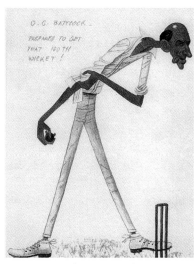

O. G. BATTCOCK.
PREPARES TO GET
THAT 100TH
WICKET!

Oliver Battcock

pantomime dames so that he could bowl all summer, he played 40 seasons for the Incogs, taking 2,204 wickets for the club at 12.99. He is remembered by the Incogs' current President, Nick Gibbs, as "a delightful chap; bowler and raconteur extraordinaire. I played with him for 20 seasons and if any one man could be said to epitomise the spirit of Incog cricket, it was Oliver Battcock."

The Second World War took a heavy toll – 50 Incogs were killed – and the club re-started tentatively in 1946 with just 21 games. But the fixture list was soon back to its pre-war dimensions, and beyond. Thanks not least to the motor car, the '50s and '60s were in some ways the heyday of wandering cricket. An all-time high was reached in 1967, when 117 games were scheduled, including four on the same day in different parts of the country. By this time, another of the Incogs' most famous characters, His Honour Judge Leslie Block, had appeared on the scene, as President. It was the irascible Block who presided at the 'Redlands Bust' drugs trial of Mick Jagger and Keith Richards, provoking William Rees-Mogg's famous 'Who breaks a butterfly on a wheel?' *Times* leader. However, he owes his Incog notoriety to the way in which he announced his retirement at the 1973 AGM, when he told the assembled company, "I'm going to do what all Presidents should do when they get too old, I'm going to fuck off"; and with that, he left the stage, never to be seen again.

From then on, and despite successful tours to Malta, Northern Ireland, Gibraltar and Canada, the club went into a period not so much of decline as of gentle contraction as both money and members became harder to come by. The early season Oxbridge tours had to be abandoned and even the Western tour to Devon was curtailed. But recent years have seen something of a renaissance. The fixture list is now at what Nick Gibbs describes as a 'sustainable' 35 games a season, all of them declaration matches rather than limited overs, and there has been a particularly welcome influx of younger cricketers – not all ex-public schoolboys, by any means – which bodes well for the future.

I suggested at the outset that it was difficult to pin down the defining characteristic of the Incogs as a wandering cricket club. Nick Gibbs says that it's the way they play "good cricket with a smile on our face", and I'm sure that is right. But there is one other club tradition which seems to me to sum them up as well as anything. For as long as anyone can remember, lunch at an Incogs game – and there is always a lunch – is concluded with port, preferably accompanied by Stilton, and woe betide any Incog who doesn't partake. Match managers are even instructed to bring a supply of port with them, just in case the home club forgets. That's the spirit!

Website: *www.incogniti.co.uk*

Bluemantle's

Founded: 1862

by Anthony Gibson

Whether the Bluemantle's can genuinely be described as a 'wandering' club is perhaps open to argument, given that it has played all of its 'home' matches at the beautiful Nevill Ground in Tunbridge Wells for over a century. But that it is wandering in its ethos, and that its history compares in distinction with the most notable wanderers in the land is beyond question. No book on wandering cricket would be complete without an account of the Bluemantle's.

The club was formed in 1862, when a notice was published declaring that 'the want of a Gentlemen's Cricket Club having been felt for the past few seasons by numerous residents and visitors to Tunbridge Wells it has been determined to meet this need by forming a Club to be called the Tunbridge Wells Blue Mantle's Cricket Club.' It was signed by H. Broadwood, President, sixteen Vice-Presidents, a committee of ten, two Honorary Secretaries and a Treasurer. The amateur cricketers of Victorian Tunbridge Wells clearly didn't believe in doing things by halves!

The new club had a lot going in its favour. Gentlemen's cricket was very much in vogue at this period – Free Foresters and the Band of Brothers having been founded, respectively, six and four years earlier – and Tunbridge Wells itself was at the height of its popularity as a spa town, thanks not least to the patronage of Queen Victoria and Prince Albert. The 'Royal' soubriquet wasn't actually awarded until 1909, by Edward VII, but Victoria was undoubtedly very fond of the place, often referring to it as "our dear Tunbridge Wells". That royal connection had particular significance for the Bluemantle's, as it accounts for their name. One of the prime movers in the new club was Henry Murray-Lane, a keen cricketer who gloried in the title of Bluemantle Pursuivant of Arms, at the College of Arms in London. We don't know whose idea it was to annex this title for the new club, but as a royal servant Murray-Lane was perfectly placed to obtain the Queen's permission to use not just the heraldic title but its colours and badge.

At this early stage in its life the club could fairly claim to be wandering. Most of its matches were two-day affairs against the military, public schools and like-minded clubs, played away from Tunbridge Wells. In so far as it had a home at all, it would have been the ground on the Common, where Tunbridge Wells CC also played. Many of the early players would have been members of both clubs, which played needle matches against each other from 1865. The strong links with the town club made it almost inevitable that, when the chance came to acquire some land from the Marquis of Abergavenney's estate for a new ground in 1895, the two would join forces to buy a 99-year lease. This became the Nevill ground – from the Marquis' family name – and was formally opened in 1898.

Its early history was distinctly eventful. Tunbridge Wells cricketers were evidently not a particularly enlightened bunch when it came to the rights of women. When the ground's new pavilion was opened in 1903, women were barred. This did not go down well when it came to the notice of the suffragette movement, still less so when one of the local cricketers attempted to explain away the policy by saying, "It is not true that women are banned from the pavilion. Who do you think makes the teas?"!

Retribution was duly exacted in April 1913, when a militant suffragette broke into the pavilion at night, set fire to the nets that were stored there, and burnt the building to the ground. Lest anyone should be in any doubt as to where responsibility lay, she left behind suffragette literature, an electric lantern and a picture of Emily Pankhurst. In the storm which followed, Sir Arthur Conan Doyle, a keen Bluemantle, attended a suffragette meeting in the town, where he branded them "female hooligans" and compared the attack (incomprehensibly) to "blowing up a blind man and his dog". The Bluemantle's were much to the fore as the cricketing community rallied round to raise the funds to build a new pavilion, which was opened in time for the Tunbridge Wells cricket week, later that summer.

After the 1913 fire
This photograph appears in a new book about Kent cricket in 1913,
A Half Forgotten Triumph *by Martin Moseling & Tony Quarrington.*
It argues that there is no evidence that Suffragettes were responsible for the fire.

Conan Doyle was by no means the only literary figure to turn out for the club. Siegfried Sassoon – whose *Flower Show Match* is one of the great classics of cricketing literature – played for the Bluemantle's all through the seasons of 1910 and 1911, averaging, he tells us, 19 in 51 innings. An entire chapter of the delightful *Weald of Youth* is devoted to his Bluemantle experiences and team-mates, including NF Druce, who had played five times for England against Australia, Osmund Scott, of the great golfing family, who also played for the Devon Dumplings, 'Camel' Casey, who captained the side and owned a car, and Conan Doyle himself, who still turned out occasionally, 'though his batting was rather on its last legs and his artful slows had lost their former effectiveness.' Druce's presence in the team shows just how strong the Bluemantle's were at this stage in their history, and whilst Sassoon is suitably modest about his own abilities, he must have been a distinctly useful cricketer to have got anywhere near the side.

The highlight of the Bluemantle's' season, then as now, is the 'Nevill Week' in early August. These days it features matches against the Band of Brothers, Old Amplefordians, Stragglers of Asia, the Moose and Emeriti, and much good cricket is still played. Legendary lunches prepared by Ros Bairamian were a feature for many years, with the washing up done by three eminent Bluemantle brigadiers! On other dates, regular opponents include the Grannies and the XL Club. The two-day games which were once the norm may long since have vanished from the fixture list, but the club still aspires to play proper declaration cricket, rather than overs matches.

From the '60s, the most important figures have been the late Herbert Hunter, a good cricketer and Club Secretary for many years, and Robert Bairamian, who has served as Fixtures Secretary for over 40 years and was a fine all-round cricketer, scoring three hundreds in the 1962 Nevill Week; as indeed was Ted Rose, Chairman until recently. Both played first-class cricket and brought competitive joviality to the scene. Nick Heroys, Richard Gracey and Colin Smith were other outstanding cricketers in this era. Records are important to a club as historic as the Bluemantle's, and for many years they have been in the safe and devoted hands of the club's archivist – and slightly eccentric wicket-keeper – Rex Roberts.

The club's playing membership is still drawn mainly from the two most prominent local public schools, Tonbridge and Eastbourne College, and indeed from their friends and neighbours at Tunbridge Wells CC. Even in the modern era, it has included many notable cricketers. Bob Woolmer, of Kent and England, was a regular, as was John Shepherd, of Kent and West Indies, not least when he was master in charge of cricket at Eastbourne College. The two Hutton boys, Ben and Ollie, are keen Bluemantle's, whilst among those who have played less regularly are James Kirtley, Ed Giddins, Dudley Owen Thomas and even, on one famous occasion, Andrew Strauss.

But the real stalwarts of the club in recent years have been cricketers like Rupert Bairamian and James Wesson, both of whom have scored over 2,000 runs, Wesson also taking over 100 wickets, as have Rupert Butler and Ted Rose. All-rounders Adrian and Ollie West and Ed Atkinson have also made major contributions, and the club is fortunate to have George Burrough and Ollie Priestman to lead the current generation of players. The club celebrated its 150th anniversary in 2012 and, with experienced wandering cricketers such as Tim Brocklehurst and Nick Ogden on the committee, can look to the future with confidence.

There have been changes for the Bluemantle's and their Nevill stamping ground over the years, perhaps the most dramatic being the demolition of the old Bluemantle's pavilion in the 1990s and its replacement by a distinctly utilitarian red-brick stand, albeit with the original Bluemantle signage incorporated. But in most respects, this is a club which gives the impression of having descended in an unbroken line, true to type, from its founding fathers, of being intensely aware of this heritage, and of being determined to maintain it for many years to come. The Bluemantle's may not have wandered very far from the Nevill, but nor have they strayed from their ethos and values.

Website: *www.bluemantles.com*

Butterflies

Founded: 1863

by Anthony Gibson

If evidence were needed of the extent of the debt which English cricket owes to the country's greatest public schools, then the Butterflies Cricket Club provides it. The Butterflies' membership is drawn exclusively from the old boys of six schools: Rugby, Westminster, Winchester, Charterhouse, Eton and Harrow. In the century and a half since the club was founded, no fewer than 37 Butterflies have played for England, 13 as captains. It is a record which is as revealing as it is remarkable.

It is also not at all what the Butterflies' two founders, Arthur Wilson and AG Guillemard, had in mind when they started the club at Rugby in 1863. They both played in the school fourth eleven and no doubt rather envied the swells in their school colours who had started their own first eleven players-only club, called the Pantaloons, three years previously. So they decided to get their own back, by forming a club from which first eleven players were specifically excluded, calling it, presumably on the grounds that it would flit gaily from place to place, the Butterflies.

The new club's first game, against the Forest School on 26 June 1863 was very much the sort of encounter that you might expect from a bunch of cricketing also-rans. The Butterflies turned up with only ten men – the eleventh being laid up on account of a 'bad wing', according to the contemporary account – but had the good fortune to enrol an 'emergency', who happened to be hanging around the ground, and who turned out to be CE Green, a fast bowler for Uppingham School. The pitch seems to have been exceptionally rough, even by the standards of those days, and Green responded in the only way that fast bowlers know. We will let Arthur Wilson himself take up the story:

> There was a hard pathway in the centre of the pitch. When Green pitched a ball on it, it went over the wicket-keeper's head, who was where long-stop normally stands; over my head, 20 yards behind him; over Guillemard's head, who was covering slip and long-stop and, as often as not, into Epping Forest for five byes.

Of Forest School's 99 runs, no fewer than 57 were extras. But when Green managed to adjust his sights he was unplayable, taking six wickets, including five clean bowled, for next to no runs.

After this auspicious beginning came Wilson and Guillemard's master-stroke: they decided to extend membership to the boys and old boys of the five other schools, and they dropped the condition regarding first eleven colours. The idea caught on; new members flooded in; even the Pantaloons swallowed their pride, disbanded and decked themselves out in the magenta, black and mauve which had been chosen as the Butterflies' colours. By 1865, they were so well established that they went on tour, to Paris no less, where several of their number managed to get themselves arrested 'for saying "goodnight" in too boisterous a manner'. Plus ça change!

Most of the club's early matches were against their six schools, although little beyond that is known of the early days, as very few records survived. But we must assume that the Butterflies flourished, first from the fact that they played over 500 matches between 1875 and 1914, and second from the quality of the cricketers who turned out for them. AN Hornby – immortalised by Francis Thomson – opened the batting for several seasons whilst fresh out of Harrow. He went on to captain England – not least in the famous loss to Australia in 1882 which gave rise to the spoof 'Ashes' obituary in the *Sporting Times* – as did AG Steel (and, in later generations, Sir Pelham Warner, Douglas Jardine, Gubby Allen and Peter May), whilst the likes of CT Studd, CFH Leslie and EFS Tylecote were just three of 13 Butterflies who played for England in the nineteenth century.

Butterflies in 1867
A photograph taken during a match against Tonbridge School

The First World War proved to be even more of a watershed for the Butterflies than for most other wandering clubs. Not only were the records lost, but also the membership list, meaning that the new Secretary, Gerald Hough (a good cricketer, who played several games for Kent), had to resort to advertising in *The Times* (where else?) in order to track down surviving members. Hough was a major influence on the post-war revival of the club as, even more so, was George Bankes, who succeeded him as Secretary in 1923. Bankes was far more than a comfortably off, crusty, cricketing ex-public school boy. He was described as "the kindest and most unselfish of men", who devoted himself not only to the Butterflies and the Old Wykehamist Football

Club, but also to the Working Men's College, for whom he was playing when he died of a heart attack at the age of just 47. It was Bankes who launched the East Kent tour, which became such a feature of a Butterflies season, and it was Bankes who persuaded cricketers as good as Douglas Jardine, Reg Bettington and Harry Altham, and as distinguished as Lord Dunglass – later Sir Alec Douglas-Home – to turn out for the club and serve on its committee.

The inter-war years were good ones for the Butterflies. Besides their six schools, they played Oxford and Cambridge Colleges, many of the better club sides, a range of army sides, and there was always the East Kent tour, with matches against the Band of Brothers, Yellowhammers and the rest, to round off the season. They were one of the last wandering clubs to maintain the tradition of presenting a bat to any member who scored a century, which survived until 1926.

Re-building was once again the order of the day after the Second World War, which claimed the lives of no fewer than 91 Butterflies (which is another very revealing statistic when you think about it). This time the responsibility fell to Bob Arrowsmith and Holcombe Read. Between them, they organised the recruitment of 126 new members in 1946 and set in train the tours of the British Army of the Rhine which would be a highlight of Butterflies cricket for the next eight years. Among the 45 Butterflies who played on these tours are some distinguished names: Peter May, Robin Marlar, Oliver Popplewell, Hubert Webb and, not least, 'Hopper' Read, who took 494 wickets at 12.4 for the club in 137 games before and after the Second World War. The cricket was of a high standard, as was the hospitality in the officers' mess afterwards.

Since those days, the Butterflies have gone on their own sweet way, as butterflies will, pausing to sip the nectar of cricket from flowers along the way, and largely impervious to the changes in the world around them. Maybe, according to the current Secretary, Patrick Cobb, the cricket is a mite less serious than it once was, but the Butterflies still like to win, and still prefer to lose than to draw. Nowadays, the club plays between 30 and 40 games a season, has 100 playing members on its books and celebrated 150 years of existence in 2012 with a match against a strong MCC side at Winchester which perhaps demonstrated the slightly erratic nature of their cricket. At one stage, MCC were 100/8, but they eventually declared at 200/8, and then bowled the Butterflies out for 100.

Good young cricketers probably have less time and more cricketing options open to them when they leave school than was once the case, and Butterflies do sometimes find themselves in competition with the respective old boys' sides for the services of the best players. But with most of the six great schools, it is still a question of being a Butterfly and an old boy, not either/or, and with a well-organised system for the recruitment of Butterflies at university in place, the future looks as secure as you would expect for a club rooted in such strong and ancient foundations.

Website: *www.butterfliescc.play-cricket.com*

Yorkshire Gentlemen

Founded: 1863

by Malcolm Watson

> Never were more enjoyable cricket matches played than those in which
> I participated on the side of the Yorkshire Gentlemen on their pretty
> ground at York. Whilst still at Eton (1874-1881) in the holidays I made
> a lot of runs for the Gentlemen.
>
> Lord Hawke

The Yorkshire Gentlemen's Cricket Club was officially formed at a meeting in York in 1863, the same year that the Yorkshire County Cricket Club started in Sheffield. Our history is closely linked to that of the county club. The original minute book has an entry stating that 'for several years previously many gentlemen in Yorkshire wished to see the county well and thoroughly represented on the cricket field both in what were termed purely county matches and also gentlemen's county matches and to have the headquarters in York.'

The Yorkshire Gentlemen's Cricket Club provided a steady supply of amateur cricketers for Yorkshire County Cricket Club from the 1880s onward, as well as 11 of the first 12 amateur captains: Lord Hawke, ERJH Ratcliffe, Sir Archibald White, DCF Burton, G Wilson, AW Lupton, Sir William Worsley, AT Barber, FE Greenwood, Norman Yardley and WH Sutcliffe. Captain (later Colonel) HS Kaye played for the county from time to time and captained it occasionally in the absence of Lord Hawke. The Right Hon The Earl Fitzwilliam was the club's first president, supported by a committee of five. After looking at various options for a ground in the York area, seven acres of the field at the back of York Lunatic Asylum (now Bootham Hospital) was leased for £50 per annum with the club responsible for levelling and fencing in the ground. This area is now covered by the modern York District Hospital.

Lillywhite's Cricket Annual said of it at the time: 'The ground is expected to be second to none in England, and when the club plays its full strength it will be about the same form as the ground. Last season, its first, it challenged all comers.'

The club played its cricket there until it moved to its current headquarters at Escrick Park, some 12 miles south of York in 1932.

Early membership of the club was made up of members of the nobility, landowners, the church, company directors, the legal profession and many army officers stationed in the York Garrison. The club flourished considerably at the end of the nineteenth century when many famous names are found in the records, including Lord Hawke, the Rev ES Carter, the Rev CM Sharp, GAB Leatham, WF Tempest, CW Landon, EM Lawson-Smith, HM Simms, CWL Fernandez and many military cricketers. Until his retirement and subsequent death in 1903, Charles Landon was the club's most regular and consistent player with both bat and ball.

The first game on the new ground was due to be played on 23 June 1864 – the year that over-arm bowling was first allowed – although, in the event, a tremendous thunderstorm caused it to be abandoned. But by the end of the month, the YGs had embarked on their first overseas tour, losing to the Vice Regal Club in Dublin by 74 runs. In the 1860s and 1870s matches were played against: the Gentlemen's Clubs of Cheshire, Lancashire, Nottinghamshire, Lincolnshire, Warwickshire and Cumberland, MCC, Harrow Wanderers, I Zingari, Northumberland Club and Ground, Scarborough, Malton, Leeds Clarence, Hull, Beverley and York Garrison. Matches against school sides have always been a feature of YG cricket, both to encourage the schools to play a good standard of cricket and as a source of potential recruits for the club. The first game against St Peter's School, York was on 12 June 1893. The first game against Leeds Grammar School was in 1887, Pocklington School in 1893, Bootham School in 1902 and Ampleforth College in 1903. We still play against St Peter's, Pocklington and Ampleforth today.

Some interesting fixtures were played in the early years, including on 13/14 July 1868 a two-day match against the Aboriginal Black Australians who were touring England. The *Yorkshire Gazette* reported: 'There was a numerous attendance of ladies and gentlemen for the occasion. The competitors were eleven men of colour, aboriginal black Australians, who have caused so much sensation of late in the country by their cricket playing. ... At the end of play each day the visitors went through a variety of exercises in throwing the boomerang and spear which they hurl a considerable distance with great precision to great applause.'

A very popular Southern Tour was started in 1880, continuing into the 1930s, consisting of three two-day games against the Royal Artillery at Woolwich, the Royal Engineers at Chatham and Aldershot Command on the Officer's Club Ground in Aldershot, plus a one-day game against the Household Brigade at Burton's Court, Chelsea. These matches were very popular occasions for both players and spectators with musical entertainment provided by various military bands at each venue.

In 1908, at the suggestion of Lord Hawke and the committee, a Northern Week was started and continued into the 1930s. Three two-day matches were played against regular touring sides including Eton Ramblers, I Zingari, Free Foresters, Oxford Authentics, the Cryptics and the Frogs.

In August 1908 the Yorkshire Gentlemen played arguably the most high-profile fixture in its history. It was a two-day game at Gilling Castle, near Ampleforth, against Ranjitsinhji's XI. Ranji had been a friend of the local vicar since his days as an undergraduate at Trinity College, Cambridge, and frequently stayed with the family at Gilling. His XI was made up of eleven first-class cricketers including CB Fry, JB King and AC MacLaren. Ranji's XI scored 361, the YGs replied with 48 and, following on, 74-6. Rain intervened and the game was abandoned as a draw.

Up to the First World War the club could rely on a nucleus of five or six regular players, including Sir Archibald White, AW Lupton, ACG Luther, Captain HS Kaye, EJ Radcliffe, DCF Burton, RC Chichester-Constable, SM Toyne and CE Anson. After the war, as the demands of earning a living became more imperative, it was not so easy

Centenary Match at Escrick Park, August 1963
Yorkshire Gentlemen versus Free Foresters
standing: RGM Quarrie, MW Cowling, IDFM Thornton, ME Taylor,
CMS Kaye, R Hinchcliffe, HNC Blenkin, M Dunnington-Jefferson, CJ Lupton,
WD Leppington, JM Watson, JB Roberts, AD Marsden, JC Burney, H Dalby
seated: TJM Smeeth, B Woodcock, WA Lupton, DC Wilson, MACP Kaye,
EJ Thornley-Taylor, DW Gillespie, WRF Chamberlain, JG Cumming, LL Toynbee

to raise good representative sides. But to these names were added Geoffrey Wilson and Sir William Worsley, both captains of Yorkshire, AO 'Pom' Elmhirst a good bat and wicket-keeper, his cousin Jack Elmhirst an outstanding leg break and googly bowler, EM Smeeth, SSM Delius, Sir K Lister-Kaye a magnificent left-arm fast bowler, Captain JES Walford the Army fast bowler, and WE Harboard who made a century against the Australians at the Oval in 1934 and toured with the MCC. Claude Anson was the most prolific batsman just before and after the First World War, regularly getting 1,000 runs per season. Sir AW White scored many runs for the Yorkshire Gentlemen, including five hundreds in 1920. The outstanding bowler was Jack Elmhirst, who took over 1,000 wickets at an average of 14.86 with his leg-breaks and googlies between 1922 and 1932, including over 100 wickets in six of those seasons.

After the Second World War other exceptional players included Derek Gillespie, who in 1950 completed the double of 1,000 runs and 100 wickets in club matches, Peter Terry, an all-round sportsman, and Michael Kaye, who took 99 wickets in 1951.

The club has been fortunate in having two long-serving scorers, Stanley Johnson from 1895 until 1935, and Paul White, who has been scorer since 1969 and is always the first person to greet visiting teams on arrival.

Although the club has its own ground, touring and away games have always featured strongly including Dublin 1864, Southern Tour 1880 to 1930s, Gibraltar 1936 and 1937, Holland 1949, Berlin 1983 to 1991, Southern Tour 1994 including a game at Arundel against the Sussex Martlets, Oxford Millennium Festival 2000, Suffolk 2002, and more recently away games against the Royal Household at Windsor and at Chatsworth.

The Yorkshire Gentlemen's Cricket Club has been well served over the years by a number of cricketing dynasties: Lord Wenlock our second President and his successors the Forbes-Adam family who own Escrick Park; Colonels Harold, Michael and Colin Kaye; Peter Terry and his son Robert; Lt Colonel Dick O'Kelly, his sons David and Richard and grandson Charlie. Among our present players there are several father-and-son combinations, including the Bartram, Brewster, Burdass, Elliot, Rossington and Reynolds families. Our current President Richard Head started in 1995 and continues to run a very well-supported and successful Sportsman's Dinner every November.

The club has always played declaration cricket, and we are probably one of the few clubs in Yorkshire still doing so. Our fixture card has, from the beginning, contained between 34 and 40 games per season. We aim to play seriously but to enjoy it, have fun and make friends. As we enter our 150th year, those traditions are as strong as ever, and long may they continue.

If you want to learn more about this long-standing cricket club and the stories and characters that make up our 150-year history, you might like to read *A Gentleman's Tale*, published to celebrate the club's anniversary in 2013.

Website: *www.ygcc.co.uk*

Escrick Park

Gentlemen of Leicestershire

Founded: 1868 (though playing from 1820)

by David Batten

Much of the early history of the club can be found in *A History of Leicestershire Cricket* by EE Snow. He records that the very first match was played in 1820 at St Margaret's Pasture in Leicester, when the Gentlemen, who fielded three Packe brothers from Prestwold Hall, took on and beat Leicester New Club. The next recorded match was against Burton-on-Trent at Wharf Street in 1831, a fixture that was repeated home and away over the following two years, Burton evidently holding a particular appeal for the Gentlemen's team!

Further fixtures against Burton and Melton followed in 1834, and in the following year they took on Stamford, Burton and the Gentlemen of Derbyshire. In 1840, they were easily outplayed by Newport Pagnall, and a further loss is recorded against the Derbyshire Gentlemen in 1846. At this time, Edward Bouchier Hartop had laid out a good ground at Burrough Hill and several games were played there against I Zingari. In 1849, the combined forces of the Gentlemen of Leicestershire and Nottinghamshire managed a draw against I Zingari in Nottingham. A year later, Richard Sutton scored the first recorded century for the club, against the Derbyshire Gentlemen, and Sir Richard Heygate hit the first recorded eight at Wharf St (these being the days before boundaries). Another unusual incident occurred in 1856, when Thompson of Derbyshire removed three Gentlemen batsmen in two balls: the first one dismissed, the second removed first ball, the third run out for backing up too far!

It is hard to say, from reading Snow's book, whether the Gentlemen were genuinely a club at this stage, or simply an intermittent gathering of Leicestershire's best amateurs. But certainly, up until 1868, when he records that it was 'revived', the club seems to have performed on a somewhat irregular, almost haphazard basis. But by the 1880s, they were firmly established again, visiting North Wales and losing to the Gentlemen of Philadelphia at Grace Road by an innings and 62, a result which makes one wonder as to what might have been, had the Americans not discovered baseball!

The fixtures against Harrow Wanderers, Uppingham Rovers and the Free Foresters – all still played today – also date from this period, but there was certainly nothing parochial about the Gentlemen's fixture list, given that they played the first Indian side to tour England, the Parsees, and also drew with a Canadian touring side at Grace Road.

But then, for whatever reason, the matches became more and more sporadic, and finally disappeared in the 1890s. It wasn't until 1904, from which the formal records of the club date, that the minute book records that, on the proposition of the Archdeacon of Leicester and seconded by Mr CE de Trafford, "the club again be re-formed", wording which suggests that it did have at least a semi-formal pre-existence.

Thereafter, the fixture list gradually expanded, so that by the 1930s, the Gentlemen were playing most of the local public schools, the local towns and a good selection of major wandering clubs, including Harrow Wanderers, Eton Ramblers, I Zingari and Free Foresters, as well as the MCC and the Leicestershire 2nd XI. Prominent figures in the club at this time were Sir Lindsay Everard, a Leicester brewer, who became Honorary Secretary from 1920 to 1933 and subsequently Vice-President and President. He and Joe Brankin-Frisby, who served as Secretary for 31 years from 1933, transformed the club, turning it into one of the country's leading wandering clubs. After the Second World War, the presidency was held by Colonel WSN Toller DSO and he in turn was succeeded by another local brewer, Sir Kenneth Ruddle, who served until the early '70s, before handing over to Paddy Swain. The present incumbent, Grahame Berkeley, took over in 1999, having previously taken on the secretaryship from Joe Brankin-Frisby's son Nick in 1969.

An article in *The Field* in June 1964 suggested that 'judged on the interpretation of the club's colours of dark green, light blue and gold, the Gentlemen of Leicestershire must be the most optimistic cricketers in the land. For the green represents the field of play, the light blue the summer sky and the gold the sunshine, a combination of colours which make up the ideal cricket day.' Fifty years on, that optimism burns as brightly as ever. However, as league cricket has become ever more dominant over the past twenty years or so, the ethos of the club has gradually changed, so that it has become very much a haven, for those who want to leave behind the demands of the league system and 'overs' cricket, and return to the more subtle attractions of the declaration game.

So, whilst the remarkable fortnight-long August Festival of cricket, played at Oakham and Uppingham schools from the '50s to the '80s has had to be cut back, as other clubs have become reluctant to wander too far, the Gentlemen still play host to the MCC and Free Foresters and continue to play many of the local schools, from whom many future members are recruited.

Wandering clubs, lacking as they do a clubhouse, ground and focal point, have perforce to rely on the enthusiasm and determination of their leadership to thrive. With the Gentlemen of Leicestershire, 200 years on from their sporadic and sometimes erratic progress through the nineteenth century, and 100 years on from their re-formation in the early twentieth, that enthusiasm and determination remain as evident as ever, promising much more cricketing enjoyment and fun during the twenty-first.

Emeriti

Founded: 1872

by Paul Mathieu

No one turned up for the AGM; it was abandoned for lack of a quorum. Fixtures were called off because the club couldn't raise a team. The committee chided members for agreeing to play in matches and then crying off. And during a two-day game, with the club well placed at the end of day one, a long, lively party was followed by a batting collapse next morning. 'Proof that dancing and cricket don't mix,' sniffed the annual results summary. None of which distinguishes Emeriti from any other touring side – except, perhaps, that all these events took place in the 1870s and 1880s.

The club was the result of divine intervention. In the 1860s, the Catholic aristocrat William Petre organised country-house cricket at his home, Thorndon Hall in Essex. Then he found a calling higher even than cricket. He took holy orders, studied for the priesthood and was ordained. Later, he became the first priest since the Reformation to sit in the House of Lords. Having declared his innings closed, Petre suggested to his friends that they should form a new club comprising old boys from the Catholic schools. They chose the name Emeriti and the motto, 'Qui stipendia legitima fecerunt', which translates as 'those who have done their lawful service', suggesting that the Emeriti themselves are 'veterans', or 'honourably retired'.

In its debut year, 1872, Emeriti had 29 members and played nine matches, among them Beaumont, Downside, Prior Park and Stonyhurst – establishing the core of subsequent fixture lists, which is the Catholic schools. The club was an immediate success: the membership grew to over 100 by the end of the 1870s, and in that time it played several county sides. In 1876 Emeriti drew with Essex and Warwickshire CCC. The following year the club beat Worcestershire by ten wickets, drew with Devon and lost to Somerset; a year on, and Devon were beaten by seven wickets.

It can be deduced that in those days touring clubs were rather stronger than today, and the counties weaker. Some accomplished players wore the Emeriti colours. Chief among them was Sir Timothy O'Brien, who played for Downside, Oxford, Middlesex, England and Ireland. At Oxford he hit a high-speed 92 in a historic win for the university over Murdoch's Australians. 'The Demon' Spofforth was among the bowlers on the receiving end. O'Brien was described by WG Grace as, 'After me, the next best batsman in England'. He scored over 11,000 first-class runs, played five times for England, and later captained Ireland. He had a volcanic temper. After a game in 1883, the Emeriti resolved, 'That TC O'Brien do write a letter of apology … in the terms dictated by the Committee, for his conduct at the Woburn Park match.' He was later blamed for 'a tremendous row' between Middlesex and Surrey.

Other notable Emeriti players included O'Brien's brother-in-law Charles de Trafford, who captained Leicestershire for many years; Bertram Bisgood, who scored 82 and 116* on his Somerset debut; Fred Welman, who kept wicket for Middlesex

A painting from 1886

*Charming a young lady outside the tea tent is clearly easier if you are wearing
the blue, black and gold of the Emeriti blazer, cap and cummerbund*

and Somerset; Cyril Wilson, another Somerset player; and in the 1920s HJ 'Tom' Enthoven, who followed heroics for Cambridge with a long career as an all-rounder with Middlesex, scoring over 7,000 runs and taking 252 wickets. Sir Arthur Conan Doyle was a lesser light, playing a few MCC games – but his sole first-class wicket was that of 'WG'.

The club's early fixture lists included one or two regional tours each season. In 1880 the club successively played Devon, Torquay, Teignbridge and Exmouth. Two years later it was Worcestershire, Malvern College and Cheltenham College. There was a hectic visit to Lancashire – nine matches in ten days. Most ambitious of all was a fortnight in Ireland in 1892 which took in six two-day games. All this activity – the fixtures and results, press cuttings, contemporary watercolours of the venues, and a report of the season past – was recorded in large leather-bound volumes. Emeriti team photos of the time show strange little caps without peaks, known as 'polo caps'. Facial hair was de rigueur. The club even had its own song. Its chorus ran:

Hurrah for the days of victory! Hurrah for the festive nights!
Hurrah for the blue and black and gold of the gallant Emerites

Fixtures could face unforeseen obstacles. A match against a Monmouth garrison was 'cancelled owing to the prevalence of smallpox'. A season notably low on player numbers was blamed on 'men called to the Anglo-Egyptian war'. Later came the Boer War. Its impact, not only on the Emeriti, can be gauged by the depletion of the fixture list: eight matches in 1901, with problems filling sides, six in 1902, and just four in 1903.

Then came 'the war to end war', and Emeriti didn't emerge from its shadow until 1922, when just three fixtures were arranged. In 1927, the club acquired its own tribute band, in the shape of the Ceylon Emeriti CC, an institution that, 'was not anything racial. It [will] include members of all communities, European, Burgher, Sinhalese, Tamil, Indian etc.' The Ceylon offshoot received many expressions of support and interest, but left no further trace in the club's archives.

By the end of the 1930s Emeriti was soundly re-established, playing a dozen or more fixtures – similar to today – when events again overtook touring cricket, and much else besides. This time, the club's officers and players were quicker to restore normality when the war ended. The Secretary, Jack Fletcher, harried pre-war committee members for a meeting as early as September 1945. The following February he persuaded *The Times* to publish a notice:

The Emeriti Cricket Club is starting up again with a few fixtures for next
season. Will those intending to play or interested in helping to revive the
Club please communicate with JB Fletcher ...

That began the third innings of Emeriti's existence – at the time of writing, 66 years without a break. Subjectively, in that time the club's best batsmen have been Hugh Watts and Peter Delisle. Watts played for Cambridge at the start of the war, and for Somerset afterwards. He was certainly a better player than his short career suggests. He lost his early 20s to war, became a schoolmaster, and from 1948 to 1952, when he retired aged 30, he played county cricket only in the school holidays, and besides he carried the effects of war wounds. He made one first-class hundred. Delisle came close to three Blues in a row at Oxford and played as an amateur for Middlesex in the university holidays, scoring three centuries. EW Swanton called him 'the most elegant of batsmen'.

The best bowlers might be Jim McConnon and Julian Murphy. McConnon, the Glamorgan off-spinner, who was the most affable of men, took over 800 first-class wickets, including a famous hat-trick against the South Africans, and played twice for England. His friend Pat Kelly (many years' cricket and hockey for Cheshire) used to take McConnon with Emeriti to Stonyhurst in the 1960s, where only the slow pitches made his off-breaks playable. Murphy sent down fast-medium seamers from a great height. His control is suggested by his analyses in consecutive matches against strong sides in 1974: 11-3-27-4 (v Bluemantle's) and 17-4-36-7 (v Martlets). Not long after, 19-7-45-6 against Incogniti – while six other bowlers shared 36-1-174-3.

Two men who best represented the ethos of Emeriti were its successive Presidents TG Hemming and Willoughby Wynne, of Downside and Ampleforth respectively. 'Gordon' Hemming served as a Commando. Having lived to tell many a tale, he wasted little time afterwards on anything unrelated to cricket. In 1947 he wrote to the Hon Sec, 'We need as never before the chance to play this noble game in the spirit of the good old days … we must do everything we can to revive Emeriti.' Gordon did work for the CBI, but that was probably so that he could lead its XI to victory over the TUC. He was a wicket-keeper; not the best, but determined. As he stiffened up, the occasional chance went down. "Sorry, bowler," he'd growl, and once, when he threw the ball back down the pitch, only to hit the bowler between the shoulders, "Sorry – sorry, bowler."

Willoughby Wynne was an economical off-break bowler and a prolific scorer of runs, for many clubs and over several decades. Like Hemming, he was a glass-half-full man, unfailingly welcoming and cheerful, unknown to have a bad word about anybody, save perhaps if they offended the spirit of cricket.

Both men were present at the most recent of Emeriti landmarks – the dinner held in the Long Room in 1996 to celebrate the club's 125th anniversary. The menu was soup, the inevitable chicken, and fruit tart. Compare that with the feast at the club's silver jubilee gathering a hundred years earlier: oysters, soup, salmon, quails with filet of beef, leg of lamb, guinea fowl with asparagus, lemon soufflé, and a savoury. And all for 5/6d (£28 today). There were seven toasts, five of them involving responses: a marathon in every respect. All being well, the Emeriti's 150th anniversary celebration awaits in 2021, with less verbiage.

William Petre left a number of legacies to schools cricket. He paid for the development of the grounds at Ampleforth and Downside, and for the pavilion at St George's, Weybridge. And he founded a club that still visits those venues, with luck doing what he intended, which is to show school XIs that there are other cricketing models than the leagues.

Website: *www.emeriti.co.uk*

Stoics

Founded: 1877

by Chris Heron

The Stoics CC was founded in 1877 as a wandering club playing midweek cricket, mostly against the strongest clubs in London and the Home Counties. Its place in cricket history was secured for all time when it was instrumental in changing Law 14, the Law of Declaration. On that occasion at least – when Andrew Stoddart scored 485 against them to demonstrate the futility of not being able to declare – the name was well deserved, and its under-pinning philosophy must have stood them in good stead (although the story that they were previously called the Revellers, and that this match caused them to change their name is, we believe, apocryphal!).

Stoicism, derived from the school of philosophy founded on the teachings of Zeno of Citium (333BC – 264BC), teaches that self-control, fortitude and detachment from distracting emotions, sometimes interpreted as an indifference to pleasure or pain, allows one to become a clear thinker, level-headed and unbiased. A primary aspect of Stoicism would be described as improving the individual's spiritual wellbeing.

Whether every Stoic cricketer could be said to subscribe to the ethos of Zeno may be open to some doubt, especially when a close LBW decision goes against them, but one who certainly does deserve that accolade was Gerald Plumbly, the former chief vet to the Queen's stables at Buckingham Palace. His two great loves were cricket and convivial company, both of which he enjoyed with the Stoics for more than 70 years in many capacities, from player to administrator to President for Life, until his death in 2010 at the age of 95.

Whilst the Stoics are proud of being a very 'English' club, to which members have to be elected, we are not a pretentious club, welcoming all those who share our passion, love of the game and its spirit. Sadly, the early records of the club have been lost but we do know that the date of foundation was 1877, that the prime mover was OR Borrodaile and that the founding members were his fellow Westminster schoolboys.

The original Stoics fixtures were mainly in Essex, but as the years went by they cast their net more widely, to include clubs like the Wanderers, Hampstead, Richmond, Woodford Wells, Old Merchant Taylors, Forest Hill, Chiswick Park, Streatham, Surbiton, Teddington, Woolwich Garrison, Sutton, Dulwich, Old Johnians, Enfield, Kenley, Witham and the Metropolitan Police, whilst a highlight of every season, until quite recently, was the Eastbourne tour.

It was on August 4 1886 that the Stoics earned their place – and earned is the right word – in cricket history. They were playing Hampstead and found themselves in the field after their captain had lost the toss. Six and a quarter hours of fielding later, they walked off – stoically, no doubt – their opponents having run up the little matter of 813 in the meantime, of which Andrew Stoddart, Punch's 'dear, victorious Stod', had scored 485, including 64 fours, 3 fives and an eight. Both the team and the individual scores were world records. Stoddart's performance was all the more remarkable given that he was only just embarking on a serious cricket career, and that he had been up the entire night before, playing poker.

It was a one-day match, and doubtless, given the choice, the Hampstead captain would have declared to give his bowlers a shot at dismissing the exhausted and demoralised Stoics, but in 1886, declarations were not allowed. Law 14 was changed just three years later, thanks not least to this particular match.

Exactly a century later, the Stoics challenged Hampstead to a re-match, under the 1886, no-declaration, rules. Sadly, that aspect of the proceedings was declined, although the match was played – Keith Miller an interested spectator – and a Stoics' victory provided a measure of revenge, thanks largely to a fine century by the future Victorian left-hander, Warren Ayres. It is possible that Stoddart played a few games for the Stoics after his history-making performance, for he was appointed President of the club in 1897, although it may just have been in tribute to a remarkable achievement, by a remarkable man. Either way, he would serve as President for ten years, before tragically taking his own life in 1915.

If Stoddart did get a game with the Stoics, he was probably the club's first Test player. The current Vice-President, Raman Subba Row, seems to be most recent England player, and the club can also boast three Australian Test players in Adam Gilchrist, Dav Whatmore and Julian Wiener. Other internationals include John Nagenda (East Africa in the 1975 World Cup) and Trevor Gripper, of Zimbabwe. Many county championship and Sheffield Shield cricketers have also turned out for the club over the years.

Gerald Plumbly

A London vet, who sometimes attended the Queen's horses, he always found time for cricket, often playing three or four games a week.

He was a Stoic for 70 years, holding the office of President from 1977 till his death, at the age of 95, in 2010.

No account of Stoics CC would be complete without reference to one of the club's most loyal, and certainly most prolific members, Jack Hyams, who died in 2012 at the age of 92. He was arguably the most successful club cricketer of all time, scoring over 125,000 runs, including 170 centuries, and taking at least 1,300 wickets, and could also lay claim to the longest unbroken playing career, covering nine decades.

Born in Hammersmith, and an accomplished footballer as well as cricketer, Jack scored his first century when he was 14. He went on to play for more than 50 clubs, including a spell in the Bradford League, ending his career at Cockfosters and Billericay. He played for the MCC, the Club Cricket Conference, the Stoics, the Forty Club, the Nomads, the Bushmen, Finchley, Alexandra Park, the Bertie Joel Eleven, and several times for the Cross Arrows at Lord's. The West Indies Test player, Wes Hall, was, he said, the fastest bowler he ever faced.

Jack played and watched cricket all over the world and was made Life President of the Barmy Army, the England fans' organisation. He was in his 70s when he scored his last century, against Edmonton at Brondesbury, and the cricket historian David Frith described him as a 'phenomenon'. In his 90th year, before a stroke laid him low, Jack played 11 times for Billericay and five for his own team. He was a talkative man, proud of his achievements, and he had plenty of reasons to be immodest – one of the most enviable of men.

In keeping with their name, the Stoics have survived the cricketing and social vicissitudes which have assailed wandering cricket over the last hundred years or so remarkably phlegmatically. There are Stoics all over the world and one significant change was in 1932 when the various branches of the club were brought together under a single headquarters in London. Another was a recent highly successful tour, to Sri Lanka; an innovation which will be repeated, once economic conditions improve. But it has mostly been a case of the same successful mixture as before: convivial company, good cricket, cheerfully and, when occasion demands, yes, stoically contested.

Website: *www.stoicscc.hitscricket.com*

In February 2008 the Stoics toured Sri Lanka. They played four matches, three of them at Test grounds, and included two former Test cricketers in their party: Aamir Sohail of Pakistan and Danny Morrison of New Zealand.

Sadly Gerald Plumbly, their President, was unable to accompany them so they carried with them wherever they went a giant version of his portrait.

By coincidence their Vice-President, Raman Subba Row, was in Sri Lanka, staying with friends. He had played for the club both before and after his first-class career, and he joined them in Kandy where he stood alongside the President for this picture.

Wanderers

Founded: 1878

by Anthony Gibson

The Wanderers Cricket Club owes both its distinguished history and its continued existence to two men, Stanley Colman and Nick Syrett. Without Colman's hard driving leadership, the original Clapham Wanderers would probably have had as ephemeral an existence as did so many other wandering clubs of the late nineteenth century; without Syrett's fortuitous but ultimately highly committed intervention, the Wanderers would most certainly have disappeared for ever a hundred or so years later.

The Wanderers started life as the Grafton CC, named for the Congregational Church in Clapham at which the majority of the founder members worshipped. Among them was a young Stanley Colman, of the famous mustard-making, cricketing, non-conformist Norfolk family. By the time he played his first game for the club, in 1876 at the age of 14, it had become Clapham CC, playing on Wandsworth Common. When it lost the use of that ground, the club became the Clapham Wanderers and then finally, in 1893, with Stanley Colman now very firmly in charge, just plain Wanderers.

Colman was a solid cricketer, who played half a dozen games for Surrey, without really ever being truly first-class. His first love was the Wanderers. He played for them from 1876 to the early 1930s, initially as an obdurate opening batsman, later being content to bat down the order. In all those years, he only ever missed a game if he was injured, and even then he would be there on the boundary, spurring his team on. During the course of his long career, he scored somewhere between 40,000 (*Wisden* obituary 1942) and 100,000 runs (*Cricketer Spring Annual* 1926), including over a hundred centuries, and took part in six opening stands of over 300. On one occasion, he shared in an opening partnership of 211 for the Wanderers with the England football international FE Saunders without either of them scoring a boundary, as the groundsman had neglected to cut the outfield all the way to the boundary fence 'and the ball could not get through'.

In the early days, it was the custom for the Wanderers not to have a club captain, but for the team to elect their leader, by ballot, on the day. From 1882 onwards, it was always Colman, to the point where they gave up bothering. The press cuttings all speak of him as 'much loved', although one suspects he may also have been a bit of a tyrant, albeit a thoroughly benevolent and deeply committed one. There is a painting of him in the Long Room at The Oval, smoking his pipe with a thoughtful look and a piercing gaze; not a man to be trifled with. Mind you, that painting does less than justice to his luxuriant moustache, which, judging by a contemporary photograph, might easily have been mistaken for a small hedge.

Anyway, Colman's influence was critical in turning the Wanderers from a small group of cricketing non-conformist friends into what the *Evening Standard* would describe in 1921 – with a fine disregard for the claims of the likes of I Zingari and the Free Foresters

The Wanderers, on tour in Kent and Sussex, 1909
back: PP Lincoln, FW Robarts, HC Pretty, JN Crawford,
RT Crawford, PH Slater, N Leicester-Clarke, R Kenward
front: AM Latham, S Colman, DLA Jephson, RB Brooks

– as the 'most famous of club touring sides'. It was Colman who arranged the fixtures, Colman who organised the transport and Colman who, using his extensive contacts, not least at Surrey, where he sometimes captained the second XI, persuaded some of the most celebrated cricketers of the time to play for his club.

One of the most unusual, in the early years, was Digby Jephson, the last lob bowler to appear regularly in first-class cricket, who has been celebrated in Anthony Meredith's book *The Demon and the Lobster*. A few years younger than Colman, he was born in Clapham, joined Surrey after Cambridge and became a regular for the Wanderers from the 1890s onwards, when he switched from fast conventional to slow lobs, his action being described as 'like setting a wood in crown green bowling'. His all-round performances were immense: all ten wickets in an innings against Chiswick Park in 1894; 301 in three and a quarter hours (while only 89 were scored at the other end) against Norwood a year later. Colman would later pay tribute to him as 'beyond doubt, the best all-round player the club has ever had'.

Jephson was very far from being the only first-class cricketer whom Colman enlisted to the cause. Many of the great names in amateur cricket from London and the Home Counties turned out for the Wanderers between 1890 and the Second World War, including the ubiquitous Jim Swanton, who played regularly for them in 1926 and '27. Colman needed to attract good players, for he lacked nothing in ambition when it came to the fixtures he organised. In 1900, these included WG Grace's London County XI, for whom the Champion scored an undefeated 167 and followed up with five wickets, although the Wanderers scraped a draw.

The Wanderers v Ealing, as featured in The Cricketer, *June 1922*
Stanley Colman, aged 60, with resplendent moustache
and still some years from retirement, takes centre stage

Another great Wanderer was George Parker, both on the field as a prolific all-rounder in the 1930s, and off it as successively Captain, Match Secretary and eventually President for the club's centenary year in 1973. It was Parker who oversaw the post-war revival, recruiting players like Giles Baring of Hampshire and Monty Garland-Wells of Surrey, although the Wanderers' real mainstay during this period was Alf Gadsby, who took 339 wickets for the club between 1945 and 1954. In 1946 came probably the Wanderers' greatest day, when they took on and beat a Surrey Second XI, featuring Jim Laker and Tony Lock, in a one-day match at The Oval.

It is a pity that a history of the Wanderers by Tommy Wheeler has been lost, and that the writer of the club's centenary brochure in 1973 elected to draw a veil over the years from 1952 onwards. It may also have been symptomatic of a slow decline in the club, for by the late 1970s its annual tour to Kent and Sussex had been abandoned and fixtures were becoming fewer and fewer. By 1983, just one fixture remained, against the Forty Club. The committee minutes record that 'no one was prepared to take on any offices', and in 1984 the Wanderers disbanded.

And that would have been that but for a stroke of pure chance. Enter Nick Syrett, erstwhile secretary of the British Racing and Sports Car Club, bon viveur, organiser of the Cricketer Cup and the owner of a moustache which has some way to go before it matches the splendour of Stanley Colman's.

He had played a few games for the Wanderers in the 1950s, but had lost touch, and in the meantime had put together his own social team, based at a members' club in Putney, of which he was Secretary. When word reached him that the Wanderers had folded, he decided that it would be a shame to allow such a hallowed name to go to waste, still less its famous colours of white, terracotta and reseda (a sort of grey-green), so appropriated both for his own use, albeit changing the reseda for British racing green. About 15 years later, in the late 1990s, word of this 'new' Wanderers eventually reached the erstwhile Secretary of the old club, Peter Marsh, who summoned Syrett to his presence.

"I was expecting a bit of a dressing down," he remembers. "But in the event I got the warmest of receptions, together with the flag, the minute books and an enormous leather case containing all the Wanderers' score-sheets from 1893 to 1939. Peter suggested that we should advertise the fact that the club had been revived, to attract players, but in the event there's been no need."

Just as Colman was central to Wanderers' early success, so has Syrett been to its resurrection. A naturally gregarious soul, known the length and breadth of the cricketing world, he has used his myriad of contacts – not least through the Cricketer Cup – to attract a mixture of good, and very good, cricketers to play for the club. They range in age from 16 to 60, and have even included ten Test players, among them Derek Randall, Hamish Marshall, Ed Giddins and Geoff Howarth, the former New Zealand captain, who is now President of the club. But the cricketing stalwart of modern times has, without question, been Charlie Redmayne, who played 108 matches for the Wanderers between 1989 and 2010, scoring 3,683 runs at an average of over 42: not quite Colman-esque figures maybe but, in the context of the times, every bit as valuable.

The 2012 fixture card listed 14 matches, against the sort of sides that the Wanderers have played throughout their history – Charterhouse Friars, Hampshire Hogs, Reigate Priory and Esher, which has become their home from home. All but one (the RAF) are on a Sunday, which ought to make it easier for league players to turn out, but doesn't always now, with the advent of the various Sunday league and cup competitions.

Still, the latter-day Wanderers seem to have carved out a solid niche for themselves and, for as long as Nick Syrett is around to organise, recruit, inspire and entertain, I have little doubt that they will flourish. Beyond that, who knows? Every wandering club without the strongest of traditions needs its Colman or its Syrett to survive and prosper, in any age. But I like to think that perhaps the revival of the Wanderers may also be symptomatic of a wider change, as cricketers come to appreciate that there is more than one way to play the game, and that, for the first time in at least 40 years, the tide may now be running in wandering cricket's favour. Let's hope so, anyway.

The Wanderers, versus The Guards, at Burton's Court, 2004
back: TP Mackenzie, FPPM Boyd, WF Burnell,
JS Weston-Simons, GFJ Booth, CH Fellows-Smith
front: DJ Brockis, MJ Taylor, CJA Goodwin, TJL Sheppard, NJ Armstrong

Hampshire Hogs

Founded: 1887

by Anthony Gibson

The Hampshire Hogs have always seemed a very happy bunch of cricketers. Whilst the fortunes of other county wanderers have ebbed and flowed, the Hogs have sailed serenely on, if not oblivious to the processes of social and cricketing change, then seemingly impervious to them, playing as hard off the field as on it, as popular with their opponents as they are with their followers. I rather doubt if there is a more sought-after fixture in the whole world of club cricket than a game against the Hogs at their beautiful ground at Warnford. There is a richness and a relish about Hampshire Hog cricket which is rare indeed.

The club was founded in April 1887 as the Northlands Rovers CC, Northlands, near the County Ground at Southampton, being the home of one of the leading protagonists, AJ Day, who would become the club's first President. Not that it kept that name for very long. By the time the first AGM was held, the following December, the committee had received a letter from a Mr Lacey, suggesting that the name be changed to the Hampshire Hogs, 'with a view to making it a more representative amateur club for the county'. When a proposal to this effect was put to the meeting, it was carried unanimously. It was the first of very many contributions that FE Lacey would make to English cricket, and which led eventually to his becoming the first man to be knighted for services to the game.

The point that Lacey made was a serious one. These were the days when, in many counties, amateur cricket was seen almost as a superior alternative to the county game, tainted – as some saw it – by professionals. It was important for the prestige of Hampshire cricket overall that the amateur side of the game was strongly and clearly represented. Only a club with the word 'Hampshire' in it could meet this criterion; as to where the 'Hogs' came from, who knows, although it might very well have been that inveterate founder of cricket clubs, Lt Colonel James Fellowes, who would go on from being a prime mover in the Hogs' creation to being midwife at the birth of the Stragglers in Somerset and the Dumplings in Devon.

The links with the Hampshire County Club could hardly have been stronger, during the Hogs' early years. As Christopher Bazalgette observes in his *Centenary History*, 'Looking at the reference books of that era, it is hard to differentiate between the Hogs and the County.' Every Hampshire captain from 1887 to 1939 was a Hog, including some of the great names of amateur Edwardian cricket, men like the Hon Lionel Tennyson, Captain Teddy Wynyard and Major RM Poore. Another fine cricketer and a hugely influential figure in the early history of Hampshire cricket was Dr (Sir, as he later became) Russell Bencraft, nephew of the great fox-hunter Jack Russell, who served the Hogs in every conceivable role, up to and including President, for the best part of 50 years.

In their early days, the Hogs played eight to ten games a season, often at either the Royal Greenjackets' ground at St Cross, or Winchester College; sometimes at one of Hampshire's many country-house grounds. They were mostly two-day fixtures, and in the officers' mess or the country-house drawing room on the evening between the two days, white tie and tails would be de rigueur. The early Hogs lacked nothing in style.

Perhaps the most significant event of the years between the wars was the formation of the Hampshire Hoggets in 1924. The idea came from Colonel R Cecil (no doubt influenced by the success of the 'Babes' in Kent), and he seems to have had no deeper motive than to give 'public school boys' some cricket in the summer holidays. But as the years went by, and the Hoggets thrived, so they became more and more important as a feeder for the main club, providing a steady infusion of good young cricketing blood which has been central to the Hogs' success ever since.

By this stage, whilst the Hogs could still attract the best amateur cricketers in Hampshire to play for the club, they tended to be schoolmasters, rather than the army officers and clergymen of the early years. One such was the splendidly nicknamed 'Lucky Lou' Lewis, a hard-hitting and fearless opening batsman who in one game knocked off the 50 runs needed to beat the Wiltshire Queries in the 12 minutes remaining, having first taken the precaution of stationing his players around the outside of the boundary to save time returning the ball. Another was Francis Irving, who, among many legendary exploits, once made 147 against the Gloucestershire Gipsies, having been up all night and fortified by Green Chartreuse!

The Second World War took a heavy toll of Hogs' members, 50 being killed, and only one match was played in 1946, against the old enemies, the Cryptics. That the club recovered so strongly thereafter was largely down to Ronald White, who had succeeded Pat Hall as Secretary in 1939 and would serve in that role for 21 years. The club showed its appreciation by electing him to serve an unprecedented three-year term as President in 1963.

The Hogs have always known how to enjoy themselves, and never more so probably than on the early-season tours to play cricket at Hunstanton and golf at Royal West Norfolk – usually with a freezing wind blowing straight in across the North Sea from the Urals – from 1961 to '74. All sorts of high jinks are recalled in the *Centenary History*. My two favourites are when Jumbo Fuller, having been up all night, decided to try pouring champagne on his cornflakes, with unhappy results; and the occasion when David Bishop wagered the snooker-playing landlord of the Neptune in Hunstanton a bottle of champagne that he could beat him, and duly did so, on the black, despite being the right side of at least 12 pints of beer. The Hogs were not invited back to that particular hostelry!

Tours to the Channel Islands from 1968 to 1974 seem to have been equally uproarious, but just because the Hogs had fun off the field, didn't mean that they gave less than 100 per cent on it – once their hangovers had cleared. They certainly needed to be at their best when they toured Barbados in 1978, where they encountered, amongst others, Wes Hall and David Holford; and in South Africa in 1987, when Barry Richards came out of retirement to play against several team-mates from his Hampshire days, among them that under-rated opening batsman and Hogs stalwart Barry Reed. There were tours as well to Australia in 1989 and Argentina in 2006, and the Hogs became the first wandering club in the modern era to take on a Test-playing country, when they played what were virtually Test strength New Zealand sides in 1978 and 1986, securing honourable draws on both occasions.

Much the biggest change in post-war Hogs cricket was the move to their now permanent home at Warnford. During the '50s and early '60s, obtaining the use of the St Cross ground had become progressively more problematic and, in 1966, the decision was taken to move to the ground on the Chester's family's estate at Warnford in the beautiful Meon Valley. That rarest of rare birds, a female groundsman, Janet Lees, worked miracles in transforming the wicket from corrugated mud into batsman's paradise, and in 1974 the picture was completed with the opening of a new pavilion. You could argue that having a home of its own does rather militate against the Hogs being described as a 'wandering club', especially as they play almost all their matches there, but Christopher Bazalgette assures me that it hasn't affected the fundamental ethos, and that's the important thing.

Among the players of the modern era, Michael Moldon, with over 10,000 runs, Peter Came (grandson of RWV Robins) who has overtaken him, star all-rounder Rupert Cox, who was on Hampshire's books for many years, and the hard-hitting Allom brothers, Dominic and Matthew (sons of Anthony, grandsons of Maurice), have all given sterling service. But, to this observer at least, the man who has done as much as anyone for the Hogs over the last 40 or so years, off as well as on the field, is the aforementioned Christopher Bazalgette, advertisement manager for many years for the *Cricketer* magazine. Between 1966 and what may or may not have been his last appearance for the Hogs in 2010, he has taken 1,405 wickets (twice as many as the next man) with his slow-medium away-swingers, invariably bowled to a 7:2 offside field. He owes his success, he says, to the fact that even the best batsmen seem unable to resist trying to hit him into the wide open spaces on the leg side, usually with fatal results.

Christopher Bazalgette in action

The ground at Warnford

The Hogs celebrated their centenary in 1987, in fine style. Since then, as other clubs which share the same approach to the game have struggled in the face of leagues, wives and breathalysers, the Hogs have carried on pretty much regardless, refreshed with new blood from the Hoggets, reinforced with refugees from the leagues and tended lovingly by committeemen and officers who show a commitment to their club which is rare and special, even by the standards of wandering cricket. They play around 50 games a season, mostly declaration cricket, against the sort of sides that they've been playing for most of their existence: public schools, old boys, jazz hats, good local clubs and touring sides, from both around Britain and overseas. The Warnford ground invariably looks a picture and boasts what must be one of the best club wickets in the country, thanks not least to the devoted efforts of ground director Bill Hughes, whose standing is such that he is the current chairman of the ECB Pitches Advisory Committee. With a total membership of 400, a playing membership of 100, and at least 15 good young players being recruited from the Hoggets each year, the future looks as secure as it can do.

What sort of club is the Hampshire Hogs?

Christopher Bazalgette is in no doubt:

> It's a wonderful club. Not cliquey in any way. We play hard on the field and have fun off it. I'm a member of 20 or so clubs around the world and I love every one of them, but nowhere do I find the same level of enthusiasm, enjoyment and sheer fun as I do with the Hogs.

Website: *www.hampshirehogs.org.uk*

Northern Nomads

Founded: 1892

by Richard McCullagh

The Northern Nomads came into the world of cricket as a club with big ambitions, and a most impressive line-up of supporters. An open letter published in November 1892 announced the intention to form a 'a Wandering Cricket Club, as far as possible on the lines of the Free Foresters in the South ... to promote the cause of amateur cricket in the North of England.' Among its 36 signatories were three existing England captains, in Lord Hawke, AN Hornby and AG Steel, and one future one, AC MacLaren.

An inaugural meeting followed on 22 December, at which the name was chosen – Northern Nomads being preferred to 'Northerners' by eight votes to seven – rules formulated, the first 95 members elected and the colours of white, black and green decided upon. The club played its first match on 27/28 June 1893, against Rossall School (a fixture that continues to this day), as well as eight further matches in 'Craven Week' and 'Westmorland and North Lonsdale Week', later in the summer.

By 1895, the fixture card showed 29 matches, and new members were flooding in. Even as early as 1894 the fixture card bore the following plea: 'Members wishing to play in matches are particularly requested to communicate with the managers and not wait for an invitation', an imprecation that continues verbatim in 2013; even if another committee decision – 'that rosettes of the Club colours should be worn by Members, with evening dress, when on tour' – is rather less likely to be followed.

From such heady beginnings the club flourished, with fixtures against Free Foresters, I Zingari, Shrewsbury, Stonyhurst, Charterhouse and even Grange in Edinburgh and SH Cochrane's XI in Westbrook Bray, County Wicklow. There were tours to Oxford and Cambridge, school matches against Repton, Rossall and Sedburgh and country-house games in all corners of the North of England. At this stage in its history, although its meetings tended to be held in North Lancashire, the Nomads were very much a regional wandering club. It played its cricket in every northern county, from Cheshire in the south to Northumberland in the north. It was only after the First World War, when the club's base moved to Liverpool, that the Nomads became a wandering club primarily for Lancashire, rather than the entire north of England.

It wasn't all plain sailing in the early years, by any means. The Nomads very nearly folded in 1913, when the members seem to have fallen out with the officers, then came the war and activities were resumed only tentatively when it was all over, with just a few games, mostly against schools, from 1921 onwards. It wasn't until 29 January 1926, when the club was reconstituted at a special general meeting at the Exchange Hotel, Liverpool, that recovery really began. Jacob Wakefield was elected President, Geoffery Wordsworth, the club's original secretary, became Vice-Chairman, and a strong committee was appointed.

From its new Liverpool base, the club reinvented and reinvigorated itself through the '20s and '30s. From five fixtures in 1926, 13 are recorded in 1934 including Eton Ramblers, Cheshire Gentlemen, Sir AD McAlpine's XI, Lord Leverhulme's XI and E Bromley-Davenport's XI. Meetings continued to be held in Liverpool either at the Exchange Hotel (for the Northern Railway line) or Exchange Club, with occasional meetings at the Union Club, Manchester. Up to 1938 a strong fixture list was maintained and many young cricketers were elected to membership, including some with whom some current members of a certain age will have played, or at least known, in the post-war years, such as Lister, Leather, McEntyre, Barlow, Legard, Pattinson, Taylor, Brocklebank, Daglish, Boult, Cranston, McAlpine, Bowman, de Figuerido, Nuttall and Spooner, to name but a few. In 1938 for the first time there was proposed a fixture against Liverpool College (to be managed by K Cranston, failing him Sir Thomas Brocklebank), thus beginning a long connection between the club and the school.

The club quickly re-established itself after the Second World War in Liverpool with fixtures proposed against the traditional schools plus Denstone. Familiar names start to be elected such as R Tyler, HGE Prescott, DDL Little, JR Crean, E Greenhalgh, AE Husband, G Sharp, Dr CW Warner, Dr J Winter and A Cohen.

Colonel DM Ritchie OBE MC was elected president in 1950, with Leslie Wethered Hon Sec and the nucleus of a strong committee that continued to 1962 when EH Hawkins became president. There is no formal record of the fixtures, but in 1952 is a minute of 'played 9, won 6, lost 1, drawn 2' and in 1953 '11 fixtures were proposed' and it can be safely assumed that the traditional fixtures were maintained.

Nor can there be any doubt as to the standing of the club in cricket circles. A meeting of February 1951 records: 'A letter was read from Mr CRK Mugliston asking if he could make his two nephews Members of the club. He was desirous of keeping the name Mugliston on the Roll of Members.' Sadly the committee could not exempt them from playing qualifying matches, and there is no record of their later election.

But perhaps the club's most notorious membership decision was reserved for the meeting of November 1959 in Liverpool. Quite apart from the fact that it was the meeting at which the current president was elected, the minutes record: 'Candidate not elected. Mr FM Worrell, proposed by Mr AJ McAlpine, seconded by Mr RJ McAlpine, was not elected a Member owing to the fact that he had only played one qualifying match and was still a professional cricketer.' And this exactly two years before the same Frank (later Sir Frank) Worrell would lead the West Indies on their inspirational tour of Australia including the tied Test and a ticker-tape farewell. It was not until 1965 that the committee decided that as 'all cricketers were now considered on a par, it was agreed they (professionals) could be elected provided the committee considered them suitable.'

On the playing side the club continued to flourish with a minimum of ten fixtures a year against traditional opponents, none more so than the away and home games against AJ McAlpine's XI at Marchwiel and Liverpool. These games epitomised the rivalry between the respective captains Ken Cranston and Jimmy McAlpine. The Marchwiel game usually took place on the Wednesday of the McAlpine Cricket Week in early July, following other games with Free Foresters, I Zingari, MCC and the like. It was universally popular because for most Nomads it was their only contact with country-house cricket, featuring as it did a lavish lunch including lobster from the McAlpine private fishery. It became known as 'The Lobster Lunch Job' and was always oversubscribed by April. The reverse fixture was a two-day affair at Liverpool CC, Aigburth, on or about 12 August when the McAlpine side stayed at the Adelphi Hotel, and was used as a gathering point for an assault on the grouse moors of Scotland.

Jmmy McAlpine would go to any lengths to prevail, and many a young Nomad found himself playing against the likes of Frank Worrell and Ted Dexter at Aigburth or Garfield Sobers at Marchwiel, not forgetting of course Jimmy's other famous cardigan-clad double-act, Ken Boles and Ian Lomax. And if at Aigburth Jimmy was ever short, the problem was usually solved by a phone-call to Lord's and a helicopter trip to Liverpool for members of the ground staff. The last record of the Liverpool game is in 1984, but the Marchwiel game continued until 2007 under Ian Cockbain's managership until sadly the McAlpine cricket operation folded.

On the administrative side the club was run from Liverpool at the Racquet Club until 1958, following which by agreement meetings alternated between Liverpool and Manchester. Things ran smoothly enough until the late 1980s when a combination of circumstances produced something approaching administrative limbo. But salvation was at hand, with the appointments of Ken Cranston as President and Steve Gardner as Secretary – the latter still in post today and in danger of matching Leslie Wethered for long and effective service.

Ken Cranston's contribution to cricket and the club has been immense. Educated at Liverpool College, he was elected in 1936. In 1947 he was appointed captain of Lancashire without having played a match, and played three Tests against South Africa, taking four wickets in an over at Headingley. In January 1948 he captained England versus West Indies in Barbados, played against Bradman's all-conquering Australians at Headingley and then retired to his dental practice in Aigburth. Lancashire and England's loss was local cricket's gain. He played for Neston, then Formby in the Liverpool Competition, managed the annual matches against AJ McAlpine's XI, became President of Lancashire and then as President of the Nomads secured its survival. He was responsible for arranging the Centenary match against MCC at Neston on 15 June 1993 and put AGMs on a convivial and well-attended basis by combining them with a golf tournament at Formby or Royal Liverpool, in which members competed for 'The Cranston Cup'.

The Cranston revival saw the restoration of fixtures against traditional schools and clubs, the addition of Cherry Hill and Cholmondely Castle as country-house matches and in October 1997 a three-match tour to Menorca under the managership of Ted Williams. This tour became hugely popular for reasons of conviviality and climate as well as cricket and continued in various forms, traditional, sixes and 20/20 until 2009 when sadly recessionary constraints forced its hopefully temporary postponement. The club maintains its school fixtures with Rossall (2012 was the 120th Anniversary) and Liverpool College as well as Cheshire Gents and local clubs. The Lobster Lunch Job at Marchwiel may be no more, but has been replaced in kind and spirit by an annual match against Bootle CC at Wadham Road where Ian Cockbain, formerly of Lancashire and the middle member of a remarkable cricket dynasty, takes a Nomads XI to play the club, followed by hospitality every bit as generous albeit in less rural surroundings than at Marchwiel.

Administratively the club's officers, President Richard McCullagh (succeeding Ken Cranston in 2003), Steve Gardner, Tim Ledsham and Fixtures Secretary Norman Cusack, four men with five prosthetic hips between them, meet at the Red Lion Inn at Parkgate to suit the Secretary's convenience. Nowadays the club can largely be regarded as Merseyside based.

These are not easy times in which to maintain the traditions of wandering cricket. School exams, club, league and knock-out fixtures, economic and social pressures, all militate against the maintenance of a strong fixture list. Yet in Merseyside and beyond, the Northern Nomads remains the club of aspiration for many good cricketers seeking an alternative to the league treadmill, and a talisman for the true spirit of cricket.

Northern Nomads versus MCC, Centenary Match, 15 June 1993
back row: A Miller, IM Taylor (scorer), RCA Thorn, RMO Cooke, DTA Cummings,
P Tipton, SP Henderson, G Monkhouse, D Otway, E Osborn, RS Dutton, M Milton,
PRA Shone, NR Davies, N Cusack (scorer), CR Fleet   front row: H Schofield (umpire),
JCB Pinnington, JP Bell, R Osborne, CFR Brown (MCC captain),
K Cranston (Northern Nomads President), RS Gardner (Northern Nomads captain),
S Dyson, PA Davis, RJ Digman, T Jones (umpire)

Craven Gentlemen

Founded: 1892 (revived in 1920)

by Brian Mason and Jim Heaton

Although the Craven Gentlemen only became fully nomadic in the last 30 years of its existence, it belongs nonetheless, from its history and its ethos, very firmly in the tradition of wandering cricket. Formed in 1892 in Skipton (hence 'Craven'), and 'Gentlemen', because in those days clubs liked to devise pretentious titles for themselves, the club participated for many years in what became known as country-house cricket. Home matches were played in Gargrave. A former secretary undertook the painstaking work of making an archive of the club from its earliest years. It is evident from this that the club enjoyed considerable success and was very well regarded from its inception to its first demise in 1896.

Revived in 1920 it switched its home from Gargrave first to Skipton, then on to Ilkley, before moving in 1939 to Mirfield and, in 1954, to Norwood Green (near Halifax), when Yorkshire CCC provided the opposition at the opening of the ground. The fixture list increased throughout the '20s, reaching 80 matches in 1928, and included annual matches against MCC and a Lancashire tour with five games.

Matches were played on Saturdays and Sundays. In the '50s and '60s there were two fixtures on Sundays. Such was the playing strength of the club after the Second World War that tours were undertaken: to Holland (1946, '47, '48 and '79), to the East Coast of Yorkshire (1950), to the East Midlands at Whitsuntide (from 1951) and to Sussex (from 1960). School fixtures, first recorded in 1894 against Leeds Grammar and Sedbergh, were started again in 1921, and in subsequent years games were also arranged at St Peter's York, Stonyhurst, Pocklington, Ashville, Giggleswick, Worksop, Oakham, Ampleforth, Rossall, Woodhouse Grove, Silcoates, and Bradford, Batley and Queen Elizabeth Wakefield grammar schools.

This proved to be a fruitful source of recruitment, as boys were able to play for the club during the holidays and join at the end of their university commitments. In 1932, *The Cricketer* magazine reported that 'this well known Northern Club has done so much for amateur cricket in Yorkshire and Lancashire.' It is also recorded, in 1938, that the headmaster of Worksop College, guest speaker at the annual dinner, expressed the opinion that Craven Gentlemen 'were helping public schools in the North in the same way as the MCC were with the Southern schools.' For many years, the club sponsored and organised a Public Schools Week, in conjunction with Yorkshire CCC. The first four days were trial matches, two teams were selected for Friday and then the best eleven chosen to play against the club on the Saturday, all of this watched by the county coaches. This festival continued until 1963 and introduced many good young players into club cricket.

Many distinguished cricketers turned out for the CG over the years, among them Frank Greenwood, Major AW Lupton, DCF Burton, Brian Sellers, MG Crawford and WHH Sutcliffe (all Yorkshire captains), together with Herbert Sutcliffe, Maurice Leyland and, more recently, Philip Sharpe.

As recently as 1970 the fixture card included over 40 matches, with a number being played midweek. The selection of individual sides was left to a small group of match managers. It was quite a privilege to receive a card inviting one to represent the CG. Matches were normally played on a 'time' basis in the best traditions of the game.

The strain of maintaining a ground caused the committee to decide, at the end of the lease of Norwood Green in 1971, that future 'home' games would be played on a ground hired for the day. From this point, it was a short step to becoming truly nomadic. The next nail in the CG coffin was the decision of the leagues to introduce Sunday cricket as the rule rather than the exception. Many promising young cricketers turned their back on clubs such as the Craven Gentlemen. Some of the innocence of our cricket disappeared as matches were played on a 40-over basis. Match managers no longer had the luxury of selecting a side from those available. Rather, they would be telephoning occasional players on the morning of a match to try to avoid arriving with a depleted team.

As older members retired and younger players were no longer forthcoming the club decided with some reluctance to draw stumps in 2004. There were only nine fixtures on the card in 2003. It was time to bid good-bye to a glorious past.

The club has been blessed with some excellent administrators over its 90 playing years. It was thanks to their hard work and the dedication of the match managers that Craven Gentlemen players were able to enjoy so many years of great cricket, camaraderie and friendship. The Farewell Dinner was held on Friday 8 February 2013.

The Craven Gentlemen Over-25 XI versus the Under-25 XI, 1976
back: Charles Furness, Charles Hartley, Tony Lydyard, Jim Heaton, John Wade, Mark Hollinrake
front: Tony Aldridge, Tim Robinson, Jim Leathley, Tony Winder, Brian Mason

Borderers

Founded: 1895 (-ish)

by Anthony Gibson

The Borderers have been flying the flag for wandering cricket in the north-east of England for over 100 years. And if they are not as well known as you might expect from such a long and distinguished history, that is probably because they have tended to stick to their native heath, which is a long way from wandering cricket's southern heartlands.

The club was founded in 'about' 1895. It is hard to be more precise as the early records are few and far between. The first matches of which the scorecards have survived were in 1899: against Mark Fenwick's XI at Morpeth on 27 July, WS Clayton's XI at Chesters on 8 August and Earl Grey's XI at Howick on 10 August. These were all country house matches, and the early encounters do seem to have had a distinctly patrician flavour. The Earl Grey in question was the 4th Earl, grandson of the famous second Earl, who introduced the Great Reform Act of 1832 and after whom the tea is named. His lordship didn't actually play, but he must have been an enthusiastic Borderer, for the 1901 minute book shows him chairing the club's annual dinner. He was also, of course, impeccably connected. Can even I Zingari ever have fielded such an aristocratic bowling attack as Lord Francis Scott, the Hon E Gordon-Lennox and the Hon C Lambton who, between them, shot the Borderers out for 129?

The club colours were typically garish of jazz-hat cricket of this era: brown, blue and pink. They were said to symbolise the three main Northumbrian rivers – brown being the Tyne (of course), blue the Coquet and pink – slightly implausibly – the Tweed. In the years up to the First World War, the club played around ten matches a season, most of them two-day, country-house jamborees, but also more serious fixtures including Durham University, Durham School and the Newcastle Garrison at Jesmond.

It was in one of these latter games that a man called Edgar Elliott played possibly the most remarkable innings in Borderers' history, scoring 332 out of 692 for 8 declared, with 13 sixes and 44 fours. The scorer must have realised that he was watching a very special innings, for we even know how long it took Edgar to compile his runs: 185 minutes. It must have been a very good pitch.

Edgar was a useful cricketer, who was a regular for Durham in minor counties games. He even played a couple of first-class matches, and that was (and is) unusual for the Borderers. Until relatively recent years, when Durham joined the county championship, all the best cricketers from the north-east had to go south – and quite a long way south, given Yorkshire's selection policy – if they wanted to play the first-class game. So good amateur cricketers either stayed at home and settled for club and minor county cricket, or moved away altogether in order to qualify by residence for a county further south.

The Borderers at Netherwitton Hall, 1902

But this did at least have the advantage of providing the Borderers with a substantial pool of good cricketers from which to select their teams. At one point, membership topped the 300 mark and, even today, the club can call upon around 60 playing members.

Not a great deal is known of the middle part of the Borderers' history, but they certainly carried on in their own, slightly isolated way, playing invitational XIs, local schools and the occasional touring side. The Harrow Wanderers and the Eton Ramblers eventually became regular visitors, there were fiercely contested local derbies against the Durham Pilgrims and the Yorkshire Gentlemen, and every season the club would travel south to play Aysgarth School in Yorkshire. They also used to play in Scotland, not just in the Border country but as far north as Edinburgh, for games against Loretto and Merchiston schools. But until very recently, when they've ventured to the deep south to play the Old Wykehamists at Winchester, that was as far as they travelled. Unlike many wandering clubs, the Borderers have never been ones for touring.

Among the more recent Borderers' players, four stand out: Nicholas Craig, the current club President, and John Jeffreys — both of whom played for Northumberland in the minor counties – as prolific batsmen, Archie Middleton for his wickets and Sir Michael Blake, not just for long service on the field but for his organisational skills off it.

Matches at Close House, once the home of the Bewicke family, now a luxury hotel, are remembered with particular affection by the older Borderers. Archie Middleton recalls "the magnificent cricket pitch, with an outfield the size of The Oval's and as good as any in the North of England." The hospitality provided by Verley Bewicke and his near-neighbour,

Tommy Ritchie, a New Zealander, whose son James serves on the current committee, was legendary. Another stalwart was Lennox Aitchison, who played for the Borderers for many years before his untimely death in an air accident in the Lake District.

In the modern era, the Borderers have faced the same sort of problems as afflict most wandering clubs. The current chairman, Julian Blake, concedes that it is becoming harder for match managers to tailor their sides to the standard of the opposition, that some of the cricket is 'friendly' rather than competitive and that 'time' cricket is becoming harder to sustain. "With quite a lot of our opponents, if you suggest a 'time' match they either don't know what you're talking about or say that they prefer an overs game." The temptation for good younger cricketers to move south to further their careers is also as strong as ever, and the age profile of the club's playing members has been increasing.

The other problem they've had is with the weather. The far north-east is not exactly renowned for its balmy springs and blazing summers. But in all the club's 118-year history, it can never have endured a year like 2012. All 13 fixtures due to be played in the north-east were rained off. In the entire season, the only game in which play was possible was the one at Winchester, which they won.

But Northumbrians are a tough and resilient bunch, and with a membership of around 200, a stable fixture list, three golf days, hard-working officers and a strong committee, the Borderers look well placed to withstand whatever social, cricketing or even climatic change can throw at them over the years ahead.

Website: *www.borderers.org.uk*

The end of an evening game against Lycetts,
the financial services company, at Eglingham, 2007

Berkshire Gentlemen

Founded: 1895

by Roy New and Ronnie Brock

When Berkshire County Cricket Club was founded in 1895 to compete in the Minor Counties Championship, the members also decided to play under the title of 'Berkshire Gentlemen' against colleges, schools and clubs within the county. By this arrangement it was considered that any promising cricketers would come to the notice of the county, and this policy still holds good more than 100 years later. Through the years the fixture list has been expanded to include neighbouring teams such as the Gentlemen of Essex, Gloucestershire Gipsies, Hampshire Hogs, Hertfordshire Gentlemen and South Oxford Amateurs. Matches have also been played against the Stragglers of Asia, the Butterflies and Toronto from Canada when they toured the UK.

The first recorded Berkshire Gentlemen fixture was in 1898 against Reading School, although the result is not known. In 1900 this game was played again when the BG scored 409 for five and dismissed the school for 91. Unfortunately, formal records have been lost prior to 1925 when all the top schools in Berkshire were played as well as a fixture against the RMC Shrivenham. This was the longest surviving fixture till 2009 when operational pressures on the military establishment caused its demise.

A full record of the 1927 season survives when 17 matches brought the BG seven victories. Local clubs Basingstoke, Wargrave and Wokingham had been added to the list to supplement the various schools, colleges and regimental opposition. The successes include Reading School, beaten by 147 runs, Newbury Grammar School, beaten by 129 runs, Bradfield College, beaten by nine wickets, and Radley College, beaten by five wickets, while the game with King Alfred's School at Wantage was tied at 81 runs each. Another win by six wickets was achieved against the Reading Biscuit Factory for whom Harry Lewis turned out. Among other Berkshire luminaries of this era, the new secretary Major Luther played in ten games, Francis Buckley in four, Guy Bennett in three, the redoubtable Doctor Woodburn in two and John Human played in the game at Wargrave.

In the late '20s and early '30s a similar pattern was maintained as the fixture list continued to expand. 1928 brought a game against Hampshire Club and Ground, whose team included John Arnold, Ossie Herman and Sam Pothecary. Herman, who was from Cowley, had earlier played for Oxfordshire. In the same year an extraordinary two-innings game against the Royal Berkshire Regiment was completed in one day between 11.35am and 6.37pm (BG 110 and 71 for 6 dec., Royal Berkshire Regiment 61 and 70). In 1930 Tom Dollery, who went on to play four Tests for England and captain Warwickshire to the county championship, played for Reading School against the BG. 1932 saw Wellington College join the programme, and 1933 brought a high scoring two-innings game with Quidnuncs for whom JGW Davies of Kent scored 161 not out and the legendary Jahangir Khan, captain of India and father of Majid Khan, scored 59 in a total of 368. In 1934 the respected cricket writer RC Robertson-Glasgow appeared in one game for the BG at Reading School in a season when 297 was totalled against Reading Biscuit Factory, who replied with 299 for one (Harry Lewis 135 not out). Matches were played against four Oxford colleges (Worcester, Exeter, Lincoln and Queen's) as well as strolling teams Romany, Incogniti, the Grasshoppers and the Frogs.

For over 40 years all Berkshire Gentlemen records disappeared, excepting only the 1946 scorebook which survived miraculously to reveal a game against Reading School, who were bowled out for 77, all ten wickets falling to WW Smith for 24 runs in 26 overs of which 16 were maidens. In the game against Beaumont College at Old Windsor, the young Alan Sears turned out beside survivors from pre-war days.

In 1968 a high-scoring game at Wokingham saw the home club declare at 256 for three and the BG finish nine runs short with five wickets in hand. Against Reading School Alan Revell scored 116 not out in a total of 204 for one, with the school replying with 182 for four; while the Privateers racked up 267 for five, only to be overhauled by the BG's 271 for nine. The season ably demonstrated one of the beauties of cricket when, having bundled Hartley Wintney out for 97, the BG then collapsed to 58 all out!

When Toronto visited from Canda in 1972, they enjoyed themselves so much that one of their players guested for the BG the following day against Douai School and scored a hundred. There were more high-scoring games in the 1980s, including three of 250-plus against Reading School, Reading CC and Hurley CC, all in 1984. In 1986 at Abingdon, the BG declared at 349 for two, of which Gary Loveday's 218 not out was believed to be the highest individual score by a BG batsman to that time The large scores kept on coming, with Simon Massey scoring 137 against Maidenhead & Bray in 1989 and Nick Pitcher 203 not out against his home club at Falkland CC.

Without their own ground and playing only away fixtures, the BG have relied on the goodwill of other Berkshire clubs. The club has always been grateful for this support, not least during the '80s and '90s, when sides came from far and wide to play the Berkshire Gentlemen. The Crusaders from Australia, Camberwell Grammar School from Victoria, Australia and Fernleaf CC from New Zealand all faced the Gents on their tours.

One of the BG's strangest victories so far was achieved in 1991 in the game against Hurley, whose number 11 batsman was recorded as 'absent – walking his dog'.

Things have changed a great deal since the Berkshire Gentlemen first took to the cricket field in 1898. It is probable that few, if any, of the eleven who played that day would have thought that it would be a Berkshire woman cricketer, Claire Taylor, who would become the first woman cricketer to be honoured by *Wisden* as one of their five Cricketers of the Year in 2009. It is certain that none of them would have thought that a woman would play for the Berkshire Gentlemen! But this did indeed happen, on 1 July 2011, when Shenica Gumbs represented the BG against the Oratory School. It was later that summer when Gary Loveday's individual record was surpassed by Richard Morris who scored 249 not out against Sou'westers, although it says something for the quality of the pitch that Sou'westers refused to be bowled out and achieved a draw.

The thought occurs, in looking back over this record of BG's cricketing achievements, that, with the notable exception of WW Smith's ten wickets in 1946, batsmen feature more prominently than bowlers. We can think of two possible explanations: the old one, that bowlers are around only to give batsmen a game; and the alternative, more honourable one, that it has always been part of the BG's cricketing ethos to involve everyone in the game, and that will often have meant giving all those who wanted it the chance to bowl.

The fixture cards tell their own story of the ebb and flow of the BG's fortunes as a wandering club: 17 matches in 1927, 26 in 1990 and just eight in 2012. Right from the start, the BG have seen it as part of their mission to identify and develop younger cricketers outside their regular club or school environment. It has also sought to attract more mature cricketers, who still wanted to enjoy the game without the rigours of batting points, bowling points and relegation battles.

The organisation and administration of the game have progressed and developed to such an extent that there is far more cricket available than there used to be, with league cricket, on Sundays now as well as Saturdays, the county age-group set-up for young cricketers, and county over-50s, over-60s and even, in partnership with Hampshire, over-70s sides, all competing in national competitions.

Something had to give to accommodate all that extra cricket, and it has often been the wandering sides like the BG who have taken the hit. But are we downcast? No, we are not. Such is the enthusiasm of the players who turn out for the BG, the commitment of the club officials and the sheer enjoyment which everyone takes from the way we play the game, that we can be confident for the future. Although it would help if the weather played its part!

Berkshire Gentlemen and Warborough Shillingford, 1997

Romany

Founded: 1895 or 1902

by Tim Halstead

The Romany Cricket Club has played non-league cricket in Yorkshire and beyond for well over 100 years. The club's archives teasingly place the date of the founding of the club, quite precisely, in both 1895 and in 1902. The club celebrated its centenary in 2002 primarily because the earlier date had long passed by the time that the centenary sub-committee had decided how it should do so.

The founder members of the club had strong ties to the Territorial Army – it is said (though no one now seems sure by whom) that the club was started by veterans of the Boer War. A newspaper cutting from 1946 refers to the revival of the Romany Cricket Club, following the Second World War:

> The members are not concerned about averages. They think more of the game than the result. Type of members: Lawyers, doctors and other professional men.

There are still lawyers, doctors and other professional men in the club, but the membership extends well beyond that.

Romany's origins are in the Leeds area – the first President was Charles Francis Tetley, chairman of the family brewing business started by his grandfather, Joshua Tetley. Over the years, the fixture list has gradually wandered more towards the old North Riding. Typical fixtures these days are against the Yorkshire Gentlemen at Escrick, York and in the classical village green setting of Crakehall, near Bedale (a tiny ground, made smaller still by the protrusion of the churchyard, such that gully to a left-hander stands right on the boundary).

For many years on either side of the Second World War 'The Romany' would tour Scarborough at Whitsuntide. It is said that the first game played at Whitby after the war was against The Romany – in front of paying spectators (quite possibly for the only time in the club's history).

The club's West Riding roots are not entirely overlooked. A current favourite in the fixture list is the annual match at Leeds against the Caribbean CC, usually played to the constant beat of music from the huge pavilion speakers. The connections with Caribbean CC can be useful on other occasions. Answering a call for two last-minute replacements for a midweek match against St Peter's School in York, Alvin Kallicharran and Collis King took the field to the disbelief (and ultimate delight) of eleven schoolboys. One of the sixes hit by Collis King was reputedly the biggest ever seen at the school in its 1300-year history.

Aside from the occasional first-class cricketer (and the even more occasional professional footballer – Peter Beagrie's famous back-flip was once displayed at Bolton Percy, following an athletic catch), The Romany has long been the home of decent club cricketers who have just passed their prime and would-be club cricketers who still dream that their prime lies ahead of them. It offers an alternative to the serious business of Yorkshire league cricket – 40 overs a side in some of the most beautiful locations in the country. One week they can be playing on the edge of a gently sloping field at Lofthouse and Middlesmoor in the Yorkshire Dales and the next at the luxury Swinton Park Hotel near Masham. Tours still take place, though now every two years, to West Sussex. In addition to a fixture in the Priory Park cricket festival week at Chichester, The Romany has played over the years at Hambledon, Arundel, Midhurst, Petworth and Singleton, among other grounds.

Perversely, the most popular games now are often those that require the longest journeys. It was not always so. Back in the 1920s, players would travel to matches in the guard's van of local trains, and the re-establishment of the club after the Second World War was slow, not least because of petrol rationing and the problems it posed for travel and therefore, by definition, for a wandering side. There were occasions, however, when members travelled in style. The club's scorer would typically cycle to matches up to 50 miles away, but was evidently rather taken by Mrs Currer-Briggs' offer to drive him to one match in a classic Rolls Royce (registration number U1). The perils of drink-driving were blissfully unknown to the players of that era, so lunch at the Queen's Hotel in Leeds would be followed by a long post-match visit to the local inn – except, that is, for the match at Castle Howard, where the teetotal Carlisle and Howard families would offer lemonade to their thirsty visitors.

A remarkably enduring character was Barry Hare, who played intermittently for the club in the 1920s and 1930s, but whose primary position was as scorer – which he held for no fewer than 60 years. As he approached the age of 80, his sharp-eyed powers of

back: B Hare, GL Watson, S Aikman, E Mylchreest, N Taylor, Goucher
front: Major Brooke, LC Bower, E Roberts, W Bower, VER Blunt

95

observation began to wane. On one occasion at Arthington the ball smashed into the pavilion about a foot above his head. As the rattling of the timber walls subsided and the ball trickled to rest at his feet, Barry was heard to enquire, "Was that a single to Hockin?"

The club's official history records an event in 1947 against 'the grammar school' (presumably at Leeds) that rather defies belief. A Romany batsman, Joe Driver, evidently hit a six out of the ground, over a passing bus, bouncing in a courtyard, through a window, to land in a bowl of trifle at a children's party. The very next entry in the records refers to a game against HMS *Ceres*, when a schoolboy from Charterhouse hit three successive sixes off the bowling of the same Joe Driver. The schoolboy in question – one PBH May – went on to many great batting achievements, but probably never landed a six in a bowl of trifle.

In its early years The Romany would have played a dozen or so fixtures a season. By the late 1980s this had grown to 50 fixtures, almost every Saturday and Sunday from late April to late September, with a few midweek fixtures besides. The fixture list has lately settled to around 20 games a year, including every Sunday from May to September. Over 100 years on, The Romany continues to offer a unique blend of (occasionally) good cricket, great locations, a traditional cricketing ethos and a healthy disrespect of anything too serious.

Website: *www.romanycricketclub.com*

Footnote
There is another club of the same name, whose profile also appears in this book. Some older members of the Yorkshire Romany say that the two are connected, but a comparison of members' names at the time of the founding of the other Romany club shows no obvious link.

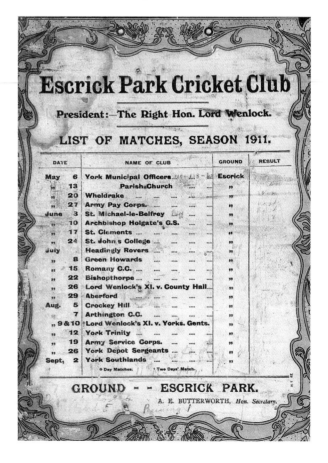

Romany among the visitors to Escrick Park, 1911

Authors

Founded: 1896 (possibly earlier), revived 2012

by Anthony Gibson

The Authors' cap is maroon, with a silver badge. Their emblem is a book surrounded by the following inscription in Latin: 'Praeter Ingenium Nihil'. This is a loose (and somewhat pretentious) translation of Kim Hughes's famous assessment of Mike Brearley after the 1981 Ashes: "He had nothing going for him except that he was intelligent." It seemed an apt motto for a team of writers, whose cricketing credentials do not always match their publishing ones.

The original Authors were just one of several literary cricket teams around at the turn of the twentieth century. Famously, JM Barrie had his Allahakbarries side, who would practise mostly on the train to matches, and PG Wodehouse and AA Milne each had their own elevens. There was a good deal of overlap between these teams but the Authors were the only one made up solely of writers. They would play each year at Lord's against the Publishers and the Actors. Arthur Conan Doyle was the central figure of the side, a formidable all-rounder who played ten matches for the MCC and once dismissed WG Grace with a long-hop. He was ably supported by Wodehouse, a short-sighted fast bowler who occasionally opened the batting with him; Milne, who was the side's best fielder; and EW Hornung, no great shakes as a cricketer, but his most famous creation, Raffles, was an excellent player at least. Occasionally the side was strengthened by the presence of the adventure story writer Hesketh Hesketh-Prichard, a fast bowler who played frequently for Hampshire, taking 106 first-class wickets in 1904. He was a great friend of Conan Doyle, sharing a common interest not only in cricket but in spiritualism and prehistoric creatures. Among his many real-life adventures was one to Argentina where he searched in vain for the mylodon – "A more hopeless task no man ever had," he wrote to his mother. He was greeted on his return to Victoria Station by Conan Doyle, Barrie and Hornung, all eager for vivid details of the creature.

This Authors side played their last match at Lord's in 1912, losing to the Publishers.

Since then, there have been various incarnations of the Authors, including a star-studded outfit in the 1950s. By then, the traditional match against the Publishers was played at Westminster School's ground in Vincent Square. In 1956, the Authors line-up featured seven internationals, with Len Hutton and Jack Fingleton opening the batting, Arthur Morris first wicket down and captain Douglas Jardine coming in at five. The writers slotted in below the former Test players in the batting order, needless to say. Alec Waugh was at eight, with Edmund Blunden, Paul Gallico and Laurence Meynell making up a distinguished tail. Hutton and Morris had only just retired from top-level cricket and were the youngsters in the side, at the ages of 40 and 35 respectively. Jardine was in his fifties by then and was described as a very pleasant captain, maintaining extremely cordial relations with his former Bodyline opponents. He made a half-century, as did Philip Snow – who wrote about this match in his memoir, *A Time of Renewal*. Snow was

The Authors and The Artists, 1903
back row: EW Hornung (creator of Raffles), EV Lucas (author and poet),
PGWodehouse, JC Smith, G Charne, Sir Arthur Conan Doyle,
Hesketh Hesketh-Prichard, LD Luard (illustrator), CMQ Orchardson (painter),
Leonard Charles Nightingale (painter), A Kinross.
front row: C Gascoyne, Shan Bullock (Irish author),
George Hillyard Swinstead (painter), Reginald Blomfield (architect), the Hon WJ James,
Edwin Austin Abbey (American painter), Albert Chevalier Taylor (painter), JM Barrie,
George Cecil Ives (poet and early gay rights activist), George Spencer Watson (painter).
sitting on ground: AEW Mason (author and politician).

also the author of *Cricket in the Fiji Islands* and founder of the first multi-racial sporting body there. In 1948, he captained the Fijian side's tour of New Zealand, where they won two of their five games.

The Authors embarked on their own foreign tour in January 2013, when they travelled to India to take on the might of the Rajasthan Royals, among others, as a prelude to the Jaipur Literary Festival. The Authors had re-formed the previous year, a century after the last of the matches at Lord's. In their first season back, they played teams of publishers and actors, the latter at the 'Home of Cricket'. They faced the Lords and Commons CC at Wormsley, Tim Rice's Heartaches and the East London Community CC in Victoria Park in Hackney. Later in the season, they travelled to the beautiful Valley of Rocks in North Devon, to historic Hambledon and then to Harold Larwood's old club, Kirkby Portland. They could have done with Len Hutton in the side, particularly in the last-mentioned game, but all season they managed to avoid the single-figure innings totals so endemic to (and beloved of) the Allahakbarries.

After the experiment with selecting some of the greatest cricketers of all time, the Authors decided to revert to the Edwardian model, which embraced all-comers, provided they'd written a book (or, in a couple of exceptional cases, were likely to). And so the Authors' squad includes both Ed Smith, of Kent, Middlesex and England and novelist

Kamila Shamsie, whose first-ever innings came against Shepperton Ladies, where she faced the former South African international all-rounder Kim Price. Many of the Authors had fallen by the cricketing wayside, thinking they'd played their last game and hoping their children might pick up a bat one day instead. But many have been successfully rehabilitated, courtesy of some pre-season nets and coaching with Warwickshire's Darren Maddy and Neil Carter. These include Anthony McGowan, author of many successful children's and adult books, Jon Hotten, whose *The Old Batsman* blog represents cricket writing at its finest, and historian and former Croatian fast bowler Peter Frankopan, who suffered from the yips and successfully reinvented himself as a destructive batsman. In his absence, his fellow historians, Tom Holland, Matthew Parker and Thomas Penn, lead the bowling attack. Its spearhead is Nicholas Hogg, the team's vice-captain, novelist and former Leicestershire Schools and U19 player. He revived the side, along with literary agent and captain, Charlie Campbell.

The Authors like to style themselves as semi-professional cricketers – which is a fairly meaningless term, particularly for a team of wordsmiths. But they are sponsored by Christie's and they have compiled a book about their comeback season, published by Bloomsbury (*The Authors XI: A Season of English Cricket from Hackney to Hambledon*) in June 2013. Other contributors include Richard Beard, Sam Carter, Sebastian Faulks, William Fiennes, James Holland, Alex Preston, Amol Rajan, Dan Stevens and Andy Zaltzman. The Authors support two tremendous charities: First Story, which promotes creative writing in challenging secondary schools; and Chance to Shine, which does the same for cricket. With a growing pool of players and fixture list, the Authors' future looks assured. They welcome new players and opposition.

Author Will Fiennes, batting at Wormsley, 2012
photographed by Ngayu Thairu

Somerset Stragglers

Founded: 1900

by Anthony Gibson

The Somerset Stragglers have their own particular niche amongst wandering clubs, in that they were set up almost as a rival to the established county side. This was in 1900, nine years after Somerset had joined the magic circle of the county championship. Then (as, to some extent, now) the Somerset cricketing public had a particular fondness for the amateur game. This was hardly surprising, given that the rollicking Mr Sam Woods was captain of the county side, the dashing Mr Lionel Palairet its principal ornament and that Somerset was home to Sir Spencer Ponsonby Fane, one of the three founders of I Zingari and thus a champion of amateurism.

But it did produce tensions, especially as Somerset went through a series of increasingly poor seasons after a promising start. As Peter Roebuck relates in his history of Somerset CC, *From Sammy to Jimmy*, 'Time and again, at area meetings and AGMs and on the executive, where Newton (Arthur), Palairet and others of the old school ruled the roost, praise was heaped on the amateur game.'

It was at this point that the Rev Edward Spurway, rector of Heathfield, not far from Taunton, appeared on the scene. Spurway was, in some ways, a typical Somerset amateur: a countryman, accomplished all-round sportsman, with time and money on his hands, who had been good enough to play two games for the county, but not good enough to have amassed more than 26 runs in his four innings. Spurway was approached by sundry other Somerset amateurs, and asked to see about forming an exclusively amateur side. Whether this really was intended as a rival to the county side isn't clear but, in any case, Spurway was sensible enough to put the idea to Somerset's founding father and all-powerful Secretary, Henry Anderton, before taking it any further. The result was a happy compromise. Somerset would be pleased to host an amateur side on the county ground (Rack Field, as it was then known), but as an adjunct to the county XI and as a way of helping to bring on good young amateurs, not as competition to it. At a meeting in the Ladies Pavilion (roughly where the second scoreboard now stands) on 27 August 1900, unanimous agreement was reached that 'an amateur cricket club for the county of Somerset be founded.' So began a relationship which continues happily to this day.

After toying with the idea of calling themselves the Nomads, the assembled company fixed instead on the Stragglers, quite possibly because someone pointed out that, with its base at Rack Field, the new club wouldn't actually be nomadic, whereas it might well be, to quote the *OED*, 'one who wanders or roves without fixed direction'. Having fixed on a name, it was time to choose the club colours. Spurway had been to Fox's mill in Wellington, where they made the traditional red and blue dress uniforms for the British army, and had also recently developed khaki, as partial camouflage against Boer snipers. So red, blue and khaki it was, although the khaki was later changed to a golden yellow – camouflage being just about the last thing that most wandering cricketers are interested in!

The new club was an immediate success. Within a year, it had over 100 members and by 1923 was strong enough financially to be able to help out the cash-strapped county club by paying for a new scoreboard, a new clock to go on the scoreboard, plus a contribution towards paying off Somerset's debts. The total bill was £94, in return for which the Stragglers asked if they could rent part of the Ladies Pavilion, and be given a small area of land in front of it, so that they would have their own pavilion and enclosure. This was agreed, and the Stragglers Pavilion, as it soon became known, was a much-loved feature of the County Ground for the next 70 years or so, until it was rather cruelly demolished in the 2008 ground redevelopment.

As co-habitees of the County Ground, it was inevitable that the relationship between the Stragglers and the county side would be close. Many of Somerset's finest cricketers, from Sammy Woods through John Daniell to RJO Meyer and Harold Gimblett, played for the Stragglers either before or after their county careers. Jack 'Farmer' White, purveyor of seemingly guileless but frequently deadly slow left-arm, was a particular terror for the Stragglers' opponents. In 1938, he took 9/9 against Queen's College Taunton, and followed that up with 14 wickets in a two-day game against the Stragglers of Asia and 9/43 against Bridgwater.

Those statistics provide a good indication of the Stragglers' typical fixture list during the inter-war years: the local public schools, the stronger local club sides, the many other wandering clubs who liked to visit Somerset on tour, and three deadly rivals from across the county boundary: Sidmouth, North Devon and the Devon Dumplings, all of whom have featured on the fixture list right from the start.

Two names stand out from this period: ER Nesfield, a land agent from Dulverton, who not only scored thousands of runs for the Stragglers during his many seasons as a player, but who went on to run the Junior Stragglers, now sadly no more, but who in their time helped nurture the likes of Vic Marks, Peter Roebuck and Jeremy Lloyds; and Hallam 'Granny' Alston, who scored over 8,000 runs and took 478 wickets for the club in seven seasons from 1932, and came as close as any Straggler ever has to doing the double, with 1,077 runs and 95 wickets in 1934 – and all this was on top of the bucket-loads of wickets and runs that he provided for many other clubs, like the Nomads, Sou'Westers, Clevedon and Guernsey. He made just one first-class appearance for Somerset, and took just one wicket. But what a wicket! Jack Hobbs.

Since the war, the biggest change has been the move away from the County Ground. The Stragglers played their last regular fixture there in 1980 and have been genuine wanderers ever since, playing at club grounds around the county with just the occasional 'special' game back at their spiritual home, most notably the centenary match against the MCC in 2000. Ironically, this wasn't long after a time in the late 1990s when the future of the club seemed to be in doubt, its finances shaky and its officers ageing. Happily, salvation was at hand, in the shape of a long-time Stragglers player, Hugh Duder, who took over the presidency in 1998 and gave the club the shot in the arm that it needed, with considerable assistance from his vice-president Michael Giles. It is now firmly established again, playing around 17 games a season, many of them long-established fixtures against the many touring sides who visit the West Country every year, and the membership list stands at a healthy 180, including plenty of younger cricketers, which bodes well for the future.

One should never fall into the trap of over-romanticising wandering cricket, but there is something about the Stragglers that speaks unmistakably of Somerset; something of cheese and cider, of long days in the sun, and long evenings in the bar or the skittle alley with old foes who have become old friends. Pat Lennard-Payne first played for the Junior Stragglers in 1936, was the club's secretary from 1956 to 63 and wrote an excellent history of the club to mark its centenary in 2000. He looks back with unashamed nostalgia to the days when Cecil Buttle, the legendary Somerset head groundsman, would roll yet another immaculate pitch, set the wickets up on a sunny morning and then spend the entire day umpiring for the Stragglers. "We played for the pleasure of playing cricket," he recalls. "Yes, we liked to win and, if we couldn't win, then to draw. But we played for the sheer joy of it, and there's really no cricket like it."

Website: *www.somersetstragglers.play-cricket.com*

The Somerset Stragglers at Instow, 1956
RJ Adamson, MJ Points
HO Hopkins, RH Foster, BW Hastilow, JP Stevinson
E Wright, PC Lennard-Payne, WR Moor

Devon Dumplings

Founded: 1902

by Anthony Gibson

'Chronic creator of cricket clubs' would have been an apt epitaph for Colonel James Fellowes, given his record in establishing them on the one hand, and his fondness for giving them alliterative names on the other. Having founded the Hampshire Hogs in 1887, he had more than a hand in the emergence of the Somerset Stragglers in 1900, and then went on to be the prime mover in the Devon Dumplings, who played their first game in 1902. Whether that name has subsequently conveyed quite the image that the club might have wanted may be open to question, but it was very much in keeping with the light-hearted, profoundly amateur spirit of the cricketing times, and it did provide the opportunity for at least one club, Holsworthy, to serve apple dumplings tied up with green ribbons as a pretty lunchtime tribute to their opponents during their early encounters.

Fellowes was a career soldier in the Royal Engineers who somehow found the time to play 23 first-class games, mainly for Hampshire and Kent, taking 60 wickets with fast round-arm, before moving back to Devon, where he had family connections, in the early 1890s. Within a few years, he had successfully resuscitated the ailing Devon county club, and when three undergraduates at Exeter College, Oxford – Lewis Cruwys, MB Baines and EH Banks – had the idea of forming a county wandering club, he must have been the obvious person to turn to.

At an inaugural meeting on 24 January 1902 in Exeter, Fellowes was elected Honorary Secretary, the name was decided upon (doubtless at Fellowes' suggestion), rules were adopted and the club colours – 'three shades of green one and a half inches wide' – chosen. The founders made no bones about the sort of club they wanted theirs to be: 'a Gentlemen's Club, along the lines of the BB, Derbyshire Friars, Somerset Stragglers, Hampshire Hogs etc'. And the founders were indeed drawn from some of the oldest and grandest families in Devon, including the Cruwyses and the Coplestones, who (along with the Crockers), 'when the Conqueror came, were all at home'. As for Fellowes, for all the clubs that he founded or revived, he seems to have been a difficult man, and it wasn't long before he'd fallen out with his fellow Dumplings and left the county.

That first season the Dumplings played four matches, all at Exeter, including two fixtures, against Free Foresters and the Somerset Stragglers, which have been contested with, in Lt Colonel the Hon Gerald French's phrase, 'the utmost zeal' virtually ever since. The fixture list expanded the following year to take in two more of the Dumplings' oldest rivals, Incogniti and Blundell's School, and by 1907 the new club already had 220 members on its books. The standard of cricket was high. The Stragglers fielded both Lionel Palairet and Sammy Woods in their 1904 match, while the first Dumpling to play first-class cricket was probably Peter Randall Johnson, a hard-driving patrician cricketer of the old school, who played over 200 games for Somerset, having qualified for the county by virtue of being born in Wellington, even though that was Wellington, New Zealand!

DEVON DUMPLINGS' CRICKET CLUB. ～ SEASON 1904.

DATE.	AGAINST.	AT.	MANAGER.
June 9	Holsworthy	Exeter	A. B. BRAMWELL, *Brampford Speke, Exeter.*
„ 13, 14	Somerset Stragglers	Exeter	F. COLERIDGE BOLES, *Bolham House, Tiverton.*
„ 20, 21	United Services	Exeter	HON. O. SCOTT, *Torridge House, Westward Ho!*
„ 28	H.M.S. Britannia	Dartmouth	A. H. GIBBS, *Clyst St. George, Topsham.*
July 6	Blundell's	Tiverton	REV. S. W. FEATHERSTONE, *Pinhoe, Exeter.*
„ 13, 14	United Services	Mount Wise	HON. O. SCOTT.
„ 18, 19	Free Foresters	Exeter	A. B. BRAMWELL.
„ 25, 26	North Devon	Exeter	G. F. C. HAMILTON, *East Budleigh.*
„ 28, 29	O.B.'s King Edward's School	Exeter	CAPT. N. R. RADCLIFFE, *Alphington, Exeter.*
August 4	Holsworthy	Holsworthy	R. M. SNOW, *Gandy Street, Exeter.*
„ 8, 9	Channel Islanders	Exeter	H. F. BRUNSKILL, *Buckland, Kingsbridge, S. Devon.*
„ 10, 11	Incogniti	Exeter	H. F. BRUNSKILL.
„ 12, 13	M. C. C.	Exeter	F. COLERIDGE BOLES.
„ 24, 25	North Devon	Instow	CAPT. N. R. RADCLIFFE.
„ 29, 30	Somerset Stragglers	Taunton	DR. W. G. GRAY, *Holsworthy.*

Members wishing to play in any Match are **particularly** requested to write to the Manager of such Match at least three weeks before the date thereof.

A. B. BRAMWELL, ⎱ *Hon. Secs.*
A. H. GIBBS, ⎰ *City Bank, Exeter.*

The Dumplings' membership suffered grievous losses in the First World War, no fewer than 140 giving their lives for their country, and recovery afterwards was slow. Fortunately, most of the pre-war stalwarts had survived, including a man who would become the Dumplings' mainstay throughout the inter-war years, the Rev Gerald Heslop. As, successively, Vicar of Upottery, Rector of Clyst St Mary, Rector of St Mary's Exeter and Prebendary of Exeter Cathedral, he obviously wasn't exactly over-stretched, for he managed to play hundreds of games for the Dumplings from 1904 to 1939, taking over 1,000 wickets with medium-pace and off-breaks and scoring at least 22,000 runs. His contribution off the field was almost equally valuable, serving as Secretary from 1921 to '39 and steering the Dumplings through probably their greatest period.

Looking back many years later, he wrote that 'such country house cricket as, before the First World War and to a lesser degree after, we were asked to play in, was something that in these days seems almost like a dream.' He recalled, in particular, Tichbourne Park in Hampshire, and Hubert Martineau's estate at Holyport near Maidenhead. But the Dumplings had a country-house venue all of their own: Bystock, not far from Exmouth, the home of Freddy Hunter, where they played many matches during the 1920s. The aforementioned Gerald French (son of Sir John), who himself played several times for the Dumplings, has left us an affectionate description of the setting:

> The beautifully-kept arena, with its irreproachable wicket, was bounded on its four sides by a drive, the park, and extensive kitchen garden, and a clump of cedars separating it from the house. There were two pavilions, one for the players and the other for the house party, while the ground's individuality revealed itself in a novel form of sight screen. This consisted of sail-cloth, fitted with rings top and bottom, and run on wires within a wooden framework – the conception, I suspect, of my genial host, Fred Hunter.

Sadly Hunter sold the house in 1929, and the cricket ground has long since disappeared.

When it comes to happy memories, the Dumplings will have inspired more than most, not just among their own players but perhaps even more so among the many wandering clubs who made the pilgrimage to Devon on their summer tours. In pre-war days, they included the Free Foresters, Incogniti, Chiswick Park, the Nondescripts, Sussex Martlets, Radley Rangers, Sheffield Collegiate and the South Oxford Amateurs. So sought after was a fixture with the Dumplings that many had to be turned away, for even in the days before league cricket there were only so many fixtures that a wandering club could sustain.

As for the individual performance of the inter-war years, that accolade must go to another pillar of Dumpling cricket, Ronnie Seldon, a master at Blundell's (like so many other Dumplings down the years) and captain of Devon. In 1929, at Exeter, he took all ten of the Somerset Stragglers' wickets and followed that with an unbeaten century, something that has only been done at this level in a single day on two other occasions in all of cricket history.

The post-war era started propitiously. By 1949, the fixture list had grown to 41 matches, about half of which were played at Exeter and the remainder at grounds like Chudleigh, Exmouth, Axminster, Tiverton and Blundell's. But pride at the club's approaching jubilee was to be followed by a painful fall, as the committee and its cantankerous secretary, Captain Jewell, hopelessly over-estimated the number of copies of Malcolm Elwin's history that would be sold – excellent piece of work though it was – and were left with a legacy of two and a half tons of unsold books and a hefty overdraft. Financial problems would haunt the club on and off for the next two decades.

Problems off the field probably didn't detract much from enjoyment on it, especially in surroundings as glorious as Instow or Knightshayes Court. For many years the County Ground at Exeter was regarded as the Dumplings' unofficial 'home' ground. More recently, as the standard of other grounds has improved, and wanting to spread their fixtures around the county, they have taken to playing more of their games at the grounds of their 'friends' – clubs like Hatherleigh, Plymouth, Sidmouth, Paignton and Shobrooke Park, as well, of course, as Exeter.

In the old days, two-day games were the rule. Nowadays, the fixtures are divided roughly half and half into all-day declaration matches, and 40-over afternoon contests, and they tend to be against old boys' sides, schools, sister county clubs, the armed forces and wandering clubs on tour. North Devon is now the only local club they play. As with most wandering clubs, the standard of cricket has ebbed and flowed down the years. In the days before the ex-public schoolboys, clergymen and schoolmasters gave way to Devon league players, the Dumplings probably lost more than they won. A notable exception to that was 1961, when they notched up 14 victories, formed the Junior Dumplings (for whom the likes of Vic Marks, Jeremy Lloyds and Roger Twose would eventually feature) and gave a debut to a man who would become (and very much remains) a Dumpling legend, Jeff Stanyer.

Over more than 50 years, he has been ever present, as player, captain, match manager and all-round moving spirit. However, it wasn't until 2008 that he first took on a formal role, when he became 'cricketing secretary', persuading his fellow academic Brian Smith to become official secretary at the same time. Both were significant appointments, for it had seemed for a time that the Dumplings might fold, for want of a secretary and treasurer.

One other 'modern' Dumpling who deserves an honourable mention is Peter Spencer, who kept wicket for the club for many years, besides serving as Secretary, President and writing the club's history, *Three Shades of Green*, which was published to mark the centenary in 2002. It would be fair to say that his final chapter was distinctly downbeat. League cricket, limited overs, social changes, alternative attractions – all were making it more and more difficult to raise sides and sustain fixtures, to the point where 'the more pessimistic among us fear that it may before too long lead to the death of the kind of cricket described in this book.'

But right at the end, he strikes a more optimistic note, suggesting that there may, after all, be a place for clubs like the Dumplings, if only to provide some light relief from the relentless pressures of the league, and expressing confidence in the spirit and resolution of his fellow Dumplings to keep the flag flying.

And so it has proved. Thanks to the efforts of its officers, and supported as it has always been by its umpires and scorers, the club has broken out of the spiral of decline which Peter Spencer bemoaned. A new generation of younger players has been recruited from a wider cross-section of clubs, the fixture list has settled down at a manageable 25 games a season and, in 2011, the ratio of wins to losses was the best ever. A 'golden season' is how it is described on the club's website, but then I guess that most cricketers would regard almost any season with the Devon Dumplings as a pretty golden one, to be able to play good cricket, in the right spirit, in such glorious surroundings.

Website: *www.devondumplingscc.co.uk*

Devon Dumplings versus Dorset Rangers, Milton Abbey, 1994
back: JH Olsen (umpire), J Barnes, P Petherbridge, J Criddle, GH Humphries, H Townsemd,
R Scott, GH Tatham front: AY Warrington (scorer), J Stanyer, PG Spencer, AWH Parr, AA Wragg

Nomads

Founded: 1903

by Anthony Gibson

From the narrowest of bases, the Nomads has developed into the broadest of cricketing churches, and is flourishing in a way that most other wandering clubs can only envy. Those two sets of circumstances are by no means unconnected, as we shall discover.

Most of the original Nomads had been schoolboys together at Peterborough Lodge prep school in Hampstead, and the club which they formed in 1903 was the Hampstead Nomads. By that time, most of them had been to Oxford or Cambridge and several were aspiring architects, an association which would last for many years. By the time war broke out in 1914, the fixture list had been built up to over 40 matches a season: against schools, old boys sides, London clubs, kindred wandering spirits and, on one occasion celebrated in the pages of *Sporting Life* in 1912, a team called Stade Francais from Paris.

The Hampstead Nomads must have been a relatively youthful side, for the war took a particularly heavy toll. Half of the members were killed, and it wasn't until 1922 that the club got going again, now known simply as the Nomads, the Hampstead connection having been broken. Memories from this period are lost although there are some fifty-odd entries in the *Cricketer* magazine between the two world wars.

The standard of their cricket must have been pretty high. Charles Poole, who had captained Northamptonshire before the war, scored 600 runs in skippering Nomads through 54 matches in 1925 and Duleepsinhji played on tour for them in the Channel Islands in the late '20s, scoring an elegant abundance of runs which were remembered by the locals for years afterwards. The highlight of the Nomads' season, for many years, was a week-long tour to Cambridge in August, playing the colleges every day, and drinking every night, as well as a regular week's tour in the UK.

By far and away the most significant figure in Nomads cricket in this era and for many years to come was Sidney Caulfield, of whom we have been left this wonderful description by his fellow Nomads' stalwart, David Morton:

> A small, almost wizened figure, he had a little beak of a nose and his flat head and wrinkled brow poked forth from his shoulders like a benevolent tortoise. No matter how hot the weather, he invariably wore a heavy grey tweed suit with a deerstalker of the same material, a Nomads tie, and he preferred boots to shoes. He was reputed to be an eminent architect, but as far as could be ascertained, his office served as the Nomads' administrative headquarters and his staff devoted the major part of their time to the arrangement and confirmation of fixtures, the notification and replacement of players and the revision of membership lists.

Sidney Caulfield had played in the very first Nomads game. Between them, he and his brother scored the Nomads' first run, took their first wicket and caught the first catch. It was a suitably propitious start to a relationship which would endure for almost 60 years, as player, secretary and finally president. He'd been a useful cricketer in his youth, but it was for his umpiring that he is most fondly remembered. Blind in one eye, and notorious for his eccentric decisions, he eventually yielded to those who pleaded with him to wear glasses. But rather than settling for a conventional pair of spectacles, he invested in a set of opera glasses, which were, of course, completely useless at a range of 22 yards.

"With this contraption in place," writes David Morton, "Sidney, when at the bowler's end, was reduced to standing with his back practically touching the sight screen in order to bring the far wicket into focus; and when over was called, he assumed a position on the boundary in the immediate vicinity of deep square leg."

Caulfield didn't have much luck with his eyesight. Having eventually dispensed with the opera glasses, he was hit a sickening blow which shattered his spectacles when umpiring at Cambridge, losing the sight of his good eye. Happily, whilst in hospital, the surgeons were able to remove the cataract which had blinded him in the other eye and, although he never umpired again, he did make more or less a full recovery. To this day, his health is drunk at Nomads' dinners.

The Nomads recovered strongly after the Second World War and by the 1950s was flourishing, organising a week's cricket at the Hurlingham Club to celebrate the club's jubilee. Peter May played for them in this era, whilst still at Cambridge, as did the West Indies captain Gerry Alexander and other top-class cricketers such as the Somerset and West Indies leg-spinner John Cameron and the Lancashire fast bowler Colin Smith who continued to play in subsequent years. This was also the decade in which that most inveterate of wandering cricketers, HNE 'Granny' Alston – so called for his preference for tea over beer whilst on tour – played most of his Nomads cricket. Several times he achieved the double of 1,000 runs and 100 wickets for the club, and continued playing for them until 1983, by which time he was well into his seventies. Pat Mean, who reputedly hit the ball as hard as any club cricketer who ever lived, was another pillar of the side.

After a successful decade in the 1950s, when they regularly played well over 50 matches a season, the Nomads went into a gentle decline in the 1960s. It was Colin Owen-Browne, energetically recruiting new players, who stopped the rot, and, with the effervescent club skipper Ian Crombie (a former Cambridge boxing Blue), set in motion a revival in both membership and fixtures. By the end of the 1970s, the club was playing as many games as it had ever done – no fewer than 77 in 1979, including the MCC's new indoor six-a-side league and the Wandsworth evening 15/15 eight-balls-an-over league.

It was at this time that, as the current Secretary, Michael Blumberg, recalls, a very conscious decision was made to broaden the base of the Nomads membership beyond the "public schoolboys, Oxbridge, military types and doctors", who up to then had been its stock in trade. "We roped in academics, actors and a string of really good

The Nomads at Iscoyd Park in Shropshire

Caribbean cricketers, many of them from Dominica. To this day, a crashing shot to the boundary is greeted by watching Nomads with the accolade 'Bacchanal!' from the Dominican patois. John Nagenda, from Uganda, captained the club for a time, and he brought in other top-class East African cricketers like Sam Walusimbi and Zahid Shah. They didn't just broaden our membership base, they broadened our horizons."

Two of the outstanding cricketers for Nomads in the late '70s and '80s were run-scoring Tony Whiteway, now Hon Treasurer, who several times scored more than 1,000 runs in a season, and Dr Mike Wilkins, a tall fast-medium bowler who one summer took 90 wickets. Nomads also benefitted enormously from the energy of two 'foreign' captains, New Zealanders Tim Bourke and Steve Hambleton, who brought a string of Antipodeans to play in a period ('85 to '95) when wandering cricket generally was in serious decline.

The other shot in the arm which Nomad cricket has received in recent years has been the popularity of their tours. Michael Blumberg, who has been a prolific wicket-taker and run-scorer for the club since the early '70s, was the editor of a magazine called *Cricket World*, which was well-known for the tours which it organised and promoted. When he sold his interest in *Cricket World* and retired from publishing in late 2000, the Cricket World XI tours were taken under the Nomads' wing and have since thrived. The club now visits the Costa Blanca twice a year, plays in Paris over the August Bank Holiday and makes at least one excursion to an unlikely European venue. Last year, it was the tiny island of Vis, off the coast of Croatia, where the locals are considerably reinforced by a former Premier Yorkshire League batsman – "get him out, and you win; fail to, and you lose" (Blumberg); in April 2003, it was

Rome. And from time to time, the Nomads travel even further afield, to places like India, East Africa and Barbados.

If the eclectic membership and the tours have been part of the explanation for the fact that the Nomads are thriving, at a time when many other wanderers are struggling, then so has an energetic and highly committed core of active members. Michael Blumberg is one of them, but great credit belongs as well to men like Richard Kershaw, who started the Dominica connection, and Charlton Lamb, Vice-President, match manager, recruiter supreme and still playing at the age of 76. Among the younger members, the club is much indebted to Charles Peerless and the current club captain Tom Brockton. Lastly the incorporation of the previously formidable Virgin XI in 2000 brought in additional members and some extra fixtures.

The loss of Saturday matches saw the fixture list shrink slowly through the 1990s. But that has been reversed since the club's centenary in 2003, to the extent that they now play around 50 games a season, not counting the tours, including such old favourites as the Eton Ramblers, Stowe Templars, Gaieties, Oxford Downs, Hampshire Hogs and Northwood. Many of the games are played midweek, just as in the good old days. Ideally the strength of the sides is tailored to that of the opposition, but they always contain a healthy mix of young and old, the good and the not quite so good. The Nomads 'prefer' declaration cricket, but, as the club's excellent website puts it, "We play cricket wherever and whenever invited."

The Nomads has become a very inclusive wandering club and seems to be all the stronger and happier for it. Why, they even have three women playing members! I'm not sure what old Sidney Caulfield would have made of it, but it is symptomatic of an approach which isn't just keeping the club afloat, but taking it on to greater things, and I'm quite sure he would have approved of that.

Website: *www.nomadscc.com*

The Nomads at Holmbury St Mary in Surrey

Frogs

Founded: 1903

by Graham Prain

The outbreak of the Great War brought most forms of cricket in Britain to a halt until 1919. The Edwardian era had seen an expansion in recreational cricket at the same time as first-class cricket was enjoying a 'golden era', with many fine players becoming household names just as 'WG' was fading from the scene. The first decade of the century also saw the start of tours to England from overseas countries other than Australia.

For a fledgling club like the Frogs, founded as a touring side on the inspiration of a couple of undergraduates at Cambridge in 1903 to play 'vacation cricket', the First World War virtually spelt 'curtains'. As Edgar Tregoning, one of the founders, wrote when it was all over: 'Of 150 members in 1914, roughly one in every five had either been killed or died on active service. Losses had been on a scale beyond all we had imagined possible, and so much seemed to have gone out of our life that none who survived from the old committee felt that we could ourselves pick up things where we had laid them down.'

The committee chose to put the club into cold storage while suitable successors could be located to revive the club. That search took much longer than first imagined. It was 1926 before Tregoning found the man he thought could take the Frogs into a new era. That man was a mere youth, Ronnie Prain, then just leaving school to begin a career in the City. It was a bold decision, but a successful one.

The reborn Frogs CC's focus became centred on London, and the club had to rebuild its fixture list and playing base. New opponents were found and a number of Sunday games introduced, an innovation in club cricket at that time. The five years from 1927 were, according to Tregoning, the most decisive in the club's history. Prain attracted new members to the club mainly from his age group, with help from some older pre-war members who re-emerged. Tours were re-established to Devon, to Hampshire and Dorset, and a new tour to Yorkshire undertaken. By the early 1930s the number of fixtures had grown to more than 50 per season.

The club's playing strength, drawn mainly from the public schools and universities, was augmented by attracting a steady flow of Blues such as FR Brown, M Tindall, AH Brodhurst, AP Singleton, TW Fraser and BH Valentine. These and others had careers in county cricket, too. The Frogs were able to field particularly strong bowling attacks, not always a prominent feature of wandering cricket. They were able to call on SJ Pegler (South Africa), FB Pinch (Glamorgan) and WT Greswell (Somerset). The latter bowled out Sir Julien Cahn's XI cheaply, much to the Frogs' host's annoyance and surprise. Indeed, EW Swanton said that he believed the Frogs were the only wandering side to beat Sir Julien's team of stars twice. Other fine bowlers for the Frogs in the inter-war years were GM Singleton, J Webster, JW Greenstock and ARN Carter, some of whom also had experience of county cricket.

The Frogs versus North Devon at Instow, 1936

The Second World War brought a further period of interruption to club cricket. The Frogs went into mothballs again, but this time they ensured they were better placed to bounce back on the resumption of cricket in 1946. A limited number of games were played in that first season, but in 1947, a summer of glorious weather and brilliant cricket (Compton and Edrich), a fixture list comprising more than 30 games, including three tours, had been restored.

The next two decades were halcyon days for wandering cricket. This was an era when it was difficult to take overseas holidays, public transport was relatively cheap and plentiful, and car ownership was becoming more widespread but roads were still uncrowded. Also the range of leisure activities available for people to pursue was smaller than now; and there were fewer constraints on post-match drinking. Cricket thrived at all levels in the immediate post-war period, and so did the Frogs.

Over 50 matches were played per season through the 1950s, with five tours annually. In 1953 the club celebrated its jubilee with a festival at Hurlingham and a grand dinner in London with a panoply of famous names present.

The Frogs were able to put out enviably strong sides in the post-war period. Many of the best players came through the Oxford and Cambridge route, strong justification for the tours of the two universities instituted after the war.

Among prominent post-war players were Bush O'Callaghan, Walter Goold, Arnold Quick, Kim Crouch and Peter Bodkin, and later Dick and John Letts, Robin Fletcher, David Fasken, Jon Fellows-Smith, Stanley Metcalfe and Peter Wenban.

The administration of the club was in the hands of an experienced committee, headed by Bob Levy and Basil Hunt. Two well-known cricketers from that time, who played for the Frogs in the two decades from the mid-1960s, were Charles Fry and Mike Griffith, who have gone on to be Presidents of MCC, as did another Frog, Sir Cyril Hawker.

By the end of the 1960s trends in leisure activities in Britain were having an impact on recreational cricket. This was also the time when league cricket arrived in the south-east. Those who had combined playing their cricket for both a home club and a wandering side or 'old boys' club, now found they were under pressure to commit to playing regularly for their home club in the leagues. This, coupled with increasing pressure on those with domestic commitments, meant that wandering clubs found the raising of good sides on a regular basis became more difficult. Saturday matches for wandering clubs virtually ceased, and for the Frogs the number of tours decreased and the total of fixtures fell by half.

From the 1970s the club continued to play between 20 and 30 matches a year, mainly against well-known clubs in the London area and south-east. Contacts and fixtures at Oxford and Cambridge were maintained, but the club also relied on connections with certain clubs like Hampstead and Oatlands Park as a source for players. Recently there has been a fruitful flow of cricketers from Exeter University.

The Frogs now play no more than 20 matches a season but the list offers entertaining cricket on attractive grounds, mostly within easy reach from London. There are matches against Hurlingham, Hampstead, Amersham, Ashtead, Hampshire Hogs and Oxford University Authentics, and against wandering clubs such as Sussex Martlets, Grasshoppers and Cryptics and 'old boys' sides such as Old Cranleighans and Stowe Templars. The club also has a long-standing fixture against the Cross Arrows at Lord's every other year. A highlight of the season is the Western Tour first undertaken as the Devon Tour in 1907. Matches are played against Gentlemen of Worcestershire, Wiltshire Queries, Devon Dumplings, North Devon and Somerset Stragglers. The Frogs have generally had success on tour, with extended runs of victories in the 1990s matching those in the inter-war and post-war years. The tour is popular with young players and students, who can get away for a week's cricket. Given good weather the tour can provide memorable cricket on some incomparable grounds.

Recent leading players include John and Harry Rawlinson, Richard Bray, Ian Martin, Mike Chetwode, Mark Rosnegk, Jeff Chapman, Marc Williams and Andrew Marshall.

The club looks to the future with hope, if not absolute confidence, for wandering cricket. It remains a small club, which aims to attract good cricketers who may have played several years of league cricket but who now want to enjoy a more relaxed version on Sundays against reasonable opposition on good grounds without committing their time every weekend. The club has only had four presidents in its 110-year history: Edgar Tregoning, Cyril Hawker, David Fasken and currently Graham Prain.

Gentlemen of Staffordshire

Founded: 1904 (some matches played earlier)

by Anthony Gibson

A certain amount of mystery surrounds the early years of the Gentlemen of Staffordshire. The first match of which a scorecard exists was against the might of I Zingari on the Earl of Stamford's Ground at Enville Hall in 1852, yet according to the club's own records, it wasn't actually formed until 1904, at a meeting in the Swan Hotel, Stafford. Perhaps the most likely explanation is that what had been a loose-knit bunch of amateur cricketers, playing occasional matches against others of their ilk, decided to put their activities on a more formal basis. At any event, the 'old' and the 'new' Gents do appear to have been essentially the same group of players. The Rev Percy Mainwaring, who became the first honorary secretary of the new club, had been playing for the unincorporated Gentlemen since 1882.

And he had been playing in some distinguished company, in both the cricketing and the social sense. Among the early Gents were Charlie Brune, a leading light in the Incogniti, who played 56 first-class matches; William Bedford, son of the William Bedford who started the Free Foresters; and the Earl of Stamford, who must have been a half-decent cricketer as well as one of the most prominent of the county's landed gentry, as he played five games for the MCC. Abraham Bass, of the brewing family, described as 'the father of Midlands cricket' by one authority, featured in that first match against IZ, as did Crispin Tinley, who played several times for early England XIs before becoming professional in 1854 for Burton-on-Trent, where he is buried.

Percy Mainwaring wasn't quite in that league, but he did play regularly for the Staffordshire county club, as have very many Gents, from that day to this. In fact, the relationship with the county club seems to have been at the heart of the debate which led up to the formalisation of Gents cricket. Concern was expressed at the inaugural meeting that 'the new organisation should not in any way be inimical to the county club.' The facts that the meeting was being chaired by Lord Dartmouth, who was at that time president of the county, that Mainwaring was a former county captain and secretary, and that one of the primary objects of the new club would be to 'bring out amateurs who would be useful members of the county team' seem to have provided more than sufficient reassurance.

However, it wasn't only the bright young things of amateur cricket that the new club was hoping to attract. In his speech to the meeting, Mainwaring explained that what he was seeking to provide was, in a telling phrase, 'a higher form of cricket'. This would attract 'amateurs who might not be considered good enough to be included in the county team, or who might be overlooked by the County Executive, or who, being old county cricketers, had had their day, but felt that there was still a little cricket left in them, yet realised that they could not play under such arduous conditions as those pertaining to County Cricket; and those who considered that they were fit to play

County Cricket and would play it under conditions of less excitement than was the case in County Cricket, and those who though not good enough to play for the county, felt that they would like something a little better than Saturday afternoon cricket.' Or, in other words, a sort of Staffordshire second XI – amateurs only, of course.

The club was intended to be nomadic, right from the start. It would play on 'different grounds in the county'. Over the years, these have included the County Ground at Stoke-on-Trent, Danescourt in Wolverhampton, Burton-on-Trent, the Oldfields ground at Uttoxeter and, in more recent years and as a throwback almost to the Victorian country-house era, Swynnerton Park, home of Lord Stafford. This was, and still is, unashamedly a club for Gentlemen, in nature as well as name. As well as being of the right background, to qualify for membership you had to have been born and to have a permanent residence in the county – a condition which the committee was empowered to waive, in respect of officers stationed at the Whittington Barracks – although prospective members were expected to play qualifying matches, to prove their cricketing credentials.

Gentlemen of Staffordshire versus Staffordshire County Police, Milford Hall, 1939
back: JH Groves (scorer), WS Robertson, ET Lawrence, FW Cumberbatch, G Ruston, H Pike, T O'Neil
middle: B Mottram (umpire), KE Tarling, RH Bennett, N Machin,
F Minshall, RE Lowe, CC Fernie, TH Potts (umpire)
front: GNR Morgan, B Meakin, WH Twigg, RSA Hardy, WWM Morgan,
Capt GWR Hearn, J Whitfield, Dr KM Barrow, RJC Evans
on grass: RHC Human, Capt K Wright, RC Blakeway, HJS Nesbitt

For many years, the pattern of the Gentlemen of Staffordshire's season would roll on from one season to the next, largely unchanged. They would play the local public schools, a few old boys' sides, notably the Old Ampleforthians, a school with which the Gents has always had strong links, and their fellow 'gentlemen' in such nearby counties as Cheshire, Shropshire and Warwickshire. Every year, they would go on tour to Yorkshire, taking in the Lincolnshire Gents en route, with fixtures against the likes of the Saints, the Yorkshire Gents and Pocklington School.

They have always played a good standard of cricket, perhaps never more so than when they took on a strong I Zingari side at Wolverhampton in 1925. Among the opposition were such luminaries of amateur cricket as Freddie Calthorpe, who played four times for England and was the current captain of Warwickshire, Ronnie Aird, who went on from a distinguished playing career with Hampshire to become Secretary and ultimately President of the MCC; the great golfer Roger Wethered, who famously declined to take part in a play-off for the Open Championship because he was already committed to playing cricket that day; and Lord Dunglass, better known as Sir Alec Douglas-Home, who failed twice with the bat, but made up for it with six wickets in the Gents' only innings. A more than usually honourable draw was the outcome.

In more recent years, the fixture list has gradually contracted from 30 or so games a season to the present 12. As with all wandering clubs, fixtures against the schools have become harder to come by, so that the majority of the opposition is made up of clubs cast in a similar mould to the Gents, although games against the Staffordshire County Police and Wrekin College have added some additional variety to the mix. They took part in the Oxford Festival of wandering cricket in 2000, celebrated their centenary – or perhaps 'one of their centenaries' would be more accurate! – in 2004 and hold a well-supported annual dinner at Trentham Park Golf Club.

To a greater extent than many county wandering sides, the Gentlemen of Staffordshire has retained its essentially gentlemanly character, if not oblivious to the social and cricketing changes of the past century and a half, then certainly unimpressed by them. The current President, Philip Evans DL, is supported by a committee drawn from the Staffordshire great and good, which runs the club efficiently and unostentatiously. What Percy Mainwaring described as 'a higher standard of cricket' is still the rule, and the occasional limited-overs game very much the exception. Old-fashioned the Gentlemen of Staffordshire may be, but there is a pedigree and a solidity about this club which should stand it in good stead for many years to come.

Glamorgan Nomads

Founded: 1904

by David Harris

Y DDRAIG GOCH A DDYRY GYCHWYN

(The Red Dragon leads the way)

The history of Glamorgan Nomads CC is steeped in a noble, if threatened, tradition, of touring cricket, the aim being to bring amateur players together to enjoy good cricket and fellowship on foreign soil.

The Nomads have never done it in small measure. Indeed, for many years, they went away for a full week, traditionally on Whit Sunday, that long forgotten holiday that greeted the onset of summer. Details of the very early tours are hazy, but for the period immediately before and after the Second World War the records are intact. The bus left the iconic Gwyn Nicholls gates at the entrance to Cardiff Arms Park in Westgate Street early on Sunday morning to travel to deepest Devon. The journey would take all day. This was before the Severn Bridge so it was via Gloucester for lunch, tea in Taunton and then to Torquay.

Bank Holiday Monday saw a game against Exeter CC at the County Ground in front of a large, appreciative crowd. Other traditional fixtures included Torquay CC on their pretty sea-front arena, ringed by deck-chairs, and the magnificent setting of Britannia Royal Naval College, high above Dartmouth. United Services at Mount Wise, Devonport, followed, as well as Paignton CC. The tour would wind up at the idyllic ground at Chudleigh, between Torquay and Exeter, before the long journey home on Sunday.

The tour parties were decided by invitation, concentrating on good-quality club players who could represent the club on and off the field. It wasn`t just about the cricket. There were suppers arranged, beer to be drunk, and chambermaids to be wooed. The records are full of team photographs of tour parties, resplendent in suits and Nomads ties, along with the tour mascot. The mascot is still with us today: a small stuffed terrier dog, wearing a tie and a collar and lead, presented by EA Parr, owner of the Roslin Hall Hotel, Torquay.

Nomads fixture cards have always borne the year 1904. The circumstances of that formation are unclear. However, what is known is that players from Cardiff and Newport Cricket Clubs, along with those from Usk, Abergavenny, St Fagans, Maesteg, Swansea, Llanelli, Neath, Bridgend and others, were brought together to enjoy what for some was to be an education. Travel and social experiences were limited, and Nomads tours were the stuff of dreams for some. Indeed, there are stories of funds being raised among some clubs to allow players to accept the prized invitation.

Historically there has always been a strong association between Glamorgan CCC and the Nomads. Glamorgan players regularly toured, hence the popularity of the fixtures at Exeter and Torquay. A scorebook found at Mount Wise, Plymouth shows that even the great JC Clay, who was captain of Glamorgan at the time, found time to play for the Nomads on tour in 1927. Other notable tourists from the county included Bernard

Glamorgan Nomads, 1938
The 'dog', their mascot, is still with them

Hedges, Jim McConnon, Peter Walker, Len Hill, Jeff Jones and Roger Davis. Latterly many 2nd XI players were afforded a trip as part of their cricketing education.

The key to the success of the Nomads was their choice of secretaries. TB Williams was a star, reportedly poached from the Welsh Cygnets, a side that toured Sussex in the 1930s. The Cygnets joined forces with the Nomads on his appointment, and tour numbers flourished. The 1950s saw the appointment of Wyndham Lewis, an entertainment impresario who owned a string of cinemas throughout South Wales. Wyndham`s influence was immense, in attracting players and providing entertainment, but, most of all, with his book of contacts. Hotels, restaurants and dance halls were all on his radar, and his knowledge and sense of fun led to heady days on the Riviera. The late 1960s saw the appointment of Jeffrey Cohen as Secretary. Cohen was a legendary Cardiff lawyer, well known for his lunches and love of life, and he ensured that the Nomads tradition was maintained.

Tours continued in the 1970s, but the 1980s brought increased pressure from league cricket. Club sides were being forced to play on Bank Holidays; indeed, the notion of a Whitsun holiday disappeared. Devon tours were reduced in length, eventually to a four-day schedule that ran well for many years. This still included games at Torquay, BRNC and Mount Wise, but the reduction in, and eventual loss of, cricket at the latter grounds made maintaining the tour even more difficult.

The Nomads celebrated their centenary in 2004 with a successful tour, an inaugural game versus MCC, thanks to the good offices of AR Lewis, and a wonderful dinner in the Park Hotel, Cardiff, which for many years had been the club's spiritual home. Speakers included Peter Walker, Steve James, himself a Nomad, and Ricky Needham, a Nomad and amateur cricketer of great repute.

The prime mover of the Nomads in the 2000s was Hubert Rees, the club's President. An Old Breconian and a player for Usk CC, Hubert was an actor and cricket enthusiast of the old school. It was largely through his hard work and many friends that the fixture list was expanded to take in games against, among others, Incogniti, Free Foresters and Stragglers of Asia. These games were played out on superb grounds such as Millfield and Blundell's, which again added to the Nomads' experience.

Hubert ensured that the MCC game became a regular fixture and that new friends were made. The Nomads list now includes games against Somerset Stragglers, Gloucestershire Gipsies, Wiltshire Queries and Herefordshire Gents, all now well established and played on excellent grounds. Regrettably the Devon tour is suspended, due in part to cost, but the Nomads tradition lives on and is thriving. The idea of new experiences, among players from different clubs and backgrounds, both on and off the field, as an antidote to relentless league cricket, is being enjoyed by young players and old Nomads alike.

Hubert Rees' words on the menu card for the Centenary Dinner sum up perfectly the spirit of Nomads cricket:

> The joy of skills without arrogance, competition without rancour, partisanship without hostility, and that good humour of shared endeavour, which sustains the ties of community among us. Long may it last.

Sussex Martlets

Founded: 1905

by Anthony Gibson

Of all England's wandering cricket clubs, and for all the affection which they command among their devotees, I doubt if any can have inspired quite so many golden memories as the Sussex Martlets. There is something about Sussex, 'Sussex by the sea', with its beautiful cricket grounds, glorious countryside and the warmth and humour of its people, which seems somehow to provide the perfect context for what, to many cricketers, is the most perfect form of the game. Sussex and wandering cricket go together like strawberries and cream.

It almost goes without saying that the Martlets were founded in the Golden Age. They actually started life in 1905 as the Hove Long Vacation Club, but it wasn't long before some bright spark (the records of those early years are lost) had the idea of naming the club after the heraldic bird on the Sussex coat of arms. The founder members were all good cricketers, not least Arthur Somerset, who captained the first two MCC sides to visit the West Indies. But the most famous of them was unquestionably Sir Arthur Conan Doyle, a keen cricketer, who was living then at Crowborough.

The new club was perfectly attuned to the times. As David Gibbs, a Martlet of many years' standing, explains in *Summers by the Sea*, his centenary history of the club, 'All along the coast of the county and in its most immediate hinterland, numerous prep schools were being founded, staffed for the most part by Oxbridge graduates who knew a little Latin, loved cricket and were bachelors.'

Having been planted in such fertile soil, the Martlets quickly took root and flourished. CB Fry and Ranjitsinhji added lustre to the list of members, and by 1907 the club was playing 26 fixtures, among them a game against Cuckfield in which CB's cousin Ken Fry scored a remarkable 330 not out, comprising 12 sixes, 56 fours and only 34 other runs. It remains, by a wide margin, the club's highest individual score.

After the First World War, the club was reorganised by its Chairman and Secretary, Arthur Belcher and ACG David, schoolmasters both, and its fixture list expanded to include public schools, fellow wanderers and tours to places like Devon, as well as the established fixtures against the better local sides. The Martlets could put strong teams into the field. All of Sussex CCC's amateurs automatically became Martlets and, for many years, there was a Martlets week at the county ground at Hove, while Sussex were away at Eastbourne.

It was in the '30s that the link with Arundel was first forged. Bernard, 16th Duke of Norfolk, was persuaded to become Patron in 1935, a role that he would fulfil with boundless enthusiasm and commitment until his death in 1975. Arundel became a base for the Martlets, if never quite a home ground, and provided the perfect stage for big games and big names, which the club has always been adept at attracting.

Sussex Martlets v Duke of Norfolk's XI, Arundel Castle, 1952

back row: JG Cox (scorer), JND Bettley, HMA Rimmer, JK Priestley, KR Jenkin, PK Collymore, AG Edwards (umpire)   front row: RG Stainton, JK Mathews, G Bolton, The Duke of Norfolk, SC Griffith, EE Harrison, KA Shearwood   seated on grass: DB Lattey, J Lattey

By this time the legendary Eddie Harrison, medium-pacer and hard-hitting lower-order batsman, was already a pillar of the club. He played for the Martlets from 1931, taking over 1,000 wickets, was Honorary Secretary from 1952 to 1984 and then President until his death in 2002. It was Harrison who cemented the relationship with Arundel and the Duke of Norfolk and who oversaw the remarkable post-war expansion of Martlet cricket. As David Gibbs writes, he was the focal point – the lynch-pin – that every wandering club needs: 'He expected high standards on and off the field and he could be cantankerous and tetchy, but his heart was devoted to the Martlets and the club owes him a tremendous debt.'

1965 was the high-water mark of Martlet cricket. No fewer than 106 games were scheduled, including the Diamond Jubilee match at Arundel, in which the Rev David Sheppard, the Nawab of Pataudi, John Snow and Hubert Doggart – Test players all – turned out for the Martlets. As the prep schools closed and league cricket took hold, it became impossible to sustain this level of commitment, and the fixture list was gradually trimmed to the 30 or so games that the Martlets play today. But there were successful tours, at home and abroad, many good young Sussex cricketers have been brought on through the junior Martlets and the standard of cricket remains as high as ever. What was once a distinctly exclusive club – in the early days, you had to have been to either public school or university or served as an officer in the armed forces even to be considered for membership – has become very much more inclusive, without losing its character or charm.

Date	Opponents	Played at	Match Manager	Umpire
AUG.				
1 Sun	Little Common ..	Little Common (11.30)..	A. G. Burke	L. Hitchcock
2 Mon	Worthing	Worthing (11.30)	J. V. Pollard	G. Downs
2 Mon.	The Old Blues ..	Christ's Hospital (11.30)	E. E. Harrison	F. H. Glogg
4 Wed	The Old Malvernians	Memorial Gr. Eastbourne Col. (11.30)	J. D. C. Vargas	F. H. Glogg
4 Wed	Old Hurst Johnians	Hurstpierpoint College (11.30)	D. F. R. Lord	L. Hitchcock
5 Thur	Horsham	Horsham (11.30)	C. J. Saunders	G. Downs
5 Thur	Priory Park	Chichester (11.30)	E. E. Harrison	L Hitchcock
7 Sat	The Grasshoppers	Christ's Hospital (11.30)	A. G. D. Corbett	L. Hitchcock
7 Sat	Southwick	Southwick (11.30)	J. L. Hope	F. H. Glogg
8 Sun	Middleton	Middleton (11.30)	J. V. Pollard	G. Downs
8 Sun	Ditchling	Ditchling (2.30)	I. W. Robertson	W. J. Rees
9 Mon	Littlehampton ..	Littlehampton (11.30) ..	D. Shore	G. Downs
9 Mon	The Buccaneers	Brighton College (11.30)	I. M. O'Brien	F. H. Glogg
10 Tues	Midhurst	Midhurst (11.30)	R. M. Burdon	G. Downs
11 Wed	Lancing Rovers	Lancing College (11.30)	J. D. C. Vargas	F. H. Glogg
12 Thur	Lancing Rovers	Lancing College (11.30)	J. D. C. Vargas	L. Hitchcock
12 Thur	Pevensey & Westham ..	Pevensey (11.30)	P. Murray Willis	F. H. Glogg
13 Fri	Old Rossallians	Brighton College (11.30)	P. C. Collymore	J. T. Jones
14 Sat	Old Rossallians	The County Ground, Hove (11.30)	A. H. H. White	J. T. Jones
14 Sat	Cuckfield	Cuckfield (11.30)	J. S. Porter	F. H. Glogg
15 Sun	Ringmer ..	Ringmer (2.30) ..	L. V. O'Callaghan	G. Downs
16 Mon	The Emeriti	The County Ground, Hove (11.30)	D. H. Glynn	L. Hitchcock
16 Mon	Mayfield	Mayfield (11.30)	C. J. Howeson	F. H. Glogg
16 Mon	The Cryptics ..		J. N. Bartlett	
17 Tues	The Cryptics ..		J. N. Bartlett	
18 Wed	The Old Amplefordians	Arundel Castle	E. E. Harrison	
19 Thur	The Eton Ramblers ..	(11.30 each day)	J. N. Bartlett	G. Downs
20 Fri	The Repton Pilgrims ..		E. E. Harrison	
21 Sat	The Harrow Wanderers		Dr M. I. A. Hunter	
	Hurlingham Week-end			
21 Sat	The Adastrians ..	Hurlingham (11.30)	J. B. F. Mathews	L. Hitchcock
22 Sun	Hurlingham ..	Hurlingham (11.30)	J. B. F. Mathews	L. Hitchcock
	Diamond Jubilee Match			
25 Wed	Sussex ..	County Ground, Hove (11.30)	The President	G. Downs
26 Thur	M.C.C.	County Ground, Hove (11.30)	D. J. Mordaunt	G. Downs
27 Fri	The Seagulls	St. Peter's School, Seaford (2.30)	B. O'Gorman	F. H. Glogg
28 Sat	Seaford ..	Seaford (2.30)	L. V. O'Callaghan	F. H. Glogg
28 Sat	Lewes Priory	Lewes (2.30)	A. H. Beadles	J. T. Jones
29 Sun	The Gemini	Itchenor Park (11.30) ..	E. E. Harrison	G. Downs
29 Sun	Ferring ..	Ferring (2.0)	P. F. Marson	L. Hitchcock
29 Sun	Bank of England	Roehampton (11.30)	J. V. Pollard	G. Downs
30 Mon	Haywards Heath	Haywards Heath (11.30)	Dr M. I. A. Hunter	F. H. Glogg

The fixture card for 1965 – 39 matches in August alone: 6 half-day, 32 whole-day, 1 two-day

It isn't all about cricket, of course. The Martlets have run a well-supported golf society almost from the club's inception, and the social side has always been important. How could it be otherwise in a county of so many splendid pubs?

We will leave the last word to David Gibbs:

> Those incomparable grounds in sight of Downs and the sea; cricket played well, with gusto, spirit and played for enjoyment and fun, not simply for winning; no helmets, no cheating, no tantrums, no inane shouting, nor excessive displays of emotion when holding a catch; umpires in white coats; and great fellowship.

Therein lies the very essence of wandering cricket.

Website: *www.sussexmartlets.co.uk*

Dorset Rangers

Founded: 1906   Deceased: 2010

by Michael Williams

The very first minutes record the inaugural meeting taking place at the Digby Hotel, now a 'school house', part of Sherborne School, on Wednesday 4 April 1906. The consequence of the meeting was the formation of a new cricket club. Those asked to serve on the nascent committee were Messrs FJB Wingfield Digby, WJ Smith-Marriott, PFC Williams, C Goodden, Sir Randolph Baker & W Vizard. The yearly subscription was set at five shillings, payable in advance on 1 May annually, and no one could become a member without the committee first approving the application, a practice that endured until the 1990s. A member also had to play two matches before getting his colours, the badge to be worn in the evenings when on tour and colours during the day. A match fee of 1/- per day was to be collected from players during a tour match to cover the umpire's and scorer's expenses. The club's chosen colours were a direct consequence of the Dorset Yeomanry Centenary Ball in 1906. The programmes printed for that evening featured illustrations of yeomen decked out in green and gold, called Dorset Rangers.

By the 1920s the club was firmly established with mounting fixtures requiring more match managers, the manager being a vital cog in the wheel. Now a benefactor of the county club, an album was acquired in which to record the scores and photographs of the club, which was available to be viewed by playing members on match days. Reports on games started to appear locally and in London journals. In fact, the contents multiplied and the details, which were recorded initially in copperplate script, were replaced by extensive cuttings.

Fixtures often occupied two days and reflected the club's diversity of membership, an amalgam of the gentry, the military, the clergy and various professions. Opposing sides were frequently of a similar, itinerant disposition including the Free Foresters, Devon Dumplings, Somerset Stragglers, Gloucester Gipsies and Hampshire Hogs. Lacking a permanent home meant that the club was obliged to hire grounds locally whilst absorbing the costs. This enabled the club to offer opponents the opportunity of playing at such venues as Hampshire's Dean Park ground at Bournemouth, North Perrott or the Upper at Sherborne School.

Indeed, local independent schools featured heavily amongst the fixtures, as the club strove to bring cricket to the young, and proved to be an excellent source for nascent members. Sadly, changes within school timetables, especially the round of examinations with which students are faced, led to a decline in fixtures.

The club possessed a 'touring' streak which, between 1956 and 1979, took it on 11 visits to European countries, notably Denmark, Germany, Greece (Corfu), Holland and Portugal. The German tour in 1957 was hosted by the Dorset Regiment which was based there. The Portugal connection was a consequence of a chance meeting between Hugh Friend, later to become the club's president, and a club member on the railway

The Dorset Rangers and the Dorset Regiment, a two-day fixture at Dorchester, August 1947

station at Estoril. Of the six visits made, three featured Carcavelos, Lisbon, and three involved Oporto, where there were links with the port and wine trade.

No history of the Dorset Rangers would be complete without reference to two major figures, the first being Wilfred Harrison, who was generally regarded as 'the greatest Dorset Ranger'. He was elected a member in 1908 and, although his duties as joint headmaster, with his brother, of the Downs School, Bristol, limited his appearances to the school holidays, he made a significant contribution with the ball and just occasionally with the bat. He became Honorary Secretary in 1939 and worked ceaselessly in this capacity for the next 30 years. Right up to 1973 he compiled the scores and averages for the yearbook and lovingly maintained the Master Scorebook which was originated by him and recorded the scores of every matched played by the Rangers.

He is closely followed by George Pinney, whose name is synonymous with Dorset Rangers. His father was a long-standing member and president of the club. George became understudy to Wilfred Harrison in 1962 before taking over the reins as Honorary Secretary in 1969. He was an accomplished performer, amassing over 10,000 runs as well as taking over 100 wickets with his tempting leg-breaks. He was a very capable wicket-keeper to boot. But he was very much the life blood of the club and, whilst he was at the helm, the club continued to flourish. However, his untimely riding accident, ultimately leading to his death, completely deflated the club. There was no succession in place and, although the club reached its century in 2006, prospects dimmed.

Finally, in 2010, the membership decided to dissolve the club. Nevertheless, its memory will linger long.

Gentlemen of Essex

Founded: 1907

by Anthony Gibson

The Gentlemen of Essex – or G of E, as they are affectionately known – seem to have played sporadic matches from as early as the 1870s, although it wasn't until November 1907 that the club was formally constituted. The man mainly responsible was Charles Green, a shipping magnate who had captained Essex in the 1880s. He was appointed President, and 30 members were signed up, representing the cream of Essex amateur cricket.

Unlike some county gentlemen sides, which set out their stalls almost as rivals to the county team, the G of E were actively encouraged by Essex CCC, as a potential conduit for good amateur cricketers from public schools and universities. It was a role that the club would fulfil with great success and distinction. By 1939, no fewer than 85 Gents had appeared for Essex, the most notable being JWHT Douglas, who captained England in 18 Test matches, but with Charles Kortright, Ken Farnes (both of England), the prolific 'Percy' Perrin and the immortal TN Pearce not far behind. In 1909, when the G of E played the Colchester garrison, the top six in the order played for Essex and two of them, CP McGahey and Douglas, for England.

Even by the standards of jazz-hat cricket long ago, the early Gents appear to have been a particularly snobbish bunch. According to Keith Alcoe, in his *Potted History of the Gentlemen of Essex Cricket Club*, to qualify for membership, you needed to be 'either a very good amateur who was able to play for Essex or the landed gentry'. The club was – and, so far as one can tell, still is – run autocratically by a self-perpetuating committee which decided long ago not to bother with the inconvenience of an AGM. Then, as now, only the committee could nominate a new member, and a man who would become one of the Gents' most distinguished servants, as player, umpire and ultimately president, Basil Hunt, was kept waiting for at least three years to be up-graded from probationer to member on the grounds that he was the son of a tradesman (the family firm manufactured agricultural machinery).

His experience is all the more remarkable when you consider that, as one of the best-known and respected umpires in club cricket, Hunt was notorious for being, in Keith Alcoe's words, 'magisterial, even pompous in his judgements, tolerating no dispute and demanding impeccable conduct from his players.' Mind you, he did get his come-uppance on one occasion, when he turned down an over-optimistic appeal from a young bowler with the words, "Young man, that was a terrible appeal and is not out." "Sir," replied the bowler, "you are here to give decisions, not opinions!"

Records are sketchy up to 1925. Since then, they have been immaculate, thanks to the 'Blue Books' which have been kept, recording fixtures, scores, dinners, members, probationers, minutes, obituaries – anything, in short, that anyone could possibly want to know about the club and its exploits. Before and after the First World War, the G of E tended to play public schools, the military and invitational sides, very often on country-house grounds, with all their attendant airs and graces. Matches against the Royal Artillery at Shoeburyness seem to have been particularly relished, to the extent that the Gents presented the Gunners with a silver tankard to serve as a loving cup at their lavish joint dinners, which has survived, and a clock for their scoreboard, which hasn't.

Quite how competitive the cricket was in this era is hard to say, although a comment from Nick Vere-Hodge, recalling the 99 he made on debut for the G of E, after coming in at number 10 with the score on 50 for 8, is possibly revealing. "After that," he added, "I had many and varied matches for Essex which was a magnificent county to play for. The professionals were gentlemen; some of the amateurs were not!"

After the Second World War, army sides and schools continued to dominate the fixture list, even if all the country-house games had by now disappeared and most of the two-day ones. In the '50s and '60s, the G of E would play as many as five fixtures against different branches of the military, and it wasn't until the late 1960s that this element of their cricket started to decline. There was a remarkable continuity in the club's post-war prime movers. Besides Basil Hunt, there was Geoffrey Rowell, who had taken over as Secretary in 1939 and would continue in that role until 1968; Donald Rankin continued to play regularly and entertain lavishly at Broomhills, where he had his own ground; and Leonard Womersley, Secretary from 1920 to 1939, was elevated to President, a position which he held until his death in 1971. Continuity has also been provided by the G of E dynasties – the Greens, the Alcoes, the Georges, the Rounds, the Cocketts, and the inevitable brewing family, in this case the Ridleys.

As the demands of county cricket increased and the old-fashioned amateur element faded away, so the G of E could boast fewer first-class cricketers than in the '20s and '30s. Even so, the post-war list is an impressive one, headed by Trevor Bailey and Doug Insole, and includes the likes of David Acfield, David East, Mike McEvoy and Peter Such (another England player), not to mention Jack Bailey, who became Secretary of the MCC.

The President's shoes
Stuck to the ceiling of the Frinton pavilion

G of E cricket has always been of a high standard, and they have won as many as they've lost over the years, invariably against strong opposition. Undoubtedly the most remarkable cricketing achievement of recent years was the five wickets in five balls – caught, bowled, caught, caught, bowled – taken by Howard Garon in the match against the Gentlemen of Suffolk at Castle Park. It wasn't a record in all cricket – that stands at nine – but it turned the game on its head and earned Garon a presentation of the match ball, suitably mounted and inscribed, at the annual dinner that winter.

The G of E celebrated their centenary in 2007 with the publication of Keith Alcoe's *History*, matches against MCC and the Cross Arrows, and a dinner which was said to be exceptional even by the standards of a club which has prided itself on the quality of its annual dinners since Keith Alcoe took over the organising of them in 1976.

These days, the G of E play around 20 games a season, almost all of them mid-week, so as not to clash with league cricket. The opposition is much as it has been for many years – public schools, the stronger local clubs, either MCC or the Cross Arrows and a match against the Frinton President's X1 in Frinton Cricket Week. And this is all proper cricket: 11.30 start, bat till you declare or are all out, 7.00 to 7.30 finish, and lunches "that have been known to last slightly longer than the usual 40 minutes". One gains the strong impression that it would be over the dead bodies of the entire committee were the G of E ever to be coerced into playing limited overs! Membership is holding up well, at around 150 in total, although it is becoming difficult to persuade many of the better players to turn out for more than the odd game, in the face of the demands of the leagues.

The Gentlemen of Essex make no bones about the sort of club theirs is, and the type of cricket they like to play. Traditional is the word, in both respects, arguably to a greater degree than with any other county wandering club. There is, I suppose, a certain irony in the fact that it should be Essex, of all counties, which is home to such a standard bearer for old-fashioned ways and old-fashioned values. But that's the way the G of E like it, and when you look at the strength of the club and the enthusiasm and commitment of its members, you certainly cannot argue with the results.

Website: *www.gentsofessex.co.uk*

Gentlemen of Essex versus Eton Ramblers, Broomhills, 2006
standing: G Mann, D de Lannoy, W Thomas, C Farquhas, R Budenburg, A Hussey, T Squier, S Went, T Fraser, T Fitzgerald, G Alcoe, C Erith, C Bowman, G Stamp, T Best, C Ashton, S Thackrah, C Devereux   seated: D Low, P Fosh, C Wilkinson, N Ridley, J Ward, M Vandome

Yellowhammers

Founded: 1909

by David Walsh

In the summer holidays of 1909, a Tonbridge schoolboy, Leonard Marzetti, took a side of his friends to play a cricket match against Heathfield Park in Sussex. They enjoyed the game so much that Marzetti resolved to form a club for '25 Tonbridgians and 15 of their friends' to play a few matches each summer holidays. Before a name for the club had been agreed, the colours were decided upon: yellow and black, the latter edged on each side with a narrow strip of French grey, the plumage of the yellowhammer. Naturalists will understand that the yellowhammer is an extremely sociable bird and this, together with the high standard of their cricket, has distinguished the Yellowhammers over the past 104 years. Not many wandering clubs have found so welcoming a home as the Yellowhammers have on The Head at Tonbridge School, their existence complementary to, rather than rivalling, the Old Tonbridgians.

Early fixtures included occasional matches against clubs such as Tunbridge Wells and the Bluemantle's, but after the Great War a bigger fixture list built up in two parts: in early summer matches within easy reach of London, such as West Kent and Sevenoaks Vine, followed by a Kent and Sussex tour in late August, mainly at Tonbridge School and Eastbourne. At Eastbourne players always stayed at the Grand Hotel, the costs for the young being generously subsidised by older members led by the 'Pres', Leonard Marzetti, who remained in this office from 1909 until his death in 1962. At the Grand Hotel an annual soccer match was played against the hotel staff for a large silver cup, while the huge dinners after cricket each evening were accompanied by large tankards of Pimms, episodes involving dressing the statue of the Duke of Devonshire with Yellowhammer colours, and many games of billiards. Younger Yellowhammers were encouraged to show their alertness next morning by joining the 'Pres' for a pre-breakfast dip in the sea, while the Secretary, Leslie Barrow, would ask for his breakfast teapot to be filled with Worthington rather than Earl Grey.

On the field the Yellowhammers have always been able to call on a very strong playing membership. In the period between the wars this included many first-class players of the calibre of Jack Davies, FH and CH Knott, Tom Crawford, Alan Hilder and Miles Howell – the Kent connection always predominating. The quality of the sides meant that they did not lose too often, but the main purpose was always to play enjoyable cricket with friends. After the war new batsmen of distinction emerged, including Colin Cowdrey, AC 'Tolly' Burnett, Roger Prideaux and Mike Bushby, while a pair of very hostile fast bowlers, Ronnie Rutter and John Farrar, were as difficult a proposition as any in club cricket. The strong umbilical cord which bound the club to Tonbridge School brought many more talented players in the late 1950s and 1960s such as Richard Gracey, Anthony Hudson, Richard Roberts, Peter Rylands, Nicholas Heroys and Tony Monteuuis who were to form the backbone of successful Old Tonbridgian sides in the early days of the Cricketer Cup.

Yellowhammers at Eastbourne College, 1958
In the centre with the umbrella is Leonard Marzetti, the Founding President.
The big man next to him is Walter Brice, who succeeded him as President in 1962.
On the other side, with pads on, is Richard Gracey, who became the third President.
At the end, with pipe, is CH 'John' Knott (Oxford Univ & Kent), a lifelong master at Tonbridge.

Leonard Marzetti died in 1962, occasioning this epitaph from EW Swanton in the *Daily Telegraph*: 'When the Yellowhammers gather on The Head at Tonbridge this week for the start of their tour, they will do so for the first time without their originator and perpetual President. Of forty-odd Yellowhammer tours the 'Pres' never missed one. In this happy and flourishing company, he has his memorial.'

By the 1980s, in common with most wandering clubs, fixtures were contracting as different pressures of finance, employment and family were beginning to be felt. The Yellowhammers retreated in good order, focusing on their August week at Tonbridge, interspersed with forays to Eastbourne (sleeping in a dormitory at the College, thanks to Yellowhammer headmaster Simon Langdale, rather than the Grand Hotel).

By now a new generation of cricketers had begun to appear, including Richard Ellison, Chris Cowdrey and John Inverarity, together with other first-class cricketers such as Graham Cowdrey, Nick Kemp, Mark Allbrook and David Walsh. Overseas opponents of the calibre of Mashonaland Country Districts of Zimbabwe, I Zingari Australia, and De Flamingos from Holland were entertained at Tonbridge, and for several years the quality of opposition was enhanced by an annual fixture with Kent Club and Ground. For a club cricketer to face Graham Dilley without benefit of a helmet was certainly a challenge!

After earlier forays to Guernsey and Ireland, the Yellowhammers undertook their most ambitious tour to Cape Town in 2002. So popular was this venture that a tour party of fifty people participated. In twelve days the club played nine cricket matches, including two sides out on the same day on three occasions, and three golf matches. The management's main problem was getting on to the team bus players who had only gone to bed an hour or two before!

In 2006 David Walsh took over as President, the record of only four presidents in over 100 years being a proud one. In keeping with Leonard Marzetti's original wish that it should be a club for Tonbridgians and their friends, it was perhaps appropriate that the fourth president should be the first non-Tonbridgian. Although Tonbridgians have always been the most numerous group within the club, many products of other schools have graced Yellowhammer teams including Robin Eliot, Peter Cattrall and Nigel Wheeler. The centenary was duly celebrated in 2009 with an opening match on a very cold day at Heathfield Park and a closing game on the Nursery Ground at Lord's against the Cross Arrows, both of them won in the same year as the Old Tonbridgians claimed the Cricketer Cup for the seventh time in 12 years.

No account of Yellowhammer cricket in recent years would be complete without fuller reference to the annual game with the Arabs, which has been the main event since at least the early 1970s. The quality of the cricket has been as high as any in wandering club cricket, both sides sprinkled with international and first-class players. No quarter has been given but the games have always been played in a good spirit, even when Tony Monteuuis bowled a red apple to Mark Faber as first ball of the match in 1976. Jim Swanton, relaxing around the open drinks cabinet in the boot of Walter Brice's car, saw the funny side of that but less so of another incident when, with nine Yellowhammer wickets down and two runs to win, the home umpire called "No ball" well after Robin Eliot's stumps had been shattered, the Yellowhammers scampering a leg-bye off the next ball.

Yellowhammer cricket is now well into its second century and is in robust health. The week at Tonbridge and Eastbourne is well supported, Matt Banes and Tim Marriott looking after us well at the latter. Teams are younger than they used to be, the over-35s now busier building their careers and dealing with family responsibilities in a more equitable way than perhaps occurred to their fathers, who dealt with them partly by expecting their wives to look after the children and make the lunches and teas, while they played cricket! The multitude of social activities which used to accompany a Yellowhammer season – annual dinners, occasional balls, many parties – have also faded into the past, as teams get younger and social habits and obligations change. There are now golf matches, too, at Royal St George's and Royal Ashdown, giving past players a chance to re-live precious moments. But the core of the cricket lives on in a way of which Leonard Marzetti would surely have approved – competitive, skilful, sociable wandering cricket played on one of the finest grounds in the country at his old school; 'a happy and flourishing company' indeed.

Cryptics

Founded: 1910

by Bill Blackshaw

The club was founded in 1910 at New College, Oxford, by three undergraduates: JG Fawcus, DMP Whitcombe and CH Campbell. The name arose when Fawcus took down a copy of a Dickens novel and his eye fell on the word 'cryptic', which fitted well with the concept of cricketing 'hidden lights' that the founders reckoned the club's members would be.

The first match was played against the staff of Bilton Grange Preparatory School and that summer there were several other matches, including the first one against a school – Aldenham – and the first tour, to the south-east in August. By the end of the season 39 cricketers had played for the club and a set of rules drawn up. The fixture list grew in the four years before the Great War. The south coast tour became a regular feature; many schools were played; and by 1914 membership had reached 160 and there was talk of limiting it to 200. But a quarter of the membership lost their lives in the conflict and there was no further talk of limitation. John Fawcus, who was secretary from 1910 until his death in 1949, pulled the club together in 1919 and arranged a tour to the British Occupying Army in Germany. A young Douglas Jardine was in the party and MC Dempsey, the future Second World War general, scored a fifty.

Matches against schools and London clubs helped build the membership and, by 1924, as well as the southern tour, there were northern and midland tours at home; and the first overseas tour to Portugal was arranged. The fixtures against schools, whilst bolstering the membership, also served to strengthen the bond with the schoolmastering world. Until changes in the exam system, these numbered a dozen or so per season and continued even in 1940 – 'intended for those on leave' – the only fixtures the club played in either war. London clubs such as Hampstead, Beckenham, Reigate Priory and Oatlands Park have been regular opponents, as have the Old Bloxhamists and the Bacchanalian Hockey Club from the midlands, which was also founded by John Fawcus.

*Cryptic transport
in the early years*

Touring, however, has been the club's driving force. The southern tour has lasted the full 100 years of the club's existence, based often, since the Second World War, on Cranleigh School. It has normally lasted nearly a fortnight and included games against the Hampshire Hogs, Old Rossalians, Lancing Rovers, Sussex Martlets and Middleton, plus the occasional country-house match in the '20s and '30s. More recently, the club has played the Hurstjohnians, Old Amplefordians, Old Cranleighans and Cranleigh CC. John Fawcus managed this tour until the Second World War; then CB Blackshaw until 1961, when Richard Russell had a short spell before handing over to Tony Beadles, who ran it for more than 20 years. Until the '60s, the two-day matches provided scope for much socialising on the intervening night, a type of cricket much praised in the cricketing press by EW Swanton, a Cryptic himself.

One fixture against Middleton deserves a mention. They were usually dominant at that time – late '50s – but were heading for a beating when they needed 70 to win in 30 minutes, with two schoolboys at the wicket. They won with five minutes to spare. The schoolboys were JM Brearley and MG Griffith.

The northern tour began in 1924, with founder member DMP Whitcombe as its manager. By 1926 it included matches against the Yorkshire Gents, Durham Pilgrims, York Garrison and Ampleforth College; they later included one against a team put out by that well-known organiser of country-house cricket, Sir Julien Cahn; and often there was a match against the Royal Corps of Signals at Catterick. After the Second World War, this tour took some time to re-establish itself, but by 1954 it was going well under the management of LH Garrett, and then for more than 20 years it flourished under the guidance of John Dean, succeeded by his son in 1978, a good example of the many father-son connections so apparent in the club. Simon Westhead then took over until the turn of the century.

Up until the '60s, two-day matches were the rule, producing the highest scores in the club's history. Among the stars of this tour in the '50s and '60s were the schoolmasters MM Walford (Somerset), GR Langdale (Somerset) and R Sale (Derbyshire). This tour included the only match with a score sheet which recorded that 'Fog stopped play'. Two Cryptics took all the wickets: PD Briggs and NP Meadows (from a family long associated with the northern tour). The club's leading century maker, Mark Williams, was a regular tourist in the 1990s and beyond, while a young Australian student called Justin Langer toured in 1988.

The current festival at Malvern grew out of earlier midland and north-western tours involving the Shropshire Gentlemen, the Cheshire Gentlemen, the Bromsgrove Martlets, Worcester Gentlemen and Gloucestershire Gipsies, and more recently the Warwickshire Imps, and now provides a congenial end to the season.

The Scottish tour began in 1974, the brainchild of Tony Beadles and Peter Lapping, and involved matches against Colonel WB Swan's XI – he was Lord Lieutenant of Berwickshire – the Grange CC, the Scottish Wayfarers, Carlton and the Glenalmond Rovers. In 1978 the tour returned to the south-west, to Galloway. Sadly this very happy tour, with its visits also to the Edinburgh Festival 'fringe', ran into difficulties in 1983, and the club has not ventured north of the border since.

From the late '20s onwards, tours to Oxford and Cambridge in April have provided some of the most distinguished cricket played by the club. As well as the colleges, the club took on the Authentics and the Crusaders, and in the '50s and '60s, these games were elevated to trial matches for the University 'A' XIs in the search for potential Blues. As well as attracting first-class players from the schoolmastering world, like MM Walford, R Sale, JD Eggar and JG Dewes, these tours also provided the club with an excellent recruiting ground. The scoresheets from that era are littered with names like Sheppard, Subba Row, Dexter, Brearley and Richard Hutton. Since 1970, however, the fixtures have been restricted to the Authentics and the Crusaders.

The Channel Islands were regularly visited in the 1930s and were very sociable events, as wives were invited as well. The club returned in 1948 and visits continued until 1955, with the Governor-General often in attendance at the matches.

The first overseas tour made by the Cryptics was to Portugal in 1924, when the club was based in Oporto. In the following year, the club went further south, to Lisbon, and followed that in 1926 with a visit to both Oporto and Lisbon which was written up in the *Cricketer* magazine by that wittiest of cricket writers, RC Robertson-Glasgow, who was also the leading wicket-taker:

> There was one Horatian evening when a certain Cryptic tried to go to bed when dressing for dinner, then, finally persuaded out of his pyjamas, he complained, in reply to the social remarks of his hostess, about some beauty who had left him because he couldn't dance the Charleston. But after dinner he danced it, then lay in triumph under a grand piano, only to resurrect himself for further terpsichorean efforts which would have made the Astaires cry and Pavlova become a channel swimmer. His last remark that night was, "How I hate Portugal!"

There were three more visits in the '30s, two in the '50s and two more in the '60s before a final visit in 1988 to help Oporto celebrate the centenary of its club. The record of that tour ends with this sentence:

> By April 10th, the Cryptics had eight matches won out of eight played: two in Mombasa, one in Gilgal, one in Nakuru, one in Nairobi and three in Oporto.

It was reckoned that during those 11 visits to Portugal from 1924 to 1988, more than a pipe of port – 115 gallons – must have been consumed by the club.

The Kenya tours of the 1980s were the brainchild of Tony Beadles; the successful 16-day tour of 1981 was inevitably followed by another one, taking in Christmas, with presents from the President, George Chesterton, for all players and family travelling. Kenya Kongonis, Robbie Armstrong's XI, Rift Valley XI, Nairobi and Mombasa were the main opponents. This tour, and the one which followed in 1987, introduced the club to a world not experienced by its players before.

All of this was followed by a tour to Malaya in 1995 – sponsored in part by Heineken, despite this being a Muslim country – where two easy wins over the Singapore Cricket Association and Singapore Cricket Club persuaded our next opponents, the Johore Rhinos, to recruit a Malaysian fast bowler and three Australian professionals and duly secure victory. From there, the club travelled on to Kuala Lumpur, Penang and Kuantan. The end-of-tour report paid tribute to 'a splendid balance of maturity and youth, of

President Tony Beadles in Ipoh, Malaysia, after a monsoon ended play early

character and characters'. Long-distance touring was maintained in the centenary year by an April visit to South Africa and since the Millennium there have been short April tours to Malta and the Iberian peninsula.

The Cryptics marked their half-century in 1960 with a festival at Oxford, featuring matches with 11 regular opponents, and a dinner at St Edward's School at which the President of the MCC was the guest speaker, while the wives went to the theatre. The 75th was a smaller but no less congenial affair at Malvern College. Annual dinners began in 1919 and have continued ever since, but no longer in London. The centenary was celebrated with a match against the Bilton Grange masters, a dinner in the Long Room at Lord's, again with the MCC President as guest speaker, and matches at Radley College against the MCC and the Free Foresters, followed by an informal dinner. It was also marked by the publication of *100 Not Out*, the history of the club written by WS Blackshaw.

There have been 128 Cryptics who have played first-class cricket, 14 of whom have played in Tests or one-day internationals, the most recent being Justin Langer and Jamie Dalrymple, whose father is the current Honorary Secretary. The club can also boast eight Presidents of the MCC, two Prime Ministers, in Sir Alec Douglas-Home and Bob Hawke of Australia, as well as John Woodcock of *The Times*, EW Swanton of the *Daily Telegraph* and Charles Collingwood (aka Brian Aldridge) of *The Archers*. The strong public school connection means that there have been far too many public school headmasters to record all their names here!

The family feel of the club can best be seen from the fact that there were only two honorary secretaries in the first 89 years of the club: John Fawcus and his son Harold. It now looks forward to reaching a double century!

Website: *www.crypticscc.org*

Invalids

Founded: 1919

by Anthony Gibson

It is a fair bet that more people have read about the Invalids than any other wandering cricket club, albeit, in most cases, without realising it. For it is the Invalids who feature in arguably the most famous cricketing short story ever written: AG Macdonell's account of a cricket match in *England, Their England*. Not by name, to be sure. The group of writers, journalists, publishers and assorted hangers-on who set off one Saturday morning in the early '20s from Charing Cross to play the village of 'Fordenden' in Kent are referred to simply as 'Mr Hodge's team'. But that Mr Hodge was, in reality, the poet and publisher JC (later Sir John) Squire, and that his team were the Invalids, has never been in question.

JC Squire was one of the leading literary figures of the age, as poet, critic and, most of all, as editor of the *London Mercury* magazine, through which he gave very many young writers their first big break. Even in his youth, he doesn't seem to have been much of a cricketer, but he loved the game none the less passionately for that, and when his uncle by marriage, EW Hornung, creator of Raffles, revealed that the West Wycombe club had re-formed after the First World War, Squire could not resist issuing a challenge. He assembled a team of authors to play the club, calling themselves 'The Old Age Pensioners' and, "with the aid of an excellent and prolonged luncheon and a considerable shower of rain", they made an honourable draw of it.

Having thus acquired a taste for captaining his own side, Squire decided to put it on a proper footing. Quite why he chose the name 'Invalids' isn't entirely clear. Squire himself had not seen active service in the war, still less been wounded, but no doubt several of his team of authors had been (the most famous of them, Edmund Blunden, had twice been reported killed in action). But the Invalids it was, complete with colours of hospital blue and old gold (the colour of army officers' hospital pyjamas) and a crest of crossed crutches.

Squire was romantic, lyrical even, in his literary tastes, and village cricket provided the perfect bridge between sport and art. Being very firmly based in London, the Invalids thus played mainly village sides in arcadian settings in Kent, Surrey and Sussex. The picture that Macdonell paints of Fordenden, on the afternoon of the match, may have been exaggerated, but, like the entire account, it speaks of the essence of what Squire and his ilk so loved about the whole experience:

> It was a hot summer's afternoon. There was no wind, and the smoke from the red-roofed cottages curled slowly up into the golden haze. The clock on the flint tower of the church struck the half-hour, and the vibrations spread slowly across the shimmering hedgerows, spangled with white blossom of the convolvulus, and lost themselves tremulously among the orchards. Bees lazily drifted.

Sir John Squire, still playing, with his wife Eileen as always the scorer

The characters whom Macdonell includes in 'Mr Hodge's' side were also authentic. Bobby Southcott, the 'boy novelist' who rattles up a quick 50 before unaccountably going into his shell and being given out lbw by the 'venerable umpire', is Alec Waugh, elder brother of Evelyn (who also turned out at least once for the Invalids), who was indeed a fine cricketer. The fierce Major Hawker, who 'terrified seven batsmen, clean bowled six of them and broke a stump' before taking refuge in the pub, was the playwright Reginald Berkeley, who opened the bowling for the Invalids for several seasons. The not entirely sober Mr Harcourt, whose shout of "No ball" whilst umpiring causes the downfall of the gigantic blacksmith was probably JB Morton, better known as Beachcomber. Mr Hodge, bowling his carefully considered, if ill-directed, slows is unmistakably Squire. The baseball-loving Shakespeare Pollock is almost certainly based on an American called Manning Pike whom Squire had enlisted as twelfth man for that very first fixture against West Wycombe.

Something else about Macdonell's account which was entirely typical of the Invalid spirit was the volume of beer consumed. Squire was a drinker, to the point where it eventually and very sadly got the better of him. So were most of his team. 'The exceptional opportunity of raising a thirst,' in Squire's words, was a major part of the attraction.

After every match, the Invalids would repair to the village pub with the locals, to drink the evening away in song, conversation and games of darts. In the winter, they would gather at the Olde Cheshire Cheese in Fleet Street for bibulous dinners. For many years, through the '20s and '30s, and again in the '50s and '60s, drinking was the hallmark of Invalids' cricket and not always, as Jeremy Paul admits in his history of the club, *Sing Willow*, to their credit:

> They drank before, during (from the boot of their motors) and after the game, and wasn't this rather boring? Late arrivals, fumbling displays in the field and generally poor behaviour must frequently have annoyed the home teams.

But it also had its funnier side, as on the famous occasion at Brook in Surrey, when Sir John Squire lumbered off in pursuit of a leg-side hit, only for his trousers to fall down. We don't know whether Squire was drunk or sober on the occasion when a shot was launched high in the sky, three fieldsmen circling underneath it, and he, as captain, called out masterfully from slip, "THOMPSON!" We do know – at least according to Neville Cardus – that all three fieldsmen stopped, and the ball fell to earth, as Thompson wasn't actually playing that day.

Alec Waugh wrote of Squire that he was no cricketer, that he knew he was no cricketer, and that he knew the Invalids knew he was no cricketer, but that everyone was in a conspiracy of silence on the matter. It was sometimes said that Squire's idea of captaincy was to steer the game to a point when he could justify giving himself a long bowl. One opposing captain is reputed to have instructed his players not to help themselves to more than 20 runs an over off him – in case he took himself off.

The Squire era lasted from the Invalids' formation in 1919 to the years immediately after the Second World War. In that time, he persuaded many distinguished writers to play for him. Alec Waugh and Edmund Blunden we have mentioned, but there were also GK Chesterton, Hilaire Belloc, JB Priestley, AP Herbert, Hugh Walpole, Clifford Bax and his brother, the composer Arnold Bax. He even managed to talk one or two top-class cricketers into making occasional appearances, the best – and most unlikely – being the great Australian wicket-keeper Bert Oldfield. Besides the village matches, Squire also arranged one or two more ambitious fixtures, including a game against the Lords and Commons XI at The Oval in 1924, while a match against the Hampshire Eskimos on Broadhalfpenny Down on New Year's Day 1929 attracted national publicity. In the winter, the Invalids played football, sometimes with the imposing figure of EW Swanton in goal.

After the war, the Invalids swiftly re-formed, and carried on much as before, albeit with a slightly altered cast of characters. Of the pre-war Invalids, only Patrick Howarth, Edmund Blunden, Ian Leslie and Sir John himself – now 61 and rarely sober – survived, but the new intake lacked nothing in enthusiasm for either cricket or beer, including as they did such future Invalid legends as Bill Foss, Tom Tatham, Edward Bishop and Roger Gray QC, who might have been a High Court Judge, had not the Lord Chief Justice turned up at the precise moment when Gray was demonstrating his prowess at drinking a pint of beer whilst standing on his head!

Squire by now was a fading force. But when he was eventually persuaded to give up the captaincy, the Invalids were fortunate indeed in the selection of his replacement, Alastair Boyd, commonly known as 'Dad'. A better cricketer and captain than Squire had ever been, and a much younger man, he became a hugely popular figure through the '50s and '60s as the Invalids cut their accustomed boozy, hilarious, sociable swathe through the villages of south-east England. Squire died in 1958 and by this stage the literary influence was less strong than it had been. Even so, the club could still field writers as distinguished as Laurence Meynell, and actors as famous as Boris Karloff, William Franklyn and Tony Hancock.

The Invalids' jubilee was celebrated in style with a swish dinner at Lord's and, when Boyd died suddenly a year later, David Pritchett proved a capable and popular successor. Boyd captained every single game the Invalids played whereas Pritchett sensibly introduced a match manager system. It is a remarkable fact, and one of the Invalids' greatest blessings, that the club has had just four captains in its 93-year history: Squire, Boyd, Pritchett and, since 1987, the dashing Ewen Gilmour. If Pritchett brought organisation to the Invalids, then Gilmour – himself good enough to have played occasionally for the Crusaders when up at Cambridge – has overseen a perceptible raising of the standard of cricket, without either of them departing for one moment from the club's fundamental ethos of joyous cricket in beautiful places. Pritchett once gave his successor a gentle ticking off for winning too many games in a season. The Invalids now like to maintain an equal balance of results and will negotiate the toss if looking strong or weak.

Now that the literary influence has faded, there isn't anything in particular – profession, school, university, background – that unites the Invalids. As Jeremy Paul, who played for the club for many years, remarked in one of the conversations quoted in *Sing Willow*, "The Invalids come from all over the shop and something quite mysterious binds us together." The mystery ingredient seems to have grown stronger with the years, judging by the numbers of fathers and sons who have turned out for the club.

The Invalids, it would appear, are in rude health. They have 25 fixtures scheduled for the 2013 season, on some of the prettiest village grounds in the home counties. Curiously, the modern world of longer working hours, less tolerant wives and girlfriends and busy social lives, has meant that young cricketers, who previously might have been attracted to league cricket or all-day wandering cricket, enjoy making periodic appearances for the Invalids. An Invalids slip cordon may still be pretty ancient but the covers can sometimes look rather useful. A group of young Invalids play in one of the hugely popular Last Man Stands London leagues on summer Wednesday evenings and, indeed, have won their division in each of the last two years. What Squire would have made of this fast and furious form of the game and the winning of a cricket match can only be surmised.

Fundamentally, though, they still play the same sort of cricket, in the same sort of relaxed spirit – if maybe not quite so shambolically – in the same sort of beautiful places as Squire and his merry men did when they captured Macdonell's imagination all those years ago.

They say that truth is stranger than fiction. In the Invalids' case, it's probably even funnier, as well.

Gentlemen of Suffolk

Founded: 1921

by Tim Bridge

The Gentlemen of Suffolk Cricket Club was founded in 1921. A little leaflet was produced to define the early structure of the club, its character and its rules. ' The colours will be light grey and black with ruby stripe and can be obtained at E.C. Devereux's, High Street, Eton. The entrance fee is one guinea, payable on election, but there is no annual subscription for those joining in 1921. The expenses of each match (for umpire, ground, ball etc) are to be divided and paid by the eleven who were playing.'

There were four fixtures in the first season, all two-day games, against the Free Foresters, Authentics, Emeriti and the Gentlemen of Essex. In 1922 the Gentlemen of Norfolk and Magdalene College Ramblers were added. The 1930s seem to have been prosperous years for Gents cricket. The Gentlemen of Suffolk went on tour for the first time in 1933, playing three two-day matches in six days in August. The first was against the Gentlemen of Worcester at Worcester, the second the Herefordshire Gentlemen in Hereford and the third the Gloucester Gipsies at Oakley Hall.

Gentlemen of Suffolk, on tour, versus Gentlemen of Herefordshire, 1933
back: CD Walker, J Huntley, EC Aitken, JH Wilson, AP Aitken
front: EW Eardle, CS Wilson, FS Beauford, RG Evans, J Venn   on grass: T Martin

This pattern of tours continued each year through the thirties with only minor changes. In 1934 the Gloucester Gipsies match was played at Badminton House and the Gentlemen of Worcester fixture was replaced by one against the Wiltshire Queries, the game being played at Marlborough College. The tour in 1939 began with the match versus the Herefordshire Gentlemen and featured a new game against the South Oxford Amateurs at St. John's College, Oxford on 23-24 August. Then, written at the foot of the page in the scorebook after this game, are the chilling words: 'Rest of tour abandoned – War'.

No matches were played during the war, but the club resumed its cricket with a two-day game against the Free Foresters on 9/10 August 1946. The tour was reinstated in 1947 and ran until 1954, by which time it had been reduced to just two matches, against the Herefordshire Gentlemen and the Gloucester Gipsies, which had featured in every tour since 1934. Another wandering club, the Bury and West Suffolk Cricket Club, had been playing matches in Suffolk since 1864 and probably for a few years earlier. By the 1960s many of the same cricketers were playing for both clubs, and the decision was taken to merge the Bury and West Suffolk Cricket Club into the Gentlemen of Suffolk Cricket Club after the 1968 season.

The make-up of the fixture list began to change from the 1970s onwards. The only two-day game was played against the Free Foresters over a weekend in August and most of the other matches were on weekdays, starting at 11.30am. We have played many matches against the Cambridge colleges, principally St John's, Emmanuel, Gonville & Caius, Selwyn and Queens', but sadly the last ten years has seen a decline in college cricket as the university is not taking in enough undergraduates who have played cricket at school and the colleges can no longer raise teams.

We have also traditionally had fixtures against the school 1st XIs in Suffolk, particularly Culford School, Framlingham College, Woodbridge School and Ipswich School. In these days of league cricket, the chance for schoolboys to play friendly, but competitive, matches against wandering sides such as ourselves is valuable for them and leads to a number of them wanting to play Gents cricket when they leave school. The remainder of our fixture list these days consists of games against club sides in Suffolk and four other wandering sides: the Gentlemen of Essex, West Norfolk, the Stoics and the Buccaneers.

The Gentlemen of Suffolk Cricket Club has survived the ravages of the years, changes in society and huge changes in cricket itself, and still aims to play a good standard of cricket, on good-quality wickets, in the right spirit of friendly competition. And if a letter printed in the *Daily Telegraph* in 1992 may have been written with tongue firmly in cheek, it did nonetheless evoke happy memories of Gentlemen's cricket in days gone by:

> SIR – Oh for that Golden Age when a cricket team comprised eight toffs, including the vicar; a member of the doctor or schoolmaster class keeping wicket and two burly, but silent, artisans providing the fast bowling and outfielding.

If it ever did exist, that stereotype has long since disappeared, but that doesn't mean to say that there isn't still much fun to be had, and the Gentlemen of Suffolk Cricket Club is no more averse than it has ever been to passing the port round the pavilion table at the end of a good lunch.

Gloucestershire Gipsies

Founded: 1922

by Anthony Gibson

The Gloucestershire Gipsies were surprisingly late arrivals to the ranks of the county-based wandering clubs. Lord Harris's Band of Brothers down in Kent had been in existence for 63 years by the time six 'gentlemen' gathered in the offices of the Bristol papermakers, ES and A Robinson (themselves a great cricketing family), in September 1921, and decided to form a County Amateur Cricket Club.

The Gipsies, as they became, were officially constituted at a first General Meeting the following January. Membership would be open to cricketers either born or resident in Gloucestershire – with one important condition: they should be the sort of men who might be regarded as 'acceptable guests in the average country house'. If that sounds alarmingly snobbish to a modern ear, those responsible could at least point to the fact that most of their matches would be played on country-house grounds, by way of justification.

But there can be no doubt that the Gipsies were very much a 'county' club, in every sense of the word. The Duke of Beaufort accepted an invitation to become their first President, supported by his fellow noble lords Bathurst, Berkeley and Bledisloe among the vice-presidents. The club's chosen colours were old gold and maroon, the same as those on the Gloucestershire coat of arms. And even as late as the 1960s, one poor chap had his membership application rejected on the grounds, first, that he had attended Cheltenham Grammar School, not Cheltenham College, and second, that he only had one initial!

The links with Cheltenham College have always been strong. Among the original list of members (published on the club's excellent website) there are at least five Cheltenham masters, whilst goodness knows how many Old Cheltonians must have turned out for the Gipsies over the years. On at least one occasion, it may have cost them more than they'd bargained for. In one season, in the early 1930s, the school bursar agreed to the Gipsies' use of the College ground only on condition that the debts owed by team members to the school tuck-shop from the previous year were settled!

This being Gloucestershire and the game being cricket, there is inevitably a Grace connection. 'Grace, Dr. E.M., Park House, Thornbury' – the name fairly leaps out at one from that early list of members. It wasn't, of course, the famous 'Coroner', Edward Mills Grace, WG's elder brother. He had died in 1910. But it was his son, Edgar Mervyn Grace, the first of the four children that the original EM had with his second wife, Annie, after fathering no fewer than 13 (or possibly 14) with his first wife, another Annie who, not surprisingly perhaps, had died in 1884 at the age of just 40. Edgar Grace's younger brother NV Grace was also a member, as were two of his (Edgar's) sons, GF Grace and yet another EM, whose son Michael played for the Gipsies for many years in the 1960s and '70s.

Grace wasn't the only famous cricketing name to be found among the Gipsies' early membership. There are Jessops there, alongside RP Keigwin, a fine all-round sportsman who played 74 first-class matches for Cambridge University, Essex and Gloucestershire from 1903 to 1923, and a BS Lyon, of Midsomer Norton, who may or may not have been related to Bev Lyon, that most spirited of cricketers, who came closer than any Gloucestershire captain since WG to lifting the county championship in the early 1930s.

All of the Gipsies' scorebooks have been carefully preserved, and in the very first one, from 1922, you will find the name of KS Duleepsinhji – nephew of the great Ranji, who might even have rivalled his famous uncle's cricketing exploits, had his career not been sadly cut short by illness. He was in the Cheltenham College side which the Gipsies took on in only their second ever match, and although he scored only 4, out of the College's mammoth 378 for six, he made ample amends with the ball, taking seven wickets with his leg spin, as the Gipsies subsided to a heavy defeat.

Most of the Gipsies' matches in those more spacious days were two-day affairs, often on the country-house grounds of which Gloucestershire enjoyed more than its fair share: houses like Badminton, Cirencester Park and Westonbirt, before it became a girls' school. When the schoolmasters were released for their summer holidays, there was a veritable avalanche of fixtures – ten two-day matches in August alone in one glorious summer. What fun it must have been. Good cricket, good company, no doubt lavish hospitality, and all in the most beautiful settings. Those golden days have mostly gone now, along with the country house cricket grounds, but the Gipsies do provide more than an echo of them, in their annual cricket week at Stowell Park, the home of their current President, Lord Vestey. Five one-day matches and a two-day encounter with the Old Cheltonians are played, and the festivities reach a climax with the annual ball – black tie or Gipsy bow tie obligatory, just like the old days.

But in many other respects, the Gipsies have changed, arguably for the better. Most of the old snobbishness has gone. The current chairman went to Marling School – a grammar school – in Stroud. These days, a cricketer can nominate himself for membership, without having to wait to be invited. You still need to hail from Gloucestershire and show that you can play a bit, and there is still no shortage of ex-public school boys and public school masters. But the key qualification these days is that you share the Gipsies' values: the comradeship, the fun, the sense of tradition, playing the game to win, but not at all costs and always in the right spirit.

The embodiment of those values is Chris Coley, the Gipsies' Honorary Secretary and longest-serving player. A former Chairman of Cricket for Gloucestershire, who organised the Cheltenham Cricket Festival for 30 years, Chris first turned out for the Gipsies as a Cheltenham schoolboy in 1959. More than 50 years later, he is still going strong, reckoning to play at least ten games a season and loving it as much as ever.

However, Chris is by no means the oldest cricketer to have played for the Gipsies. That honour belongs to the remarkable Cyril Hollinshead, long-time treasurer and secretary of the club, who played his final game for the Gipsies in 1992, at the age of 90. Nor was it a token appearance. The redoubtable Cyril, who by this time was bowling slow left-arm, opened the bowling against the Gloucestershire Clergy and conceded just 16 runs in his six overs.

Over 86 and did not get a bowl!

A headline-catching performance by Cyril Hollinshead in 1988
Playing against the Cryptics at Malvern College he did not bowl in a Gipsies match
for the first time in his 40-year career with the club.
He was also out second ball for nought, but he did not seem downhearted:
"I hared after the ball two or three times from mid-off, but always saw something go past me
like an express train – another fielder. But I did manage to get to the ball first once."

Thanks to the enthusiasm of men like Cyril Hollinshead, the Gipsies continue to thrive, even in these league-dominated times. They have over 200 playing members on their books and the 2012 fixture list extended to 60 matches, each organised by a different match manager. His task, which is made very clear, is to raise a team which will roughly match the opposition for cricketing skill. Sometimes that may mean including one or more of the many first-class cricketers who are Gipsies' members. There have been more than 20 of them in the last three years, including the likes of Steve Kirby, now hurling his Yorkshire thunderbolts on Somerset's behalf, and former Derbyshire, Gloucestershire and England batsman Kim Barnett. Or it may mean selecting a judicious mixture of old guard and young bloods. The idea is to make a good game of it, one that preferably goes down to the final few overs, ideally to the last ball.

The Gipsies' match managers are an interesting bunch, to be sure. Besides former Gloucestershire stalwarts such as Andy Stovold and Mike Smith, they have recently included such giants of the racing world as champion National Hunt jockey Peter Scudamore and Cheltenham supremo Edward Gillespie, not to mention the former *Times* cricket correspondent now racing, Alan Lee. They even get celebrities from time to time, always provided they are proper cricketers, of course. John Cleese certainly qualifies on both counts. He once took six for 58 against a decent Wiltshire Queries side.

At a slightly different level, I do like the story of the distinguished musician, Roger Smith, who lived at Highnam Court. In a match against Bourton Vale, he scored a century before lunch, retired so that he could conduct a choir at the Guiting Power music festival, and then returned after tea to keep wicket!

Another key ingredient in the Gipsies' continuing success is the annual tour. They've been all over the world, winning the international six-a-side tournament at Chang Mai in Thailand on three occasions, and even playing a match on the ice at St Moritz. According to Chris Coley, the three most enjoyable tours were probably to South Africa in 1998, with a side which included Gloucestershire's Jon Lewis and Bobby Dawson, to the scenic magnificence of the Canadian Rocky Mountains in 2006 and to Zimbabwe in the winter of 1994/95. This sounds as if it was a real cricketing safari, staying as guests at the game lodges of the Streak and Whittle families, in the days before the worst excesses of the Mugabe regime.

So, what sort of a bunch are the modern Gloucestershire Gipsies? Well, they love their cricket, that's for sure, and they love their county almost as much, with that fierce, Gloucestrian pride. There's a good strong whiff of farming in there, and a well-developed Cheltenham National Hunt racing connection. This was started by Chris Coley, whose company organises hospitality facilities at the racecourse, and has been carried on through Lord Vestey, who until 2011 was Chairman of the Steeplechase Company, and Edward Gillespie, its Managing Director and by all accounts a most obdurate batsman, who once shared in a partnership of 75 at Malmesbury without scoring a run!

The Gipsies may indeed have been relatively late arrivals on the wandering county clubs scene but, where some other more venerable clubs are struggling, they seem to be thriving. "We somehow make it work," says Chris Coley, and to this observer, it seems to be working very well indeed.

Website: *www.glosgipsiescc.co.uk*

Winners of the 2007 Chiangmai International Cricket Sixes
left to right: the guide, the driver, Karl Pearson, Mark Briers, David Terrington,
Dom Hewson, Paul Lazenbury, Chris Coley and (in front) Ben Gannon
The final was against a Bangladeshi Six which included two Test cricketers.
With six to win off the final delivery, Dom Hewson hit the ball in the air to leg, towards the spot
where the team were gathered. They watched it as it landed six inches over the boundary.

Durham Pilgrims

Founded: 1922

by John Bailey

The Pilgrims were born in 1922, when a pillar of the county club, the Rev WLM Law, asked Mr WJ Nimmo "to try to arrange some decent mid-week cricket". Nimmo responded by inviting 14 of the leading Durham cricketers of the day to join the new club and appointed Tommy Kinch, skipper of the county side, as captain. The club regalia were entirely appropriate for a venture that was evidently at least partly sociable in nature: a tie in port wine and brimstone and a port-coloured blazer with gold buttons embossed with a 'P'. The tie was subsequently altered to include a blue stripe and thus avoid confusion with two other wandering clubs, the Hawks and Armstrong College, whilst the motto which appeared below the club crest of a Mayflower ship was 'Semper Vagrantes' – always wandering.

In their first match, the Pilgrims played Durham University. The match report in the club records is commendably terse: 'Our first match, fine day, bad wicket, victory for the Pilgrims by 58 runs.' A second game against the university was also won, thanks mainly to J Turnbull, who scored 103 and took five wickets. There followed a defeat to Cumberland on a horribly wet wicket, but the Pilgrims had their revenge in the return fixture six weeks later, winning by 17 runs. That first season concluded with a match against a Public Schools XI, won by the Pilgrims fairly easily. The report describes the schools' XI's fielding as 'very bad and slack'.

Among the Pilgrims' earliest fixtures were encounters which still feature prominently today. The match against the Cryptics dates from 1924, and that with the Yorkshire Gentlemen from a year later. Visiting clubs always enjoyed playing the Pilgrims on the Brewery field of J Nimmo and Son at Castle Eden, with its flat outfield, perfect wicket, boundaries so short that a hit over the ropes only counted for four and the enticing aroma of malt and hops wafting over the ground. The brewery has sadly gone now, but the ground is still there, larger than it used to be, so sixes can be scored, and its current occupants, the Castle Eden Cricket Club, still very kindly make it available to the Pilgrims for their annual two-day match with the Cryptics.

The Pilgrims have lacked nothing in continuity over their 90-year life. There have been just five secretaries, in WJ Nimmo, CA Macfarlane, WD Edgar, HJ Bailey and B Stone, and even fewer presidents. Records do not reveal exactly how many, but probably just four.

Four Test cricketers, CL Townsend, DCH Townsend, NS Mitchell-Innes and SJE Brown, have played for the Pilgrims. And if that is fewer than some other county wanderers, the Pilgrims more than make up for it in the number of rugby internationals they have fielded. They include Brian and Carl Aarvold, Laurie Gloag, Cliff Harrison, Mike Weston and Charlie Adamson. Another brilliant all-round sportsman to play for the Pilgrims was Micky Walford, who won Blues at Oxford for cricket, rugby and hockey and went on to play hockey for England and to captain Somerset at cricket. His brother David, another hockey international, was a long-time Pilgrims' treasurer.

The fact that Durham was a minor county till 1992 inevitably reduced the opportunities for past generations of Durham cricketers to play first-class cricket. Even so, several Pilgrims' regulars have played first-class matches, either for the Minor Counties against touring sides, or for other counties, among them RB Proud for Oxford University and Hampshire, David Bailey for Lancashire, Philip Weston for Worcestershire, Robin Weston for Durham and HJ Bailey and BR Lander for the Minor Counties.

The Pilgrims have five fixtures scheduled for the 2013 season: against Durham School, Barnard Castle School, St Bees School, the Yorkshire Gentlemen and Cryptics (two days). They are all in midweek, thus maximising the chances of the best players being free from the obligations of league and cup cricket and domestic duties.

Like many other wandering clubs, the Pilgrims don't find it as easy to assemble sides as they once did. But thanks to the dedication of the match managers and secretaries down the years, the club remains in good heart, and is looking forward eagerly to its centenary in nine years' time. Only one small mystery remains, and that is how it came to be known as the Durham Pilgrims, rather than just plain Pilgrims, as its founders seem to have intended, for no formal decision to change the name seems ever to have been recorded. No matter. The name was well chosen – "who would true valour see" and all that – and the club has been living up to it splendidly throughout its 91-year history.

Durham Pilgrims versus Cumberland, East Boldon, 24 August 1922

Penguins

Founded: 1923

by Tom Kemp

It was in 1923 that Dr Reginald Lee suggested a friendly match at Thorp Arch, Yorkshire, between the Thorp Arch club, of which he was captain, and a team organised by George Armitage from among the staff of the Leeds General Infirmary. Dr Lee had recently entered practice locally, while George Armitage was house surgeon to Sir Berkeley, later Lord, Moynihan. Although there is no record of the result, the match appears to have been an enjoyable success, for in the pavilion after the match, while scantily clothed, George Armitage suggested that the team be kept together and play regularly; formal baptism of the idea being performed that evening in the nearby Pax Inn. The first name suggested was the Pelicans, but it was felt that there could be objections from the owner of the Pelican Tobacco Factory in Leeds, and eventually, for no clearly remembered reason, the club became Penguins, with a first season in 1924.

George Armitage, whose medical student days at Leeds were interrupted by the Great War, won a Military Cross on the Somme and a bar to that decoration at Passchendaele. He became an eminent and much loved Leeds surgeon, and was ahead of his time concerning audit, writing in 1959: "Surgery like cricket is only interesting if you keep the score." He was a good shot and an accomplished golfer, and he developed a pedigree herd of Friesian cattle. After retirement from surgical practice he became chairman of the family brick manufacturing firm, George Armitage & Sons Ltd. He was known to arrive late for matches, with the largest cricket bag the other players had ever seen – and with a man to carry it.

George was the first captain of the club, and the only other skipper before the Second World War was insurance broker Allan Denison, another recipient of the Military Cross – as a pilot after an aerial dogfight during which he acquired German metal in his arm, which remained in place throughout his playing career. When writing after the war, Denison gave the closest one is likely to get to an explanation of the club's name by describing some of the first players as being like penguins, on account of their webbed feet and their preference for liking their drinks iced! He also exhorted future Penguins to "play good cricket ... in the Yorkshire style, and to relax as much as possible after the game, not during it."

The first president was George Armitage's father, and the first centurion was his brother Leonard – against Coal Exporters CC in Hull in 1926, although he was responsible for running out three men while amassing his century. George recruited the former Yorkshire batsman Charles Hardisty, who was employed at the infirmary. This was 15 years after he had finished playing for Yorkshire and, although large scores for the Penguins eluded him, he was good company and an excellent drinker. Other Yorkshire players who appeared occasionally for the Penguins included Frank Greenwood, Maurice Leyland, Sandy Jacques, Norman Yardley, Paul Gibb and Ken Taylor. The club was fortunate that for many years the brothers Fred and Arthur Potter from York acted respectively as umpire and scorer.

For some years club meetings were held at Leeds General Infirmary, and in the earliest days most Penguins were medical men or their relatives. When Armitage went as a Rockefeller travelling fellow to Boston and Denison became captain, the medical contribution diminished rapidly to nothing, apparently with improvement in the playing standards. Several pre-war players, including Armitage and Denison, had attended Ackworth School, with whom Penguins had a fixture until 2002. Another Ackworth Old Scholar is the club's oldest current player, Peter Dibb aged 79, an economical opening bowler and once formidable opening batsman (in 1951 he opened an innings with Ken Taylor) now insisting on batting at number 11.

When play was resumed after the war, a large fixture list was developed, with two matches each weekend, and in many years a midweek tour. Having several members of a family playing for the club started with the Armitages, and the Emmett family in Dewsbury were particularly notable in continuing the tradition. Until around 20 years ago there were still about 40 fixtures a year, but opponents and grounds have since proved more elusive. Former regular opponents have entered leagues, Sundays are often cup match days, and each year recently has seen at least one of the previously regular opposition teams go out of existence. Matches against schools have disappeared as summer terms have become shorter and more exam-focused. The regular fixture with Silcoates School helped to provide a steady intake of Penguins, and in the 1970s and 1980s many Penguins were Old Silcoatians.

The club is fortunate now to be able to rent a ground with excellent facilities (including hot showers, by no means universally available on the club's travels) at Silcoates School, with good wickets prepared by the school groundstaff. Thus, although still largely a wandering club, it is able to host some home matches in July and August. Without the availability of this fine ground, the fixture list would have become more severely restricted. Twenty matches a year, one each weekend, are now played.

Over the last 20 years the club has been returning to its medical roots. Most of each team are now usually either doctors or the sons of doctors. It is also common for there to be several father-son pairs in a team. Recruitment has been particularly active at Dewsbury

& District Hospital where one of the older current players used to work as a physician. He manages to keep his place in the side by virtue of being married to the lady who organises the home teas, generally regarded as being the best in the local non-league circuit, and by being the fixture secretary, match manager, and father of the captain. It is that sort of club!

About 35 men play for the club during a season, some only very occasionally. With the re-emergence of the medical connection the club has benefitted from the company and performances of many fine players originating from India, Pakistan and Sri Lanka. The highest individual innings was achieved in 2011 by Ashish Rana, a psychiatrist, who scored 230 not out against Almondbury Casuals; the previous highest score by a Penguin against that club was 161 in 1984 by the young New Zealander Ron Hart, who guested for Penguins over several years. Another famous Kiwi, Martin Crowe, contributed a couple of centuries in 1982. The habit of inviting southern hemisphere professionals to play on Sundays died out twenty years ago, and the strength of the club is now in its regular local members. To continue name dropping, mention should be made of recent MCC President Phillip Hodson, who performed notably with bat and ball in 1970.

The ethos of the club would still be approved of by Allan Denison. Play is serious – and quiet – and passionate concern is evinced about which team is going to win, but not (or not much) afterwards about which team has won. Recriminations when they occur are only in jest. When a certain player received a knighthood a few years ago he was rapidly disabused of any idea that this honour could advance him up the batting order, and he continues diligently to act as scorer for most of the Penguins' innings. Penguins vary considerably in ability, age and visual acuity, and the composition of the team changes substantially from week to week; it is not unusual for five bus-pass holders to take the field, together with some more vigorous younger men. Penguins cricket is played for the enjoyment of participation, win or lose; it is viewed as a relaxing diversion from more serious matters, and as excellent value for the £3 match fee.

Teams of Yorkshire Gentlemen and Penguins in 2012 on the 60th anniversary of the first appearance in this fixture of Peter Dibb (seated, centre)

Grasshoppers

Founded: 1923

by Barrie Lloyd and Patrick Strachan

The club was formed in 1923 by Henry 'Shrimp' Leveson Gower and Hilary Chadwyck-Healey, amongst others, as a Surrey wandering club on the lines of the Sussex Martlets, Hampshire Hogs and the Band of Brothers. The objectives were to attract membership from a Surrey base and to encourage and foster cricket in Surrey schools.

The cricketing background and ability of the two principal founding members could not have been more different. Leveson Gower had played first-class cricket for Surrey for many years, had captained England, was chairman of selectors for several years in the 1920s and Surrey President from 1929 to 1939. Chadwyck-Healey was the son of a baronet and was as unathletic and physically unco-ordinated as can be imagined. He was a composer of church music and a march dedicated to the club. It was rumoured that his role in the foundation of the club was driven by his wish to secure a place in a cricket team, a motivation in which, among wandering club founders, he was certainly not alone!

The influence of Leveson Gower in Surrey cricket, however, ensured that strong sides were raised from the outset and members included C'I'A Wilkinson, a former Surrey captain, and Guy Earle, who played for Surrey before going on to captain Somerset. Douglas Jardine also played for them. In fact, when the Grasshoppers played a Canadian XI at The Oval in 1936, he suggested 'tongue in cheek' that the club's opening bowler, Gavin Bell, should bowl short at the batsman's ribs with a few close catchers on the leg side!

Interestingly, the MCC goodwill tour of Australia and New Zealand in 1935/36 – a tour designed to make good the damage caused by Jardine's bodyline tour of 1932/33 – included two future members of the Grasshoppers, the appropriately named 'Hopper' Read, the fiercely fast but wild Essex fast bowler, and Adam Powell, the Essex wicket-

THIS CARD DOES NOT NECESSARILY INCLUDE THE FALL OF THE LAST WICKET

Surrey County Cricket Club 2d.
KENNINGTON OVAL
Grasshoppers v Mr. R. C. Matthews Canadian XI.
WEDNESDAY, AUGUST 12th, 1936. (One-Day Match)

GRASSHOPPERS	First Innings		Second Innings
1 J. C. Christopherson	c Davies, b G. Percival	36	
2 G. Howland-Jackson	c Loney, b Scott	28	
3 S. A. Block	c & b Carlton	27	
4 D. R. Jardine	c Loney, b L. A. Percival	30	
5 M. H. Bell	c Carey, b L. A. Percival	30	
*6 D. A. Strachan	b L. A. Percival	16	
7 Capt. A. P. Block	b L. A. Percival	11	
‡8 R. S. Machin	c Carey, b Loney	1	
9 B. B. Waddy	not out	18	
10 G. G. Hill	b L. A. Percival	0	
11 Hon. R. R. Blades	c Carlton, b Loney	0	
12 N. G. H. Bell	B , l-b 6, w , n-b	6	B , l-b , w , n-b
	Total	203	Total

FALL OF THE WICKETS

1–51	2–83	3–107	4–148	5–161	6–176	7–183	8–184	9–202	10–202	11–203
1–	2–	3–	4–	5–	6–	7–	8–	9–	10–	11–

BOWLING ANALYSIS — First Innings — Second Innings

	O.	M.	R.	W.	Wd.	N-b.	O.	M.	R.	W.	Wd.	N-b.
Seagram	11	2	32	0								
Scott	10	1	20	1								
Loney	20.5	2	47	2								
Carlton	9	1	31	1								
G. Percival	8	1	28	1								
L. A. Percival	13	2	39	6								

CANADIANS	First Innings		Second Innings
1 E. F. Loney	c Machin, b	13	
2 L. A. Percival	b N. G. H. Bell	0	
3 K. H. Ross	c Blades, b Waddy	7	
4 D. E. Carey	b Waddy	1	
5 N. F. Pearson	b Waddy	0	
*6 W. E. N. Bell	l.b.w., (n) b Waddy	0	
7 L. C. Bell	l.b.w., b N. G. H. Bell	30	
8 W. G. Scott	b N. G. H. Bell	30	
‡9 M. I. Davies	b Waddy	17	
10 C. A. Seagram	l.b.w., b N. G. H. Bell	6	
11 E. Carlton	not out	9	
12 G. Percival	l.b.w., b Howl'd-Jackson	15	
	B 4, l-b 9, w , n-b 5	18	B , l-b , w , n-b
	Total	146	Total

FALL OF THE WICKETS

1–2	2–15	3–.7	4–27	5–27	6–28	7–93	8–96	9–116	10–120	11–146
1–	2–	3–	4–	5–	6–	7–	8–	9–	10–	11–

BOWLING ANALYSIS — First Innings — Second Innings

	O.	M.	R.	W.	Wd.	N-b.	O.	M.	R.	W.	Wd.	N-b.
Waddy	19	11	31	6		3						
W. Bell	21	9	40	4		1						
Hill	6	1	18	0		1						
Capt. Block	3	0	13	0								
Howl'd-Jackson	6	0	26	1								

*Captain   ‡Wkt.-keeper
Umpires— Gravett & Harris

Toss won by GRASSHOPPERS
RESULT— Grasshoppers won by 57 runs
(n) Signifies L.B.W. under the new experimental rule

CUSHIONS MAY BE HIRED 3d. EACH PER DAY

The Grasshoppers versus the Free Foresters, Busbridge Hall, circa 1929

back: EM Wellings, EAW Taylor, CG Bambridge, HF Lucas, CJ Wilson, RLH Green, LMT Castle   middle: W West, RW Kettlewell, HR Glover, PS Whitcombe, CA Barlow, DA Strachan, WR Lawson, D McCall, M Gravett (umpire)   front: TNF Wilson, B Clarke, JHR Dickson, ESB Williams, R Earle, EL Armitage, SA Block, R Clarke, LKA Block

keeper, both of whom had strong Surrey qualifications and played first-class cricket as amateurs. 'Hopper' Read played successfully against South Africa in the final Test of 1935. He owed his selection to an astonishing piece of bowling for Essex against a strong Yorkshire side at Huddersfield when Yorkshire were bowled out on the first morning of the match for 31, Read taking six wickets for 11 runs. The story goes that a diehard Yorkshire spectator, who was late for the start of the match, asked the gateman for the score and, on hearing that there had been a batting collapse, was heard to mutter disconsolately, "It is always the same with these weak Southern counties. They are not really worth playing." Essex went on to win the match by an innings and 204 runs.

Adam Powell played for the club up until the end of the 1960s. Poker-faced, he declined to stand back to any of the club's bowlers, no matter the pace, and rarely (if ever) let through a bye, dropped a catch or missed a stumping chance. To see him standing up to the wicket when 'Hopper' Read was bowling was a sight to behold!

All non-school fixtures before the war were played at Busbridge Hall, near Godalming, epitomising all that was best in country-house cricket. The matches were joyful occasions for players, families and locals alike. The club thrived up to the start of the Second War and although fixtures were reduced in number, the club was able to keep going. This was largely thanks to the then secretary, Douglas Strachan, another of the early stalwarts who more or less ran the club single-handed during the war years. Douglas Strachan was a medium-pace, away-swing bowler who could bowl all day and who delighted in luring batsmen to their destruction with his seemingly guileless offerings. Not that he showed his delight, mind you. Excessive exuberance has never been part of Grasshoppers' cricket. He was President of the club from 1965 to 1985 and played until well into his sixties and thereafter appeared at almost every game, until his death at the age of 98 in January 1997. His son, Patrick Strachan, a useful mid-order batsman and hitter, followed in his footsteps as

Douglas Strachan (left) with Derek Fenner

one-time secretary and now President of the club, and his grandson, Jamie Strachan, is currently one of the club's leading young players.

During the 1950s, the club's sides continued to be drawn largely from pre-war members to the point where the lack of mobility in the field became embarrassing. Things came to a head when an enthusiastic officer cadet playing for the RMA Sandhurst was run out attempting a fifth run. It had taken a posse of five ageing Grasshoppers to return the ball to the wicket-keeper, the last of whom, much to the surprise and dismay of the officer cadet, proved to be able to throw.

The club was rejuvenated in the 1960s whilst Derek Fenner, then a schoolmaster at Epsom College (and later the headmaster of Alleyn's School, Dulwich), was its secretary. The club attracted many good players from the leading Surrey schools and played competitively and to a high standard. Fenner was himself a tall left-arm spin bowler with a high rhythmical action and a devastating and well-concealed in-swinging faster ball.

The club was also able to call upon the services of MH Bushby, a Cambridge University captain, and a wonderfully correct and clean-striking opening bat, as well as Richard Jefferson, also of Cambridge University and distinguished opening bowler for Surrey. Jefferson played as an amateur and as such was free to play club cricket on Sundays, the normal rest day, from which the club benefited on a number of occasions. This did not endear him to the Surrey coach, Arthur MacIntyre, but seems to have done him no harm as he was awarded his county cap at the end of August 1964.

Another of the club's characters of the 1960s was the talented composer, Edward Harper, a nuggety opening batsman with a wry sense of humour. Amongst other compositions, Harper set the love poems of e.e. cummings to music, and the piece was sung at the BBC Promenade Concerts at the Albert Hall on 28 August 1978. The advertising billboards read "Mozart, Debussy, Harper, Strauss", a batting order of which Hilary Chadwyck-Healey would surely have been proud.

Edward Harper often found himself in the same side as Peter Adams, a local butcher, who was described by Christopher Martin-Jenkins in his autobiography, *CMJ, a Cricketing Life*, as 'a brilliant stocky little wicket-keeper'. Adams was a dedicated member of the club and served as its treasurer for many years.

The team of that era might well have included Martin Lawrence, a regular and loyal club member, who bowled away swing and batted in cavalier style. After a successful career in marketing, he has for some years been Chairman of the Northants County Cricket Club and influential with others in pressing the case through the ECB for a World Test Match Championship and other reforms. Another regular player was Barrie Lloyd, a fine opening batsman and wicket-keeper and very competitive cricketer with a fine record. Renowned for his vociferous appealing he contributed a huge amount to the club serving as both secretary and later as president.

The club continued to field competitive sides throughout the closing years of the millennium and was especially well represented, thanks to the selfless enthusiasm of Nigel Williams, at the Wandering Clubs Festival held at Oxford in 2000. The highlight of the Festival for the club was the match against the Romany. The club was set a target of over 300 runs to win the match on a beautiful wicket and lovely day. The challenge was accepted and, with Romany keeping the game open by seeking to buy wickets, a thrilling finish ensued, with Grasshoppers reaching their target in the very last over. It was a match in the finest traditions of wandering cricket.

The club throughout its history has been served by a series of dedicated umpires, among them Johnny Hill, Bill Hook, Peter Parker, a classical music devotee, and David Havenhand. All have in their own way added greatly to the character of the club and the enjoyment of the game. The club has also been well served by family members throughout its history, and mention should be made of Miles Dorman, a fine cricketer and all-round games player, who now serves the club as treasurer, and his son, Christopher who served as secretary for a number of years.

The original purpose of the club has sadly been eroded because Surrey schools, now with a much reduced summer term, have opted to play against other schools, often on a limited-overs basis. The club has, however, an attractive fixture list against club sides, and the playing membership has recently been increased thanks to the determined efforts of a group of young members who find wandering cricket a welcome change from the pressures of league cricket. Lifelong friendships continue to be formed by playing for the club, competitive cricket is played in excellent spirit, and laughter and fun prevail. May it long be so.

Stragglers of Asia

Founded: 1925

by Jack Hyde-Blake and Willy Boulter

Colonel PB Sanger, late of the Royal Artillery, a founder member, described the formation of the club thus:

> In the early 1920s, when stationed in Ambala in the Gunners, I was invited by the late Maharajah of Patiala, to take a cricket team to Chail every summer. Chail was in the Simla Hills, 7000 ft up. The Maharajah had cut off the top of one of the peaks and made a cricket ground. It was the most tremendous fun and we played them at everything. Cricket, hockey, tennis, billiards and we even did our best in the whisky stakes. The Patiala Peg was two fingers, measured with the first and little fingers. After we had done this for a few years, we discussed the possibility of forming a Club.

The first match was played at Eastbourne College, where the club maintains a fixture to this day. The scoresheet refers to 'H.A.V. Maynard's XI' but coins the name Stragglers of Asia as 'given to the team of Officers and Civil Servants home on leave, and (it) was the most enjoyable match of the season.' One of the players was a certain AJ Trollope, who is referred to in the secretary's pen pictures of each member as 'one armed – bowls a little'. Sadly, the bowling analysis does not survive, but the luckless Trollope took no wickets and was bowled out for a duck!

The young men who entered the army, civil service or the big trading companies in those days tended to come out to India quite early in life, before they had time to join cricket clubs in England. In those more spacious days, six months' leave was allowed every three years and was generally taken in the summer. The idea was to give young cricketers at home on leave a team to play for.

Alleyne Coldwell and Vernon Maynard were the great instigators of the venture and it was in 1925 that they, together with Colonel Sanger and Mason MacFarlayne (later Governor of Gibraltar) drove to London to fix the final details of the Stragglers of Asia, as they had decided their club would be called. The next morning they went round to the tailors, Fosters, to choose a club tie and then headed off to the Savoy for lunch with the Maharajah of Patiala, whom they promptly made a member for life.

Alleyne Coldwell, a colonel in the Northamptonshire Regiment, became 'Hon Home Secretary' based at the regimental depot in Northampton. A great many of his brother officers joined. At the same time an Hon Foreign Secretary was appointed in Calcutta. Under the benign leadership of Vernon Maynard, who became known as the Founder, the club was immediately successful. Representatives were appointed all over the Far East as far as China. Membership was by introduction only and Representatives introduced potential candidates to the Foreign Secretary who forwarded all details to the UK, where the Home Secretary helped candidates to play their qualifiers when on leave. The qualification for membership was 'to have been in residence for at least two years East of Suez'. The fixture list rapidly developed and consisted, in the main, of a tour of Oxford colleges, a tour of Cambridge colleges and a West Country tour.

In 1939 18 fixtures were played, but then came the war and the club ceased to function. In 1945, a small advertisement appeared in *The Times* asking any interested Stragglers to meet. Six Stragglers appeared, and it was decided to start again. Six matches were arranged for 1946, printed on a fixture card the size of a cigarette packet.

Revival was swift, thanks not least to the fact that so many cricketers were able to qualify under the Eastern residence rule through their wartime service. By 1948 the membership was over 400, including one Lieutenant General, one Major General, 12 Brigadiers, 23 Colonels and 84 Lieutenant Colonels.

In 1954 Colonel Sanger arranged the first fixtures in Germany. This was fruitful ground for the Stragglers, and up to ten games a year were played against military establishments, touring sides and the occasional Dutch club. However, as the British civilian and military presence East of Suez diminished, so did the main source of membership. Eventually, notwithstanding the best efforts of the committee and much agonising, the club was left with no option but to open membership to all like-minded cricketers, if it was to survive. The decision was taken at a meeting in the Star Tavern, Belgravia, in 1982, and marked the birth of the Stragglers of Asia of the modern era.

The Hong Kong Stragglers continue to play one or two matches each year, but Stragglers in Germany played their last fixture in 1994. With the reduction in the armed forces, new players are now mainly civilian, and the military flavour of the club has become much less pronounced. Even most military fixtures have faded away due to the understandable difficulty of producing a cricket team in the UK whilst simultaneously conducting operations in Iraq and Afghanistan

The Stragglers are fortunate to have been served by some outstanding chairmen and presidents through the years. Paul van der Gucht was an active member in the pre- and post-war eras, later serving as president 1973-81. He has been described as 'probably the best wicket-keeper Radley has ever had' and 'one of the very best timers of the ball'. He played numerous first-class matches for Gloucestershire, alongside Wally Hammond, and then for Bengal and the Europeans in India. He still holds the record for the Stragglers' highest individual score, with 204.

Among others who stand out is Brigadier Johnny King-Martin CBE DSO MC, who shepherded the club through the difficult 1970s and was chairman 1982-84. He was a formidable character, who didn't mince his words. If the club had had a disappointing season, or the organisation was in a muddle, he said so, in his annual newsletter. More lightheartedly, he commented on the 1973 cocktail party that "wives and attractive girlfriends provided a backcloth for hopes of better things to come and members are asked to keep this in mind and are encouraged to bring wives and girlfriends in the future."

Another distinguished soldier to serve Stragglers well has been General Sir Geoffrey Howlett KBE, MC, a no-nonsense paratrooper with a penchant for lending staff cars and

The Stragglers of Asia, playing the Cross Arrows at Lord's, 2006
back: Alex Garman, Fergus Boyd, Sam Chapman, Mark Ferrao, Robert Pollock-Hill, Ben Rogers
front: Willie Boulter, Tim Lerwill, Sye Razvi, Harvey Anderson, Teddy Bostock

credit cards to Stragglers on tour – in Denmark in this case. He served as president of the club from 1989 to 1993 and remains an honorary member. In the nineties, largely thanks to the General, the Stragglers were fortunate to be able to appoint as President Lt Col John Stephenson CBE, the well-known and visionary Secretary of the MCC. As a result, Straggler committee meetings are held at the home of cricket to this day.

From the very earliest expeditions to Oxford, Cambridge and the West Country, the club has prided itself on the quality of its tours. Many are the Stragglers described as 'good tourists' in the club records! In the heyday of BAOR (British Army of the Rhine), there were several tours to Holland and Denmark, and, fondly remembered by many, Berlin – when West Berlin was a NATO enclave surrounded by Communist East Germany. Barbed wire and minefields seemed to give the nightlife a certain edge.

In 1986 the committee resolved that 'Tours need to be planned well ahead, and not be too ambitious', but immediately disregarded the latter point. In 1993 a hugely successful venture to Hong Kong went ahead (one tourist stayed on in Hong Kong for the next five years or so!) and this was followed by the Western Cape, South Africa, in 1997, the 75th anniversary tour to India in 2000, and Sri Lanka in 2004.

The 2000 tour to India enjoyed the active co-operation and assistance of HH Captain Amarinder Singh, Maharajah of Patiala – grandson of the 'original' Maharajah. A symbolic match was played on the Chail ground – and the tour culminated with a great match against HH's XI containing six members of the Patiala family, as well as Bishen Bedi and Mushtaq Mohammad. The touring party enjoyed extravagant hospitality and a warm reception wherever it went.

In 2007 a touring party flew once again to India, this time to play eight matches, including a day-night match in Mumbai. A diary of the tour, *Tales from the Raj*, was published each day and posted on our website. Between major tours, our short tours have been most successful and have included long weekends in Portugal, Cyprus, Malta and a memorable six-a-side tournament in the Algarve in 2007. In the UK the club continues to tour both the West Country and the North from time to time.

Sye Razvi under guard on the 2007 India tour. He has scored almost 7,000 runs for the club to date.

The club has always been concerned to bring on younger cricketers and since 1988 has awarded the Hugh Lindsay Trophy to the 'young cricketer of the year' in memory of the Equerry to the Queen, who was tragically killed in a skiing accident at Klosters, and who played many matches for the Stragglers as an aggressive early order bat.

The Stragglers of Asia have not been immune to changes in the world around it and have been hit hard by the global downturn and associated financial crises, which have made it difficult for many members to find the time and the money to go on overseas tours. But the club maintains strong links with cricketers the world over and is determined not to lose its touring ethos.

In the meantime, at home, successive committees have concentrated on improving the fixture list and maintaining membership, to such good effect that the club now has over 400 members, and plays 30 high-quality matches every summer. The Stragglers of Asia may have moved some way from its East of Suez roots, but this is a club which has adjusted well to the modern age and looks to the future with confidence.

Website: *www.stragglersofasia.co.uk*

South Wales Hunts

Founded: 1926

by Charles Brain

The South Wales Hunts Cricket Club had its origin at the Royal Hotel in Cardiff on a certain Tuesday during the winter of 1925/26. It was custom for Messrs JC (Johnny) and Peter Clay, Charlie Jenour and 'Tip' Williams to convene at the Royal Hotel once a week for lunch. On one of these occasions the aforementioned thought that it would be sensible to have an activity to keep the hunting fraternity occupied during the closed hunting season, and the idea of forming a wandering cricket club was born.

Following an encouraging response from a circular letter sent to hunts in the local area, an inaugural meeting was held in the bar at Chepstow Racecourse where the first committee was appointed. Many of the South Walian hunt members would have been regulars at the racecourse but the venue was most appropriate as it was held in a bar, a practice that the current members continue with great enthusiasm today.

One of the items that was agreed at the meeting was the magnificent club colours of green, black, claret and primrose with a red fox on the cap, supposedly derived from the colours of the various hunts across South Wales.

Membership was confined to landowners and those who hunt or had hunted regularly and fairly as members or supporters of one of the following packs of foxhounds: Brecon, Carmarthenshire, Curre, Glamorgan, Golden Valley, Llangeinor, Llangibby, Monmouthshire, Pentyrch, Tredegar Farmers, Pembrokeshire and South Pembrokeshire.

There is a reference on file that even into the 1970s a qualification for new members was that they were expected to own at least one acre of land. On being told of this rule, a cricketer who had recently been invited to become a member declared that he was indeed eligible as he owned an acre of land, although not on this planet but on the moon!

Qualification to become a member has been relaxed somewhat since the formation of the club although the principles still remain of being a sociable person who enjoys wandering cricket played in a sportsmanlike manner. A South Wales connection is desirable and, although there are some 'tidy' cricketers amongst its members, cricketing ability is not a crucial factor so much as playing the game with enthusiasm. The match managers try to ensure all players have the opportunity of being involved in the match in some way.

In July 1926 the South Wales Hunts, known as the Hunts, played their first fixture against the Heythrop Hunt at Bourton-on-the-Water in Gloucestershire. The team travelled from Swansea on the Newcastle Express, which stopped specially for the cricketers to alight at Bourton. It wasn't an entirely auspicious start as the Hunts lost, although they did manage to acquit themselves rather better in the next four seasons with either victories or draws.

The South Wales Hunts and their opposition, date unknown
front row: JC Clay third from left, 'Tip' Williams centre, Mike Brain third from right

Viscount Tredegar proved himself to be an excellent, and popular, first president. Not only did he make his Tredegar Park available for a number of matches, but he laid on the most splendid four- or five-course lunches accompanied with at least three different wines. During lunch at one game, two of the Hunts team were detailed to look after Nigel Haig of our opponents, the Free Foresters, which they did without stinting Haig or themselves. Notwithstanding the Hunts strategy, Haig proved unplayable, which was hardly surprising as only two years previously he had bowled out the Australians at Lord's.

During the first ten years the Hunts fixture card grew, and by the late 1930s the club had become firmly established. 'A club of character and characters' is how it was described by 'First Slip' in *The Cricketer* in November 1976. It currently has about 300 members, of whom roughly 100 are playing members, including some who are descendants of the founders of the club and of those who played in the first few seasons. Among many distinguished cricketers who have been members of the Hunts are JT Morgan, Wilf Wooller, Tony Lewis and Hugh Morris, besides, of course, the great JC Clay.

The club's longest-running fixture is against the Army, in some form or another. From the late 1920s the club played against the South Wales Borderers and the Royal Welch Fusiliers. Following the disbandment of the regiments, the Hunts played against other Welsh Army sides at various locations within the Principality, including the Old Welsh Brigade. A few of these matches were two-day games held in Brecon on the same weekend as the renowned Brecon Jazz Festival where the players enjoyed the jazz music drifting over the ground as the overs were being bowled. The Hunts played many of their Army fixtures as well as other fixtures at the Cwrt-y-Gollen Army base, a picturesque ground in the foothills of the Black Mountains near Abergavenny. The club still plays the Army, in the shape of the Guards CC, at Burton's Court.

Another of the early fixtures was against the Gloucestershire Gipsies. Although there was a gap of a number of years the fixture has featured on the card for the last ten years. Another established fixture is against I Zingari which has been played at various locations in both Wales and England since 1965 and still continues.

Including the Heythrop Hunt, the club has enjoyed playing other hunt XIs with a match against the Berkeley Hunt being the longest standing fixture, dating from 1964. Other hunt matches have included the Duke of Beaufort's Hunt, the Old Berks Hunt and Llangibby Hunt & Lady Curre's XI.

Over the years the Hunts have played several 'old boy' sides, such as the Eton Ramblers, the Harrow Wanderers, the Old Wykehamists, the Old Hurst Johnians, Shrewsbury Saracens and the Sherborne Pilgrims. In 2000 the club celebrated 70 years of playing the Downside Wanderers, and the fixture continues to be included on the card today.

Many of the Hunts fixtures used to be two-day games with a dinner party after the first day's play, held at one of the club members' houses. There was a time in the 1950 season when a one-day game was sandwiched between two two-day matches, with the core of the team playing in all three games. Unfortunately, such are the pressures on players' time and family commitments that we now no longer have two-day matches. The last was played in 2002, although that's not to say that we will not have a 'two-dayer' sometime in the future.

The club used to tour, both overseas and within the UK. The annual UK tour tended to be three matches played in Devon at Devonport. On one occasion accommodation was secured at the Royal Naval College in Dartmouth, and one late evening/early morning after plenty of rehydration, a game of corridor cricket ensued. A bin, being used as a wicket, was stood against a door – on the other side of which, unbeknown to the tourists, a visiting admiral was trying to get some sleep!

Overseas tours included trips to Jersey and Corfu where, unusually for that island, rain delayed play. Both sides wanted a result, so play got under way again. The only problem was that shots hit towards the boundary on one side of the ground, and any fielders in pursuit of them, had to negotiate a deep ditch with running water which formed part of the infield, before returning the ball to the keeper.

All good wandering clubs enjoy an exciting match, and the Hunts try to ensure a tight finish whenever possible. There have been many matches where any one of the four results has been possible at the start of the final over. One match against Abergavenny in 1949 saw the Hunts, after an all-too-excellent lunch, lose nine wickets for 51 runs. However, two of the founders of the club, JC Clay and Tip Williams, batting at 10 and 11, added a further 71. The tension mounted as the opposition wickets started to fall and the Hunts proceeded to bowl out Abergavenny with just one run to spare. In another match, against the Earl of Carnarvon's XI at the picturesque ground at Highclere, the Hunts required 16 runs off the last three balls. Our number 11 batsman, William Taylor, hoicked two sixes and, with all the spectators on their feet, he clubbed the last ball which was stopped just inside the boundary rope and the Hunts fell short of their target. However, we cannot claim that all Hunts matches have reached the dying overs, There was one encounter with Southerndown CC where the Hunts replied to 180 for eight with 15 all out!

The Hunts was one of 32 sides that took part in the four-day International Millennium Cricket Festival for Wandering Clubs held in 2000 in Oxford. And, although it may not have enjoyed the greatest success in terms of results, the team yielded to no one in playing in the true spirit of the game. The spectators enjoyed themselves, too, thanks not least to our chairman's travelling champagne tent. The club has always had a social aspect to it, including holding dinner dances from time to time, to raise funds, strengthen bonds and give everyone concerned a jolly good time.

In its heyday, the Hunts played over 20 games a season, plus a golf match against the Sparrows at Royal Porthcawl. Nowadays, it would be closer to ten, although several strong fixtures have recently been added to reflect a very welcome increase in membership in the last few years.

All in all, the South Wales Hunts CC loves its wandering cricket because of the people who make the game so pleasurable.

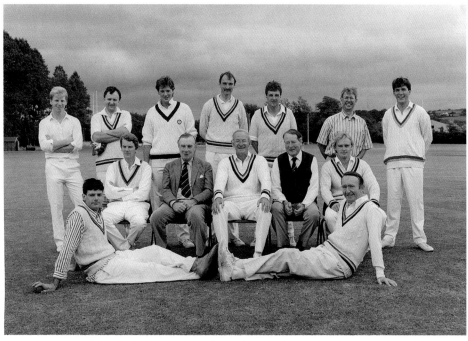

South Wales Hunts, inaugural two-day match versus Cowbridge, 1990
back row: Charles Brain, Jeremy Rawlins, James Prichard, Anthony Alexander, Harry Lewis,
unknown scorer, Johnny Morgan   middle row: Charles Williams, Henry Lewis,
Nigel Anderson, Ivor Pugh, Ali Eynon   bottom row: Geoffrey Meggitt, Griffy Phillips

Lincolnshire Gentlemen

Founded: 1928

by Andrew Scoley

The Lincolnshire Gentlemen's minute book opens with a meeting held at the Saracen's Head Hotel, Lincoln, on Friday 13 January 1928, to form an amateur cricket club in Lincolnshire. The attendance list and apologies include many names familiar to Lincolnshire cricketers today. The idea behind the formation of the cricket club was to help support cricket in the county, and to produce players to represent the county.

That meant attracting good cricketers, but also the right sort of cricketers, and there was much debate over the wording of the qualification for membership with that in mind. In the end, it was decided that the club wouldn't go too far wrong if members 1) were supporters of and members of the County Cricket Club; and 2) must not have been known to have argued with the umpire. And so it has proved!

However, as the minutes of this meeting make clear, this was not the first incarnation of the Lincolnshire Gentlemen. A club of that name had played with some distinction in the second half of the 19th century, its first recorded match being against the Gentlemen of Norfolk in 1863 at FL Hopkins' ground at Boston, and its last against Lord Yarborough's XI at Grimsby in 1881. Judging by the names of those who played for and against the Lincs Gents in that era, the standard of cricket must have been reasonably high, and there was at least one noteworthy performance. In the match against a reasonably strong Harrow Wanderers side, captained by ID Walker and including the England Test captain AN Hornby, in 1873, Arthur Appleby and David Buchanan scored 123 out of the 238 runs amassed by the Gents in their two innings, including a match-saving opening partnership of 101, and took all but one of the 18 wickets that fell to bowlers. The fact that both were established first-class cricketers – Appleby bowled fast left-hand round-arm for Lancashire – is a clear indication of the quality of cricket played by the Gents of this era.

Exactly what happened from 1881 onwards, isn't clear. Possibly they faded away, or maybe it is just that the records of their matches have disappeared, and that they carried on until the First World War. But that didn't mean that the meeting at the Saracen's Head constituted a re-birth, not least because there was an extended debate over a name for what was evidently regarded as a new club. It came down to a ballot. 'Gentlemen of Lincolnshire' garnered 2 votes; 'Lincolnshire Poachers', 6 votes; and 'Lincolnshire Gentlemen', 12 votes. Apart from membership of the county club, candidates were further required to be connected with the county by either birth, residence, land ownership or business.

The late '20s was a tough time for the land-owning classes in Lincolnshire, which possibly explains the decision not to supply lunch or tea unless they had been suitably refreshed by the opposition at the away fixture! Club colours would be left to the committee, so long as the background was Lincoln green. The secretary was then asked to write to Ryder and Amies of King's Parade, Cambridge to ask for samples and quotations for caps, blazers, ties and so on.

Lord Yarborough was elected President, despite his protestations that the post should be filled by a more prominent cricketer, while match managers were appointed to raise sides for particular games, exactly as they are today. In the event of a manager finding himself short of players at the eleventh hour it was agreed that he should be able to invite a non-member to play, neatly circumventing the qualification rules of the club. An account was opened with the Midland Bank, who remain the club's bankers to this day – albeit now in the guise of the HSBC. The first accounts show a surplus of £37 from an income of £67. A gap appears in the minutes between 1939 and 1945, and at the first meeting after the war, on 26 October 1945, a list of club members killed in action was read out. Both the Woodhall cricket week and the Southern tour were cancelled in '39 due to the imminence of war.

Fixture lists prior to 1953 do not exist, but in a year strangely reminiscent of 2012, the secretary's report on the '53 season describes how it was spoilt to a considerable extent by the weather. There were 28 fixtures on the card that season, including four two-day away games, a Norfolk tour and a cricket week at Woodhall Spa, as well as an annual dance. The report goes on to say it was becoming increasingly difficult to collect a side in midweek. Nine years later there is still frustration: 'One of the more irritating problems of the Match Manager is finding some 48 hours before a match that he has only 8 players whereas two weeks before he had some 12 to 15 wishing to play. It is felt that people who have accepted, and then are unable to play, within the last three days prior to the start of the match, should find their own replacement.' The more things change, the more they stay the same!

The fixture list continued to include a high proportion of school matches through the '50s and '60s, including Kings, Grantham, Repton, grammar schools in Spalding, King Edward VI in Louth, Carres at Sleaford, De Aston at Market Rasen, Loughborough, as well as Stamford, Oakham and Lincoln Schools. The RAF College team at Cranwell were also played on the Orange in front of the magnificent College building, and the Lincolnshire RAF team were hosted during the cricket week. This was particularly apposite as the 617 Dambusters Squadron officers' wartime mess was just across the road from the Woodhall Spa ground, in the Petwood Hotel.

It was reported at one point that 'a certain person had purchased a Lincolnshire Gentlemen's cap from Wingad Ltd, although he was not a member of the club, because it was the only one that fitted him. The secretary was instructed to take the matter up with Mr Wingad so there should be no repetition of this sort of sale!'

In the late '40s and early '50s a Dutch touring side visited Woodhall to play the LGs. The fixture was duly confirmed for 1950 and entertainment promised during the match. The following year, the treasurer's report caused considerable discussion, relating particularly to the Dutch match and the annual cricket week. After a full explanation had been wheeled out of the then treasurer, it was resolved 'that no Dutch Team be entertained in 1951 except to the extent of lunches and teas.'

Unfortunately the number of fixtures the club plays has declined over the years from the highs of 28 or so matches per season to around a dozen today. That isn't to say that the process could not be reversed but, outside the school holidays, it is not easy to find as many youngsters as the club would like, especially when they are maybe playing twice every weekend for a league club. The greater choice enjoyed by good young cricketers can obviously pose problems for wandering clubs like the LGs, but against that, many cricketers prefer to play a form of the game in which, whilst still playing to win, they don't have to put up with constant calling out and sometimes even sledging in the field. Comment has often been passed on how much more enjoyable a match has been because of this more relaxed atmosphere on the playing field.

Perhaps in keeping with many wanderers clubs, the activities focus on the field of play, and the bar after or indeed during the game. The same dozen or so diehards attend the AGM out of the 220 or so playing and non-playing members of the club. To be elected to office is a privilege from which it is not always easy to extract oneself! The LGs range into Yorkshire, Norfolk, Derbyshire and Nottinghamshire, as well as various Lincolnshire venues for their matches, whilst Woodhall Spa CC provides an unofficial 'home' ground, as and when required.

There are still county cricket office-holders on the LGs' committee, which consists of a good mix of current and past players, although it can sometimes be difficult to decide which is which. As club secretary I battle to get the entire membership into the electronic era; it is a glacial process, but with postage costs spiralling up it is a measure which will have to be taken. We are guided by our current President, Mick Marsh of Grantham CC, and our Chairman, Jeff Kirkham of Collingham CC, who keeps a wary eye on our finances too.

It may be anachronistic now, but the Lincolnshire Gentlemen still hold to the mantra that it is not whether we win or lose, it is how we play the game. Many lasting friendships have been fostered between LGs and the opposition on the cricket field, and may there be many more in the future.

Gentlemen of Lincolnshire at Holkham
back four: Martin Philips, John Lawrence, Tom Robinson, Peter Robinson
front: Sam Coates, Ian Walter, John Robinson, Jim Robinson, Will Bale (Holkham)

Jesters

Founded: 1928

by Anthony Gibson

Rule 2 of the Jesters Cricket Club explains that 'the purpose of the Club shall be to play cricket in a spirit not unworthy of the name of the Club' and, as the club enters its 86th year, that remains its guiding principle. Jesters cricket is played to win, but with a big smile on its face.

The Jesters were founded in 1928 by Jock Burnet and a group of his friends at St Paul's School in London who thought it would be fun to start a cricket club for holiday matches, where the main thing would be to enjoy cricket in the company of friends. The club's original name was 'The Jokers' but, in replying to the invitation to become President of the club, Pelham Warner pointed out that a club of cricketing golfers already existed with that name. So 'The Jesters' it became; and 'Plum' Warner remained President until his death in 1963. Jock was an inveterate organiser and about the same date founded the Jesters Squash Rackets and Fives Club which, as The Jesters Club, continues to this day as a prominent organisation in the world of those who enjoy playing games in courts with walls.

The first ever Jesters cricket match took place on 28 April 1928 against Beaconsfield. The result, a defeat by two wickets, with the winning boundary coming from a dropped catch in the deep in the last over, should raise a wry smile from anyone familiar with Jesters cricket. "How typical," they will say.

Throughout the 1930s the club maintained strong links with St Paul's. Many players were current or recent pupils, masters there, or friends at other schools. Indeed, the most successful bowler in those early years was a St Paul's master, Pat Cotter, who in only four seasons took nearly 200 wickets with flighted leg-breaks (and, in a varied life, went on to represent England at croquet and bridge and compile crosswords for the *Financial Times*).

The most distinguished Jester from those early days was Jackie Grant. He was a regular during the first season, 1928, before going up to Cambridge and subsequently captaining the West Indies against both England and Australia.

Before the days of foreign holidays, the bulk of matches took place in August. By 1933 the fixture list had grown to 55 games with no fewer than 37 between late July and early September. These games were played against much the same mix of Home Counties club and village sides that the Jesters play today. There was also a New Forest tour, an array of military opposition – the Royal Tank Corps, 2nd Battalion Scots Guards, RAF Duxford – and a regular September fixture at Lord's against Cross Arrows. The club even faced the might of the Eton College Servants XI.

The early records of the Jesters tell of journeys by steam train from Fenchurch Street to play the Royal Artillery at Shoeburyness; of inadequate maps landing expensive cars in ploughed fields after dark; and of motoring to the New Forest in Kenneth Gandar Dower's chauffeur-driven Lagonda. It all seems impossibly romantic to the modern observer more used to battling round the M25 en route to Jesters cricket.

Outside the Jockey House, near Wimborne, on the New Forest tour of 1937
The old house, now demolished, had medieval chains, a secret passage and a fabled ghost.
The Jesters slept in the orchard in chalets which, one member wrote, "could be revolved very rapidly,
involving permanent damage to their bearings and temporary giddiness to their occupants."

Gandar Dower was one of the more remarkable Jesters. An all-round sportsman of great distinction and unorthodoxy, he competed at Wimbledon, made one of the first flights from England to India, explored Africa, wrote successfully, and attempted to introduce cheetah racing into England, once causing uproar at the Queen's Club when he brought a male cheetah into the bar on a leash.

After the Second World War, links with St Paul's fell away as the club evolved into a typical London wandering side. The last relic of the old days was the annual match on the St Paul's School ground with the Jesters Club which finally came to an end in the early 1970s. Throughout the post-war period the Jesters remained – as it does today – a small, unpretentious club that tries not to take itself too seriously. That there should be no speeches at the annual dinner is a firm club tradition; nor are averages produced at the end of each season.

By the 1950s Jock Burnet had become bursar of Magdalene College, Cambridge, from where he directed a steady stream of cricketers towards the Jesters. Cambridge remains a fertile recruiting ground to this day – as does Oxford – and the club mirrors London professional life, with lawyers, accountants, property people, academics, media and literary types all among the current playing membership.

Like most wandering clubs, the Jesters owe a huge debt to the few individuals who have given up their time to run the club, steering that fine line between unobtrusive administration and total chaos. At this point Robin Atkins – retiring in 2013 after 16 years as President and 50 years' membership of the club – should perhaps take a bow.

Not that it hasn't sometimes been a close call. One annual general meeting is notorious for having taken place 'on a sofa, in the Quadrant Restaurant, Regent Street', only two Jesters being present; while on more than one occasion the club minute book notes there were insufficient members of the committee to form a quorum, those present 'invoking the spirits of their blood-relations' to overcome the problem.

The shape of the modern Jesters Cricket Club perhaps owes most to Ranald Phillips' 15-year tenure as Hon Secretary in the 1980s and '90s, which brought great stability at a time when league cricket had disrupted the traditional fixture lists of many wandering sides and made increasing demands on their players. Fixtures had to be pruned, younger members recruited and new directions sought as league clubs paid much less attention to their Sunday cricket.

Today, the club still plays most of its cricket within a 50-mile radius of London. But there are many fewer games against conventional club sides than 30 years ago, and many more where other wandering sides, old boys teams and 'occasional' XIs are the opponents. The Cambridge weekend, playing college sides, remains as a hangover from more leisurely days when weekend tours to Oxford, Norfolk, Bristol and Bassingbourn also featured on the fixture card. Vindicating these efforts, the club has undergone a real renaissance since the 1990s, recruiting many younger members disillusioned by leagues and seeking good-quality cricket played in the right spirit. The sides turned out today are probably as strong, and possibly younger, than at any time in the club's history.

Best of all, the spirit of the club is unchanged. Members eagerly await the club's annual prize for the 'most Jester-like performance' of the season – usually awarded for a moment of spectacular embarrassment, lunacy or glorious failure – suggesting Rule 2 is as alive today as it ever was in the balmy, carefree days of the 1930s.

In 1975, Michael Meyer wrote the history of the Jesters Cricket Club. Its concluding paragraphs are as true today as they were then:

> It is in the character of Jesters cricket that we should lose rather more games than we win. At full strength we are still, as we were forty years ago, a match for any club side in the country.
>
> But three sacred traditions of the club have always been, firstly, that humble minnows such as the writer of these words should be as welcome (well – nearly as welcome) as the titans in whose shadows he weakly trembles; secondly, to give all members a chance of a game as often as possible, which inevitably means that in our gentler fixtures we sometimes field sides rich in character but somewhat less rich in talent; and thirdly that, although we like to win, we would rather go for a win and lose than settle for a draw at tea-time.
>
> It is for this reason that the phrase so often recurs in letters which members have written to the editor of this history: "Jesters cricket has been the cricket I have most enjoyed." This is the end to which Jock Burnet and his companions founded the Jesters Cricket Club half a century ago, and that will always remain the chief purpose of Jesters cricket.

Website: *www.jesterscc.com*

Romany

Founded: 1929

by Anthony Gibson

This Romany Cricket Club – and it is not to be confused with the Yorkshire one – is perhaps best known, certainly in the modern era, for its tours. Founded in 1929 by one of EW Swanton's predecessors as *Daily Telegraph* cricket correspondent, Colonel Philip Trevor, the club made its first major expedition to foreign parts (although there had been a weekend in Paris in the '30s) when it became the first club (apart from the MCC) to visit South Africa in 1960/61. Since then, there has been no stopping it.

That first South African tour came about almost by chance. A South African called Brian Mirchell had played for Romany regularly in 1957 but had decided to go back to Johannesburg at the end of the season and so had missed what proved to be a hugely successful club tour of Devon in 1958. "What a shame that old Brian wasn't around to enjoy the trip," lamented one Romany, during the match against the Met Police at Imber Court at the end of the 1958 season. "Yes," chimed in another, "I don't suppose we'll ever play with or against him again."

"Not unless we tour South Africa," chipped in a third.

"Well, why not?" said one and all.

With Brian Mirchell's considerable assistance, the tour was duly arranged and proved to be a great success. Although they won only two of their 14 matches, several of the six defeats were by narrow margins, whilst rain denied them at least one other win. In the match with Natal Estates , their host, Colonel Campbell, laid on half-naked Zulu maidens to dance before the start of play. In the event, the lorry bringing the dancers broke down, so they had to do their thing between innings instead. The account which appeared subsequently in *The Cricketer* relates that "after that, we lost three quick wickets and the match by 30 runs!"

Seven further tours of South Africa have followed, the most recent being in 2004, when they won six out of the seven games played. The results haven't always been so much in Romany's favour on these expeditions, but they have played against top-class opposition – including provincial and even Test players – and have always given a spirited account of themselves under captains like Stuart 'Tiger' Surridge, who led the 1983/84 tour.

Romany tours have never been anything less than globe-trotting. In 1979, they enjoyed an outstandingly successful tour of Sri Lanka, organised for them by Chandra Pereira. The highlight was a match against the powerful Singalese CC when a last-wicket partnership of over 100 between the team's 'little and large' – 5'6" Hugh Suter and 6'5" Tim Verity – saw them to a thrilling victory. That was followed by visits to India, Thailand and Hong Kong in 1981/82 and Australia in 1985/86. In more recent years they have taken wandering cricket to outposts as far-flung as Kenya (1997/98), Brazil and Argentina (2000), India again (in 2001) and, most recently, a highly successful expedition to Sri Lanka in 2006. With that sort of record, it is hardly surprising that it should have been two Romany leading lights, 'Tiger' Surridge and Tony Matharu, who organised the International Festival of Wandering Cricket in Portugal in 2005 and in which Romany were enthusiastic participants for the four years that it lasted.

If this all, on the face of it, seems a long way from the travelling band of public schoolboys and military types that Colonel Trevor put together to play matches against clubs and schools in the Home Counties, it is worth remembering that the good colonel was a cricketing tourist himself, having managed AO Jones' MCC tour to Australia in 1907/08, no less. I'm sure he would have approved of how his club – which is very much what it was in the early days – has broadened its horizons.

The founder members of the Romany were a formidable bunch of cricketers. Names such as Gubby Allen, RC Robertson-Glasgow, Sir Pelham Warner, The Hon FSG Calthorpe, FR Brown and, of course, EW Swanton fairly leap off the page of the Romany history. Not that most of them played all that often, although Swanton would have captained the club in its very first match, against Hornsey in 1930, had torrential rain permitted any play.

Country-house matches became a feature of the Romany fixture list as the '30s wore on. From 1932 onwards, Jim Swanton organised a two-day match against Sir Julien Cahn's XI at Stamford Hall, and there were games as well at Cliveden, where the opposition was the Hon ML Astor's XI. These were high-class encounters, with Test and county players on both sides. No wonder that, during those years, Romany were able to recruit cricketers are accomplished as Ian Peebles, Arthur Gilligan, Bev Lyon and Hugh Bartlett; and as distinguished as HH The Jam Saheb of Nawangar – better known as Ranji – and John Brocklebank, later Chairman of Cunard.

However, the two men who did most to revive, sustain and eventually develop the club in the post-war era were Terry Sutton Mattocks, Secretary 1954-70, and Dick Hawkey, Match Secretary 1957-64. Both were decent cricketers, although Hawkey's greatest proficiency was as a squash player, at which he represented England. Between them, they expanded the Romany's fixture list from around 25 games a season to over 60 in the 1960s, recruited enough good players to sustain the increased commitment, and were responsible both for the first West Country tour in 1958 and, as we have seen, the first South African tour in 1960. In the diary that he kept for many years, Hawkey was quick to acknowledge the debt which Romany owed to their West Country hosts, such as Seaton, who lent them their ground to play another touring club, the Boffins, and the Wiltshire Queries, who originally hosted a two-day game at the start of the tour, which later became two one-day games, the Queries on one day, Chippenham on the other.

The fortunes of the club have ebbed and flowed in more recent years. There were complaints in the '70s and '80s that the membership was getting too old – "too many players and too many match managers qualifying for membership of the Forty Club" was how it was expressed – and Romany have not been immune from the pressures of social change and cricketing change, to which all wandering clubs have been subject. The fixture list has gradually contracted, so that they now play no more than around ten games a season – a mixture of overs and declaration cricket – against clubs such as Tunbridge Wells, Epsom, Radley School and the Gloucestershire Gipsies.

Like many wandering clubs, Romany relies on a dedicated group of active members to keep the flame alive: men like Fulton Paterson, who has played for the club since 1963, and who once scored nearly a thousand runs for them in a season; Tony Matharu and Jon King, who host all of their meetings at the Grange Rochester Hotel backing onto the Vincent Square cricket pitch in Westminster; and long-time supporters like Andrew Page, Tom McKewan and the current president, Will Smith. The club also owes a great debt of gratitude to Margot and Geoff Harrison, respectively scorer and umpire for all its overseas tours. In 2012, Romany toured again overseas to Malta, and it is hoped that this will become a regular event and will lead to a resurgence of interest for some younger potential members.

Romany's motto is 'Ambulando', from the Latin 'Ambulando solvitur' – you can solve it by walking. I'm not sure it is a sentiment to which all batsmen would subscribe, but walking the highways and byways of the world of cricket for the last 80 years, no doubt solving a few problems along the way, has certainly done Romany no harm, and must have brought a great deal of pleasure to both them and the teams they've played against, not just in England but all over the world.

Website: *www.romanycricketclub.co.uk*

Romany at Four Elms in Kent, 2012
George Bunn, Torquil Deacon, Martin Corbett, Jonathan King, Nick Clark,
Paul Lack, Clive Grierson, Clive Offer, Dicky Clark, Nigel Angus, Bill Johnson

Sou'westers

Founded: 1930

by A Sou'wester

In April 1930 a group of Cambridge undergraduates met to form a cricket club. It played only once that year, but the seed had been sown. The following year it enjoyed briefly a split personality: the Hoboes played in and around Cambridge, and the Cambridge Sou'westers undertook a Devon tour to 'prolong the West Country season'. We have been doing the latter ever since, and the two personalities soon merged simply as the Sou'westers.

Activity in Cambridge had ended by the 1980s. Cambridge term dates, the timing of school holidays and the East Anglian spring climate all combined to kill off the annual Cambridge Easter tour. It has been replaced by an occasional series of overseas tours of increasing ambition. Early visits to Portugal and Spain have been followed by two tours to Cape Town and its glorious surroundings and to Bermuda, where our perspectives on big hitting were much altered.

The two-week West Country tour in late summer has continued, interrupted only by the Second World War. Timings have shifted and fixtures have come and gone, but four Devon clubs, Bridgetown, North Devon, Seaton and Sidmouth, have featured almost every year. It was our privilege for many years to play the Somerset Stragglers at the County Ground in Taunton and for a couple of years the Gloucestershire Gipsies entertained

Bermuda 2009

Groot Drakenstein, South Africa, 2012

us at the Bristol County Ground. Now we limit ourselves to two county wandering sides, the Devon Dumplings and the Berkshire Gents. We have over the years enjoyed many grounds of outstanding character and beauty, and, breathe it not too loud, some spectacular catering. The spreads at Bridgetown and Seaton and the legendary Dorset Rangers lunches of Dawn Pinney linger long in the memory, as do the hot lunches provided by the very much lamented Miss Dennis at Instow.

The playing strength has evolved from the Cambridge undergraduates of the early years and their friends. Schoolmasters, initially mostly bachelors with long summer holidays to fill, featured heavily, and mainly through them themes have developed. In Cambridge in the spring the Leys School provided lots of able players. Appleblossoms, who derive their soubriquet from an unfortunate correlation between the charms of scrumpy and a set of false teeth, came originally through Forest School and South Woodford Cricket Club. There was a stream of Millhillians and Eastbournians. For some time Reading University sent us her sons. There is a strong connection with the Cryptics. Now the membership has a much more local West Country flavour, to blend with yet another new strand from the Falkland club at Newbury.

Family traditions flourish too. In 2010 three generations of the Peet family took the field against Bridgetown, and over the years three generations of Olivers, Spragues and Haynes have appeared. Indeed, in 2013 we expect Martin Oliver to celebrate the golden jubilee of his first appearance for the club, fortuitously hauled off a North Devon beach by his cricket master to make up Sou'wester numbers. There have been numerous father-and-son combinations; in 2012 at Chulmleigh four fathers and five sons took the field together in the presence of one grandfather and two grandmothers, with another two grandfathers probably looking down proudly from on high.

The club has long worked on the principle that we are willing to travel considerable distances to play, but that we try to offer cheap and cheerful accommodation for tourists. In easier times, before and just after the war, large private houses and small hotels served. For some time Feniton, the extensive house of founder member and club secretary Bruce Hart, was our base. Since the 1960s we have been able to use the dormitory facilities of countless West Country boarding schools, though the George at South Molton came into use for many years for the North Devon games (and still has a strong sentimental attachment for some senior members). The longest serving of these and perhaps most fondly remembered is Hazlegrove House, in Sparkford, where for many years we were hosted by its then headmaster and our current President, Paddy Heazell. Mirrors and showers set at the right height for prep school boys posed problems for some, but the school cricket pitch, which we used more than once, the swimming pool, croquet and floodlit hockey played with unusual hazards and the large kitchen which produced such magnificent breakfasts more than compensated. Now the need for schools to generate income during their holidays is making it increasingly hard for our long-suffering management to alight upon a willing host. We have long been indebted to Stewart Peet for the annual miracle of our West Country fixture list and for his immaculately organised overseas tours, and to Martin and Marion Oliver for their team management and bursarial skills in the West.

Our playing membership has included some distinguished headmasters, an England rugby cap in Peter Henderson, one of the great characters of the club and the master of the circular conversation, some hockey Olympic medallists and Blues galore. Bruce Hart ran the club and dominated bowling figures in the early years, to be followed by 'Granny' Alston (known as such from his teens) who started in the 1930s as a prolific batsman and finished in the 1970s as a wily and inelegant but very successful phantom spinner. In between he entertained us with a series of stories which seemed to have neither beginning nor end, but still left his audience in stitches. More recently Christopher Dean has dominated the bowling scene with his medium-pace swing as our most prolific wicket-taker. He now often surprises unwary batsmen as an umpire with his deliberate decisions and his bowler's-eye view. Among batsmen Geoff Courtenay, also a talented keeper and a Dorset stalwart, scored heavily in the 1940s and 1950s. Since then the ruthless efficiency of Mike Barford, now our Chairman, the precise elegance of Mark Williams and the pragmatic style of Simon Halliday have been our mainstays. Among keepers, the silky hands of Tony Leek stand out.

Three of our members have the distinction of a single first-class wicket to their name: 'Granny' Alston, who claimed the scalp of Jack Hobbs for Somerset, and for Cambridge Robert Wiggs (his victim was an extremely unhappy Raymond Illingworth) and John Haynes.

A feature of the club is that it has always welcomed what PG Wodehouse would have described as 'good eggs' who happen to be very modest cricketers. Their qualities shone through in the dressing room and bar, and sometimes on the field. In December 2012 the 'good eggs' took on the Eggheads, setting a first for wandering cricket clubs by appearing on the BBC2 quiz. Unfortunately there was only one question on cricket, and their ignorance was exposed on American horror fiction, German playwrights and the pop songs of Engelbert Humperdinck.

The club keeps careful statistical records which are published every five years and produces a comprehensive year book. Rather sketchy early reports on tours and opaque profiles of players have now developed into full, often quite amusing match reports, statistics, funny (often unintentionally so) remarks made on tour with an elaborate explanation and from time to time a sermon from the president on the state of the game.

We like to think we have a unique club, which exists only to tour, and generates an atmosphere all its own. We are really quite proud of our club.

Website: *www.souwesters.co.uk*

Buccaneers

Founded: 1930

by Richard Gwynn

The Buccaneers was founded in 1930 by a young Geoffrey Moore to provide a more enjoyable brand of cricket than was offered at BP's Lensbury club in Teddington. Geoffrey insisted that fine fellowship and fun in the bar was at least as important as strong and stylish play on the field. It is an unspoken rule that Buccaneers never leave a ground before their hosts and this spirit is enshrined in the club's motto:

> *Let us take our Stand, and play the Game,*
> *But rather for the Cause than for the Fame.*

Geoffrey drove his brainchild with messianic zeal for over 70 years, developing an enviable fixture list of south-east England's leading clubs, schools and universities, from which he shamelessly recruited the most promising players. Few could resist Geoffrey's persuasive summons, even early on Christmas morning, when he infamously rang one young blade to remind him of next August's Sussex tour.

By the outbreak of war in 1939, in ironic defiance of their motto, the Buccaneers were able to attract famous names to play in exhibition matches at Lord's in aid of the Red Cross Fund. In 1940 Freddie Brown and Laurie Fishlock turned out for the Buccaneers at Lord's against a British Empire XI containing Private Jack Davies and Hugh Bartlett. A year later at Lord's, Gubby Allen took 2/25 against a London Counties side featuring Denis and Leslie Compton.

In June 1945, at the Saffrons in Eastbourne, the rapidly promoted Colonel Jack Davies captained the Buccaneers against an Australian Imperial Forces side containing future Test skipper Lindsay Hassett. After the Aussies had just edged a close game by one wicket, both sides celebrated the end of hostilities until 4am. In 1950 one Wally Hammond creamed a dazzling 128 not out for Esher against the Buccs.

A fairly decent England side could be selected from the famous names who have turned out for the club over the years, including David Gower, Colin Cowdrey, John Snow, Alec Bedser, Gubby Allen, Raman Subba Row, Percy Fender, Freddie Brown and Ashley Giles. But a candidate had to be more than just a good player before Geoffrey would elect him a member. Shortly after leaving King's Canterbury in 1975, David Gower stroked an elegant 165 not out for the Buccaneers against his old school. However, he didn't pass muster with Geoffrey who blocked his membership on the grounds that his hair was too long and he had holes in his jeans.

Jack Davies, of whom *Wisden* wrote 'In 1945 he was as good an all-rounder as any other English player', made 5,904 runs, including 11 centuries, and took 287 wickets with his off-spin in 190 matches for the Buccaneers. But even Jack's record is eclipsed by the achievements of a very different Cambridge Blue who also proved a thorn in the side of the Aussies. Gwyn Hughes made 94 for Glamorgan against the 1964 Australians but then chose to lend his intense professionalism to St Paul's School and the Buccaneers.

In 17 seasons from 1967 to 1983, he bowled 4,387 overs of immaculate left-arm spin, snaring no fewer than 838 scalps at 11.71 apiece. Treating every Sunday friendly with the gravity of a Test match, the tall, blond Welshman also crafted 7,604 runs at 47.23 with the rectitude of a Baptist minister.

A recent legend was more cavalier than roundhead, though. New Zealander Doug Murphy made a nonsense of many a declaration as a crash-bang opening bat who was known to drive his first ball for six. After several near-misses, Doug cracked the club's highest score: a dashing 200 out of 273 against Adastrians (RAF officers) at Uxbridge in 1999. Amid all the back-slapping in the changing room, Doug was asked if this double century was his career-best. Ever reserved and thoughtful, Doug replied; "No, I once made 310." "Was that in a three-day game, Doug?" an astonished team-mate inquired. "No, it was in a 40-over game. I went in in the 10th over," murmured the Kiwi almost apologetically.

Hurlingham, that Elysian country club in Fulham, was the idyllic scene of another memorable record in 2006 when the Buccaneers' current run-machine/wicket-keeper/disc jockey Jim Harcourt joined Cambridge Blue Mel Ragnauth at an unpromising 8/2 in pursuit of an improbable 308. They were never parted and with a roaring blaze of strokeplay cruised to a famous eight-wicket victory with 15 overs to spare in the club's highest-ever stand of exactly 300.

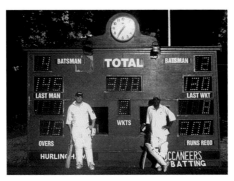

Jim Harcourt and Mel Ragnauth after their
record 300 partnership at Hurlingham, 2006

Hurstpierpoint has also hosted several legendary matches. In 1973 yeoman seamer Stuart Rankin achieved that rarest of cricketing feats by taking all ten Old Hurst Johnians' wickets for 31, following a dropped catch off the unforgiving Gwyn Hughes. There was an equally epic encounter on the same Sussex school ground in August 1984. Playing from memory after two brain-threatening days at the Oval Test, Paul Thompson and Richard Gwynn rescued the Buccs from a torpid collapse in a madcap stand which doubled the score to a competitive 240 for six declared.

Gwynn then took a hat-trick with the first three balls of the Old Hurst Johnian innings, Keith Jenkin, himself a Buccaneer, was yorked first ball, number three was improbably caught by Thompson at gully and number four played on. By tea, the OHJs had 'recovered' to 36 for six with Gwynn taking all six and opener John Goodacre, who had watched the carnage from the other end, 20 not out. Assuming the game was virtually in the bag, the Buccaneers took their foot off the gas as Goodacre flogged a wilting attack to all parts in the innings of his life, finishing 170 not out to snatch an unforgettable victory by one wicket.

During their first 50 years, the Buccaneers had wandered throughout southern England, as they still do, from Framlingham to Taunton, Oundle and Cambridge to Canterbury, Winchester and Godalming. But in 1980 they embarked on their first overseas tour, to Thailand, Malaysia and Singapore. Delayed 24 hours at Heathrow on New Year's Day, the sleepless tourists were stunned by the wall of heat and humidity as they stumbled off the long flight in Bangkok.

In no fit state for the first fixture, which was due to start within two hours of touchdown, the unlucky XI was selected from those drawing the shortest straws. Miraculously the club's honour was upheld by a heroic Rorke's Drift of an opening stand by current President Simon Woolfries and the prolific Peter Kaufmann who defied unbearable heat and fatigue to put on over 100 and launch the tour in style at Royal Bangkok Sports Club.

Culturally, Singapore was fascinating, but the cricket was washed out and the party moved on to Kuala Lumpur eager for action. Struggling to contain the strong Selangor batting, Richard 'The Hack' Gwynn was barracked by a raucous "Load of rubbish, Gwynn," bellowed from the far pavilion. Traipsing off for tea, Gwynn was greeted by a jovial stout Malaysian whom he remembered in the nick of time as Pete Jaafar, a fellow student at Nottingham University twelve years earlier.

"Hello, Pete," ventured Richard. "What are you doing here these days?"

"I'm chairman of a few companies now."

"Oh yeah, what sort of companies, Pete?" asked the sceptical reporter.

"Shell, Dunlop, ICI and RTZ are some of them," answered the former law student.

"That's amazing, Pete. How on earth have you managed that?"

"Well, my dad's the King. What are you doing after the game?"

"We're all going out for a meal to celebrate Simon's birthday."

"Afterwards, why don't you all come round to the nightclub under the Hilton?"

After dinner, the whole touring party arrived at the Hilton to be red-carpeted like royalty by the Prince. After an hour or so of Bolly and Beluga and a line of local lovelies, a clap of the princely hands seemed to open double doors from which emerged four coolies bearing a cake the size of a pool table inscribed with icing wishing 'Happy Birthday to Simon'. Pete had apparently had the national bakery opened specially.

Acquiring a taste for touring, Geoffrey proceeded to organise no fewer than six enjoyable tours to South Africa between 1982 and 1996 plus a less successful foray to Australia, Hong Kong and Singapore in 1986/87. In the 21st century the Buccaneers have stayed closer to home to devote more time to the wine bars of the City, the golf clubs of Europe and, especially, to the cricket grounds of the south-east.

Website: *www.buccaneerscricketclub.co.uk*

Stage

Founded: 1931

by Brian Jackson

Phone most club match managers or skippers on the day of a match or even the evening before a fixture, to say you've got a last minute voice-over job or an audition and 'can't make it' and you might never play for that club again. This probably would be the case should you be a member of the average cricket club with its own ground and particularly so if your withdrawal from the relevant match happened be a vital league game. Not so with Stage Cricket Club.

Can you imagine a vital fixture where the outcome could make your club top dog of the league and your side is batting second and one of your best bowlers, who can't bat for toffee, asks to 'go in early' because he has a show to do that evening? This happens with us and there you have it, the essence of why Stage Cricket Club exists.

Stage CC print two Shakespeare quotes on its fixture card. One, inherited through at least fifty years, is from Act One of *Coriolanus*: "What works, my countrymen, in hand? Where go you with bats and club?" The second quote, from Act One of *Love's Labour's Lost*, was decided on because of the ever-increasing tendency, surprisingly so for friendly matches, for some batsmen not to 'walk' even after a snick is heard in the pavilion: " ... and, as I am a gentleman, betook myself to walk."

The chairman's pre-season homily to members always repeats two reminders: the first that we are, in the main, guests and must always behave as such, even though the opposition's umpire may be obviously as blind as a bat; the second, if a ball has been tickled, 'Stage walk' despite the umpire being as deaf as a post and as blind as a bat in adjudicating a 'not out.'

Stage CC was born the same year as me, in 1931, and, like the troubadours of old, its players were destined ever to wander the village greens of England. Our club was created out of necessity by a collection of actors who had a simple love of the game and, with actor-like modesty about their skills, displayed some ability with bat or ball, sometimes both; they simply got together and sought out like-minded opposition, particularly host clubs, which provided 'a good tea'. Another necessary governing factor for founding member cricketing actors was, and still is, that in the world of theatre, Saturdays are usually occupied with two performances, a matinée and evening show, so our fixtures have to be played on Sundays and midweek.

In the early days, Stage CC's weekday fixtures were rarely played on Wednesdays, again because Wednesday was the favoured day for West End theatre matinée performances. The midweek fixture was usually a day match starting at 11 with the important proviso of a decent lunch as well as requisite good tea, was available at tolerable cost, and that stumps would be drawn in good time to travel from wherever the green sward happened to be, to theatre-land for an evening show.

Stage CC, 1931 or 1932

Second left, standing, is Atholl Fleming, who later founded Stage and Radio Cricket Club in Sydney. He is said to have been 'a useful bat, a good slip fielder and a Machiavellian captain'. Third from the left is Nigel Porter, fifth is Rex Harrison, sixth is Aubrey Dexter. Seventh, next to the umpire, is Boris Karloff.
Seated are (first) Evan Thomas, (second) Abraham Sofaer, (third) Garry Marsh, (sixth) Errol Flynn and (seventh) W Earle Grey, the prime motivator in the forming of Stage CC.
The club would love to hear from anybody who can identify any of the others.

Even today, the physical theatre stage is referred to as The Green, a reference back to when wandering players performed Miracle Plays on village greens. In most theatres there is a communal back stage area specifically designated for actors in which to relax and take refreshments, which is always known as The Green Room.

We have had opportunities to acquire our own ground, but this has never been seriously entertained by different committees, the reasons being manifold: you may persuade an actor to open and even run the bar but to get him to prepare a wicket which hasn't been mown or to paint a popping crease, or discover the assigned actor has taken the pavilion keys with him to South Africa at short notice to film a television commercial, were factors in declining such heavy responsibility.

When people first hear the words 'Stage Cricket Club' they visualise its players being stars of stage, screen, theatre and television. We see this expectancy whenever we are invited to play a new fixture and, on arrival at the ground, find a good turn-out of the opposition's families and supporters who are expecting to set eyes on at least someone from *Corrie* or *Strictly*, but mostly they are disappointed and the star struck are not seen again the following season, providing, always, the venue is renewed.

We have always maintained a club rule that Stage CC cricket should be played as cheaply as possible; the rule is important because the very nature of the acting profession creates a high percentage ratio of actors who may be 'resting', something which is perhaps particularly true of our members, the majority of whom are jobbing actors and not highly paid 'stars'.

Over the years, many notable actors have appeared in Stage CC sides, many of them so-called stars; one of our players won *Celebrity Mastermind* recently and his specialist subject was, naturally, cricket. But in the main we are cricketers for the working day and our prowess is good enough to renew fixtures year after year with top clubs in the Home Counties and Greater London area, culminating with a match at Lord's, a fixture which I know has been held since the late 1940s when Stage CC thrashed Cross Arrows. (The following year the Arrows took revenge by playing a 'ringer' by the name of FJ Titmus. I have the scorebooks.)

In recent times members of Stage CC have literally 'sung for their supper'. It happened in the season 2000 when an event known as Oxford 2000 – the International Millennium Cricket Festival for Wandering Clubs – took place on the many splendid grounds gracing the City of Oxford. It was like this: we received an invitation to take part in this cricketing jamboree but then discovered that the fees to participate in this princely shindig were high, too high for us poor players to strut our stuff midst Oxford's spires; what to do? We offer to put on a show? Yes! The deal was done; we paid only a modest fee in return for an in-house Stage CC Revue – it was *A Load of Old Bails* and very successful it was too. The performance was a resounding success, which provoked invitations to present the show for other clubs together with invites for fixtures, one of them a semi-sponsored swatch of matches at the home ground of Gentlemen of Philadelphia, USA.

Stage CC has two tours each season; currently we have a four-day tour in Kent starting off with a popular fixture against Provender and a happy Gallic long weekend knock-about in Entrecasteaux in France. Both tours seem set to continue.

"Time!"

Website: *stagecc.co.uk*

Cartoon by Bill Tidy

South Oxfordshire Amateurs

Founded: 1933

by Anthony Gibson

One puts pen to paper on the subject of the South Oxfordshire Amateurs with a certain amount of diffidence, given that this is a club with a strong literary tradition and that David Money and Tony Lurcock's *75 years of the SOA* is amongst the most amusing and best written of all the wandering club histories that I have had the pleasure to read. If I quote liberally from it, you will understand why.

The literary legacy, in common really with the entire ethos of the SOA, is owed to its founder, Malcolm Elwin, who wrote biographies, articles for JC Squire's *London Mercury* and letters: hundreds and hundreds of invariably humorous, fluent and above all lengthy letters – "Three or four immaculately typed quarto pages would be a typical reply to an enquiry about a player for next Tuesday," David Money recalls. When he died in 1974, a tribute in the *Journal of the Cricket Society* remembered him as being 'in the great tradition of literary cricketers'.

He was a big man, with a Van Dyke beard, a dominating personality and an irresistible flow of conversation, who, in the '30s, was invariably accompanied by his enormous bull mastiff, Jon, sometimes with spectacular results. "He excelled himself at Wallingford, where, having inserted the opposition, Malcolm took the field, followed by the SOA, followed by Jon, followed by the railings of the old pavilion. The fixture had been obtained with some difficulty, and shortly after disappeared from the pre-war list!"

Elwin was a decent cricketer, who bowled accurate inswingers, well enough to have represented both Oxfordshire and Devon in Minor Counties cricket. But his first love was club cricket, played in the right spirit. It was Stephen Fry, son of CB, who suggested to Elwin that he should put together his own sides, to play mid-week matches against local Oxfordshire opposition in the summer of 1933. The experiment worked so well that, that winter, they decided to put it on a formal basis as the South Oxfordshire Amateurs – 'the term amateurs being preferred to 'gentlemen' as implying a love of the game for its own sake, and therefore being more descriptive of the way in which the club intends to play its cricket.'

Elwin and his self-appointed executive committee ran the club as an unashamed autocracy. They alone had the power to appoint new members, and they did so on the basis of much more than just cricketing ability, as Elwin's Code of Membership explains: 'A batsman equal to Bradman or a bowler to Larwood is no good to us if he is not congenial with the spirit of the Club. We want good cricketers, but they must also be 'good fellows'.'

By a mixture of force of character and organisational ability, Elwin soon had his new club flourishing. Membership grew rapidly, partly by recruiting from opposition teams, and partly because Oxfordshire had no county wandering club, like the Hampshire Hogs or the Devon Dumplings, so the SOA was able to attract good players, not least from the University, who were glad of the chance to play the midweek matches which have always been the SOA's stock in trade. By 1939, the fixture list had topped 50. They played schools, old boys' sides, the bigger local clubs and, of course, the Oxford colleges, where the standard was vastly higher than it is now. The first of what would become the highlight of the club's year – the Western Tour, via Wiltshire to Devon – was made in 1938. By the time war came, the SOA was very firmly on the cricketing map.

Recovery after the war was swift. 1947 was a golden summer for the SOA as well as for Compton, Edrich and the game as a whole. The Western Tour now took in the Wiltshire Queries, the Somerset Stragglers, the Devon Dumplings, Sidmouth, Budleigh Salterton and North Devon at the famous Instow ground. This last fixture, and the one at nearby Westleigh, seems to have had a special resonance, perhaps because Malcolm Elwin had moved to North Devon during the war and lived for the rest of his life at Westward Ho! That didn't stop him turning out for the SOA whenever he could, but it did mean the advent of match managers, and that Freddie Nunn had to shoulder much of the burden of assembling teams, recruiting new players and keeping the club's finances on an even keel.

Petrol rationing was a big problem for wandering clubs in the '40s, which David Money remembers that the SOA overcame with typical ingenuity: "Stuart Edmonds got two vital cars for the match against the Queries at Bledlow by recruiting Dick Crawshay, who could legitimately deliver goose eggs, and Norris Bazzard, who drove over professionally to draw up Stuart's Will!"

Social change and cricketing change have inevitably meant changes to the SOA's membership and fixture list. The gentlemen of leisure, farmers, schoolmasters (in the holidays) and dons who used to make up the bulk of the membership are no longer so readily available, whilst, as Tony Lurcock remarks, in his section of the history, 'Midweek cricket, which used to be as rare and thrilling as pre-marital sex, is, like that, now available to all.'

Malcom Elwin and Stuart Pether, Instow, 1952

The games against the Oxford colleges have mostly fallen by the wayside, since the advent of mixed colleges diluted the available cricketing talent; the demise of club cricketing 'weeks' and the predominance of league cricket has also taken its toll. Against that, the number of matches against other county wanderers has grown from seven in 1983 to nine today, the highlight being the encounter with the Gloucestershire Gipsies, whose hospitality at Bourton-on-the-Water in the early 1980s, laid on by Mrs Hiram, was such that proceedings were described as "an all-day lunch with cricketing interludes"!

But there is continuity as well. In 2008, Tony Lurcock reported that nearly 30 players were sons of members and, in the case of the Florey family, grandsons. The Western Tour continues to be vastly enjoyed, and the club has spread its wings even further afield, with highly successful tours to South Africa in 1997 and 2009, and Australia in 2004, as well as entertaining touring sides from overseas, on grounds all over Oxfordshire. Most important of all, the club's ethos of playing cricket in the right spirit remains intact.

For the 2012 season the club had 50 matches on the card, nine of them on the West Country Tour. Sixteen of them were all-day fixtures, and two were Twenty/20 evening games, which raises the vexed question of 'overs' cricket. The SOA's guiding principle on this issue is clear enough: they much prefer proper declaration cricket. But they are also pragmatic enough to move with the times. As Tony Lurcock laments, "Year by year it becomes more difficult to observe the club's stated aim not to play limited-over cricket, and to convince opposition teams that a close draw is a better result for everyone than winning or losing by a margin of 200 runs. A sad feature is that several of our opposite numbers have to have declaration cricket explained to them, and then play as if an all-day fixture against, often, a team of elderly players from Oxfordshire needs to be pursued in the spirit (if you could call it that) of a cut-throat league match."

But it is not all one-way traffic, by any means. Recently, there have been signs of leading local league players turning to SOA cricket as a welcome break from the sometimes unpleasant pressures of the league. Maybe, in time, declaration cricket will come back into fashion. In the meantime, as Tony Lurcock concludes, "The SOA will remain true to its traditions and ethos, whilst also being prepared to adapt to meet the demands and pressures of modern times."

Website: *www.soacc.co.uk*

South Oxfordshire Amateurs, at Albert Park, Melbourne, February 2004

Wiltshire Queries

Founded: 1933

by Barry Aitken

> The Club cap, Wiltshire green with a large white question mark on it, perhaps symbolises the Club, when playing for which anything may happen to you but for which you may be sure of getting either a bat or a bowl. Those who play for or against it say it is quite unlike any other Club and perhaps 'Jika' Travers summed it up by muttering after a game against the Queries, 'None of this could have happened in Australia.' The Club plays hard to win, but above all revels in exciting finishes and there can be few clubs that have such a high proportion of its matches ending as the clock strikes. The tone of the Club was set by some of its founding fathers WJM Llewellyn, RG Hurn, AW Newsome, REF Moloney and James Wort. It was under Wort that there developed the fanatical belief in the value of putting the other side behind the clock and then getting them out with 'slow rubbish', possibly aided by a certain amount of vocal gamesmanship. The secretary (Chris Cutforth) bowls slower and talks more than any other cricketer in England, save possibly the captain himself.

As today's members are coming to the close of the 2012 season they might reflect upon these words taken from *The World of Cricket* published in 1966. They were written about one of Wiltshire's long-established county nomadic or wandering cricket teams, the Wiltshire Queries.

The genesis of the Wiltshire Queries lay in the Wiltshire Under-19 sides of the late 1920s and '30s. They played their cricket seriously and had a nucleus of good players, but above all they had a great capacity for enjoyment and fun. At the end of the 1932 season they realised that because most of the side were moving on to university or working locally they would be available for the next three years to play cricket in Wiltshire in August and September. Michael Llewellyn wrote to county player Dick Hurn to say that he, James Wort and Pat Moloney, all at Cambridge, thought it a pity to let old associations break up and, if they started a cricket side, would Hurn be prepared to play. He was pleased to say yes.

Subsequently a small group met for dinner in the Bath Arms at Warminster on 27 December 1932 to discuss the formation of a club with an age limit of 21, to play clubs and village sides all over the county during the summer holidays of 1933. That first rule was quickly set aside, and the only other club rule, 'that no player suffering from persistent boils on the neck shall be eligible for membership', was never applied.

After an unbeaten inaugural season the Queries began to play better sides – local towns, South Wilts at Bemerton, Frome, Chippenham. In 1937 the county club offered

The first Queries XI at Winterbourne Gunner, 7 August 1933
from left: HA Bennett, SI Jones, JW Parsons, WJM Llewellyn, FD Hollick, J Wort, RG Moloney,
RWD Pawle, AW Newsom, FAH Ling   (11th man – taking the photo? – CE Blake)
The Queries won by 4 wickets

to provide the Queries with an umpire and balls, if the Queries would take on the county's Club and Ground matches. The county reserved the right to nominate two players for each game, a practice that continued until well after the war. As a result a number of county players enjoyed their cricket as Query members: DM Richards, David Milford, Norman Creek, Dick Knight and Reggie Forrester, to name a few.

In the late 1940s the membership consisted largely of schoolmasters and boys on holiday. The fixture list comprised two tours, Oxford in April and South Hampshire in August, and cricket on most days in the remainder of August. The card continued to grow and grow, until the present day when it stands at some 40 matches stretching from the end of April until mid-September, including a tour to Yorkshire. The list of playing, past and candidate members stands today at a healthy 243 and of those playing there is still a solid mix of county, ex-county and club players.

The guidelines that were set out so many years ago still hold good today:
>   that cricket should be enjoyable and fun,
>   that one purpose of the Club was to provide the opportunity and enable young people to play cricket and not to create barriers to prevent them from doing so,
>   that the actual process of playing should be carried out seriously,
>   that as far as possible no-one should go home without having had a chance to bat, bowl or keep wicket,
>   that dull draws should be avoided at all costs, and
>   that those who played against the Queries should want to do so again the following season.

Today the club secretary Barry Aitken has need of computers and the internet, text messaging and Facebook to keep track of players, match managers and the fixture card, but he still manages to perpetuate the Queries' healthy disregard for 'bumph'. On the financial side it is a fact that the three treasurers who have served the club so loyally over the last 79 years accepted the office only on the understanding that any demand for an audited account would result in their immediate resignation! The committee meets almost once a year, and there is an AGM which is traditionally sparsely attended. It is clear that the business of the club, under the watchful gaze of their president David Haywood, is cricket and not administration!

And the business of Queries cricket continues to flourish. New players continue to apply to become members. New fixtures appear on the list each year. And the reputation of the club continues to strengthen as each season goes by.

As was reported in *The Field* on 3 June 1965, 'These were players at cricket's light-hearted best. The Queries stand as a vindication of England's genius at combining cricket at a level of almost lunatic levity with a purpose that is genuinely in earnest.'

Long may they flourish!

Website: *www.wiltshirequeriescc.co.uk*

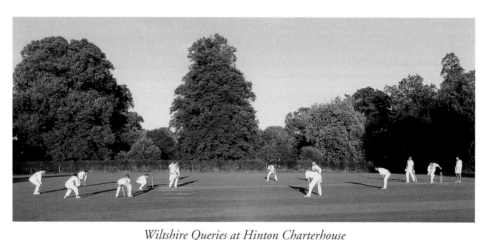

Wiltshire Queries at Hinton Charterhouse
The batsman is the former editor of Wisden, *Scyld Berry*
Keeper: Brian Thompson, 1st slip: David Haywood, 2nd slip: Geoff Ramsey,
Gully: Charlie Palmer, Leg slip: Paul Roberts, Short mid wkt: Will Thomas,
Short mid-on: Joe Dorgan, Short extra cover: Jon Moore, Short mid-off: Tom Palmer,
Square leg: Andy Palmer, Bowler: Tom Haywood

Flycatchers

Founded: 1934

by Anthony Gibson

Like many wandering clubs, the Flycatchers were effectively the creation of one man: in this case Freddy Macdonald, a clubbable man who loved his cricket with a passion. Sadly – or perhaps happily in view of subsequent events – his enthusiasm was not matched by his ability and he found it hard to get a game on a regular basis, a fact that he was bemoaning one evening at the Gargoyle Club in London's West End, no doubt over a sociable glass or two with some of his many cricketing friends. It was then that the brainwave came to him: how best to ensure you were always selected? Form your own club.

That was in late 1934, and by the 1935 season the Gargoyles, as they were initially known, were up and running with matches against 14 assorted village and business-based sides, including the BBC. By 1938, Freddy had fixed on the club colours – green and blue stripes against a brown background, chosen to symbolise what he considered to be the perfect cricketing day: green grass, blue skies and plenty of beer! From this you will gather that the Flycatchers were, are and have always been a convivial bunch, who believe above all that cricket should be fun. Freddy insisted that, in the pavilion or pub after the game, both sides must have enjoyed the day, win, lose or draw. Winning mattered, of course, but not to the point where it became more important than a good day's cricket, keenly fought and with a barrel of Benskins to follow. In fact, there was a time when Freddy Macdonald called a meeting, as the club had played eight matches and won them all, and he was concerned that this might have been at the expense of enjoyment. True to form, the club lost their next six games!

The Second World War inevitably took its toll of the early Gargoyles, and by 1945 Freddy Macdonald had moved out of London to Hertfordshire. With a new location and new players, it seemed the obvious thing to give the club a new name, and Freddy chose the Flycatchers from the little birds he would often see sitting on boundary railings around his beloved village grounds. He knew a lot of good cricketers and, right from the outset, he saw it as part of his mission to bring good cricket to the village sides which were, and are, at the heart of the game.

And some of the cricket was very good. An early Flycatcher, and the founder of what has become a Flycatcher dynasty, was Hugh Bartlett, who had been, in Jim Swanton's words, 'a youthful phenomenon, a tall, left-handed hitter of remarkable power'. For the Gentlemen at Lord's in 1938, Bartlett had scored 175 against Frank Woolley's Players, the second highest score ever in these matches, and he followed that with 157 against Bradman's Australians, reaching his century in just 57 minutes. After distinguished war service he returned to cricket to captain Sussex from 1947 to '49 and would turn out for the Flycatchers as often as he could. For a village bowler, his arrival at the crease must have been a truly daunting prospect. In all, 15 Flycatchers have played Test or county cricket, not counting Douglas Jardine, an early and active President of the club.

Flycatcher dinner, 1949
standing: Guy Patterson, Freddy Macdonald, Douglas Jardine, John Haslam, Hugh Bartlett, Miles Howell

Flycatchers at Hertford, 1952
back: Umpire, N Smales, J Burnham, M Nunn, P Ashley, M Churchill-Dawes, J Purves (scorer)
front: F Cammaerts, B Purves, R Wallers, F Macdonald, E Parker, A Glover

There are four or five families who have been associated with the club from its inception, both as players and as committee members, and this tradition continues today, with the third and fourth generations on from the founding fathers turning out for the side. But that doesn't mean to say that it is cliquey. One of the key requirements for the match managers is to identify potential members and bring them in. The typical Flycatcher will be a half-decent club cricketer and a thoroughly decent bloke.

Stories of Flycatcher exploits are legion and have been recorded for posterity by Freddy Macdonald's son, Roddy, in a delightful little book called *Reminiscences of a Flycatcher*. The early 'Catchers certainly knew how to drink. After one match against Horsmonden in the 1950s, the team and their followers got through 265 pints of beer! And they certainly had their characters, one of the most eccentric of whom was known, simply, as McGusty. If he had a Christian name, it was never used. He wasn't much of a cricketer, although he did have an ancient bat, on which was stencilled 'My name is Biffo. If found, return to McGusty'. But his main claim to fame was as an umpire. "At Hurlingham, in the game against the Nogs," Roddy Macdonald recalls, "McGusty was umpiring at square leg when there was a run out appeal – unfortunately, McGusty was lighting his pipe with his back to the game, but on turning round, quite undeterred, raised his finger. Jack Crisp (the 'Catchers captain), always the master in difficult situations, advised the batsman that he was definitely not out and should stay put until McGusty lowered his finger. The game continued with McGusty serenely untroubled."

Things aren't quite so convivial in these days of breathalysers and 'new men', but the Flycatchers' ethos that cricket should be fun is still strong and the club is as close-knit as ever. They play 15 or so fixtures a year, mostly against Home County village sides, hold an annual dinner and two golf days, and the match managers' reports – published on the website – still make delightful and sometimes hilarious reading.

The Flycatchers may not be the biggest or best-known club in the land, but they are unquestionably one of the truest to the spirit of wandering cricket.

Website: *www.groupspaces.com/flycatchers*

The end of a victorious run chase against the Gentlemen of Philadephia, Oxford 2000
The Flycatchers' Janet Sawyer is hard at work with her coloured pens

Arabs

Founded: 1935

by Anthony Gibson

'The Arabs'. The name has an oddly dissonant ring to it for a club that has the reputation of being the crème de la crème of modern-day wandering cricket – an I Zingari for the 21st century. Credit for it goes to EW Swanton's great friend, RC 'Crusoe' Robertson-Glasgow who suggested it when the then relatively youthful EWS (this was 1935 and Jim was 28) was wondering what to call his recently assembled side after an intended tour to Bermuda became instead a trip to Jersey.

"Nomads, wanderers?" mused Crusoe. "How about Arabs?"

It was a strange choice on the face of it because Arabs are no more nomadic than other races. Perhaps he meant Bedouin. More likely, it was a reference to the Victorian slang word for street urchin, the lowest of the low, and as such maybe a bit of a leg pull. If so, whilst Crusoe may have been the first Arab to make gentle mock of The Founder's pretensions, he most certainly was not the last!

The Arabs has always been and, 13 years after his death, very much remains a club created in its founder's image. Jim was an immensely keen cricketer, and also a very good cricketer, playing three first-class matches for Middlesex against Oxford and Cambridge in the late 1930s, and he took his cricket with all due seriousness. As Tony Lewis observes, in his sparkling foreword to Jim's history of his club, *Arabs in Aspic*: "He understands the everlasting truth – that there is no fun to be had from cricket that is played for fun alone."

But taking the game seriously and playing it competitively is a long way from wanting to win at all costs, which is something of which the Arabs have never been guilty.

"Like any other touring club we came into being for no deeper purpose than to enjoy ourselves," writes Jim in *Arabs in Aspic*. "If we succeeded in that, our opponents would naturally become our friends, irrespective of how hard we played the game. It mattered a great deal to win while one was on the field, afterwards not at all. That was our subconscious philosophy and has remained so."

That first tour to Jersey was notable not only as marking the inception of a club which has become a cricketing institution but also as being the first one in which a side travelled by air. There is a lovely photograph of the team standing by their aircraft at Heston airport, nervous smiles not quite masking the apprehension within. But all was well. Jersey were beaten in a two-day match, Jim making 52, while that ubiquitous and hugely talented wandering cricketer, Hugh Bartlett, savaged the local bowling in the second innings to record the first Arab century. The Channel Islands had their revenge in the second match, a combined Jersey and Guernsey XI winning by an innings, with the Arabs rounding things off with a win in a final one-day encounter.

Heston, 1935, waiting to board the plane to Jersey
JD Eggar, RC Robertson-Glasgow, RG Tindall, JC Bune, AJ Wreford-Brown, EW Swanton,
NS Hotchkin, JM Brocklebank, JSO Haslewood, AA Muir, Umpire Hicks Absent: HT Bartlett

Three further tours to Jersey would follow before the outbreak of war. Almost to a man, the Arabs enlisted. Many of them served with distinction, not least Jim himself, and five paid the ultimate price. When peace finally returned, Swanton and his Arabs had to decide whether to tour elsewhere, as the Channel Islands were in no state to host a cricket tour, or fold their tents and melt away into the desert. Happily for all concerned, they chose the former. A two-day game against Cambridge University was followed by a morale-raising visit to the British Army of the Rhine, a tour which marked an Arab debut for a promising Oxford undergraduate by the name of John Woodcock.

It was Jim, of course, who chose his Arabs: three or four a year, as others retired, moved away or turned to golf. They were men who, if not quite in the inimitable Swanton mould, were nonetheless very definitely of a type: right sort of family background, public school, Oxbridge, as befitted a club whose colours are narrow stripes of Oxford and Cambridge blue on a green background, and invariably very good cricketers. Over 125 Arabs have played first-class cricket, including such luminaries as Gubby Allen, Ian Peebles, Colin Ingleby-Mackenzie, Henry Blofeld, Freddie Brown, Billy Griffith, Jack Fingleton, Richie Benaud, Tony Lewis and Colin Cowdrey – and more recently Ed Smith, Alex Loudon, Ben Hutton, James Bruce, Mark Wagh, Andy Whittall, Will House and Richard Montgomerie.

But they had their characters as well, not least the splendidly named 'Loopy' Legard, an 'idiosyncratic' (Jim's description) bowler, who liked to fortify himself throughout a game with the quart bottles of beer with which he filled his cricket bag. He went on to become Secretary of Delamere Forest GC and when he retired, part of his pension was two pints of beer, on the house, every day for life! Goodness knows what the Founder made of all that.

By the '50s, the pattern of an Arabs season had become pretty well set: ten or a dozen games, against fellow wanderers, the armed services, a tour either to the north or to Kent and Sussex, and the annual visit to Horris Hill preparatory school, to play sides raised by its headmaster Monty Stow. Touring overseas didn't become part of the picture again until the late 1960s, by which time Jim and his wife Ann had bought a house in Barbados, and it seemed the obvious thing to bring the Arabs across. Ingleby-Mackenzie captained for that first tour in 1967, with Tony Lewis following in 1973/74, when they encountered some ferocious fast bowling from the likes of Gregory Armstrong and Charlie Griffith. A further tour followed to Kenya in 1979/80 and the first one since that time set off for Dubai and Abu Dhabi in December 2012.

The 91-year-old former England captain Bob Wyatt at Wormsley, with Paul Getty, Mrs Wyatt and EWS

The Founder played his last match for the Arabs in 1967, at the age of 60, with 2,376 runs and 148 wickets under his majestic belt. He did think of winding the club up but the members decided, by a majority of 2 to 1, to carry on, with Jim assuming the role of an anxious, protective, demanding but also very proud father figure, writing a 'Letter' each year, to keep the membership up to date with the club's progress. But he continued to play in the Annual Arabs' golf day at his home club of Royal St George's until well into the 1990s, golf having been an important aspect of the Arabs as a club, right from the outset, as indeed it still is.

Jim died in 2000 at the age of 92 without, slightly surprisingly, leaving any instructions as to what should happen to his beloved Arabs. Some of the older members wanted to call it a day; the playing members tended to favour carrying on. After much agonising, the consensus was to continue; tentatively at first, with a pared-down fixture list, but with increasing confidence and success as time went by. At the time of writing, under Charles Fry as President and James Martin-Jenkins as Secretary, the Arabs are as strong as they have ever been. Membership stands at around 250, with as high a proportion as ever of former first-class cricketers; a fixture list of around eight games a season – at some of the country's finest grounds – more than makes up in quality whatever it lacks in quantity, and includes MCC, Oxford University, Arundel Castle, Sir Paul Getty's XI and the Yellowhammers.

right: Christopher Martin-Jenkins

left: Charles Fry

Perhaps it is their competitive spirit, or maybe the strength of their sides, or possibly even the influence of their Founder, but for whatever reason, the Arabs have always been, as Tony Lewis acknowledged in that Foreword, 'a club that others have wanted to beat with undisguised relish'. But to accuse them of big-headedness is as mistaken as it would be to brand EW Swanton as nothing more than a stuffy old snob. Jim certainly gave the Arabs their competitiveness, but their other defining characteristic is not his pomposity, but a diametrically opposite, conscious, irreverent reaction to it. As Jim himself wrote of his great friend Crusoe, 'If there is such a thing as the Arab spirit – defined perhaps as a strong distaste for solemnity and pomposity – no-one did more to create it than he.' Except, of course, and even if it wasn't quite what he intended, Jim Swanton himself.

The Arabs in Dubai, 2013
back: Spencer Crawley, Hugo Loudon, Rory MacLeay, Henry Watkinson, Tom Hemingway,
Mark Wagh, Rick Johnson   front: Mumtaz Habib, Tom Crump, Henry Rudd,
Charlie Duffell, Mathew Crump, Alex Loudon, James Martin-Jenkins
Also on tour were Will House, Ben Hutton, Harry Chetwood and Rob Bruce

Woodpeckers

Founded: 1936

by Brian Scovell

Woodpeckers CC was formed in 1936 by a group of toffs, mainly public school boys who loved cricket, particularly village cricket. One of them had been inspired by reading AG Macdonell's book *England, their England* published three years earlier. They arranged fixtures, similar to the game Macdonell wrote about, at distant villages, enabling them to have a good, boozy day out. Not many matches were won, but they talked a good game. After the Second World War Hugh Stoneman, a private detective who specialised in exposing rich folks' adultery, skippered the side. His son Bingo, an artist, was also a good all-rounder and the history of the club is littered with instances of family involvement. Nigel Phethean, who retired at 42, made a comeback 15 years later, and in 2011 two of his grandsons played with him at Four Elms.

In 1969 Brian Scovell, the *Daily Mail* sports writer and author, replied to an ad in *The Times* as a joke and met the officers at the Dorchester Hotel. He said he was another Garry Sobers – actually he wrote a column for Sobers for many years and wrote his autobiography in 1988 – and they accepted him with alacrity. Having scored a duck and failing to take a wicket, he was voted captain, stayed in charge until 2008 and is Life President. John Boyd-Carpenter, the secretary, died at the wheel from a heart attack, and Scovell took over the job and the other posts. After the takeover, no subscriptions were charged. "With an all-sorts group of people, some of whom might not have been very good, you don't want someone coming up and saying, 'I've paid my sub and I ought to play!'" he explained.

The Peckers started winning, as younger players were recruited, as well as lots of colonials. One such was Bradman Benka-Coker who bowled very fast and hit the ball very hard, without being terribly reliable. The only pity was that he never played in the same side as his twin, Ponsford Benka-Coker. They'd been named for the record 451 that the two Australians added against England in 1934.

Most of the recruits came from state schools in the London inner city. One, a teacher named Paul Davidson, a small, ginger-haired medium-pacer who bowled line and length, took a record 451 wickets. He was a diabetic, and one day a group of rebellious school boys were seen approaching the main drive of the school carrying bricks in their hands, ready to attack the staff. The police hadn't yet arrived, and Paul came out to meet them on his own and persuaded them to drop the bricks and go back to their classes. He died from MRSA at the age of 58, and 600 people honoured him at his funeral. His friend Matt Wall, at a nearby school, had the same fearless approach, and he played his cricket as a successful opening batsman in the same manner.

The best naturally talented player in the club's history was Mick Hogan, a wayward Irish teenager who had Botham-like qualities – fast swing bowling, hurricane hitting and Sobers-like catching. After failing to turn up for trials at The Oval and Lord's, he disappeared. He preferred Guinness.

In the early days, lady scorers were the rule, one of whom left her husband, provoking quite a scandal. Whereupon Scovell banned lady scorers and instead encouraged his players to bring their wives, children and girlfriends, to make it a family day out, as it still is. When Scovell's wife Audrey, a top-class etcher, died on Christmas Day 2000 he changed the name of the Texaco Cup – played for between sponsors Texaco and the Cricket Writers' Club until the fixture was dropped – to the Audrey Scovell Memorial Cup, to be presented to the lady who contributed most to the Woodies' ethos.

The standard of fixtures slowly improved. A long-standing one at the Royal Household at Windsor Castle was eventually cancelled when TA Sekhar, a Test player, bowled them out for 40. He was one of around a dozen Test players to have appeared for the Peckers, others being Sarfraz Nawaz, Aftab Gul, Aamir Sohail, Danny Morrison, Geoff Lawson, Michael Slater, Ian Bishop, BS Chandrasekhar and Willie Rodriguez.

In 2010 a weakened side lost by eight wickets to the Windsor Great Park side which consisted of members of Her Majesty's staff. The following year the Woodies were told that the Queen was available for the players to be presented to, to commemorate the 150th anniversary of the WGP club. The wives were all set to buy new clothes when the Woodies were gazumped. Swan Richards, who ran the Australian Crusaders touring side, had a fixture arranged at WGP on the following Sunday but insisted on switching his game so as to be able to meet the Queen.

A very exciting game at the HAC was reaching its climax when in the middle of an over the groundsman Len Fortiss started to push the first of four covers onto the square.

The Woodpeckers at Leigh, 2006

He then pushed another one towards the middle which crashed into the first one being pushed by several Woodies players in the opposite way. It quickly became a cover-jousting contest, with Len shouting, "I'm in charge here and the game is off" and the senior umpire saying, "Oh no, I'm in charge." After a minute of two pushing and shoving, the groundsman relented. And the drizzle stopped. Mr Fortiss is now chief groundsman at The Oval and, as Alec Stewart said, "He's one of the very best in the country."

Scovell father and son at Brook
Gavin holds most of the batting records – 184* the highest score, 27 centuries,
56 fifties, one every four innings, and Woodpecker of the Year four times.

There have been some great stories from the 1,200-odd matches, many of them related in my recently published book *Our Beloved Cricket – from village green to Lord's*. One of the best concerns the Australian swing bowler from Perth, Simon Hare. Woodies were looking as though they would lose at Tilford, and the number six batsman was pulling a succession of sixes over the Barley Mow pub. As the rain fell harder, the ball became almost impossible to hold. The captain said to Simon, who fielded on that side of the ground on the boundary, "Next time the ball is thrown back, lose it. That's our only chance of using a dry ball." A six went over the pub, someone threw it back and Simon promptly hurled the ball into the nearby river. The umpire looked at the captain and said, "Have you seen that? That man has thrown the ball into the river!" The captain said, "Yes, I did but he is from Western Australia and they're all batty!" After a short interval of back-chat the game resumed and, with a dry ball, the Woodies achieved a worthy draw.

Today the Woodies are still going strong under the enthusiastic leadership of Patrick Owen-Browne whose father and uncle, twins, were early pace-setters. Five other Owen-Brownes have played – once all in the same game, another record.

Forty Club

Founded: 1937

by Barry Aitken

When Benjamin Franklin wrote, "At 20 years of age, the will reigns, at 30 the wit and at 40 the judgement", could he have been thinking about the Forty Club? Franklin, though American, may have been interested in cricket as he visited England many times in the late eighteenth century, but it would be another century and a half before Henry Grierson would bring will, wit and judgement together when he founded the Forty Club.

Happening to be in Bedford in the summer of 1935 he went to watch his old school playing the Incogniti, captained for the day by Shirley Snell. Snell upbraided him for having given up cricket in favour of golf. Slightly stung, Grierson reflected on this and eventually decided that "if it were possible to raise a sufficient number of fellows of forty years and over who were reasonably good players, we might be sharp enough to handle some of the schools." He thought that the batting might be adequate but had some qualms about the fielding. As to the bowling he felt that if the professionals joined in – a devout hope – the bowling would be good enough for what he had in mind.

He set about writing to some 50 cricketing friends, 40 of whom replied that they quite liked the idea, a few were doubtful and the remainder said they did not consider it a practical proposition or alternatively that Grierson had gone crackers. Thus encouraged, he decided to go ahead and started by taking a side in 1936 to Wellingborough School. The match was won, rather easily, and enthusiasm was generated. During the following winter Grierson started to lay the foundations of a club. He persuaded Captain CEB Stevens to become Secretary, and Sir Pelham Warner and Mr Jack Hobbs (as he was then) to become President and Vice President respectively. As Grierson says, "These two names were sufficient to ensure the success of the enterprise," which was then christened The Forty Club and the letters XL adopted as the logo. The first game under the new title was played in 1937, Wellingborough School again providing the opposition. In the years leading up to the Second World War, seven or eight games were played in each season. Rules of the club were drawn up in 1937; in 1938 the match fee was established at two shillings and the club dinner was held at the Carlton Club at a cost of 10s 6d per head.

Mighty oaks from little acorns!

With little cricket generally available during the war, former Test players were only too happy to play in Forty Club matches. One can imagine that school teams must have been somewhat overawed when facing Vallance Jupp, the former England all-rounder, who took five wickets in an innings on five occasions for the club, or when having to bowl at Herbert Sutclifffe who scored a century on his only appearance.

Henry Grierson was determined to continue to expand the club after the war and from time to time he press-ganged a few under-40s to play. One such was David

Money, a schoolmaster at Bedford School, who was asked to make up the numbers in 1948 at the age of 28 and who then proceeded to keep wicket for the club for another 51 seasons!

By 1961 the fixtures card had grown to 36 and by 1978 to 73. The Grierson gospel appealed to 40-year-olds and, with his unquenchable enthusiasm, membership grew and cricketers of the calibre of Denis Compton, Fred Trueman, Reg Simpson, Ian Peebles, Brian Sellers, Jack Young, Billy Griffith and Freddie Brown were playing. By 1992 the fixtures card included 143 schools.

As a wandering club, the Forty Club does not own a ground. Membership is nationwide with a sizeable number of overseas members. Under a central administration the UK is divided into a number of districts, each with its own chairman responsible for the matches in his own area. In the early days former county and minor county players were the basis of most sides. Today, although there are a number of ex-first-class players as members, membership is focused more on players of a reasonable club standard.

Age is less of a handicap to ability than it once was. Centuries are scored by 50- and 60-year-olds, and five- or six-wicket hauls are often achieved. It is only in the area of fielding and throwing that the experience of the Forty Club players tends to be outmatched by their opponents' youthfulness. Ageing bones and enfeebled legs and arms require a well-organised system for the return of the ball from the boundary!

Schools cricket finishes quite early in the season nowadays and so, from July onwards, XL has a number of fixtures against club sides. In addition there is a domestic tournament between all the UK districts and an international tournament, called the Triangular Tournament, playing SGS Holland and Dansk XL from Denmark; this is held in each country in rotation. Further afield, tours have taken place each year for the past 15 years or so to countries around the world.

Yet taking cricket to schools will always be the mission statement of the Forty Club, and this objective has been strengthened by the award annually of a silver cup to the winning school – that is the school adjudged to have performed best in the season of schools' fixtures. The school or youth XI team is assessed not only in the skills of bowling, batting, fielding and teamwork but also in the 'Spirit of Cricket' subjects such as captaincy, behaviour on and off the field, turnout and, most importantly, sportsmanship. Winning the Forty Club Trophy (The Henry Grierson Cup) is a major achievement for a school, and the winning team captain and master-in-charge are invited to attend the club's annual dinner where the cup is presented.

Public schools are the main Forty Club opposition, but the club is conscious that the fixtures card needs to include more schools from the state system and steps are being taken to that end. Further – and in response to the growing number of county over-50s, 60s and 70s sides – the club has lowered the entry age limit to 35 and will experiment with a complete withdrawal of an age limit. Not only does this introduce some younger legs and stronger arms to the sides, it also significantly enlarges the 'playing window' for members. This change is bearing fruit as more and more league cricketers are looking for less intensive cricket at around the age of 35 and they are attracted by the opportunity to play fine school first XIs all over the UK on some of the finest grounds in the country.

The Forty Club playing Crathie CC on the Queen's estate at Balmoral

There is also a flourishing Golfing Society within the Forty Club, many members of which used to be seen at the crease, but who now enjoy the prospect of about 36 matches and two meetings a season. The Society is a popular section of the club and something that it is hoped will expand across the country. It is an important tool in the effort to increase the visibility and 'footprint' of the Forty Club.

The club's remarkable expansion shows the affection in which it is held by both members and opponents, and it is due to the dedication over the years of scores of cricketers who have been and still are prepared to give time to administration.

The fixtures card today, in 2013, has some 220 matches. The club continues to play the Inter-District Tournament and the Triangular Tournament (now in its 51st season) and to tour to all sorts of interesting countries. Membership stands at around 2,400 and, keeping up with the times, they are supported by websites, e-newsletters, on-line shopping for club colours and so on.

Father Time is the patron saint of cricketers, and it is certain he will not be removing the bails while will, wit and judgement continue to characterise the Forty Club.

Website: *www.thefortyclub.co.uk*

Bushmen

Founded: 1942

by Alastair Lack

According to legend, the Bushmen first played in the Second World War, taking the field in June 1942. As Maurice Latey, the first historian of the club and one of the founding fathers observed, "The field they took was in the park at Woburn Abbey, since then the scene of many strange diversions, but of none stranger than this."

Woburn Abbey was then the headquarters of the Political Warfare Executive (PWE) where senior members of the BBC German Service would visit to discuss mutual matters of war. The two most regular visitors were Hugh Greene (later Sir Hugh Greene, Director-General of the BBC) and Lindley Fraser. Both were experts in the field of finding a decent pint – sometimes difficult in those times – and both loved cricket. A match was soon arranged between the BBC and PWE, with much enjoyable pre-match psychological warfare, as befitted the two outfits.

So, on a bright Saturday afternoon in June 1942, the secret weapon of Bush House went into action. As The Historian relates: "Imagine the scene: the deer browsing round the meadow scurried for cover in the trees as the burly Berrmann (the leading German Service announcer), profiled like one of the more formidable Roman Emperors, thundered up to the wicket; at the other end, standing well back, wicket-keeper HC Greene crouched, his six-foot six-inches bent double or treble; in between, the PWE opener, looking pale and defenceless in his one pad and no gloves." It was an eventful opening over: the first ball flew straight to second slip, hitting him a painful blow and the second went for four wides down the leg-side. It was also a long over and set up PWE for a good score. At the end of it, Berrmann pulled up lame. Not surprising perhaps, as it was the first time he'd bowled for twenty years.

As the afternoon wore on the Bush House team began to take a hold, until an American from the US Office of War Information, stationed at Woburn, strode to the wicket. He took up his stance in baseball style. His first hit scattered the deer among the trees, and he continued in this vein for several overs. In a move that was either a desperate measure or a stroke of genius, the Bush House skipper, Hugh Greene, called on Maurice Latey, a purveyor of very slow donkey drops. He immediately performed the first hat-trick in the proto-club's history.

But this great event was soon overshadowed by a greater one. At this moment a messenger ran onto on the field to announce the fall of Tobruk. The Historian takes up the story again: "Dismissing the unworthy thought that this was a political warfare trick to put us off our game, we took council. There was not much the broadcasters could do about it. Our colleagues back at Bush House had plenty of practice in dealing with defeats. They could handle it. We played on. We reminded ourselves of Sir Francis Drake and his bowls on Plymouth Hoe. But it was all something of an anti-climax after that, even if it did bring the proto-Bushmen their first victory."

The game had cheered everyone up and further wartime cricket was played. With peace in 1945 came the idea of founding a cricket and dining club to carry on the wartime traditions of Bush House. To name the club was not difficult: The Bushmen. For some twenty years the Bushmen flourished without any rules, relying on the verbal traditions of the elders (this had its drawbacks, when it was discovered that the first game had not coincided with the fall of Tobruk, but had taken place a year earlier). Indoor nets began in the corridors of the BBC and cherished traditions soon emerged: the traditional Bushmen middle-order collapse, the varying complaints of wicket-keepers ("I'm dazzled by the light of the buttercups") and the vital question of where to slake the thirst after a game. By 1966 the club had reached the comparative respectability of acquiring a bank account. The bank required to see the rules of the club and so the chairman, Christopher Dilke, obliged by writing them. The first two clauses are clear enough:

(1) The Bushmen shall play cricket during the proper season.
(2) During the winter the Bushmen shall dine.

The final clause of the rules reads: 'The Bushmen, founded in war-time, exists to celebrate the arts and pleasures of peace', a celebration that continues to this day.

And Great Officers were created, among them to this day a Keeper of the Wardrobe, who does not keep the wardrobe, an Umpire who does not umpire, a Senior Scorer who does not score and an Auditor General who does not audit and probably would not know how to begin.

But if the rules were relatively clear, much less so is the motto of the club, 'Nec tamen consumebatur'. The Latin tag has been a continuing source of mystery to generations of Bushmen. Clearly it has something to do with Bush House. Some old hands will quote from Exodus: 'Behold the bush burned; but it was not consumed.' An even more learned member may add that it is also the motto of the Church of Scotland. And there we have a clue. A founder member, Lindley Fraser, was a son of the manse, and it was he that commissioned the Bushmen crest in the form of a burning bush. According to The Historian, 'The fiery bush symbolises the Bushmen's untiring activity on and off the field, on a green cap, symbolising the eternal youth of the Bushmen.' The emblem has struck terror – or sometimes the reverse – into the hearts of many an opposing team in many a hard-fought struggle.

After the club's creation, the Bushmen entered what The Historian called the Dark Ages, to be followed by the Middle Ages, because of the lack of documentary evidence in terms of scorebooks and menus. Nevertheless, Bushmen tended to prosper in these Ages, three of them becoming the Director-General of the BBC and others holding top posts in radio and television. Robin Day was moved to write in the *News Chronicle* on the appointment of Hugh Greene as Director-General: 'At the top of the BBC hierarchy is a small exclusive circle. Very few people even in the BBC know of its existence. This select society calls itself The Bushmen. One by one the Bushmen have been moving up to key positions in the Corporation.' The Bushmen were moved to reply: 'Mr Day's blend of audacity and pure imagination seems to us highly Bushmanlike. We look forward to welcome him as a guest to one of our winter dinners.' And indeed, Robin Day was later a speaker as well as attending Bushmen cricketing weekends in Dorset.

Over the years the fixture list expanded from some six matches a year to the present 20-plus. And some well-known and diverse names have turned out for the club. Apart from founding members like Sir Hugh Greene, others have included Patrick Gordon Walker, the former Foreign Secretary who once scored 93, Julian Yeatman of *1066 And All That* fame, Edmund Blunden the poet, Sir Ian Jacob, another Director-General, and the biographer Michael Meyer (sometimes known as the Boycott of the Bushmen). Later Sir Trevor MacDonald played for several years and took a hat-trick in the first over of a game in 1970. Others include the Faulks brothers, Edward and Sebastian, and many names from the media world, as well as the odd MP and member of the House of Lords.

Alex Barnett is the only Bushman ever to play in a one-day final at Lord's and to field for England at Lord's in a Test match, albeit as twelfth man. But the palm must go to Sir Learie Constantine. An old friend to Bush House, he made his debut in 1964 against Great Missenden. Their brisk in-swing bowler was making inroads. Sir Learie strode to the crease with the words: "I will show you how to deal with him." And he did. He thrust his leg down the wicket and swept. The first ball flew over square leg onto the other side of the road, the second into the hedge. And so it continued. His last game was against Herongate, in Essex. The second Historian of the Bushmen, Peter Hill, remembers Sir Learie's words of advice: "Whether you hit the ball or I hit the ball, I do the calling!" The umpire was nearly lynched when he gave Sir Learie out.

To get a flavour of Bushmen cricket, one can do no better than read the captain's annual log. In 1977 skipper Peter Herrmann reflects on the bowling of Laurence Gretton and Michael Birley (both fine bowlers who took many wickets over long careers): 'Gretton's victims were usually bemused by the packed offside field and his legside bowling, while Birley's victims were simply amazed by his ability to bowl after two hours in the pub.'

A few years later, Mark Jones noticed a curious fact in the Brickbats game: 'Our number one (Hill) and our number five (Cockerell) had both been named and censured in the House of Commons the previous week.' He added: 'The Historian confirmed that this had not happened in June for some little time.' Michael Cockerell's log included the following: 'Michael: now he is very unusual. He is the only man I know who called for a runner – and he was bowling at the time.' And here's a view of the Bushmen changing room before the game: 'There we are changing, joking light-heartedly about whose turn it is to wear the communal jockstrap. In a corner one of our older brethren is taking Phyllosan – intraveneously. I lead the team out on to the field, followed by the other ten captains.'

Captains miss matches 'for contemplation and spiritual renewal' (or to save their sanity), while others record a season as 'the usual mix of farce and brilliance'. Another notes that, whereas Bushmen used the thicket at Newdigate to relieve themselves, the opposition used it to strike a succession of sixes. And as Peter Hill records, 'Michael Kaye inherited the captain's mantle in 2008 as a kind of retirement present.' Michael records an all too typical Bushmen misunderstanding: with both batsmen at the same end, 'one calls but disdains to run, the latter runs speedily but disdains to call.' It was a season, he concluded, 'that I shall never forget, try as I might.' And to pen a personal note, I remember the first time I captained the side. I won the toss and decided to bowl on a green wicket. The match started at 2pm, but where was the Bushmen opening bowler? He arrived at 3, smiled and said: 'Sorry, I thought the game began at 2.30.'

The Bushmen have also enjoyed many a battle on a foreign field, from a pioneering visit to Holland in the 1950s to a recent end-of-summer visit to Menorca. The letter M seems to figure prominently in destinations, from Milan through Munich to Monte Carlo and beyond. The most ambitious tour was to Kerala in southern India. Four close matches were played and enjoyed, not least against the Swanton Veterans club in Cochin. On being told about this, the doyen of cricket journalists EW Swanton thanked both clubs warmly: 'I am indeed flattered and delighted by this recollection of my broadcast work of long ago.'

Perhaps the best way to understand the generally engaging and occasionally perplexing philosophy of Bushmen cricket is to attend a match and enjoy the banter before, during and after at the pub. An alternative would be through the annual award of the Berle Adams trophy, given by an eminent American media executive, presumably impressed (unlike some others) by his first experience of Bushmen cricket. It is awarded to the individual who has performed the most Bushmanlike achievement of the cricketing season. It sometimes celebrates a dazzling century, fine bowling or a wonderful catch. But it is awarded equally to a batsman who scores one run in 56 minutes, or the fielder who drops the sitter that loses the match. Both categories are valued as being essentially Bushmanlike.

The BBC correspondent John Simpson once wrote this about the Bushmen, after returning from the Kalahari desert, their chief hunting grounds: 'They are a small, hardy, intelligent and gentle people, who have eked out life for themselves, while the rest of humanity developed along completely different lines.'

The Bushmen live on: nec tamen consumebatur ...

Website: *www.myspace.com/thebushmencc*

Bushmen in Suffolk, 2008
(from left to right) Michael Kaye, Laurence Gretton, Clyde Jeavons, Bobby Ancil,
Peter Herrmann, Michael Cockerell, David Morley, Bernard Jacobs (scorer),
Francis Gretton, Pianki Assegai, Chris Ancil, Javed Soomro, Andy Popperwell

Cricket Society XI

Founded: 1949

by Peter Hartland

The Cricket Society itself was founded in London in November 1945, originally as a body for statisticians starved of cricket during the war. Its first formal title was The Society of Cricket Statisticians. There had been nothing like it before, apart from a short-lived Cricketana Society set up for collectors back in 1929. As cricket returned to Britain at all levels, its followers felt a need to share its pleasures and communicate amongst themselves by way of something more than facts and figures and, in recognition of this, the AGM of November 1948 led to the organisation being renamed The Cricket Society.

The wider remit duly attracted new members. Meetings covering more general cricketing matters were scheduled and a dinner arranged, all in London. It was also decided that the society would field an occasional wandering team. Three fixtures were arranged for the summer of 1949 against West Chiltington in Sussex, BBC Second XI and the recently nationalised National Bank. The early teams to represent the Cricket Society were informal scratch elevens playing a handful of matches a season, mainly against villages in south-east England. Regular players included the prominent statistician and book collector Geoffrey Copinger, and Ayton Whitaker, producer of plays for the BBC.

A tour to Paris took place in 1954, followed by two trips to Holland, the first of which was led by Con Davies, arguably the greatest club cricketer who ever lived. During a long career Davies captured over 5,000 wickets with his left-arm spin and hit 126 centuries. Unsurprisingly he registered the Cricket Society's first three-figure score. Around this time a conflict of interest arose within the team between those who wanted to continue playing for fun, and others with grander ambitions. By and large the former held sway throughout the 1950s and 1960s. Distinguished cricketers, such as the Pakistan Test player Shujauddin Butt, did turn out for a side that was now playing a dozen games a season, but the Society XI remained a social team at heart, carried on the field by accurate seam bowlers taking advantage of helpful village pitches. The profile of the XI was raised under the enthusiastic, charismatic captaincy of Chris Box-Grainger (1957-67) and diligent management of Anthony Robinson.

Box-Grainger led a party of Cricket Society members to Australia to watch some of the 1970/71 Ashes Tests. A game was arranged against the recently formed Australian Cricket Society in Melbourne, with a rematch at Shepherd's Bush in London on the rest day of the 1972 Lord's Test. One of the Australian openers in the rematch, Kevan Carroll, decided to stay in England, playing for several years for the Society. In his first season, 1973, he amassed 1,198 runs, which is still the only instance of a four-figure aggregate for the club within a calendar year.

During the 1970s the fixture list took a leap forward in quality and quantity. By the end of the decade there were 40 games a year. Tours to various destinations were organised, including Australia, Barbados, Corfu, Jersey and Philadelphia. Overseas stars and county second XI men were recruited. Illustrious occasional players included Chris Cowdrey, Paul Sheahan, Jack Robertson and Bill Frindall. At Blenheim Palace, Sheahan stroked a memorable, effortless hundred.

The Society XI became a serious cricket team, albeit still a nomadic one intent on enjoying itself. The vision and ambition to expand upwards and outwards, while retaining something of the village roots, were shared by three men in particular. Jeremy Burford transformed the fixture list while Michael de Navarro managed with gusto the increasingly demanding organisation of the team. John Douglas, according to Society chronicler Nigel Haygarth, displayed manifold talents as captain, opening batsman, wicket-keeper, photographer and cartoonist. Between them these three turned out more than 1,200 times for the Society XI. Burford and de Navarro became QCs. Other key figures of the period were the stylish Old Tonbridgian batsman Bill Gunyon and seam bowlers Ron Stern and John Kershaw, whose 421 wickets are still a record. This halcyon period lasted well into the 1980s, when the giant former West Indian Test cricketer Reg Scarlett joined the ranks. Off-spinners Barry Goddard and Tim Lowry took over the bulk of the bowling, wheedling many a batsman out against the clock.

League cricket had dominated the North and Midlands since the turn of the twentieth century. The town clubs of the South held out against it for seventy years, but once resistance was broken, smaller clubs began to go with the flow. It became a rush in the 1990s, and by the turn of the millennium virtually every club with a home ground participated in a Saturday league. In parts of the Home Counties, Sunday leagues were introduced as well.

The Cricket Society XI at its Diamond Jubilee match, Arundel, 2005
back: Robin Butchard (umpire), Barney Douglas, Paul Fielding, Paul Pennock,
John Symons, Adnan Mohammed, Neil Holmes, Adrian Gale, Geoffrey Hartley (umpire)
front: Robin Burns (scorer), Tom Carmichael, Ronald Paterson,
Charles Noakes, Andrew Moss, Tony Warrington

The Cricket Society XI was bound to be affected. Without a home ground it could not join a league, which meant the end of Saturday fixtures and a halving of the overall programme. Many of the stronger fixtures had to go: Bath, Finchley, Malmesbury, Streatham, St Lawrence & Highland Court and others of similar stature. There were no overseas tours after 1992, though the May Bank Holiday excursion to the Isle of Wight remained intact. By the year 2000 the Society XI had become in essence a Sunday side playing villages, its membership growing steadily older.

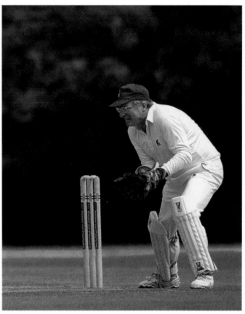

With the growth of inter-county senior cricket, combinations made up of players in their 50s and 60s have learned to make the most of their experience. Canny, accurate bowling to thoughtfully-set fields, and years of timing run chases to the minute, compensate in part for the inevitable deterioration in eyesight, reactions and mobility. This was increasingly the case with the Cricket Society XI, which more than held its own against much younger opponents. In 2010 the Society enjoyed one of its most successful seasons, winning 14 matches and losing five. Of the 11 most regular players, only three were under 50 years of age, and one under 40. The position remained unchanged in 2012 and looks set to continue.

Tom Carmichael, wicket-keeper and chief organiser of the Cricket Society XI since 1999

The Society's most prolific batsmen of the past twenty years have been Ronald Paterson (leading all-time run-scorer with over 10,000 runs), Tony Crockert (record 13 centuries), Andrew Moss, Adrian Gale, Rob Humphreys and Tony Warrington, a heavy scorer in Minor Counties cricket who made 92 against the 1973 West Indian tourists. During this time five bowlers have reached 200 wickets: Charles Noakes (407 wickets and the longest-serving captain), Norman Jones, Neil Holmes, Paul Fielding and John Symons. They have been ably supported by wicket-keeper Tom Carmichael, who has conscientiously undertaken much of the team organisation.

Wandering clubs tend by nature to be a little less parochial than those with a fixed base, and the Cricket Society XI over the years has welcomed into its ranks a range of professions and nationalities, abilities and personalities. While holding its own on the field throughout the sixty or so years of its history, the team has always sought to embrace the sensitivity and fellowship of cricket, in the true spirit of the Cricket Society itself.

Website: *www.cricketsociety.com/cricket*

Boffins

Founded: 1949

by Paul Mathieu

The Boffins blossom briefly at the same time every year. They exist for only a week each summer, playing the same six fixtures. Starting on the Sunday before the August Bank Holiday, the Boffins' fields of dreams are Seaton, Sidmouth, Tipton St John, Chardstock, Kilmington and Chard, in a lovely stretch of East Devon and the Somerset border.

The Boffins tour began in 1949, though it had a forerunner 50 years earlier: a side led by a Mr Burrows. The Great War did for Burrows' XI, but a tour including its fixtures took over between the wars, in the shape of the Hampstead Itinerants. They failed to re-form after World War Two, and the Boffins emerged – so-called because some of the players were from research establishments like RAE Farnborough. They were joined by a number of notably unscientific players whose qualification was simply that they wanted to play friendly cricket against genial opposition. Their enthusiasm mostly outran their ability. Among them was an accountant, George Arbuthnot, who handled the tour's logistics and acquired the title, 'King Boffin'. Other pioneers included the tiny and eccentric Sir Wolstan Dixie and Hugh Talbot, a London stockbroker. Their commitment was absolute; their competence suggested by Dixie's total of 99 Boffins runs – spread over several tours.

It can be a challenge to find accommodation for touring cricket teams, especially those with a penchant for late, well-refreshed nights. The early Boffins were housed in a long-gone pub in Seaton, the Golden Lion. It offered bed and board for £7 a week. Tales of the Golden Lion suggest something close to primordial squalor, but it was sufficiently beloved to inspire the Boffins' flag, which is a recovering lion, prone on its back, with hung-over red eyes, on a cricket-field green background.

Later Boffins' boltholes included a pub in Ottery St Mary, where a burnt-out armchair (our opening bowler fell asleep with a cigarette) gave the landlord cause to expel us; and a motel where every footstep stuck to the carpets, and water dripped from the light fittings after rain. But cricket tour paradise arrived thanks to Brian Dillon, in his time a dashing Boffins batsman. On retirement, he bought a farm near Sidford. Its outbuildings had been converted into holiday cottages, and there the Boffins have stayed for the last dozen or so years. Brian has sadly passed, but his wife Linda continues to preside over the perfect base for a cricket tour.

Time was, the tour began at Whimple on the Saturday, but the arrival of league cricket put paid to that. Seaton is the Boffins' foundation fixture, and that now starts the tour on Sunday, followed by Sidmouth and its panoramic Channel view on the Bank Holiday. Sidmouth has long been the toughest fixture of the week, and down the years Boffins have earned transient fame there by snatching victory or (more likely) staving off defeat. John Nagenda can claim more glory than most. In his pomp he was a high-class quick bowler, including opening for East Africa in the first Prudential World Cup. Something about the sea air brought him bristling back to his best; more than once, he reduced the top half of a strong batting side to ruin by lunchtime. At that point the

Sidmouth president would wrap an arm round Nagenda's shoulders, grab a bottle of port with the other, and let thirst take its course.

Tony Fairbairn took on the leadership of the Boffins after George Artbuthnot, and ran the tour for over 30 years. His particular concern was to field a competitive side at Sidmouth, and to that end he recruited ringers of the quality of Farokh Engineer and John Price. 'Rooky' ignored the script, declined to keep wicket, batted down the order – and took six for 51 bowling leg-breaks.

Having, with luck, survived Sidmouth, the Boffins moved on to Budleigh Salterton. After many years, the fixture was lost because of a log-jam of home matches. When it was restored, the usual format was a Budleigh team comprising three or four seniors, a rising Devon player, and the rest youngsters. Then came a year when, with a key league match to prepare for, Budleigh fielded a side whose first six batsmen had all played – or were playing – representative cricket. They had a sweep for the fastest 50. The winner took 14 balls.

The Boffins spent the winter plotting revenge. Keith Arthurton was recruited. Come the day, Budleigh turned up with only eight players, divided equally between seniors and children. The Boffins lent them the two Faulks brothers, Sebastian and Edward. Arthurton raced to 30-odd, at which point he got an edge and the ball stuck in a Budleigh elder's midriff. Afterwards, Edward remarked, "I've been bowling that inswinger for years, and at last I've found a batsman good enough to touch it." He's now a peer, and one would like to think that bagging a West Indian Test player was a factor.

Sadly, the Budleigh fixture re-lapsed, and the Boffins tried various alternatives before, in 2012, finding what appeals as the perfect replacement at Tipton St John: a lovely ground by the river Otter, good-natured hosts, an epic tea and a nearby pub called (a reminder of times past) the Golden Lion.

From Wednesday the tour moves towards Somerset, beginning with the incomparable Recreation Ground at Chardstock, tilted above a beguiling valley. Its pronounced slope has done for many a visiting batsman, shouldering arms to a ball a foot or more outside the off-stump and regretting it a moment later. A fondly remembered Boffins umpire, Chris Poole, used his *London Evening Standard* column to promote the excellence of Chardstock's cream teas. Self-interest was involved: Poole had the silhouette of a well-lunched WG Grace. After his first outing with the Boffins, Poole enthused to his fellow racing correspondent, Claude Duval of the *Sun*, about the rich pickings available for a decent off-spinner. At the time, Duval was homing in on 100 wickets for the season in the Sussex leagues and elsewhere. Poole told him the target was "just waiting to be picked up" in Devon. So it was, including an eight-fer at Chardstock – bowling down the slope with four short legs.

There's a photograph from Chardstock which shows the Boffins' and home team's wicket-keepers together. The Boffin is in his late 60s (at least); the Chardstock 'keeper is about ten. He's Julien Fountain, and he became one of the best-known international cricket coaches. His companion is the late TG 'Gordon' Hemming, 40 years or so a player for the Boffins, Emeriti, Free Foresters and many others besides. Even after a reluctant retirement, he continued to keep his gloves and pads in the boot of his car – just in case. Taking leave of Chardstock, it's necessary to note that, as Hemming and many others have found out, it's no place for a wicket-keeper. Byes sometimes top-score.

Chardstock – 'tilted above a beguiling valley'
The bowler is Paul Mathieu, the keeper is his son Mark;
the batsman is wondering which county to hit the ball into.
The missing fielders are probably huddled together at long on.

The same certainly isn't true at the Boffins' Thursday fixture, Kilmington. There, on a tranquil ground in easy reach of the New and Old inns, is a square like a billiards table. There's also strong evidence of the continuity that makes touring cricket so enjoyable. The Boffins now field a third-generation player and several second-generation, and you'd need to go back a long way in the score books to find a Kilmington side vs Boffins without a Lavender or a Rockett in their team. With a quick outfield and a true pitch, Kilmington is a batting idyll, and it's commonplace for 550 runs to be shared in an afternoon there.

The Boffins tour ends at Chard on Friday. The tourists are usually depleted by injury or summonses back to the office. The survivors are flat-footed. There's a collective sadness that the week's finale has arrived. Chard is a tough exit. Like Chardstock, it has a steep slope; many an exhausted Boffins fielder has seemed to be chasing a ball to the uphill boundary, but is barely running on the spot. And Chard is a big club with several Saturday sides, allowing their veteran groundsman Bruce Crabbe to spring the occasional sharp shock as he picks his team.

The Boffins tour is now in its seventh decade; well past middle age, but seemingly good for a few years yet – a feeling encouraged by playing at Tipton St John against a ramrod-straight left-arm spinner, aged 76. The current King Boffin, Bob Lo, is only the third bearer of the title. Part of the tour's attraction is that its members come from far and wide; only a handful play their cricket together in the rest of the summer. The sole qualification is an invitation. So if one day you're resting outside a pavilion, flushed with the century you've just scored or the five-fer freshly taken, and someone sidles up to ask if you're available on the August Bank Holiday Monday, then it's time to take directions down the A303. You might become a Boffin.

Lord's Taverners

Founded: 1950

by Richard Anstey

Such is the fame of the Lord's Taverners the length and breadth of the cricket world that it is easy to forget that the club's founders were just that: actors, writers and other artistic types who enjoyed watching cricket from the old Tavern at Lord's, pint of beer in hand. It was an opera singer turned jobbing actor called Martin Boddey who, in the summer of 1949, had the notion of putting this fellowship of like-minded individuals onto a more formal basis, to play cricket matches and raise a few bob for the National Playing Fields Association in the process. He was encouraged by the initial response of fellow Tavernites Spike Hughes and Michael Shepley but, according to Leslie Frewin, in his *Tavern in the Town*, it was the enthusiasm shown by the actor Bruce Seton that was the clincher. It was one thing to have a bright idea; quite another to find someone, in Seton, who was prepared to do everything he could to make it a reality.

Between them, the two actors drummed up supporters, not just in the Tavern itself but seemingly in half the pubs of London. One such was Captain Jack Broome, who had served in the navy with Prince Philip and thought he might be interested. Through the good offices of Lt-Commander Michael Parker, the Prince's Equerry, an audience was arranged, at which Prince Philip was asked if he might be prepared to serve as the club's first President. That would be too big a commitment, he replied, but he would be willing to act as Patron.

Leslie Frewin takes up the story:

> The overjoyed visitors prepared to take their leave. Before doing so, they casually mentioned that the honorary and honourable position of 'Twelfth Man' had been hopefully left vacant. Much amused, Prince Philip inquired the significance of the position. He was told – if he needed to be told! – that the traditional duties of that indispensable and always keenest member of a cricket side were to (a) carry the bag from the station, (b) look after the score-book, (c) bring out the drinks, (d) 'sub' in the field, and (e) run for anybody who didn't feel like it after lunch ... 'Exactly what I thought you meant,' he said, and thereupon claimed the right to fill the role!

Thus royally patronised, Boddey and co called a meeting of their supporters in the Circle Bar of the Comedy Theatre, Panton St, Haymarket on 3 July 1950 to put their new venture on a proper basis. The name was agreed, draft rules ratified and the foundation stone laid for all of the Taverners' subsequent charitable giving when it was agreed that the entrance fee 'shall be a donation to the National Playing Fields Association.'

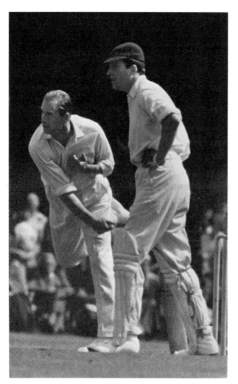

Prince Philip – during and after the game

In the early days, the NPFA (also a favourite cause of Prince Philip) was the only charity that the Taverners supported, most of the money going towards the installation of artificial pitches. But it gave the club a charitable purpose which, far more than any link with the acting profession or fondness for drinking in the various Lord's Taverns, has been its raison d'être ever since.

By the time of the first annual dinner in September 1951, the Lord's Taverners had developed a membership and programme of activities that are mirrored in much of what is done today. Within the first year the membership included Laurence Olivier, Jack Hawkins, Trevor Howard and Richard Attenborough from the world of acting, alongside John Arlott, Brian Johnston, FR Brown, AER Gilligan, RC Robertson-Glasgow, Rex Alston and Sir Pelham Warner from cricket. This eclectic mix of show business and cricket continues to form the core of the club, although other sports, notably golf, are now well represented, as is the world of big business.

The first ball at the Grosvenor House in April 1951 was a huge success, raising £1,000 for the NPFA. Princess Elizabeth and Prince Philip attended, and a cricket match between the Lord's Taverners and the Rest of the World took place in the middle of the dance floor, with commentary by John Arlott. Law 1, coined for the occasion, read 'The batsman is out when and if the umpire decides he ought to be out; such dismissal shall be entered as "umpired out".'

The next milestone in the Lord's Taverners' history was its first proper cricket match on 12 July 1952 against Bishops Stortford CC. From this developed the celebrity cricket matches, which continue to be one of the core fund-raising activities. The make-up of these teams remains a judicious mixture of former Test and county cricketers, together with stars of stage, screen and sound, along with those from other sports. If the great cricketers of recent years are now largely precluded from turning out for the Lord's Taverners regularly by their contracts with BBC, Sky or Channel 4, celebrity cricket continues to make a substantial contribution to the club's overall fundraising.

Celebrity cricket
Disc jockey Pete Murray and comedian Norman Wisdom collide in mid-pitch

The target of raising more than £100,000 in a season was first hit when the former Kent wicketkeeper Derek Ufton was cricket chairman from 1982-94. His successor, John Price, the former Middlesex and England fast bowler, ensured that this figure was comfortably exceeded every year, his best season being 2000 when over £200,000 was raised from 17 matches. Since then, the amount raised each year has gradually increased, recession notwithstanding, to the extent that over £250,000 was achieved annually under the chairmanship of Roger Oakley (2004-12). Martyn Ball, the former Gloucestershire all-rounder, is the current chairman of cricket.

The club's 21st birthday in 1971 was celebrated in style, with a dinner at the Mansion House in the presence of the Lord Mayor of London. But if the Lord's Taverners was at this time still a club with a small membership largely confined to the south-east of England, the appointment of Captain Tony Swainson RN as the secretary, later director, in 1972 was swiftly to change all that.

Swainson's lasting contribution was to turn the Taverners from being essentially a club, to being a club and a charity, without losing in any way the special atmosphere and camaraderie that had been built up over the first 21 years. The membership expanded, largely through the new category of 'Friends of The Lord's Taverners' – a sort of half-way house to full membership. And there was gradual expansion outwards from London, through the development of a series of regional bases, of which there are now 25, all of them vibrant fund-raising entities in their own right, contributing a large percentage of current income.

In 1987 the Lady Taverners was set up, and in 2012 celebrated their 25th anniversary. Over that period, they have raised over £12 million for the charity and there are now 24 Lady Taverners' regions around the country.

Next on Swainson's agenda was an expansion of the charitable remit. While support for youth cricket now extended well beyond funding for non-turf pitches and junior cricket bags and has remained a core activity to this day, the charity added a major string to its bow in 1975 when it first channelled money towards providing recreation for young people with disabilities.

The new programme initially focused on the provision of the Lord's Taverners' trademark green minibuses which provide recreational opportunities for organisations looking after young people with special needs. The delivery of the 1,000th minibus in 2012 was a vivid testimony to the success of the programme. More slowly, but equally vitally, a programme of providing sporting opportunities for young people with disabilities was built up alongside the minibuses. The focus today is on supporting disabled youngsters through the junior wheelchair sports development programme, sensory rooms and outdoor play spaces. In 2002 the Sports Wheelchair Sponsorship Scheme was set up, Patron Dame Tanni Grey Thompson. To date the charity has funded over 800 wheelchairs.

The way the LTs spend the funds they raise on cricket is constantly under review, but the focus is firmly on providing more and better opportunities for young people to play the game. The club works closely with the England and Wales Cricket Board (ECB). In addition to the non-turf pitch programme for clubs with youth sections and schools, the LTs now give away 1,000 bags of Youth (Under-16), Colts (Under-13) and Junior (Under 11) cricket equipment each year as well as a girl's bag and a softball bag.

In late 1999, the Brian Johnston Memorial Trust was taken under the Lord's Taverners' wing and became its sole corporate trustee. The BJMT has twin objectives, complementary to but different from the club's, of providing scholarships to promising young cricketers in financial need and helping blind cricketers. The BJMT also supports the ECB's national spin-bowling programme at county academy and university level. We are sure that Johnners (Taverner no.160, elected 18 December 1951) would have approved. He more than anyone epitomised the Taverner spirit of having fun while working for a serious purpose.

Very many distinguished cricketers have turned out for the Taverners' cricket teams over the years. Mike Denness holds the record for the most runs scored in a career (1,934), with another pillar of the club, Mike Gatting, not far behind; the old Middlesex and England fast bowler, John Price, has made the most appearances (129); whilst Len Hutton and Colin Cowdrey – as formidable an alliance of regal English batsmanship as could possibly be conceived – once put on 123 for the club in sweeping all before them against the might of Hoover in 1963. But star performers from other sports, and indeed celebrities from the world of entertainment, have also demonstrated noteworthy cricketing prowess in Taverners' colours. Chris Tarrant is high on the list of run-scorers, Harry Secombe once added exactly 100 in the urbane company of Neil Durden-Smith, and the record for the highest partnership by professional sportsmen other than cricketers is held by two legends of Welsh rugby: JPR Williams and Barry John, who put on 78 against the whipping boys of Hoover in 1988. The great Bill Edrich holds the record for the most wickets in an innings, with 8/42, although neither William Franklyn's 6/44 nor Ian Carmichael's 5/27 are to be sniffed at.

Since the late 1970s, in addition to all the games played in the UK, the Taverners have played cricket all around the world, including Canada, Hong Kong, Dubai, Corfu,

Arsenal's Bob Wilson

Monte Carlo, Menorca, Paris, The Hague, Berlin, Florida and California. Probably the strongest Taverners' side ever to take the field was the eleven assembled by Roger Oakley to exact revenge on the Fly Emirates XI in Dubai in 2005, after an unexpected defeat at Windsor Castle the previous season. The team that took the field that day included nine England cricketers, in Mike Gatting, John Snow, Derek Underwood, John Emburey, Rob Bailey, Chris Adams, Graham Roope, Tim Munton and John Stephenson, plus Zimbabwe's Andy Flower, Gloucestershire's Andy Stovold, and Tim Rice as 12th man to bowl slow left-arm when Underwood got tired. Ah, the best laid plans of mice and men and all that: after the Emirates had made 193 for six in their 35 overs, they shot out the Taverners' all-stars for a humiliating 63. But there were no hard feelings, as is evidenced by the fact that the match against the Emirates at Windsor and the return in Dubai have since become regular fixtures, in which the Emirates still lead the Taverners, by 14 wins to ten.

Ainsley Harriott and Devon Malcolm

But of all cricket's wandering clubs, this is the one to which results probably matter least of all. For the Lord's Taverners, cricket is a means to an end, not an end in itself, the end being to give disadvantaged and disabled young people the chance to fulfil their potential through sport. In that they have succeeded triumphantly, at the same time as bringing a great deal of pleasure to countless cricket lovers, as well as, not least, having a lot of fun themselves along the way.

Website: *www.lordstaverners.org*

Almondbury Casuals

Founded: 1952

by David Walker

Over one hundred years after the formation of I Zingari, in readiness for the 1952 season, four enthusiastic young cricketers invited 21 of their friends, relatives and colleagues to meetings held in the Woolpack pub, Almondbury, near Huddersfield, to discuss the proposal 'that next Summer the Almondbury Casuals should become a small cricket club and should be put on a more organised basis.' The four founders took turns to be skipper (getting a side out, managing the game and providing a tea) and were the nucleus of the committee, under the chairmanship of Phillip Haigh (1952-1960).

The first Sunday home fixtures, played at Thurstonland CC, were against WR Wanderers (a nomadic West Riding team), the Stafford Arms (a pub in Stainborough, near Barnsley), The Old Boys (Huddersfield RUFC) and The Amateurs (Huddersfield Amateur Association Football Club). Away games included RAF Lindholme with Len Hutton, where the entertainment in the officers' mess was much appreciated. Harry Taylor, headmaster of the King James Grammar School, was approached about a pitch and maybe an outdoor net. He became a Casual in 1953.

Those 25 members, and subsequent 1950s and 1960s recruits, knew each other well through work, family, marriage and leisure (rugby, soccer, golf, hockey and the Borough gentleman's club). The names of their businesses read like a directory of Huddersfield textiles: E Haigh (wool merchants), Jarmain & Sons (scourers), Z Hinchliffe (spinners), Learoyd & Sons (worsteds), Robinson & Co (dyeing) and Shires & Co (vertical mills that did some or all of the processes). Supply businesses were also represented: Broadbent's hydro-extraction, Whitley's loom and mule makers, Garnett's card cloth manufacture and Brook Motors. Add in accountants, bankers, builders, medics, architects, funeral directors, teachers, printers and caterers and the Casuals membership looks like a slice of Huddersfield's sporting middle classes. Many were newly returned from war service. Prior to the war, most had learned their cricket away at school. Some had continued at university. They didn't claim to be good cricketers; there was no desire to play against strong sides and they lost more games than they won. The amateur ethos was important and enjoyment of each other's company was paramount.

Guy Overton (Chairman 1961-1964) summarised The Casuals' purpose 'to form a team of cricket lovers ... Sunday was the chosen day, when wives, fiancées and girlfriends could all join together for a happy, convivial and social afternoon/evening together.'

In the 1960s, due to an influx of league cricketers who enjoyed a run-out on a Sunday, the Casuals' performances improved. Jack Taylor (Kirkburton), Billy Bolt (Bradley Mills) and Alan Priestley (Thurstonland) were joined by Richard Taylor, the headmaster's son, who first played when he was 14 and went on to a league career with Almondbury and Old Almondburians.

These then were the strengths: playing purely for enjoyment, great networks and contacts, strong leaders with sound organisational skills, and no property to argue over. Regularly changing skippers ensured fresh blood, especially if a team could not be raised from current members. Friends and colleagues were invited and, if they fitted in after two or three games, they became members too, the rules of membership being adjusted appropriately. When textiles declined and the early members retired or moved on, they were replaced by sons and nephews, friends from rugby and other local sports and professional and business contacts. There were more league men, notably Rod Kelly, who enjoyed less competitive Sunday cricket, and there was always room for hopeless cricketers who simply loved the game and the craic.

One further strength was needed to complete the picture: good fixtures in delightful locations, against strong and/or clubbable opposition. Starting with fewer than ten games per season, the list grew to 18 in 1968, gradually increased to 27 in the 1990s, and then back to 15 or so by 2009.

You cannot overstate the virtues of friendly cricket in beautiful settings, yet it is so hard to describe precisely. It's not all alcohol and slapstick. Nor is it about results. The memories of Casuals' stalwarts are as good a way as any of capturing the essence of the club. Guy Overton remembers that once the opening partnership was broken on a Sunday afternoon, everyone down to number 11 would get padded up. Michael Hallas, who was chairman in the late 1960s, recalls Philip Haigh's remarkable recruitment skills: 27 in all, and enough to guarantee that we could field at least eight players every Sunday, even if three of them were wicket-keepers.

President's XI v Chairman's XI, Thongsbridge, September 2005

Then there are the grounds we played on, like Dorney Reaches at Windsor, where Guy Overton has fond memories of lobster at the Hind's Head in Bray, with next day a lunchtime session in the Pineapple, followed by a match which might be interrupted from time to time as a herd of cows made their slow way across the meadow. For David Pedley, chairman 1977 to '94, the best place to play was Tusmore Park, arranged by his friends, the Stephenson brothers. The ground was idyllic, situated in the middle of the park near the mansion, with its pavilion and sheltering trees. The result always seemed to matter even less than usual, such was the hospitality and good fellowship.

We had our characters as well, like Jack Wade, who hadn't played for 20-odd years before he joined us as a scorer, and didn't take the field for another season and a half, whereupon he spent most of his time fielding with his ankles. Or Roy Saunders, remembered by Tim Beaumont (chairman 1994-2000) as "a man who couldn't walk down the nave of an abbey without wondering if it took spin".

I think of Burge (John Burgess), almost impaling his backside on the stumps at the bowler's end as he backed into them to take a throw from the deep, or Rupert Wilson and Will Ward opening the batting together, the former crashing it to all parts, the latter prodding and poking it about so painfully that, if it hadn't have been for the tavern, some of us watchers would have lost the will to live.

Two men have played and been involved in running the Casuals through five decades and more. First, Jim Netherwood, who became a Casual around 1956. His last game was in 2004 or thereabouts, when he turned out for us one Saturday morning at Paddock CC against touring side, Wealdstone Corinthians. It was an annual tribute to his son, Stephen, a Wealdstone player, who died in 1992. Between 1956 and 2004, Jim was a Casuals skipper, chairman from 1969 to 1976, a regular at committee meetings well into the 1990s and the writer of *Cricket in Perspective*. For nearly 40 years he was the archetype Casual: an enthusiastic if limited cricketer. He died in 2010.

Second, Alan Priestley, who is the Casuals' most valuable player. Around 1968, Jim Netherwood asked him to play one week when the Casuals were short. He was still playing in the early noughties. He also served on the committee for many years and helped set up the tours to Helmsley, including a round of golf next to Ampleforth School. With over 5,000 runs in 227 innings, including three centuries, and 1,093 wickets, he has made more appearances, scored more runs, and taken more wickets than any other Casual.

It is not easy to keep a wandering club going these days, what with the gradual reduction in the rich networks of the 1950s and 1960s, low replacement rates through family, work and local sports clubs (with the honourable exception of Huddersfield RUFC), the abundance of other attractions and a culture which isn't always appreciated by the modern cricketer. Sadly, the Casuals had to suspend their fixtures in 2012 and the future looks uncertain. But whatever happens, we who have known Casuals cricket have been left with a host of wonderful memories of delightful grounds, clubbable opponents and glorious days of friendly cricket in the sunshine, in which enjoyment of the game comes first, and the result a distant second.

Grannies

Founded: 1956

by Mark Pougatch

A good lunch cannot often have been the sole reason for the birth of a wandering cricket club, but that was certainly the case with the Grannies. In the summer of 1956 three undergraduates playing for Corpus Christi College in Cambridge found their movements and reflexes a little slower in the afternoon session while fielding in the covers, so much so that, as another drive pierced this ring of silk, an exasperated captain cried out, "You lot are fielding like a load of grannies."

In truth the three students – my father Michael Pougatch, Michael Broke and David Ramsbotham – hadn't by then found a cricket club that appealed to their characteristics: a club where the purpose of the game was, of course, to try to win but also where everyone had the chance to contribute with bat or ball and, just as importantly, enjoy themselves. The Grannies adopted this as their raison d'être from the off and created a rocking chair as their emblem and a suitable motto to go with it : 'Unbending but unbowed'.

Early matches were played against schoolmasters' elevens including an annual match at Malvern, Michael Pougatch's old school, which provided many players in the first

An early game at Corpus Christi College, Cambridge
Standing: Michael Preece, John Bloxcidge, John Hamilton, Graeme Buckingham,
Jeremy Hogben, Tony Peel, Chris Minter, Albert Jaggard (umpire and head porter at Corpus).
Sitting: Tony Bromage, Peter Nicholson. On the ground: Michael Broke, Michael Pougatch

few years and where the late George Chesterton always ensured a healthy opposition. The fixture list for the first decade or so totalled about a dozen games, but that changed when Michael Pougatch moved his family to the East Sussex village of Stonegate in 1966. Spotting a suitable field on the edge of the village, he asked the parish council whether he could turn it into a cricket ground and was told, "Yes, as long as you re-start the village team as well."

Thus for the next quarter of a century he was chairman of the village club as well as, paradoxically, ensuring his wandering club had a home base for a good dozen fixtures a year. That helped widen the fixture list so that, in addition to the village sides they faced in the south-east, they could play some of the established wandering sides of the time like Stragglers of Asia and the Invalids and some esoteric sides like the Wine Trade. That all-day game had a slightly lop-sided look: two and a half hours for lunch, to test out exactly what the opposition had brought with them, and a quick 20-minute tea interval.

Although by the late '60s Michael Pougatch was the driving force behind the Grannies, there was always a huge team effort behind him. His great friend Tim Villiers-Smith was like a second groundsman and on many a Friday afternoon before a game Michael's wife, Sonia, could be found gang-mowing the outfield. As a boy I helped my father paint the creases, put out the boundary markers and set up the bar. The Grannies were pulling off the trick of being a thriving wandering club which also had a permanent base that clubs enjoyed visiting.

Undoubtedly part of the attraction was quite simply the best tea in the whole of the south-east. At about 3.45 every match day, a green wheelbarrow powered by a large orange wheel would appear on the outfield and Mary James, known simply to one and all as 'Mrs James', would start unloading her winning fare of jam butties, chocolate cake, coffee cake, coconut macaroons and plates of sandwiches, each plateful labelled with a little flag atop a cocktail stick. Many a fast bowler, having over-indulged in Mrs James' legendary tea, was unable to open the bowling.

The club also enjoyed touring in the '70s and '80s with a trip to Corfu in 1974, to Hong Kong in 1981 and some years later to the Maldives where they were greeted as if MCC themselves had arrived. More recently Portugal, Paris and Scotland have enjoyed exposure to Grannies' cricket and the Parisienne boulevards are preparing for another visit in 2013.

The Grannies' great strength has always lain in its ability to adapt to the current times. Hence it managed the transition smoothly from a small fixture list to a wider 40 games a season when Stonegate was in full swing, and it had to face another challenge when Michael Pougatch died in 1991, aged 57. With his passing and the retirement of Tim Villiers-Smith – but not before he'd taken 1,000 wickets for the club – the decision was ultimately taken to give Stonegate up as a permanent home and resume a more traditional wandering life. Several key figures played a hugely important role in stabilising the club at a time when its future could have been in jeopardy: Nigel Draffan proved a rock as chairman, the late Michael Rogers carried on his excellent work and the current chairman Bob Percival – when not playing in the Lawyers' World Cup – continues to keep wicket with style and lead the club from the front.

The Grannies on tour in Devon, c. 1980
back: Joe Frampton, Anthony Sykes, Michael Broke, Nigel Creffield, Michael Bluett,
Julian Mercer   front: John Rayer, Henry Beckwith, Vera Broke,
Caroline Creffield, Martin Lindsay, Andrew Don, Geraint Norris

Today the Grannies' fixture list remains in the 35-40 games a season bracket with a healthy mix of village sides, some old boys' sides and traditional clubs. There are heavyweight fixtures against clubs like the Band of Brothers, the Hurlingham Club and the Yellowhammers. The Grannies can field an extremely good eleven when the occasion demands it but, because the club's appeal has always been based on its insistence that everyone should enjoy their cricket, whatever their ability, the diversity of the fixture list means every cricketer will always find a game that suits their needs.

This means the Grannies have always been a very popular club with about 150 players over a season and a very inexpensive club as well. Subs are just £18 a year and students play for free. It has also been a very inclusive club right from the start, actively encouraging wives, girlfriends and children to come along and watch and have tea. Many a Granny cricketer has graduated from a game on the boundary's edge while watching to pulling on the rocking-chair cap. The probationary rules are also very straightforward: know someone who will invite you to play, enjoy yourself and then ask to play again.

Perhaps not surprisingly for a club born out of camaraderie, the Grannies know how to celebrate their milestones. From a 25th anniversary party on the Thames, to the 50th in the Long Room at Lord's and an evening's racing at Goodwood, to the 55th at The Oval. Some 57 years after that shambolic fielding display in Cambridge, they are still smiling as they play.

Website: *www.thegrannies.org.uk*

Badgers

Founded: 1958

by Anthony Gibson

The Badgers got their name almost by accident. They were going to be called Willows, until someone discovered that that had been taken, several times over, and they needed a name to fit with their colours of black and white. But it was a happy accident, for badgers are highly sociable animals, living in extended families and can be fierce or playful as the mood takes them. As in nature, so in cricket. For this companionable, clannish and sometimes distinctly competitive cricket club, the name Badgers could hardly be more appropriate.

The club has its roots in south-west London, Sutton to be precise. In 1958 members of the Lind Road Methodist Church Youth Club and the Belmont Methodist Church Club were challenged to a game of cricket at Epsom by members of Banstead Methodist Church. Whilst the outcome has not survived, the game was evidently a success, for the following winter, over a late-night rubber of bridge, some of the leading protagonists decided to put their cricket on a permanent basis by forming a club. So the following March, at a meeting at Belmont Methodist Church, the Willows CC was duly formed: captain Mike Law, vice-captain Alan Preston, chairman Derek Beadle and secretary Laurence Pitts. It became the Badgers at the subsequent committee meeting.

The first game was against Riverside from Battersea on the Morden Sports Ground on 19 May 1959. It was lost, heavily, as were all too many of the early encounters. Founder member, current president and father of the present captain, Roy Gordon remembers that: "In the early days, matches were often over before tea. Badgers were pleased to reach three figures when batting as scores below 100 were frequent. So we then had a ten-over-a-side match with everyone having to bowl an over."

For such wins as they did secure, they could usually thank Brian Moore, an erstwhile Essex triallist, who bowled fast and hit hard. He set the tone as early as the club's third game (his first), when he took eight wickets, and made the national press in 1966 with the remarkable figures of ten wickets for two runs against Montrose. He was the leading run-scorer and wicket-taker in the 1960s and topped the bowling performances again in the '70s and '80s, before eventually being forced to retire by knee problems in 1992. All told, he scored 5,827 runs for the Badgers at 26.9 and took 965 wickets at a remarkable 6.9.

The Badgers' first president – and a significant benefactor in many ways – was Frank Butt, the first of four generations to be involved with the club. His son, Allan, who also played in that first season, is the current chairman, still playing regularly at 72, alongside Frank's grandson and great-grandson on the distaff side, Steve and Darrell Pitts. Other early members were Mike Law, who scored the club's first century, the aforementioned Roy Gordon, a wicket-keeper so enthusiastic that he would scream an appeal even if all three stumps were lying flat on the ground, and Laurence Pitts, who was the heart and soul of the club, off the field as well as on it. And how could we possibly ignore Barry Passmore, a club stalwart for over twenty years and treasurer for six, who lived at Stump Cottage, Square Drive?!

After struggling to raise sides throughout the 1960s, the Badgers enjoyed almost an embarrassment of playing riches through the 1970s, and results improved accordingly. Brent Noble made a stack of runs, out-scoring even Brian Moore, while the Tickner brothers, Alan and David, were major contributors with both bat and ball, both of them going on to be popular and effective captains in the '70s and '80s and David to write a distinctly off-beat history of the club to celebrate its 21st birthday. Besides listing the usual club records, this also celebrates some less conventional achievements, like the 'swimming record' awarded to Steve Goldman, for making it across the Thames after the match against Sunbury in 1977 to win a £5 bet, or the 'throwing the cricket bat' record, which went to Brent Noble for his performance against the BBC in 1976.

I suppose it was inevitable, given their name and their fondness for beer, that a link would eventually be forged between Badgers CC and Hall and Woodhouse's Badger Brewery in Dorset. This duly came about in 1980, when the team made its first expedition to Blandford Forum, followed by several similar excursions through the 1980s. I daresay that the following note by Richard Kemp captures the general ambience of these affairs pretty well: "coach trip in rain – plied with beer, team paralytic in brewery bar – still won." Having got the taste for breweries, further tours would follow to Hook Norton in the Cotswolds and the villages around, including many memorable stays at the Lygon Arms, Chipping Campden.

Alan and David Tickner shared the captaincy through the 1980s with Simon Fox, a decade that was marked by the outstanding batting of Chris Morgan – 2,942 runs at an average of just over 40 – and the first instance of a Badger being called up for international duty. This was Adrian Cowell, who was selected to play for Japan against Vanatu in a World Cup pre-qualifier and, in Dave Tickner's words, "on opening the batting, received two consecutive beamers from their opening bowler who just happened to be their Olympic javelin thrower!" Simon Fox also played international cricket, in friendlies for both Thailand (against Hong Kong) and Mexico (against Belize).

The departure of Simon Fox and Adrian Cowell at the end of the 1989 season marked a significant change in Badgers' personnel. Of the regulars at the start of the decade, only the Tickner brothers and the new captain, Steve Pitts (son of Laurence), remained at the end of it. Among many useful cricketers who took the places of the old guard was Mark Gordon, son of Roy, who, in Steve Pitts' words, has developed into "arguably the best all-round cricketer who has ever played for the club" – which is some accolade.

Mark took over as captain in 2001 and has led from the front, as leading wicket-taker, outstanding fielder and second only to Patrick Redding with the bat. While wandering clubs have lost a lot of players to league cricket, Patrick is an interesting example of a cricketer who has gone the other way, having come across the Badgers through their website whilst in search of friendlier cricket. He certainly found it, and enjoyed it to the extent that he scored five centuries in his first two seasons, contributing to what was something of a purple patch in the club's results on the field. The Badgers have always liked to win, and, apart from the early days, have usually won more than they've lost – played 957, won 427, lost 290, to be precise. But it is central to the club's ethos that, whilst it's good to win, it's much more important to play the game in the right spirit.

The Badgers initially played most of their games at Rose Hill recreation ground in Sutton; that was until the local council decided that tennis was more important than cricket. Other suburban clubs have suffered similarly, as costs have escalated and standards of ground maintenance fallen away to little more than a cursory mow. So the Badgers tend now to wander through the villages of Surrey, rather than the suburbs of London, playing 20 or so Sunday games a season, and the occasional 20-over thrash on a weekday evening. They are popular visitors, thanks not least to the amount that they put over the bar after close of play.

The secret of the Badgers' success? Steve Pitts, who's been a Badger all his life, and whose son Darrell is the third generation of Butt/Pitts to play for the club, puts it down to friendship and family at one level, and good organisation, not least through the club's excellent website, at another. "Basically, we're a bunch of mates who love our cricket. The thread of continuity provided by the family connections – Mark Gordon's pre-teenage son Jake has already played 32 games for the club – combined with the fact that new players are generally friends of existing players, helps to keep it all together."

Simon Fox thinks that getting everyone involved in the game has a lot to do with it – "the 'long leg both ends, number 11, did not bowl' doesn't feature – unless the game is rained off and there's a pub at both ends!" To Dave Tickner, with 489 Badgers appearances under his belt, it is "the perfect balance struck between trying to win and having an enjoyable afternoon amongst friends." But whatever it is, it seems to work. This is a thriving, successful, happy wandering club of the modern era.

Website: *www.badgerscc.org.uk*

back: Alan Wilkes, Ian Gregg, Mark Gordon, Barry Davenport, Dave Tickner,
David Aldwinckle, Richard Kemp, Mick Willmott
front: Keith Miller, Darren Hanley, Steve Pitts, Alan Tickner, Graham Davenport

Saints

Founded: 1959

by John Raybould

In the early hours of Easter Sunday 1959, three cricketing enthusiasts and friends decided to form a club with a membership of people with whom they wanted to play cricket. Cricketing ability was taken for granted as a qualification for membership, but just as important was that the members should be thoroughly decent blokes. And so it was that, with the considerable assistance of the remarkable administrative skills of Desmond Bailey, who was to become a prominent member of the Yorkshire County Club, members were recruited and fixtures arranged. Originally these were with leading clubs, schools and touring sides in the north, but as the club grew and thrived so the net was extended further south, taking in prominent clubs like Hampstead, Harrow Wanderers and Eton Ramblers.

The key to the development of such a strong fixture list was the cricketing calibre of the club's membership. What made the Saints unusual as a wandering club was that its public school and university players were augmented by an impressive group of professionals, mostly from Yorkshire. Before long, the club could boast a whole host of Test players, including Fred Trueman, Brian Bolus, Philip Sharpe, Richard Hutton, Alan Smith, John Hampshire, Peter Parfitt, 'Pom Pom' Fellows-Smith from South Africa, Don Brennan, Geoff Cope and Don Wilson. The Saints also provided valuable experience for young Yorkshire Second XI hopefuls, such as Andrew Dalton, Peter Kippax, Barrie Leadbeater and Brian Bainbridge, all of whom went on to play for Yorkshire with distinction.

So high was the standard of Saints' cricket that the mighty Yorkshire county side would play them in a two-day warm-up match before the start of every season. It was in one of these matches, when Trueman was actually captaining the Saints, that Geoffrey Boycott took it upon himself to bat for the entire second day, for 96, not out of course. Even Fred was almost rendered speechless – but not quite!

The fixture list also had an international flavour, with matches against two very powerful South African touring sides, the Wanderers from Johannesburg and the Grasshoppers from Natal, as well as a game against All Holland, in the run-up to a World Cup.

The Saints has always been run as a benevolent autocracy. The committee saw to it that no one, not even the great Trueman, could be admitted to membership without playing the obligatory three qualifying matches, and took to holding the AGMs in secret, to make it as difficult as possible for any troublesome members to attend. Never has a club been run more smoothly!

Yorkshire being Yorkshire, so-called 'friendly' cricket has been at a premium. League cricket has always dominated, and has always attracted the best players. But, fortunately for the Saints, league matches were played on a Saturday, leaving Sunday free for less competitive encounters. Not that the standard wasn't very high. Matches were played against some of the stronger league clubs, as well as the likes of the Yorkshire Gentlemen and Craven Gentlemen and leading local schools. The standing of the club also made it possible to find grounds on which touring clubs from the south, or overseas, could be entertained, not least because it was well known that a Saints fixture was a guarantee of good bar takings!

Midweek cricket was very much a feature of the Saints' early years, as was enthusiastic post-match socialising, before the advent of the breathalyser made every fixture an away game. Many are the Yorkshire hostelries whose takings have been boosted by a Saints Annual Dinner over the years, and memorable was the entertainment for the members who attended, much of it provided by the inimitable Fred Trueman, who was in his element. The annual dinners continue to thrive, still drawing members from across the county and still able to attract first-rate speakers, who don't seem at all put off by the reputation which these occasions have for barracking which is at least the equal of the Sydney Hill! It would certainly make a good preparation for Prime Minister's Questions, even if the club cannot yet claim an MP amongst its members, although we do boast the recently retired President of MCC, Phillip Hodson.

Social changes, the rise of one-day cricket, the plethora of local league competitions and the trials of travelling have all taken their toll on the Saints' fixture list in recent years, so that from 20 games a season the club now plays only six. But membership is still strong, with 60 playing members, plus qualifiers, 80 retired members and 10 Honorary Life Members, our surviving Test players. And if the cricketing side of the club's activities may have been in decline, the social side is as important as ever, providing as it does plenty of opportunities for like-minded people from across Yorkshire to gather and bemoan the death of proper cricket.

back: Harry Neilson, Richard Hodson, Charlie Metcalfe, Martin Laidler,
Edward Broadley, Charlie Cowell, William Hodson, Mark Cowell, Graham Wilson
front: Richard Hutchinson, Phillip Hodson, Chris Farrell

Jack Frost XI

Founded: 1961

by David Lipop

The Jack Frost XI was founded in 1961 by HAC 'Tony' Gill who agreed to raise a side to play against the Leverets, a team who played on a small ground with a matting wicket outside the Swan Inn at Claygate, Surrey. This inaugural match, played on a sunny day 'out of season' on 4 October, set the tone for the future XI. The match was such a success that Tony and his team were invited to return the following year, as well as playing two fixtures against other clubs.

Tony reasoned that, having played in the autumn when frost may occur at any time, the name would be appropriate. In 1963 Ockham CC was added to the fixture list and in this match one of the great traditions of Jack Frost cricket originated: the Man of the Match award – a triple Scotch to be downed in one! For the club tie Tony remembered a character in the *Rupert Bear* strip cartoon named Jack Frost and designed the silver figure on a green ground as the club logo. Ties were presented to players who had played all three matches in 1962. In later years a baggy green cap with a silver Froster was designed and still worn to this date.

A constitution was drawn up which had as its aim to 'extend the season at both ends'. Subject to committee approval, an invitation and the playing of three matches would qualify a player for membership. Frost sought to find opponents where it was thought all would have a good time in the bar afterwards. The club elected to play most matches on Sundays when they would not be poaching players from their regular clubs, and in 1968 a match manager system was adopted, which still operates.

By the mid-sixties 20 matches a season were being played, mainly in Surrey, Sussex, Hampshire and Kent, and the extended season games attracted a host of good players keen to play more cricket of our kind. Warnham CC, our oldest fixture, dates from this time as well as long-standing fixtures against Ockham, Thursley, Blackheath, Reigate Pilgrims and Rudgwick. By the early seventies the Jack Frost XI were prepared to take on a number of stronger clubs, mainly in their cricket weeks. By this time, membership had reached over 100 (which is where it is today), many of them good club cricketers who were available to play midweek.

In 1964 another great Frost tradition was started – touring. To date, 30 domestic tours have been undertaken. The first was to the New Forest in 1964, playing Ringwood and Burley. We did not return to the New Forest until the late 1970s, then 1990 and again in 2003. Many of the New Forest matches were played on New Year's Day, and we also played regular matches on Boxing Day in the 1970s and 1980s. Over the years that followed, Frost toured Dorset, the Midlands, Wiltshire, Northern Ireland, Alderney, Scotland, Norfolk, Cambridgeshire, Devon and Essex. The first overseas tour was to Eire in 1970 where matches were played against Cork County, Waterford and the South of Ireland. Besides the visit to Alderney, the club also toured Spain for three years from 1994.

However, the crowning glory of the early years came in 1975 when the Jack Frost XI toured California. A tour committee, with various areas of expertise, did a wonderful job organising and obtaining sponsorship for a three-week tour based in Los Angeles. A party of 31 departed from Gatwick Airport in a snow storm, and a day later a warm-up fixture was played against Walter Beeney's XI in temperatures nearing 100 degrees.

The following day we were victorious against the Cricket Club of British Columbia who had come down from Vancouver to tour LA. On day three we played Hollywood CC, led by an Englishman who had the Rolls-Royce franchise for Southern California and who went on to become Ian Botham's agent. Twelve matches were scheduled including the University of California Los Angeles, Santa Barbara, San Jose, Marin County and Pasadena. This tour was probably the most successful enterprise ever undertaken by the club and did a great deal to spread its popularity not only in the USA but in English cricket circles.

The next big tour took place in the winter of 1998/99 to Australia, which was planned to coincide with England's visit. Seven fixtures were arranged in and around Sydney for the touring party of thirty, the highlight being the match at the Bradman Oval against Bowral. Frost won three matches and enjoyed receiving and providing great hospitality to our hosts. Since then, Frost have toured five times to Des Ormes, France, twice to the International Sixes Tournament in Sarasota, Florida and three times to the Chiang Mai Sixes in Thailand. In 2006 we played in the Ice Cricket Tournament in Tallinn, Estonia and the following year toured to Latvia. The Jubilee Tour in 2011 was to the island of Vis in Croatia.

The Jack Frost XI are famous for their annual dinners, the first of which was held in 1968. An infamous tradition at the dinner is the award of the Annual Gnome to the member considered to have caused the cock-up of the year. Besides receiving the Gnome statue, which he must display at all matches and events, he has to down in one the infamous 'Traffic Light' drink in one. For 34 years the dinners were chaired by the founder, Tony Gill, and no-one who attended will ever forget his brilliantly eccentric

Intrepid Frosters on tour in Estonia with a local interpreter

*Jubilee Dinner,
Lord's, 2011.
CMJ chats to
club chairman
Nigel Fowler*

delivery and wonderful speeches. Sadly, Tony died in 2011 at the age of 75, his obituary appearing in the 2012 *Wisden*.

The club has also had the good fortune to welcome some distinguished guest speakers over the years, not just from the world of cricket, but from business, sport, the arts and journalism. They have included three Presidents of the MCC and 20 first-class cricketers, 15 of whom were Test players. In November 2011 the Jubilee Dinner was held in the Long Room at Lord's where the 164 members and guests celebrated the 50th Anniversary of the Jack Frost XI. The guest speaker was the immediate past President of the MCC, Christopher Martin-Jenkins.

The activities of the Jack Frost XI have not passed unnoticed by the media over the years. The club's first match in 1961 was recorded in the *Daily Telegraph*, while the BBC filled some of the gap left by the cancellation of racing and football over the snowy new year of 1969 by screening film of the club's match at Burley in *Grandstand*. Photographs of the game appeared in the national press and in some overseas newspapers, and unseasonal cricket produced another television appearance when the club competed in the Ice Cricket Tournament in Tallinn.

The club has also had more than its fair share of mentions on *Test Match Special*, especially when Bill Frindall, who had been a Frost player in the early years, was doing the scoring, although Henry Blofeld also referred to us in commentary in September 2011.

More than 50 years on from the club's foundation, the Jack Frost XI is thriving and continues to qualify new members every year, playing over 20 fixtures each season excluding tours. Declaration cricket may be something of a rarity these days, but it is undoubtedly being greatly enjoyed by a new generation of cricketers, brought up on limited-overs league cricket, when they turn out for the Frost.

It is also heartening for the future of the game that a club which sets such store by playing cricket in the right spirit should be enjoying such success, even in an age when standards of behaviour in cricket more generally are not always as high as they should be.

Website: *www.jackfrostxi.org*

Lord Gnome's XI

Founded: 1963

by Peter Gillman

This is the ideal year to commemorate Lord Gnome's XI's role in wandering cricket, as it is fifty years since our team played its first match in its original guise. Our provenance is closely linked with that of the satirical magazine *Private Eye*, whose first issue appeared in 1961. Although its founders were cast as radicals and subversives, most came from a public school background and so it should come as no surprise that many were keen cricketers. In 1963 the William Rushton XII played the village of Aldworth in Berkshire, home of Richard Ingrams, the magazine's editor. Besides Rushton, the cartoonist who helped found the magazine, other team members from those pioneering years included the radical journalist Paul Foot; the writer (and first editor) Christopher Booker; the actor Roy Kinnear; Peter Jay, future British Ambassador in Washington; the multi-talented Barry Fantoni; the magazine designer Tony Rushton; and the journalist Patrick Marnham. The team formally adopted the name Private Eye CC in 1969, and in 1971 it placed an advertisement in the magazine looking for fixtures, marking the transition from an occasional side to an organised wandering team.

It was Marnham, then fixture secretary, who invited me to play for the team that year, after our paths crossed through journalism. My first match was on a bumpy pitch at Marcham, an Oxfordshire village in some way connected with the literary agent Michael Sissons. By some miracle I scored 50 and took a couple of wickets, which was enough to secure a place. On discovering that the team was looking for more players, I recruited several friends who went on to play for the team for 30 years or more. They included the artist Norman Ackroyd, now an accomplished etcher and print-maker and Fellow of the Royal Academy; the journalist Wynford Hicks (we both wrote for *Isis* at Oxford); and another journalist, Lew Chester, who like me worked for the *Sunday Times*.

Already in the team was the architect and painter Richard Napper, a friend of the *Private Eye* crew. Other long-standing recruits were the architect John Dunthorne; the BBC reporter and marine knick-knack entrepreneur Lynn Lewis; and Matt Cannon, son of journalist Geoffrey Cannon, an aggressive all-rounder and the only one of that early group still playing for the side. He is now its leading run-scorer, wicket-taker and catcher and for a long time had the record innings of 167.

A number of our fixtures were played in or around the Windrush Valley in Oxfordshire, largely because Marnham had asserted his fixture secretary's prerogative to arrange matches near his home. We established an Oxfordshire tour over August Bank Holiday weekend, with matches against the villages of Swinbrook – our longest-standing fixture – and nearby Minster Lovell. Our tradition of camping in Swinbrook's cricket field dates from those days.

We also convened at the Old Vicarage in the village of Asthall Leigh, the home of Andrew Osmond, a founder of *Private Eye* and co-author of a successful thriller with foreign secretary Douglas Hurd. It has been rumoured that not only did alcohol flow but also that sweet-smelling substances were ingested during those balmy nights. If so, that can only be a hangover from the '60s and obviously occurred without the knowledge, let alone consent, of any of the aforementioned personages.

There were other elements to give the team its character. Our cricket was a family affair, with wives and partners welcomed. (Since we were mostly a wandering side, they did not even have to make tea.) Our children attended too and it was natural for them to graduate into the team. My elder son Danny played more than 300 matches, forming a formidable fast-bowling partnership with Matt Cannon, and one of only three bowlers to notch a nine-wicket haul (the others were Norman Ackroyd and the *Private Eye* journalist Martin Tomkinson). Danny's brother Seth played over 100 matches, and enlisted sons included Cal Chester, Tom Napper, Lyndon Lewis and Conan Hicks. The consequent spread of ages has been another appealing characteristic of the team, with teenagers playing alongside old geezers in their sixties, presenting captains with delicate decisions over field placings.

Meanwhile the proportion of real *Private Eye* members dwindled: eventually Tony Rushton was the last survivor. Invitations for fixtures still arrived at the magazine office but we noticed that our hosts appeared disappointed that our sides were conspicuously lacking in satirists or celebrities. For that reason we changed our name to Lord Gnome's XI in 1977, although a separate Lord Gnome's Invitation XI continued to play an annual match against Aldworth until 1984.

During the 1980s our fixture list grew, swelling to more than 30 at its lengthiest. While we retained the rural element, we also played in suburban purlieus such as Sidcup, Norwood and Twickenham. We organised tours to Kent, Cornwall and notably to the Dordogne where Wynford Hicks had a summer home and we played against the British community in Bordeaux – all out for 12, our opponents' lowest ever score. It was in this period that we played our most celebrated match. It took place at Swinbrook on 23 August 1986 and ended in a tie: we were 197-9 dec, Swinbrook were 197 all out. Norman Ackroyd produced an evocative etching, *The Great Match*, to record these events and admitted that, since he had taken seven for 55 with his wily medium-pacers, this was "a disgraceful act of self-indulgence".

We also joined the media circuit, playing teams from what was still Fleet Street or its environs. Our matches against *The Times* and *Sunday Times* were memorable for being played at the magnificent *Times* sports ground at Ravensbourne in Bromley which had been gifted to the staff by the proprietor, Lord Astor, in the 1930s. Sadly the ground did not survive the vandalism of the Murdoch era, as it was sold to property developers who appeared unaware that local planning rules meant it could not be built on. On my last visit several years ago, it was a wasteland with only a rusting roller in the undergrowth to testify to its years of glory.

While the core of the team remained stable, other recruits arrived, including Matt Patten, until recently chief executive of the Lord's Taverners; Mark Feltham, like my son

Norman Ackroyd's etching

Danny a graduate of Jesus College, Cambridge; the script writer Chris Gill; the painter John Butterworth; and restaurant and property magnate Fenton Ramsahoye. There were two sets of brothers: Tom and Nick Godfrey, who for ten years held the partnership record of 192 (for first wicket v Washington in 1998); and Eric and Bernard Chapman. Our guest players have included no fewer than five international women cricketers: Sarah Potter, Cathy Mowat, Claire Taylor, Isa Guha and Issey Cannon.

Throughout this period we reckoned to play within what we regarded as the spirit of wandering cricket. Those of us who have also played league cricket dislike the gamesmanship, sledging, dissent and general bad temper it seems to foster. Although we have been competitive and like to win as much as the next man (or woman), we hope we have accorded our opponents all due respect. We regarded the after-match socialising as a key part of the occasion – drinking at our hosts' bar rather than sloping off to the nearest pub. Since we usually umpired our own innings, we made it a rule to walk for catches behind rather than risk embarrassing our umpire. We had one member who made it clear that he did not feel obliged to walk, so we always gave him out anyway. We still took our cricket seriously enough to practise in the winter nets at the Indoor School at Lord's, and we won the indoor competition for the net teams several times – thus enabling us to make the grandiose claim on our fixture card that we were the World Indoor Cricket Champions.

Although the team contained a predictable number of assertive characters, it has largely been a harmonious fifty years, with two exceptions. The first is the annual blood-letting known as the Annual General Meeting, held for a long time at the infamous *Private Eye* Soho pub the Coach and Horses, when long-held grievances over issues such as the batting order and umpiring decisions erupted to the surface.

The second was what is still referred to as the Great Schism – one of those rifts that can afflict even the most benign of organisations and which occurred during the 1980s. It began as a personality clash and escalated into an all-embracing row over issues from team tactics to members' drinking habits and sexuality. Since I was the team captain (we mostly captained by rota, taking two-year stints at a time) it fell to me to try to resolve matters. After failing to parlay a solution, I proposed that the member I held most to blame should be expelled. My proposal was carried at an emergency meeting by a nerve-racking one-vote margin and he was thrown out. His three leading supporters resigned en masse which at least cleansed the team of one of the offending factions.

I retired from the side in 2004. (Since I have mentioned nearly everyone else, I would like to record that in the 2003 season, when I was 62, I took most wickets, 42, and most fielding catches, 12.) It is reassuring to report that the team has continued its wandering ways – it has now played more than 900 matches and is going strong in the 2013 season – although to my eyes its make-up has changed. John Dunthorne's son Ollie became one of its leading figures, and its players tend to be proficient and fashionable young men like him. They own enormous wheelie cricket bags, wear baggy trousers and reflective sun glasses, and are much given to youthful joshing.

They have established important new records (highest innings, Max Fernie, 174* v Dunsfold in 2008; highest partnership, Fernie and Ollie Dunthorne, 250* for first wicket, same match). They have a Facebook page where they exchange insults with other teams, although two of the oldies – John Dunthorne and myself – have infiltrated the site and post photographs and memories of those golden early days. I have qualified as an umpire and have stood in Gnome matches, which appear to be conducted in the same civilised spirit as when we began. At fifty years we probably still rank as a newcomer among wandering sides. But I look back on matches played in wonderful company and enchanting surroundings that have given me among the most scintillating memories of my life.

Mandarins

Founded: 1963 or 1964

by Michael Richardson

Who is the only freshman to make a century against the Australians for Oxford or Cambridge; and for which wandering side did he subsequently play? A subtle clue to the second question can be gleaned from the title of this chapter; the answer to the first is probably best left to Douglas Miller.

Yet the last thing the Mandarins would expect – or wish – to be remembered for is their cricketing prowess. Their oral tradition is one of cock-ups and disasters, of defeat snatched from the jaws of victory. Yes, there have been seasons with more wins than losses, but the folk memory does not dwell on them. Not that the Mandarins ever took a game less than seriously – far from it; but their survival owes less to that seriousness than to an indispensable sense of humour.

The club emerged, in the obscure way that eccentric British institutions sometimes do, from a civil service training course in the year that Larkin's sexual intercourse began (or in 1964; recollections differ). It (the course, not Larkin's pursuit) was run by the Treasury in an elegant Regency house in Cambridge Terrace NW1. The more athletic trainees fixed up a scratch game in Regent's Park (pitch hire: £1.12s.6d). Unsuspected talents were revealed; the only blight on proceedings was the whiff from a wolf nearby whose ideas of personal hygiene were not well developed.

The first match was played against Kew, on Kew Green, in the late summer of 1964. The defeat set a long-standing precedent. Mandarins were and are a – strictly unofficial – civil service-based team whose administrative ability has often outstripped its playing prowess. Over the years, the Whitehall element became diluted as players privatised themselves, or worked in the wider public sector (BBC, CEGB, NCB), or arrived with a playing qualification almost as nebulous as that needed for international sport. But the boundary chat still exchanges Whitehall gossip, including appreciations of ministers and special advisers.

A fixture list grew by serendipity: clubs in villages where members lived, or had played as an undergraduate, which had pretty grounds and a pub serving real ale. Some clubs remain on the fixture list – Pink Elephants, Thursley, Reading University, Peper Harow, Monks Risborough, Brill, Lords and Commons (Parliament's annual opportunity to put the executive firmly in its place; and it often has). Far more opponents, alas, have fallen by the wayside – among them Kew, Aldworth, Chaldon, Weald, Woldingham, Mayfield, Grannies, Grayshott, Begbroke, Chalgrove, Great Tew. In the '80s, fixtures swung towards the sabbath as clubs' Saturdays were increasingly pre-empted by league cricket. Since then, occasional ventures into limited overs have had tactical consequences – for the art of the declaration, of keeping the opposition in the game by taking somebody off (or putting him on), or of holding out in the gloaming for a dishonourable draw. More recently the list has been refreshed in diverse ways: Brigands host on the hallowed Broadhalfpenny Down, and there is Twenty20 in Battersea Park.

Tours have been a happy feature. There was an early visit to Paris, often recalled but never repeated; was there undiplomatic behaviour? Thereafter, the Mandarins soon settled into the seductive annual rhythm of Suffolk in mid-August, initiated by John Chapman around his home village of Easton. Based initially at The Crown (first in Framlingham, then in Westleton), the team now stays at Framlingham College, its lovely ground overlooked by the castle. A variety of après-cricket has included skinny-dipping at Dunwich and midnight poker; more dependable delights are the coast and heathland, Adnams and medieval churches. In the 1990s there were also tours to North Yorkshire, based at the Royal Oak Tavern in Great Ayton; and now to Dorset, every June, around Shaftesbury.

In the early years, batting stars included Sidney Fremantle, whose energy did so much to establish the club; Robin Butler, later to become the Mandarins' first (of three, so far) Cabinet Secretary (and now club president); John Baker; and Neville Abraham, the first Mandarin to score a century (but not against the Australians). Bowling talent included the Davids Hartridge and Pentecost; and John Coles, subsequently the club's first head of the Diplomatic Service. A noble tradition of rabbitry, which Christopher Roberts modestly claims to have founded, also flourished.

By the mid-'70s left-arm quicks Murphy and Pattison were in their pomp, but in their absence O'Shea had to bowl from both ends; and the batting relied too heavily on Holmes, Hadley and Gavyn Davies (who combined opening with discussion of the money supply). The end of the decade, however, saw the success of *Yes Minister*, an upsurge in Mandarins' fortunes, and then Sir Humphrey's progression to Cabinet Secretary.

A former Cabinet Secretary in action
Gus O'Donnell, 2012

There developed a nexus of young (well, youngish) players who extracted permission to play every week and sometimes twice of a weekend: O'Shea (whose six wickets in six balls once curtailed a promising afternoon at Brill), McIntyre, Lewy, Richardson, Baker, McKeon, and then Eastaway (whose book explained what a googly was, even if he never picked one). This hard core was supplemented with less regularity by Mayhew, Wilmot, and then Healey. With these such mighty cricketers twas but natural, if not to win, then to play a more expansive game and engage opponents on more equal terms. The boundary was adorned by faithful and long-suffering WAGs – Lesley, Milly, Angie, Polly, Hilary, Jenny, Diane – and their children, some of whom grew up to supplement the Mandarins' ranks. The club acquired its own colours: orange (for mandarins, of course) and charcoal grey (for civil servants). In the late '80s it averaged 40 fixtures a season.

And so into the 1990s – Crump, Hurst, Gardiner, Jarvis ... and, above all, Rob Foot, an MoD civil servant who combined unparalleled athleticism with a deep love of the game (and of much else), outstanding all-round ability and a yen for the Mandarins' amateur ethos: Keith Miller comingled with Siegfried, Rupert Brooke, Duncan Edwards. Et in arcadia ... After distinguished service in Bosnia and Sierra Leone, Rob was diagnosed with leukaemia and finally dismissed in 2002. There is now played annually a memorial game at Burton's Court, Mandarins v the RCDS, with proceeds going to the Robert Foot Leukaemia Fund.

Rob Foot

Twenty-first century Mandarins have a website, of course (emcc?) which can attract surprising numbers of hits. The tradition continues in capable hands – O'Donnell, Heard, Porter, Gray fils. And in addition to some golden(ish) oldies who still turn out, the club has attracted youthful energy: the Mayer brothers, Jon (a civil servant) and Josh, both injected antipodean panache during their sadly brief UK stay.

A golden jubilee celebration is planned for 2014. Members are sustained meanwhile by memories – of settings, grounds, lunches, teas, pubs, opponents, companionship, banter, and even occasionally of the cricket. Over the years, some anecdotes may have grown in the telling (though not the one about Lord Orr-Ewing's collision with Michael Latham MP); but all are true, even when, like the club's bowling, less than accurate. Oh, and that Cambridge fresher? In 1956, RM James became the third (and last) undergraduate in the twentieth century to take 100 off an Australian attack. Other Mandarins boasted Blues or half-Blues – for football (the association game as well as the rugby code), for squash, for lacrosse, for rugby league. But never for cricket; what sort of club do you think this is?

Website: *www.mandarins.org.uk*

Old England

Founded: 1968

by Stephen Chalke

Old England began life in 1968 as the Whitbread Wanderers, the brainchild of Frank Twiselton, the brewers' managing director in the south-west. A year or two earlier he had got up a team, mostly of Whitbread employees but with two or three professional cricketers in their midst, to play against a school side near Exeter, and so happy was the occasion that during the after-match dinner he started to work out how he could turn it into a permanent side.

'Twizzy', a fine all-round sportsman, had played football in the war with Stanley Matthews, he managed a local football club Stonehouse, and he was later to become chairman of Gloucestershire County Cricket Club. So, as well as the former cricketers working for the company, he had plenty of contacts in the world of sport.

In the first years of the Whitbread Wanderers they played one week of cricket: five matches against top Devon club sides such as Paignton, Sidmouth, Torquay and Exmouth, the sixth in or near Bristol on the way home. 'Twizzy' would choose the week to coincide with gaps in the fixture list for the three West Country counties – Somerset, Gloucestershire and Worcestershire – and he was never short of volunteers from their playing staffs. It is hard to imagine now, but there they were, professional cricketers in mid-season, enjoying their days off on a brewery-sponsored cricket tour.

Tom Graveney was involved from the start, as was David Carpenter, the former Gloucestershire batsman who was now working for Whitbread. Then came David Allen, Len Coldwell, Basil D'Oliveira, Arthur Milton, Mike Procter and David Green. Even the long-retired Godfrey Evans travelled down to join them, staying with them all at the fifteenth-century Sea Trout Inn at Staverton near Totnes.

This was not highly paid celebrity cricket like Lashings. The players were given accommodation, food and perhaps a ten-pound note if they stayed the week. But they were all of a generation who, in the words of David Allen, "were happy to play for the love of the game and the friendship." The drink flowed as befitted a brewery side – 'Twizzy' loved to sing The Barley Mow, and 'caught Stella, bowled Artois' summed up a few dismissals – but they were always too strong for the local sides. The convention was to bat first, then in the field to make the game last long enough to entertain the good crowds that came to see them.

Such was their appeal that they attracted several Australians: Somerset's Bill Alley, never far away when there was fun (and drink) to be had, Graeme McKenzie, and Neil Hawke, who became a regular. On one occasion, at Thornbury north of Bristol, Hawke hit the former Gloucestershire off-spinner Derek Hawkins for six sixes in an over. In another match, at Sidmouth, his first ball parted the hair of a startled club batsman, who had travelled down from north Bristol to play. "I thought there was one off the mark in this game," the man protested, only to get the reply, "You've just bloody had it."

In 1978 Frank Twiselton retired from Whitbread, and responsibility for the team passed to Jim Parks, the former Sussex and England batsman-keeper who was working at the time for Heineken. At this point the fixtures spread outwards across the whole south of England, and the pool of players grew wider, too: John Snow, Tom Cartwright, Alan Oakman, John Jameson, Robin Hobbs, Pat Pocock, Derek Underwood, Derek Randall. Now they played Sunday games as Whitbread Old England, raising money for local clubs and for charities.

For the players, no longer enjoying the fraternity of county cricket, the days together were magical, with the accompanying wives (and John Snow's dogs) creating a family atmosphere. The late Tom Cartwright recalled it all with a great glow: "Joan and I used to leave Neath on Sunday morning, drive maybe 250 miles, play a game of cricket, then drive back. About 12.30 or one o'clock in the night, if you called in at the Leigh Delamere service station on the M4, you'd always find Joan and me, David Allen and Joyce and sometimes Jeff Jones having a cup of coffee. D.A. and I were still playing together thirty-odd years after we'd toured South Africa."

Tom had so many happy memories: John Edrich's superb century at Shepperton, the cluster of spectators that gathered whenever Derek Randall fielded on the boundary, the devotion with which Raye Luckhurst compiled scoring charts of her husband Brian's innings, the sight of Basil D'Oliveira fielding deeper and deeper in the slips as the years went by, the rainy day at Eaton Hall when Brian Close fell from grace by tipping his cigarette ash into the Duke of Westminster's precious ornaments … and a wonderful innings by Arthur Milton at Bromyard: "He was in his sixties, and he came at the last minute, got his bat out of the attic. He played in his pumps. It was a wet ground, and he never fell over. He had an incredible balance. He got a hundred that day. Days like that, they're very special in your life."

David Allen captained from 1984 to 2000, with a fixture list of eight to ten games each summer. His favourite memory is of a game in Surrey when they reached the final over needing to take one wicket for victory. "The batsman struck it over Derek Randall in the covers, and he turned and ran, catching it over his head. He threw the ball up, caught it behind his back, then ran into the tent and presented it to the Lady Mayoress. He was a tremendous crowd pleaser."

Sometimes the youngsters in the opposition can be looking to make a name for themselves in the game, but mostly the old pros are capable of handling themselves. In fact, D.A. can only recall one bad defeat – against, of all teams, the London Fire Brigade, playing somewhere near the North Circular Road. "Cartwright and I were left trying to score some runs to make a game of it."

Robin Hobbs, his leg spin losing its bite as he played well into his sixties, recalls a more recent game down at Sittingbourne in Kent. A first sight of the opposition revealed most of them to be young schoolboys. "I can see some easy pickings here," he said confidently, only for one of them, a Cowdrey grandchild, to hit him repeatedly out of the ground, mostly over extra cover. "I bowled six overs for 105 runs," he tells. "It wouldn't have been so bad, but he came into our dressing room afterwards and thanked me very much for playing."

Sponsorship of the team passed in 1991 from Whitbread to NatWest, then to Amex. Now each match is sponsored locally. The current captain is the former Essex and England left-arm bowler John Lever.

The team plays fewer games than in its heyday. With longer distances to travel, the players are paid expenses more generous than 'Twizzy' ever offered, but fewer former Test players make themselves available. Nevertheless, according to the calculation of Jim Parks, still a stalwart of the club, their games have raised more than a million and a half pounds.

Whitbread Wanderers
back row: David Carpenter (Glos), Roy Booth (Worcs), Ray Digman (Cheshire),
Ron Headley (West Indies), Mark Fryer (Swindon), Ken Webb (Whitbread), Chris Lowe (Glos),
Norman Gifford (England), Basil D'Oliveira (England), John Knott (Whitbread)
front row: Neil Hawke (Australia), Len Coldwell (England), Frank Twiselton (team manager),
Tom Graveney (England, captain), Bill Alley (Somerset), Godfrey Evans (England)

Heartaches

Founded: 1973

by Tim Rice

One of the most important creations of my life has been Heartaches Cricket Club. As I write this in 2013, it is about to celebrate its 40th anniversary, something unimaginable to me and eleven friends (it was a 12-a-side match) as we wandered out onto a pitch at Bicester in Oxfordshire on Sunday 8 July 1973 to pit our skills against those of William Heath's Gentlemen. The second game of 2013 will be our 600th, and on 8 July we plan to re-create the original fixture with as many of the original players as we can find who are still able to run, or at least stand up. Unfortunately the ground has long since been built over, but we should have no difficulty in borrowing one of the 100+ grounds we have visited over the years for this important celebration.

Heartaches CC was launched because I played a couple of charity matches in 1972. I had not played cricket in earnest since I had left school ten years before, and so much did I enjoy the experience I decided to organise a game of my own before the end of that summer. That was a huge social success, and a repeat the following year was not hard to arrange. In fact, it was repeated five times in 1973, and the fledgling side acquired a name, colours (red, pink and green) and even a motto – *Clava Recta*. This is the nearest Latin can get to 'a straight bat'. 'Clava' is the Latin for 'bat', but as in flying nocturnal mouse rather than as in willowy blade. 'Recta' means 'upright' or 'erect', the full motto thus translating as 'Erect flying mouse' which is probably an aeronautical and anatomical impossibility. But it looks impressive on the team's writing paper.

Why the name Heartaches? At the time, with the top tax rate at 83 per cent, and no guarantee that I would have any worthwhile income for more than a year or two, I had recently formed a company to employ myself and a few close relatives, which (legally) managed to reduce the insane demands of the Inland Revenue to a level that was merely outrageous. I called the company created for this purpose Heartaches Ltd, itself a tribute to one of my favourite Elvis Presley songs, *That's When Your Heartaches Begin*. Perhaps in the hope that cricket teas and equipment could be charged to the company, I named the team after Heartaches Ltd.

Obviously we were to be a wandering side as we had no home ground. I did move to the Oxfordshire village of Great Milton in 1974 and considered laying down a wicket in a field next to the property, but the field was just a tad too small and anyway very close to the house. By then Heartaches had caught on in a big way, and my wife Jane was not sure she fancied entertaining thirty or forty people every other weekend. Thus we played wherever anyone would put up with us.

Heartaches was never conceived as anything other than a private pastime, deliberately non-show-business, non-charity and low profile. It has proved to be a wonderful way for me to keep in close touch with a score and more of friends and their families, without actually having to write a musical with them. The line-up of players has changed gradually over the years, but not significantly in that many sons (and to date, one grandson) of the pioneers are now regulars and at least a dozen who played in the 1970s still clock in for the odd match, some even still available for nearly every game, whether selected or not. Those who have retired still appear at the pre-season parties, close-season parties and Christmas lunches – the loyalty to the Clava Rectan cause has been staggering over four decades.

The Hearts, as we affectionately call ourselves, have wandered far and wide over the seasons. Most of our games are played within 75 miles of London, in Surrey, Oxfordshire, Bucks and Berks, but every September we travel to Cornwall for three or four matches and we have also toured Yorkshire on two or three occasions. The two grounds we have graced most frequently (over 100 matches between them) have been the Oxfordshire grounds of Great Haseley and Stonor Park. In both cases, thanks to the generosity of the grounds' owners, we have been able to act as the home side and entertain other wandering sides. Overall, roughly half our matches have been with other homeless teams, and half have been played with Heartaches as the grateful guests of opponents with a permanent abode, many of whom we have now visited over 30 times.

But our wandering has taken us way beyond England. To date we have visited South Africa, Charlotte (North Carolina), Estonia, Berlin and St Petersburg. Apart from South Africa in 1993, when we stayed for three weeks and visited the Cape, Natal and Johannesburg, playing six games, these trips have been three- or four-day jaunts. Tourism is as vital a factor (especially for the wives, lovers and girlfriends) as the actual cricket, which can often be of quite a high standard in the most unlikely places. We had hoped for an easy win or two in Russia, but on that trip even Peter the Great's XI contained a selection of Sri Lankans and Australians and we failed to impress. This might have been in part due to the fact that the local groundsman (who clearly was Russian) marked out the pitch in metres rather than yards and it took some time for our attack to realise the batsman was about five feet further away than he would have been in England. As our 41st season approaches, in addition to the 40th birthday extravaganza after the match on 8 July, we are planning a trip to Budapest.

Tim Rice

Heartaches v Tiddington, 2011
back row: P Harding (scorer), T Riley-Smith, J Cohen, R Stoneham, T Whittome,
J Pressland, P Boreham (umpire)   front row: W Deal, T Graveney, D Glenn,
T Rice, M Gatting, A Rossdale   very front: Toast, Sparkle

Every year since 1975 I have produced a privately printed Heartaches Cricketers' Almanack, modelled on *Wisden*, which contains a ludicrously detailed literary and statistical account of the season just past. I spend a happy week or two at the end of every summer writing it, including updating the almost deranged Records Section, which, sad to say, reveals my career batting average, after more than 500 appearances, to be a shade over 7. I am at least remarkably consistent as I was dismissed in that first ever game against Heath's Gents for 7. I have slightly better bowling figures, including, amazingly, two hat-tricks featuring six very unlucky batsmen, but none Estonian I hasten to add. By enabling me to return to my childhood delight of playing with numbers without too much embarrassment, my Almanack is of enormous therapeutic value. All in all, it usually takes up more of my time than lyric writing. Designed by the cartoonist Robert Duncan, and with match reports (often of a thousand words or more) of every game played, it costs a packet to produce, but the briefest and most pathetic innings by the most transient of players is recorded therein with mind-numbing accuracy for all time. It is the nearest I have come to keeping a diary.

As we prepare for the forthcoming campaign, I also look back. I have easily as many great memories of my life as the Hearts leader as I do theatrical and musical ones. I have easily as many good friends in Heartaches circles as I do in show business – many more, to be honest. And there is nothing in my other life with which I feel more satisfaction than that which I get from being part of a wandering cricket team, taking on villages and fellow nomads in peaceful English surroundings without crowds, fanfare, publicity or opulence.

Website: *www.heartaches.co.uk*

Touring Theatre

Founded: 1974

by Anthony Gibson and Anthony Fowles

The association between cricket and the theatre goes back as far as I Zingari and the Old Stagers, and there is certainly no shortage of teams of cricketing actors, be they wandering, like the Gaieties, or rather more rooted, like the National Theatre. But there is, as far as I am aware, only one sprung from the unseen and largely unsung heroes of the theatrical world, the backstage technicians – the scene crew, lighting men, ASMs, carpenters, etc., who make it all happen. That team is the Touring Theatre Cricket Club.

TTCC was founded in 1974 by three backstage 'techies': Max Alphonso, Peter Cascarino and George Yerby who, to the detriment of his lifetime aggregate, combined fine technique as an opener with an astonishing susceptibility to hay fever. It was christened West End Touring Theatre on birth but some dozen years later the 'West End' was dropped as at 'an increasingly jovial AGM' it became clear that few of the star players felt comfortable at the prospect of being selected for a WETT dream team. In the early days, links with the Lyric Theatre, Hammersmith were strong and in so far as TTCC ever had a geographical centre it would be Shepherd's Bush. Fixtures were mainly against sides from south of the river down Surbiton way, but forays to the fastnesses of Enfield, Perry Vale and Windlesham in Berkshire were courageously stage managed.

This is a wandering club of modest rather than massive pretensions. Its current president, the novelist Anthony Fowles ("I was once an emergency follow-spot operator and drank in the same pub") puts the prevailing standard as "around club two and a half XI standard" and cheerfully admits "we lose more than we win but who's counting?" From the stories he tells, however, it does sound as though they notch up more than their fair share of fun along the way.

There was, for example, the occasion when, having reached an efficiently rapid century, the captain of Windlesham, a seriously decent cricketer who went on to play in the northern leagues, opted to throw his wicket away. He threw up a towering catch into the covers. Actually he did so thirteen times. The first twelve of his generous offers were spurned – spurned as in spilled. Seven of them were put down by the same fielder. The thirteenth and held catch was not so unlucky for the batsman as by then his scientific slogging had brought him 235 in less than three hours.

Lapses in the field, most notably off his own bowling, were also the bane of a short-fused quickie who played regularly for TTCC in the '80s. "Like McEnroe on a bad day or Broad on a good" is how Fowles remembers him. Every time a catch went down or a misfield cost runs he would mutter not quite under his breath as he stalked back to his mark. One day, against a particularly good batsman, he slipped in his slower one. It worked. The batsman lobbed back the easiest of dollies. Hands quivering in anticipation the bowler reached to accept the gift. And dropped it. His team-mates were gifted the spectacle of a strong man face down in the middle of the track beating with both fists at the grass he was biting into. "We were less shocked than silently but richly gratified," Fowles fondly recalls.

It sounds as though sides taking on Touring Theatre would be well advised to check their First Aid kits on the match-day morning. A Perry Vale lower order player had the habit of gripping his bat at the handle's very bottom when scampering the (very occasional) run. Came the day when running full pelt and attempting to slide the bat home ahead of the fielder's return, he only succeeded in jamming its toe end into a council rec clump of weed. He impaled his right groin and thus fainted dead away. He was carried away by ambulance to the nearest A&E department where it transpired he had ruptured a major artery and diverted a life-threatening amount of blood away from his heart. Happily, a full recovery duly made, he was able a year later to answer the elementary question – "What did it feel like?" – with commendable economy of expression: "Like I'd rammed a fucking bat handle into it."

Less fortunate by a distance was the South Indian Railway Taverners' batsman who after contributing 70-odd to an as yet unbroken first-wicket partnership of 170 gave the Touring Theatre attack the breakthrough they had been toiling for by dropping dead at the wicket. Actor Ben Martin gallantly attempted mouth-to-mouth, but it emerged that the deceased had been dead before he hit the ground. It was nothing but a tragedy for his family but, as the ambulance was leaving the ground, one of his erstwhile team-mates was heard saying: "Pity to let the tea go to waste."

Coming from the world of theatre production TTCC have naturally played many matches against teams of actors over the years (though, interestingly, not many against their good friends the musicians). They have thus encountered a cluster of wandering stars from the stage's great and the (not so) good. Hugh Laurie, a useful cricketer as well as a Cambridge rowing Blue, featured for the National; William Franklyn, cursed by the "Schh ..." of tonic water in his later years, captained the Sargent's Men; Richard Bean, adaptor of Goldini's *Servant of Two Masters*, was a regular for the modestly entitled Actors Anonymous team; the Troughtons, pére David et fils Jim (aged thirteen), were in the same RSC side; Jack Shepherd unchivalrously caught out the author whose lines had just given him employment; and Sam Mendes, as good a bat as TTCC encountered, preceded his Hollywood Oscar by scoring a lightning Stratford 70 before gifting his wicket away to an actor he has yet to cast.

Famous names in TTCC's own ranks are harder to seek although Ed Yardley, son of Norman, the English captain up against Bradman's '48 Aussies, added a measure of steel and class during the few seasons he played in the '80s. One of the best players – a class number four and a good wrist spinner – was founder member Max Alphonso. Hockey was Max's real game, and he was good enough to play for Kenya in the Olympic games when they were semi-finalists. He is described by Anthony Fowles as "highly intelligent and articulate, but in the manner of Stanley Unwin – only with more inscrutable trains of thought and ways of expressing them. One of TTCC's favourite after-match gambits with an opposition player who had earned their disapprobation (by not walking, for example) was to send Max over to him in the bar for a bit of a chin wag. The target would become pinned glassy-eyed to the wall baffled by Max's effortlessly unrelenting stream of alternative consciousness for at least the next incomprehensible half hour. Max, bless his memory, was utterly oblivious."

Touring Theatre 1984

Operating often in the nether regions of wandering cricket, TTCC have come up against all sorts. They used to play a team of Buddhists from whom, naturally, you might expect a peaceable, almost spiritual, approach to the game, all good manners and courtesy. On the contrary, according to Fowles, they were the most consistently aggressive side that Touring Theatre ever encountered. "Their ground was on the top of a high ridge overlooking the Thames," he remembers. "One year the wind was so strong the bails kept blowing off. Their skipper was also their opener so I suggested we do without them. He agreed – and very next ball just got the toe of his bat on a yorker. The ball rolled on under the bat and dead straight on to the stumps. He was morally out but he didn't budge an inch. 'Well, we'll never know,' I said, trying to shame him, 'so you'd better stay there.' The bastard did – and went on to get a hundred. That was another evening Max earned his ale."

In their salad days TTCC played some 18 games a season. That admirable total has gradually declined as encroaching age has taken its toll and a few old cricketers have left the crease. It has become more difficult and, indeed, unrealistic to hang on to the best-quality fixtures. But latterly, under present captain John Warnaby, a youth policy has been introduced and the introduction of a classy band of young Indian and Pakistani players, deriving less from the theatre than the Catholic Church, has begun a perceptible renaissance. That didn't prevent TTCC's being so short on three occasions last summer (2012) that Anthony Fowles had to come out of retirement at the age of 73. He covered himself in dubious glory in his last game by top-scoring while trying to hang around for the draw. He totalled 4. "All singles," he insists.

So what might the future hold for the Touring Theatre Cricket Club? Well, John Warnaby is confident that they will "carry on" contributing to the vagaries of wandering cricket for at least the next couple of seasons. And if they continue to have as much fun as they seem to have had for the last 38 years, it should be for a lot longer than that.

Weekenders

Founded: 1970-something

by Christopher Douglas

According to our fixture card, the Weekenders CC was established in 1979. If you go by the website it was 1974. The actors Clive and David Swift who founded the club will tell you it started on Hampstead Heath in 1977 – or the year before. They can't agree.

Vagueness about time and dates has been a defining characteristic of the club over the past however many years it is. A recent AGM began with the secretary in the wrong pub and the captain enjoying dinner on the other side of town. But the evening somehow came cheerfully together in the way that our games tend to, that's to say shambolically to begin with but then with a surge of enthusiasm that comes from no one quite knows where. The enthusiasm can sometimes disappear again without warning but the point is we're still going so a philosophy of not giving a toss appears to have served us well.

To experience the chaos of running a wandering cricket club is to appreciate the miracle of human progress. Many of our regulars occupy prominent positions in banking, the law, journalism, medicine, broadcasting etc., men used to making things happen and to defending their organisations when things go awry. But we seem to regard the Sunday match as an opportunity for competitive misjudgement, for outdoing one another in decision-making of spectacular wrongheadedness without any obligation to account for our actions.

Friendly cricket offers stupidity therapy for the professional classes. I have seen lawyers pick fights with the opposition, a doctor suggest vodka and fags as a remedy for a torn rotator muscle, a graphic designer claim the ball that bowled him was a wide, a professor of mathematics unable to work out that with one ball to block for the draw a six over mid-wicket isn't much use if you're 125 behind. We had a civil servant in the Department for Transport who drove to Chippenham in Wiltshire unaware that there was another Chippenham in Cambridgeshire where we were already about 25 for six by the time he phoned to ask where the hell we all were.

And then there are the actors. It would be wrong to call actors the backbone of friendly cricket because that would imply a degree of reliability which could be misleading. But it would be hard to make up the numbers without them. Some actors are brilliant cricketers, others aren't but are regularly available which is almost as good. Another significant group of thespians is drawn not so much to the game of cricket as to the prospect of being driven somewhere and a good chance that one of the lawyers will buy them some beer and crisps.

Then there is a further subcategory of actors, too small to register statistically: those with jobs. Several have played for us. The distinguished Shakespearean David Troughton (father of the current Warwickshire captain) skippered us for several years in the '70s. He was a lively swing bowler and a straight hitter with a Jessop-like follow-through. Clive Swift (*Keeping up Appearances*) and his brother David (*Drop the Dead Donkey*) retired only recently. Ian McKellen once played a game – or perhaps half a game. And last but not

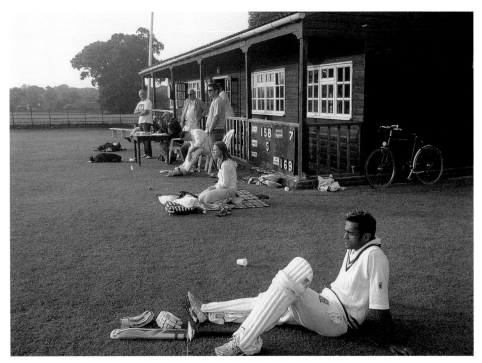

Twelve to win at Turville Park – Tim Rice's dog feels the tension

least, we can claim the face of Captain Birdseye throughout the noughties. This brings the conversation to a gratifying halt if anyone tries to take us on at the name-dropping game.

We played a team called London Theatres for some years, the fixture being named in memory of Anthony Ainley, the actor who played The Master in the old *Dr Who*. It would be hard to imagine a less fitting memorial to this delightful, courteous and scrupulously fair opponent. Tempers were often lost before a ball was bowled and we fell out for good after a furious on-field altercation, not helped by the emotional intervention of the square-leg umpire who was a member of the *Evita!* chorus. As our out-of-control bowler charged in, the batsman pleaded, "Not in the face. I'm an actor!"

"There's always radio," chirped our short-leg. The fixture remains in abeyance.

Cricket clubs develop their own sense of humour over the years. Some find it killingly funny to shout 'jug avoidance' when anyone makes a mistake. We think it hilarious to offer each other meaningless encouragement 'Join the dots!', 'Bake the pie!' 'Cat's-arse tight, lads!', that kind of thing. Side-splitting, no? During a dull passage of play one of us will call out, "Come on boys, let's have some pointless clapping", and we'll amuse ourselves by unnecessarily putting our hands together. As I say, it's an individual thing.

The most poignant words of encouragement I ever heard on a cricket field were "Well kept out, Mum", spoken by a little boy at the non-striker's end on a day when we were struggling for players and found ourselves about 80 runs adrift with the last pair at the crease. *Well kept out, Mum* could be the title of a sentimental Victorian painting depicting filial duty and plucky optimism in the face of hopeless odds. I almost cry when I think of it.

The Weekenders have had their good days, too. Chasing down 248 to beat Hertford CC on the county ground, and doing it without a ringer, was probably our finest. We have played on manicured Oxbridge college squares, south London recs where you change in the bushes and mark your run-up with dried dog poo. I can't believe there's a lovelier village ground than Boughton in Kent where the views and the pre-match Whitstable oysters render the result an irrelevance. In our early days we would travel anywhere in search of a win, 'Heathrow Terminal 3 Baggage Handlers' for example, and if anyone knows what's become of 'The Dregs of Humanity' please drop me a line because they were a pushover.

We have played other wandering sides of similar vintage to ourselves, Tim Rice's Heartaches, Captain Scott's XI and its schismatic offshoot Rain Men, run by the writer Marcus Berkmann. It was during a game against Marcus's team that I heard my all-time favourite exchange between batting partners. The Rain Men's number nine was looking for quick runs as tea approached. He hit the ball to a fielder standing on a ludicrously short offside boundary and bellowed, "Come on, Camilla! There's two there – oh, sorry, darling."

The low points in the Weekenders' history include being bowled out for 26 by bloody London Theatres, and last year's game against Hoddesdon. Harold Pinter, in his last filmed interview, remembered with pride the day his beloved Gaieties beat Hoddesdon. I'm not surprised it was in the forefront of the great man's mind. Hoddesdon took us for 493 in forty overs. Fortunately the fourth wicket stand of 323 prevented the South African pro getting to the wicket or we'd have been chasing four figures. The loss was certainly a club record and possibly a global one too.

Chaotic we may be but our records are carefully kept and memorised. Captain Birdseye has the most consecutive ducks. Walking off after the eighth, he hurled his bat over the boundary. It smashed the offside headlight of his car. The record for the highest innings in a pair of black trainers is 30. And then there's the longest over, 14 deliveries in all. If the umpire had applied the wides law more scrupulously the over would still be continuing.

Time for some pointless clapping, I think.

Website: *www.weekenderscc.org*

The pre-match warm-up, Telegraph Road Ground, Putney Common

Fleet Street Strollers

Founded: 1976

by Peter Patston

Fleet Street is long gone as the centre of the British newspaper industry, but some of its more acceptable traditions live on in the Fleet Street Strollers. The club was founded in 1976 by journalists on the now defunct *London Evening News* with the original name of the Northcliffe Strollers, in recognition of the media group that owned the newspaper.

The early '70s were good times for Fleet Street cricket, with many papers fielding occasional teams able to call on columnists such as Denis Compton and Ted Dexter to supplement more modest in-house talents. The games were convivial affairs played on pristine pitches where always the sun poured down like honey. Naturally, it was essential for players to keep their fluid levels high. The *Evening News* had held an inter-departmental cricket competition for many years and also played an annual match against its arch rival, the *Evening Standard*.

It was against this background that features sub-editor Simon Brodbeck set up the Strollers. The idea was to play decent, enjoyable, friendly cricket every Sunday at pleasant club and village grounds in the Home Counties. Volunteers were sought from all corners of the newsroom on the understanding that enthusiasm was as important as ability. Step forward television editor Patrick Stoddart, who became one of the keenest and most popular Strollers, even though he would be the first to admit that his contribution with the bat was decidedly average: 1.4 in 131 matches, to be precise.

Player numbers were also boosted from beyond Whitefriars Street. I was on the *Standard* news subs' desk and, having captained the aforementioned rival team, was welcomed to the fold. Of the first recorded Strollers team to take the field – against West India and Millwall Docks at Sidcup on 25 April 1976 – Simon and I are the only members still in active service today.

The Strollers bandwagon drew on apace – with 'drew' being the operative word. Limited-over, win-or-lose cricket was the staple of league sides; our friendly matches relied on a sporting declaration and allowed for nine, ten and jack to hang on stoically, honours even. If any of the opposition took offence, we were adept at 'drinking back' the fixture.

Wives, girlfriends, parents, children, friends, relations and pets are as much a part of the club as the players. Pat Stoddart's wife Nicki worked for Laurie Lee's literary agents and was instrumental in securing us a fixture on the writer's fabled sloping pitch at Sheepscombe in the Cotswolds. On our first visit Laurie greeted us warmly at the Butcher's Arms, offered to buy a round and promptly tripped up on his way to the bar. "Laurie Lee tripped here," growled the publicity-conscious poet in his best *Cider With Rosie* burr.

The Northcliffe Strollers became the Fleet Street Strollers in 1980 after the demise of the *Evening News*. By then it was a more fitting name anyway, as we spread the net wider to find more players to meet the demands of a growing fixture list. Little by little our results improved, although sometimes the team appeared stronger on paper than in the field. O'Kill and Slaughter, for example, gave many opposing batsmen cause for concern – until the pair in question started to bowl. Peter O'Kill's strange windmill action was mostly harmless, and Stan Slaughter's beguiling left-arm spin far from terrifying.

Can any team ever have boasted a more opinionated opening bowler than Richard Littlejohn, at that time industrial editor on the *Standard*? His rapid off-cutters were unsubtle, belligerent and aimed at the jugular, much like his later columns on *The Sun* and *Daily Mail*. His best-bowling return of eight for 9 stood for more than ten years as a club record.

Another Strollers talent was Peter Hayter, now cricket correspondent of the *Mail On Sunday*. Peter was in the side that set a club record at Blackfordby, an old Leicestershire mining village, in 1988. It was August bank holiday, Saturday morning saw it chucking it down, and a dreadful pile-up stranded half our party on the M1. The few of us who arrived in good time took refuge in the Bluebell Inn and proceeded to lunch voluminously, expecting to be there all afternoon. But at 2.30 the deluge abruptly ceased and our hosts, without a care for their wicket, suggested a start in 20 minutes. So after five pints each of Marston's Pedigree, Peter and I sallied forth to open the Strollers' innings. "If you need me, I'll be at the other end," he reassured me. Indeed he was, but only for the first delivery which I glided adroitly through the slips for a single. Next ball Peter, shaping up for a more expansive shot, was bowled. The rest of us fared little better. The harassed stragglers finally began to turn up; they parked, frantically scrambled across to the pavilion, changed, rapidly marched out to the sodden wicket, then trudged back in, having succumbed to bowling which was, if truth were told, nothing out of the ordinary. We were all out for the grand total of eight – though, to our credit, we did win the beer match. To Peter's credit he entertained us handsomely with his mellifluous baritone crooning later that evening.

Ah, the crooning. You don't have to be mad about community sing-along to play for the Strollers, but it helps. It was his precise back-up vocals to *Running Bear* ("oompa-oompa, oompa-oompa") that added value to Kimball Bailey's contribution to the club when we first recruited him. His arrival coincided with a seismic shift in the British newspaper industry, the diaspora of the national press to undiscovered countries such as Wapping, Canary Wharf and Kensington. Until then, if we were struggling to raise a side, we could walk into The Harrow, Poppinjay, Cheshire Cheese, King & Keys or practically any other EC4 watering hole and rustle up a body or two for the weekend.

The exodus from Fleet Street left us with a chasm – and into it Kimball poured his vast network of business and social contacts, as befitted his calling as a management consultant. We were also helped by the demise of another wandering cricket side, the Non-Conformists. Six of their best took the attitude "If you can't beat them join them" and remain committed Strollers to this day.

Another aid to recruitment was the introduction of midweek Twenty20 fixtures, which were originally aimed at raising money for charity. It was hearing of another feat of charity cricket on *Test Match Special* that led us to send a cheque to Krishna Lester, an expat Englishman who managed the Chateau de Chaintres vineyard near Saumur and ran the local cricket club (Hon President, Mick Jagger). Krishna called Kimball and invited him to bring a team over. That first 'rebel' tour was in 1998, and it took a few years for the event to receive the club's official recognition. Now, however, we wouldn't be without our

Stanton by Dale in Derbyshire, where the Strollers compete annually for the David Tranter Cup

French connections. It was on the banks of the River Loire that the Strollers finally met their match when it came to *Running Bear*. Not only did the Montagu Toller team who were also touring there know all the words, they also did the accompanying whoops and war dances, much to the bemusement of locals passing the Irish Bar in the small hours.

Another tour takes us to the South of France each autumn, for matches against, among others, Riviera and Monte Carlo cricket clubs, on a quaint daisy-strewn ground north of Grasse on the Route Napoleon. More recently we have ventured to Geneva to take on the CERN nuclear research establishment. A guided tour of the Large Hadron Collider facility sets you up nicely to face the quickest bowling.

The 21st century has seen the influx of a new generation of players, mostly keen Kiwi 30-somethings introduced to us by Hamish McDougall, who as communications manager for the Canary Wharf Group has genuine press credentials. Of his friends, James Timperley has already overhauled the club record for the number of centuries and total runs in a season while Jono Addis has shown a penchant for scoring double centuries.

Keeping immaculate track of such statistics is another key Stroller without whom the club wouldn't be what it is today – my wife Maggie. Cricket scoring is in her blood, which no doubt runs the colour of the different pencils she uses for each bowler. It's a comforting thought that, as Simon Brodbeck and I approach the twilight of our cricket careers, we both play for the team we set up nearly 40 years ago alongside the bright younger things who will keep it strolling on. In Simon's case it is because he is still our 'Main Man' and still bowls a mean spell – 1,000th wicket coming up in a year or two.

Me? Well, as they used to say in the team song (to the tune of *The Laughing Policeman*): "He really only keeps his place, 'cos his missus keeps the book!"

Website: *www.fsscc.org.uk*

Captain Scott Invitation XI

Founded: 1980

by Sean Reilly

"Why must you always be so fucking late?" Founder and long-term captain Harry Thompson's memorable words to his successor Sean Reilly, as he was bravely batting and battling with advanced and ultimately terminal lung cancer, were followed by a huge embrace. The mantle Harry had been carrying for 25 years was finally being handed over, and with it the responsibility of safeguarding the legacy of one of the world's most notorious and adventurous travelling cricket teams – Captain Scott Invitation XI.

Very few travelling amateur cricket teams merit one best-selling book. Captain Scott's boasts two. *Penguins Stopped Play* and *Rain Men* both chart different aspects of the same notorious band of multicultural ragtag cricketers who have played thousands of games over a third of a century and graced cricket grounds from Antarctica to Argentina, Oxford to Oslo, Switzerland to South Africa, Trinidad to Tanzania.

Founded by Thompson when a weedy Oxford undergraduate denied a place in his college team on the woefully thin grounds that he had never actually played the game before, from the beginning Captain Scott's achieved notoriety and a permanent place in cricket lore. For the first decade and a half the team took glorious failure to dizzy heights. Its domestic motto *Modo Egredior* ('I'm just going out…', in tribute to Captain Oates' honourable sacrifice) demonstrated a very English desire to revel in gentlemanly failure and celebrate the contributions and participation of those with mixed and often no ability or whose talents had been affected by one too many pints of Tanglefoot. Thompson and friends were so obsessed with cricket that they even had the teams first twenty years of scorecards and averages bound in a yellow hardback version of *Wisden's Cricketers' Almanack*.

A picture in the Almanack

v Trinity Triflers, 1980
S Lewis, M Hetherington,
RA Corden, M Berkmann,
I Hislop, D Child

Thompson's caption reads:
This is the earliest extant Scott photo.
The pavilion and Hislop's hair
have since been demolished.

Another photo page from the Almanack

Thompson writes of Hugh Grant:

The release of Four Weddings *made any sort of public life utterly impossible. He tried playing once, at Ardley-with-Fewcott in 1994 – he even made it to the tea interval without being noticed – but once his presence had been rumbled, that was it. Every single girl for about thirty miles around "just happened" to pop down to the ground to watch the game, in stilettoes, mini-skirts and halter-neck tops.*

At the end of the match he was besieged in the shower, the pavilion surrounded by panting women desperate to get in, while his team-mates trailed off (grinning unsupportively) to the pub. Afterwards he made the reluctant decision to give up Captain Scott, although he did wear his Scott cap to the première of Sirens. *Despite the millions he made from that and other films, he cunningly managed to avoid ever paying his membership fee.*

C. Williams 1995

H. Thompson 1988

W. Matthews 1995

A. J. Leonard 1995

H. Grant 1995

J. Moore 1994

Yet Thompson and his band of journalists, comedy writers and louche wags overlooked one thing. After fifteen years of playing over fifty matches per year, they had got rather good. At least some of them had. There followed what can only be described as a very English squabble and Thompson led the club into a new era, shorn of some of the less cricket-focused members and with a new-found zest for pushing the boundaries of cricket and international relations.

Having moved, at least partially, from the cricketing mission of glorious failure, Thompson and his team-mates decided to follow Robert Falcon Scott more literally and take cricket, for the first time, to Antarctica. Having conquered Antarctica, and managed not be pipped at the post by a devious Norwegian, and then beaten a country, Malaysia, Captain Scott's hatched the idea of taking cricket to every continent. In one trip. The administrative, diplomatic, interpersonal and cricketing challenges that such an undertaking posed are hilariously dealt with in Thompson's bestseller *Penguins Stopped Play*, a must-read for anyone who loves cricket.

It started on Boxing Day 2002 with somewhat inebriated cricket played with a guitar and a tennis ball (9/11 had banished cricket bats from hand luggage) in front of bemused throngs of Americans in Miami airport. The guitar, belonging to Sean's brother Eiran, was permanently damaged by the batsman digging out a devilish yorker from Sean's other brother James, an incident which prompted such a vocal family row that airport police nearly removed the entire team.

Harry Thompson

A sound thumping by the champions of Barbados was followed by a narrow defeat by an Argentina XI in the refined Victorian setting of the Hurlingham club in Buenos Aires. A battling defeat in 110 degrees in Perth was avenged by a stunning one-wicket victory over a Singapore Development XI, and the whole five-week bonanza was wrapped up with a losing runfest at the foot of Table Mountain. After a month of drinking, flying, narrowly avoiding deportation and making friends in the five corners of the globe, the Scotties returned home tired but determined to continue the new tradition of touring far-flung places. For the tour the club introduced a new travelling motto for international games, which can be seen on their trademark yellow and blue striped caps: *Jou Ma Buk Fir Renoster*. In Afrikaans, this translates as 'Your mother bends over for a rhino'.

Sadly, Harry himself was to make only one more tour. The team's resident diplomat, Tony Brennan, happened to have a plum posting in Prague and had established a cricket network in Prague and neighbouring central European countries. Harry and Captain Scott's jumped at the chance to take part in the inaugural Central European Indoor Cricket Championships in Prague in 2004.

In the depths of an icy Prague winter an elite Scotties team took on a trio of Central European teams. Harry seemed to have a bad hacking cough and flu-like symptoms but soldiered on as always, snaffled a few wickets and eked out a few runs against some wily opposition. It was only later that year when he was diagnosed with terminal lung cancer (having never smoked) that his team-mates realised what had been going on. While he turned out in the poorest of health for a few more summer appearances after Prague, this was really his last hurrah. Captain Scott's won in the final in Prague with Harry taking the winning catch.

Since these championships have yet to be repeated, Captain Scott's victory means that the club can claim to be the reigning European Indoor Champions as well as the Antarctic cricket champions and the only club to play a Test series in all five continents.

Harry's funeral was attended by many luminaries of British television and radio comedy (all of whom had donned the white flannels at various times for Captain Scott's) and he is still sorely missed. He was buried with his bat in Kensington, and the Scotties also threw in a cricket ball as the coffin was lowered to give Harry his last half-volley in the corridor of uncertainty that is the after-life.

Harry needn't have worried about his legacy. His trusted lieutenant, Sean Reilly, along with his brothers and a core of regular tourists drawn from many nationalities and unified in the spirit of friendly, charismatic, competitive cricket and world-class socialising, have carried on the torch with gusto. After a period of consolidation and a bit of fixture rationalisation (Captain Scott's now mainly plays on Sundays), the club has remained in vibrant health. It retains some of the traditional 30-year-old fixtures against the Oxford colleges and in pretty Cotswold villages, with some plum recent additions such as the Royal Household and the Honourable Artillery Company. And the tours to far-flung places have become a central focal point of the club's life. These are now fully mixed affairs with wives, girlfriends, partners and children all taking part.

To celebrate his 40th, Paul 'Magic' Daniels, one of the longest serving players, thought cricket in the West Indies would be a suitable backdrop for a party. He was correct. So we all packed off to Tobago for ten days which would include the ODI between West Indies and Sri Lanka at the Queen's Park Oval. Tobago is a fabulous place to holiday. No crime to speak of. Tour: three games, a narrow loss verses Airport, face-saving big six hits against the island champions Sunday School at Buckoo, goat curry, rum punch and 'liming' are often fondly remembered. Not to mention the drone of a conch that can be heard at many a Scott do.

In May 2010, it was time for Harry's widow Lisa to organise a tour to the land of cuckoo clocks and fondue, at the original suggestion of Simon Hewitt, a former player for the French national side, old pal of Harry's from Oxford and Scotty from long ago. Now settled in Cossonay near Gruyere, he didn't end up playing in the end, but it didn't stop this from being the first ever tour in 33 seasons where we were 100 per cent unbeaten.

We didn't beat a country but this time but we weren't far off – the team we beat on the drizzly Saturday were basically the Swiss national side and they were dispatched by four wickets with three overs to spare – plus an easy victory over our hosts the next day. Marred slightly by the hotel owner accusing us of burning the sheets (it was actually mascara staining), this was a satisfying trip.

Malaysia is a fantastic place to tour, so we decided to visit once more, this time in November 2010. Ten days' brilliant weather, good hosts and fabulous food. Our dear friends at Kelawar CC hosted us and treated us like royalty. The match at the Selangor Turf Club was close but on the fifth anniversary of Harry's passing there was only ever going to be one winner. We paused at 3pm to drink a toast to our absent skipper and, galvanised by the sentiment, we fielded like dervishes. The midweek Malaysian team were able to return home with the satisfaction that a 100 per cent tour record doesn't mean it's any easier to work off the excess baggage that comes with visiting Fat Mums in Langkawi. We rounded off the tour with a trip to Penang to play the Penang Sports Club who were duly dispatched.

In 2011 our resident diplomat Tone suggested that since he was now posted in Sudan, it would be easy to arrange a tour to his previous posting in Tanzania. This would include three games, a safari and a trip to Zanzibar. We almost won the first game but alcohol and match fitness are not bed buddies and we succumbed to keen youthful opposition and a six-hour trip in the back of a safari Landy!

The first game had been at the Gymkhana Club against The Dik Diks, Tony Brennan's old club. The sight of Tony in a Scott club shirt galvanised The Dik Diks to a rain-affected victory. The last game of the tour, against a Tanzania development side, was a mismatch. Half the team had Dar Belly, and the rest had added to their own bellies with Serengeti lager to the extent of all sorts of muscle tears and pulls, not to mention Jock's lack of sleep due to his nocturnal attempt at Anglo-American relations.

As the centenary of Robert Falcon Scott's fatal final expedition loomed, Magic mooted a second cricket trip to Antarctica to play an Amundsen XI and avenge the defeat in the race to the Pole! We wouldn't use pit ponies or hot air balloons but cricket bats and balls. Sadly Antarctica is a £10k round trip per person and rustling up eleven Norwegians proved difficult, so we went to Norway for the 17-1-12 Scott's anniversary of reaching the South Pole and played The Oslo Aliens, masquerading as An Amundsen XI, at night on the ice in minus 20. We hooked up with *Cricket Without Boundaries* charity and raised a few pounds for them. Revenge was exacted by The Scott XI. We now play the Aliens as part of their English Tour in April, whilst they have been promoted to the Elite league in Norway and continue to help raise funds for CWB and The Roy Castle Foundation.

As this ode to wandering cricket is being compiled, the Captain Scott Invitation XI are planning Barcelona in May. A tour down under is nailed on for November as Tone has answered Her Majesty's call to deputise for the commissioner in Canberra! Of course, it wouldn't have anything to do with an Ashes series, now would it?

We always have room to accommodate new members, experienced or not, the only caveat being that you try your best, whether it be on the field or in the post-match boat race, in which we boast a six-continent unbeaten record (and as for post boat race relief, as the late great Tony Greig would say, "If you're going to slash, slash hard"). Our evergreen core members Paul Daniels, Sean and James, Dan 'Jocky' Vale, Jimmy Slatter, Mike Stepney, Uncle James and our very own KP, bound together with the organisational and diplomatic skills of Lisa Thompson and Tone, exhibit enough continuing joie de vivre, flat-track bullying and mystery spin to mean the club is in safe hands and we can look forward to many more years of global cricket wandering.

Website: *www.captainscottscricket.com*

Boxbusters

Founded: 1980   Deceased: 2001

by Chris Herring *(once ct. Spratt, b. Salmon)*

They say if you can remember the Boxbusters you weren't there. This was, after all, the '80s. And in the '80s' advertising industry, for whose London agencies the Boxbusters agreeably toiled, keeping fit came a very poor second to getting slaughtered.

Take lunch. Lunch meant an hour in the pub deciding where to go for lunch. Two hours in the expensive restaurant on which we'd decided. Followed by a 'cleansing ale' back in the pub to discuss the events of lunch, frequently into the night. Looking back it's a wonder any of us survived, let alone did any work, let alone played cricket. That we did is as much a testament to our apparently indestructible livers as to our desire to get out of London at weekends in our expensive company cars – usually German, usually black – to bucolic village greens, preferably with an adjacent pub, preferably thatched.

The team had many incarnations over the years, but could usually be described as five or six who could play, four or five who couldn't but thought they could and one or two who couldn't and didn't but agreed to turn up, after frantic Friday night phone calls, as long as beer was involved. But in whatever category they were found, each brought something of their own to the team. For example, the Falstaffian figure of Cliff 'Full English' Feraday would undoubtedly fall in to the first category with the bat, but he also performed an even greater service in the field when wet weather looked like it might close in. It was then that all eyes were on him in case he lay down.

Derek Payne, always known as Sir Derek, certainly looked the part and was voted Boxbuster of the Decade, but perhaps more for the Golden Age insouciance he brought to the side, rather than the prowess he took to the crease. Whilst pavilion purists purred at the elegance of his cover drive, in its execution the ball and his bat so rarely inhabited the same space-time continuum they could have lived in parallel universes. And Alan Midgley, professional Yorkshireman and campaigner for the return of timeless Tests. He scored over 1,500 runs opening the batting, but they came at a rate so glacial that onlookers would be dismayed to find that their clothes had gone out of fashion between singles.

Then there was our backroom team led by our scorer and occasional player, Dennis Lewis. Dennis produced annually what must be the most detailed statistical analysis ever lavished on a dysfunctional wandering cricket team, the astonishing *Denwis Boxbusters' Almanack*. In the 1992 edition, for example, you can glean that of the 19,045 runs the Boxbusters had scored up to the end of that year, 1,950 had been extras. Although quite what you'd do with information like that still puzzles experts.

Many of those runs were amassed in places with names redolent of the sort of English rural idyll we craved: Knotty Green and Ley Hill in Bucks, Brightling Park and Rotherfield in East Sussex, Little Waldingfield in Suffolk and Thaxted in Essex (against Bill Philpott's All-Stars for the Great Turd of Thaxted Trophy, of which less later). Burwash in East Sussex, whom we finally managed to beat, narrowly, at the sixth attempt, was a stone's throw from the stately pile and trout farm of Roger Daltrey of The Who. What was it we took to these otherwise sensible clubs, who for reasons best known to themselves invited us to their unspoilt parts of the country, and amazingly invited us back?

Well, we took our club motto emblazoned on our sweaters – *Per Violentium Victi* – approximately Latin for *Victory Through Violence*. And our badge, a gentleman's abdominal protector, whose last wearer now presumably has a speaking voice an octave or two higher. (*Victory Through Violence* had come out best in exhaustive focus groups – we were in advertising – narrowly outscoring *Overbearing In Victory, Surly In Defeat*.) Naturally, we took our sweaters with the tasteful club colours of red, black and blue. Blood and bruises, you see, it was all thought through.

We took our penchant for the official team drink – the Dark & Stormy, dark rum and ginger beer. A cocktail that tended to get darker and more lethal as the evening wore on. And we took our WAGs, otherwise known as the Boxbiters. Quite where this dubious appellation came from or why it was thought appropriate is unknown, but it does explain the name of another group of usually more enthusiastic supporters, the Boxnippers.

We generally spared domestic opposition our team dance, Fish Dancing, which we reserved for foreign tours. What you required for Fish Dancing, often Formation Fish Dancing, was a chair, more often a barstool, on which to lay across on your stomach, the ability to breast-stroke in time to music, or out of time, it didn't seem to matter, and beforehand prodigious quantities of Dark & Stormy. It was introduced to the team by regular tourist, Ric Hawkes, first breaking out on our 1987 tour to Ibiza.

Ibiza? Yes, they have a cricket team, or had in 1987, Eivissa CC. And fine hosts they were. A bit too fine, in fact. Their tactic of getting us hammered the night before only worsened the hammering we were to suffer the following day. Our first foreign tour had been to Corfu, where we played three matches in front of understandably large crowds. Understandable because one side of the pitch was lined with tavernas where people habitually gathered in large numbers for lunch al fresco whether there was any cricket on or not. Nevertheless, even the most indifferent diner had to be impressed with our bowling. Some of the sixes hit off it threatened to violate Albanian airspace.

A tour followed to Ireland, where we played the rather alarmingly abbreviated Irish Research & Advertising in Dublin and the MCC (Murphy's (Stout) Cricket Club) in Cork – followed by what can only be described quite literally as a piss-up in a brewery. Our tours to France, a week in the Dordogne to play Cricket-Club De Perigueux, and several long-weekend trips to Cabris near Grasse, were our most successful in cricketing terms (despite a Cabris resident once striding defiantly across the wicket mid-over shouting, "Jouez a Londres!"). Unlike our one and only trip to Belgium to play Royal Brussels CC. Tom Rodwell, later Chairman of the Lord's Taverners, was familiar with their ground, on the battlefield at Waterloo, but still managed to get us hopelessly lost, twice. Posterity would be the sufferer here. In the grandly appointed RBCC pavilion, there is a large leather-bound book containing quite long, hand-written entries faithfully describing visiting teams and the games. So impressed with us were our hosts that we have been immortalised with 'The Boxbusters turned up late'.

Back home two decidedly damp tours to the Lakes and Northumberland were remarkable only for the first Boxbusters century, scored by Dave Tyler. It was a feat

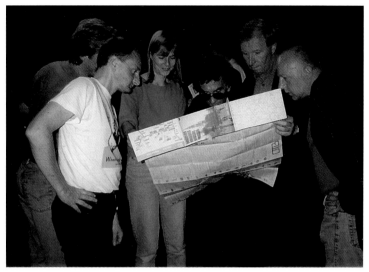

Lost – the all-too-common fate of the wandering team, this time in Brussels

celebrated by leaving the Riverdale Hall Hotel bereft of Copperhead Cider. Also at home we occasionally played other wandering teams in neutral, albeit agreeable, surroundings. Among them were The Magpies, The Heavy Rollers and most notoriously Tim Rice's Heartaches. The latter remain the only opposition to do the unthinkable. They batted on after tea. Even having tea prepared by Lulu couldn't make up for that. No autographs were sought after the game, and the fixture quietly dropped.

No Boxbusters' retrospective would be complete without mention of our Dinner & Dances, always introduced by the club's theme tune, Ray Parker Jnr's *Ghostbusters* ('Who you gonna call? Boxbusters!'). Starting at the Thames Rowing Club in Putney and then moving to The Oval and eventually Lord's, we were entertained by the likes of guest speakers Peter Parfitt, the very funny David 'Bumble' Lloyd and dear old Bill Frindall, who startled everyone at the end of his after-dinner speech by congratulating the club on "the finest collection of crumpet I've ever seen at one of these things."

The Boxbusters Hall of Fame, if there was one, would have to include the following; Alan Lofthouse, the Bat Out of Hull; Dave Buonaguidi, the Boxbusters' only Italian international (and we suspect the only one in amateur cricket); Warren Brown, our token Australian; and of course Ken Mullen (our only multi-centurion) and Brian Seaward, who between them scored well over 4,000 runs and took nearly 400 wickets. There would also have to be a Boxbusters Hall of Infamy with two occupants. Kevin 'Shabby' Kneale and his dog, Mr Patch. Shabby (you'd only have to see him to know how he got the nickname) kept wicket as if the ball was a live grenade, while the long-suffering Mr Patch hid his head in his paws on the boundary as successive chances hit the deck. My final reflection is of a knock by Richard White-Smith whose fifty, said locals with long memories, was the best they'd witnessed on a Hinton Charterhouse sticky.

It's hard to remember sometimes, through all the disasters, cock-ups and, of course, the Dark & Stormies, that on our day we could actually play a bit, too.

Kensington

Founded: 1982 (previously 1848)

by Anthony Gibson

Kensington has two main claims to fame as a wandering cricket club. The first is that it went into a state of suspended animation for more years – 123, to be precise – than any other club of which we are aware; and the second is that it claims to be the only truly international nomadic side, in that it makes a very conscious effort to draw its players from as many different nationalities as possible.

The original Kensington CC was founded as long ago as 1848 by four gentlemen who met at the home of a Mr Pickering-Clark in Earl's Terrace, to discuss that possibility. They obviously decided to give it a try, for at a meeting soon afterwards in the King's Arms, the club was formally incorporated. The founders had no intention of being nomadic. Indeed, they signed an agreement with a Mrs Johnson of Holland Farm, to rent one of her fields as their ground. But Mrs Johnson evidently drove a hard bargain, for the £15 a year rent that she charged for her three-acre field was the equivalent in today's money of £1,230! It evidently proved too much of a financial burden for the infant club to sustain. Even though the subscription was raised by four shillings to 25 shillings for its second year (just over £100 in today's money), it wasn't enough. Despite a riotous party, which it took no fewer than five pages of the minute book to describe, the club folded at the end of the 1849 season.

That wasn't the end of cricket in Kensington, by any means. The *Kensington Gazette* reported on matches in 1853 and 1855, and the scorebook of Bishop's Stortford, a club which the modern Kensington plays regularly, records matches against Kensington in 1905 and 1906. The Rev Geoffrey Whitfield even owns a bat presented by the club to Mr R Berryman in 1877 for scoring the most runs during that season. But to all intents and purposes Kensington CC was, if not dead, then certainly dormant, and would stay that way for very many years.

The first green shoots of revival showed themselves in 1973, in the shape of a side called 'The Devonshire XI' (after the pub in Marloes Road) which was put together by Sunil Amar and Anthony Rickard to play a charity match in aid of Help the Aged against the Lamb Inn at Andover, whose landlady, Anthony's mother, had just turned 50. It raised only £10, but all concerned had such a splendid time that they resolved there and then to put their cricket on a more organised basis.

After a short spell at the Scarsdale in Edwardes Square, the new club found its spiritual home at the Britannia in Allen St, and was re-named the True Brits. The number of fixtures gradually increased, as did the number of members, and in 1982 Sunil Amar obtained the Royal Borough's permission to use their name, a committee was elected at an extraordinary general meeting and Kensington CC was officially re-born.

Sunil Amar was the first captain, with Anthony Rickard chairman, Richard Waters secretary and Bill Rodwell fixtures secretary. They made a strong and effective team. The fixture list grew, and with it the number of members. Initially, they were mainly English, with a seasoning of Indians and West Indians, but then came an influx of Australians, giving the club a cosmopolitan flavour which it has never lost and now actively cultivates.

*Sunil Amar with Farokh Engineer
at the Annual Ball, 2011*

"We like to think of ourselves as an international wandering club," explains Sunil Amar, now the club's president. "If variety is the spice of life then, as far as we are concerned, diversity is the spice of cricket. The key is to attract a good balance of cricketers from all sorts of backgrounds, ethnic and otherwise. We're a real mixed bag, and I think we enjoy ourselves all the more on that account."

It has proved to be a highly successful formula. The playing membership and fixture list have been increased in tandem, so that everyone who wants a game can get one fairly regularly, and they are now playing over 40 matches a season – sometimes two on the same Sunday – mostly against good club sides on picturesque grounds in London and the Home Counties, but also on tour. They've toured Europe regularly, taking in cities like Rome, Antwerp, Paris, Amsterdam and Oporto, as well as less likely venues such as Brittany, Corfu and Menorca, and in 2008, travelled all the way to India. There is a strong and very sensible emphasis on bringing younger players on. In the mid-'90s, there was a very welcome influx of young cricketers from St James' School, several of whom are still playing for the club today, and a feature of the fixture list is Youths v Veterans, always a hard-fought but sociable encounter in which historically the Youths have, quite rightly, been dominant.

Kensington CC believes in remaining true to the spirit of wandering cricket, off the field as well as on it. They've become one of the few wandering clubs to have succeeded in attracting sponsorship: mainly in kind – from Cobra beer and Johnnie Walker Black Label whisky. The beer they take with them to drink in the changing room as a post-match thirst-quencher. Of the two bottles of whisky provided per match by the sponsor, one is presented to the opposition team's 'man of the match', while the other is donated to the club bar. This is a club which sets great store by rewarding hospitality with generosity. "Our opponents always say that we put more over the bar after a game than anyone else they play," says Sunil Amar, "and in all our 40 years, we have hardly ever lost a fixture."

Nor is sponsorship their only innovation. Inspired by watching The Masters, with its green jacket to the winner, Sunil decided that a maroon jacket should be awarded to any player who had given particularly outstanding service to the club. He earned one himself last year, and not before time, considering that he's taken 390 wickets for the club over its lifetime with his medium-pace swingers, and plans to carry on for a few years yet. Another good idea, which other wanderers would do well to consider copying, is to include the cost of the black tie annual dinner and prize-giving in the membership sub, so guaranteeing a good attendance – wives and girlfriends included – for what sounds like a riotous evening.

Kensington are a good cricketing side. Test players like Sarfraz Nawaz, Kapil Dev, Arun Lal, Kirti Azad and the Australian quick bowler, Rodney Hogg, who enjoyed the cricket so much that he stayed for half a dozen games, have turned out for them. Off the field, Farokh Engineer, the former Indian wicket-keeper, and Keith Bradshaw, the Tasmanian cricketer who went on to be Secretary of the MCC, have been highly influential supporters. Among their recent players, Jamie Kelleher from Melbourne, now recovering from a serious eye injury, has probably been the batting star, with captain Chris Ledger a tower of strength in the middle order and Michael Blumberg still going strong, if not very rapidly, at 71. The long-serving fixtures secretary San Gore has also played a big part in Kensington's success, not only with his bat and gloves but with his tireless organisation behind the scenes. Whilst cricketing ability is a help, what matters even more, according to Sunil, is that the Kensington members play the game in the right spirit. "Characters are more important than skills," he insists, and Kensington CC has had more than its fair share, among them Neeraj Nayar, the club's marketing guru, Vino Nath and Navneet Ball, now happily back playing again after an injury which cost him an eye.

Kensington CC stands out among wandering clubs not just for its international flavour but for its success. The modern incarnation strikes me as the diametric opposite of the Victorian original. They seem to have been a fairly clueless bunch of local gentry who gave up at the first reverse. Their modern equivalents are bright, innovative, classless, cosmopolitan and going great guns.

"Continuity, commitment and delegation are the keys," says Sunil Amar, "as well as ensuring that everyone gets a game. Combine all of that with players who are characters, who enjoy their cricket and who play it in the right way, and you've got a winning formula." It certainly works with Kensington.

Website: *www.kensingtoncricketclub.com*

Gouvia Marina, Corfu

Chelsea Arts Club

Founded: 1984

by David Maddocks and Stephen Bartley

The club was founded in 1984 by David Maddocks and Stephen Bartley at the suggestion of Dudley Winterbottom. It played its inaugural match against a side representing the Arts Council of Great Britain captained by Anthony Reynolds at London Fields on 15 July 1984. The CACCC, facing a total of 139, were bowled out for 49, losing by 90 runs, with D Maddocks top-scoring with 15. Another defeat followed two weeks later at Durrington, and the first season ended with a hailstorm at Tormarton in an eventful match against the Salutation Sloggers. This match was notable for the inclusion of Reg Scarlett of the West Indies in the CACCC XI, the only time that a Test cricketer has played for the club to date.

The next season kicked off with a local Chelsea match against the Phene Arms CC played in Battersea Park. This resulted in a defeat by 78 runs, despite having the opposition three wickets down for just four runs, including a wicket with the first ball of the match. Unfortunately A de Keller responded with seven for 10. A memorable dinner was held at the Chelsea Arts Club afterwards. A nine-wicket defeat by Alfriston followed. However, on 23 June the club avoided defeat for the first time, by tying a contest against the ACME XI captained by Jonathan Harvey. This epic game was played at Victoria Park. ACME, set to make 70, were coasting to victory at 63 for six, when their last four wickets fell for six runs, Bartley finishing with figures of six for 13. The ACME opening bat Christopher Le Brun, now President of the Royal Academy, was caught by Charles Hickey off the bowling of Maddocks for 0.

On 25 July of that second season the CACCC recorded its first victory by two wickets in another match against the Salutation Sloggers who were captained by Eric Defty, architect and one-time drinking buddy of the famous American sculptor David Smith, partner of Sandra Blow RA. He claimed to have once captained a Durham University XI that included Frank 'Typhoon' Tyson. A loss against Fenn Ditton was followed by two more victories against the National Trust XI at Dorney and the Full Tossers at Ashwell. Nine fixtures were played in all during this second season, and the club could now be said to be firmly established.

The 1986 season began with another match against the Phene Arms on 3 May in Battersea Park with the CACCC winning by three wickets. The fixture list included games against the Wimbledon Wanderers captained by Chris Potter, the Imperial War Museum, West Norwood, ACME CC, Market Lavington All Stars, Keevil CC, the Slug & Lettuce, the Arts Council, the Bystanders, Salutation Sloggers, Rode CC, Leverett CC, Snettisham, The General Trading Company, and Dornay CC.

The 1987 fixture list was notable for the inclusion of a match against the V&A XI captained by Nicky Bird which was played at Stonor. This fixture is still played today, along with our matches against the Phene Philanderers and Keevil CC. The Keevil game, which is still played in the picturesque private ground at Keevil Manor in Wiltshire,

Chelsea Arts Club CC at Keevil Manor, by Liz Wright
photograph coutesy of the artist at Chelsea Arts Club

courtesy of Christopher Vernon, was notable for a memorable draw, thanks mainly to a match-saving innings of 68 not out by Bartley.

1988 started badly with a pounding at the hands of the Phene Philanderers. Their opening bowler F Bushby had the fine figures of nine for 22 as the CACCC subsided to an 81-run defeat in Battersea Park. Several more drubbings followed until we were invited to play a match at Brympton D'Evercy, the home of the Ponsonby-Fane family, one of whose members had been a founder of I Zingari. The match against Patrick Haran's Invitation XI, The Plunkneteers, was to provide the occasion on which the first century was scored for the CACCC, 110 out of 145 by S Bartley. Fred Ingrams chipped in with 84, enabling the Club to declare at its highest ever score – 266 for five. A fixture against Urchfont preceded our Sunday game at Keevil, making for an excellent Wiltshire weekend of cricket with many unforgettable evenings at the Lamb on the Saturday night.

At the end of 1989 we played our first match against Mark Mason's Morris Men from Hell at Dunsfold. Later we came to adopt Dunsfold as our unofficial 'home' ground, and it has provided an attractive and enjoyable venue for many of our games over the past 20 years. The same year we played against the Groucho Club for the first time. Their opening bat notched up 152, and they scored a resounding victory by 139 runs. When we played them again two years later, we gained sweet revenge by bowling them out for 25 and, for some reason, the fixture has never been renewed.

The 1990s saw the club broaden its horizons with a Whitsun tour to Cornwall where we played the Penzance Arts Club and later added a match at Trengilly Wartha. In 1991 a match to celebrate the 100th Anniversary of the founding of the Chelsea Arts Club was played at Burton's Court. The players and spectators dressed up in period costume of the 1890s, and a Whistler XV played a Ruskin XV for the prize money of one farthing. Among the players invited were Roland Butcher, Clive Radley, Geoff Howarth, Nicholas Pocock, Roger McGough and Brian Glover. Jeffrey Bernard umpired – until he had to retire 'unwell'. The event was attended by over 1,000 people but still managed to lose an inordinate amount of money.

The teams after the Centenary match

The late 1990s and start of the present century saw the fixture list expand to about 25 fixtures a season and the beginning of the overseas tours. It also saw us attracting better players who, although they had played at a higher level, enjoyed the craich of the club. We started winning many more matches than we were losing and in 2003 had our most successful season ever, losing just two matches out of 25. The flavour of the club was also changing, taking on an international slant. Although we had had players from overseas previously, we now had two Australians, two Sri Lankans, two South Africans, a West Indian and an Indian, all of whom played regularly.

The overseas tours, of which there have been five, have been to Malta (twice), France, Estonia, Portugal and 2013 will see us touring in Paris (well, just outside!). The first Malta tour was undertaken over a dull few February days, and we lost both games badly. However, the social side was one of the most entertaining ever, with a local bar of dubious standards and women taking centre stage. One player woke up one morning to discover a bill for over £1,000 on his credit card, with the receipt showing a bottle of vodka and one of champagne. Some evening!

The Estonia tour saw the tobogganing division of the Chelsea Arts Club competing in the first Ice Cricket World Championships and, much to our surprise, we won the damn thing! There were about 16 teams competing, and the pitch was sheet ice (as opposed to the matting used in St Moritz), with a composite ball which moved viciously off the pitch. The batsmen wore pads and gloves, as much against the bitter cold (-29°C!) as for cricketing purposes. As there was about four to five centimetres of snow on the 'outfield', we became very adept at hitting the ball over the infield and running as many as possible whilst they scrabbled around for the ball in the snow. Happily, the captain and joint author of this piece was spared the tradition of dunking the winning skipper in the frozen lake. The victory was all the more remarkable for the fact that most of our players had had no sleep the night before, having been locked out of the hotel! And as there is no evidence that a second championships has ever been held, we're entitled to consider ourselves the reigning Ice Cricket World Champions.

The Portugal tour to Oporto was all about the vast quantities of port consumed, as might be expected. We stayed at the splendidly English Lawn Tennis and Cricket Club and could walk out of the back door straight onto the pitch. We won our first match quite comfortably and did well to escape with a draw in the second, given that we started it with only six players, the others all nursing sore heads from the night before.

As we head into our 29th year, we are pleased to be able to report that the club is in rude health, with an excellent fixture list, a good pool of players and a distinguished and active president in Henry Blofeld, who says that he enjoys watching the CACCC play as much as any cricket anywhere. This year will see us play our 500th fixture. As co-founders, back in 1984, we could certainly never have envisaged that.

Harry Baldwin Occasionals

Founded: 1986-ish

by Michael Simkins

I can't remember where and how the Harry Baldwin Occasionals was formed, except that its genesis was, as with so many dilettante teams, the rich primordial swamp of cricket and showbiz. One moment we were just a load of mates playing impromptu matches on Sunday morning in a park in my home town of Brighton, our only kit a set of battered stumps and with a pair of motorcycle gauntlets for wicket-keeping gloves – the next, we were in our 27th year, with fixture lists, averages, annual subscriptions, yearbooks and even a small mobile scoreboard. (I'd been out for 99 twice in matches in which there wasn't one available, and I'd frankly had enough.) We even celebrated our longevity a couple of years back by managing to wangle a game on the most hallowed of all turfs, the main strip at the Sussex County Ground, where I'd watched my heroes – Parks, Greig and Snow – as a schoolboy nearly five decades before.

I do know that a love of cricket, formed while watching Sussex on that very ground as a kid and nurtured through an education at Brighton Grammar School (captains during my time there included Gehan Mendis and John Spencer), kindled a love of the game, and that, years later, having by now trained as an actor at RADA and appearing at Chichester Festival Theatre (in Shakespeare's *Anthony & Cleopatra*, if you're wondering), I was asked if I would organise a team to play the theatre side in a charity match. One by one I rustled up a motley collection from my past: actors from London, old friends and schoolmates from Brighton, and other assorted loafers and deadbeats, until I had a team. We all had two things in common: a deep-seated love of playing (and talking about) the game and a collective disenchantment with competitive club cricket, a world which most of us had sampled in our early twenties and which, to our jaundiced eye, was a world that had long since lost its charms. We'd all experienced the same thing: a culture in which winning had supplanted enjoyment as the reason for playing, in which personal failure was met with sour admonishment, and whose protagonists seemed to have no subject of conversation in the pub afterwards except the inner workings of motor cars and the latest football results. Perhaps we'd all just played for the wrong clubs.

Our aim was simple: to play with maximum keenness and maximum fun. The first game against Chichester Festival Theatre proved such a success that a return fixture was organised at Preston Park in Brighton on the old velodrome, where a decade before I'd had some of my most miserable moments as a weekend cricketer. The following season a list of 18 fixtures was organised, against sides ranging from flourishing local clubs to the National Theatre, the RSC and dog-eared pub sides.

For our emblem only one man would suffice: the famous image, taken at the turn of the 19th century, by the Victorian photographer George Beldam, of Hampshire's Harry

Baldwin. If you've seen the photograph you'll need no reminding. A small rotund man, about 4' 6" inches tall and nearly as wide, with a cap clamped to his head, a rubicund face, impressive moustache and a girth that would have had Colin Milburn purring with pleasure. He was famously described by CB Fry as 'a cheery bowler. The ideal net bowler'. That would do for us. Better still, he'd actually be hitching up his trousers as the shutter clicks. This was a man who was used to life in the slow lane, purveying his amiable trundlers for many years and with great success, and obviously no stranger to the joys of the pork pie. Baldwin would be our lodestar.

The club motto followed as night follows day: a line from WS Gilbert's half-forgotten operetta *The Mountebanks* describing a gang of lily-livered brigands. Their motto? 'Heroism Without Risk'. Perfect. We've not yet got round to club colours, but someone recently suggested white with a yellow stripe down the back might be appropriate, given our ability to fold against quick bowling faster than a collapsing picnic chair.

The next two decades became a blur of cricketing memories: endless trips up and down the M23 and round the M25, making 24 rounds of tuna and sweetcorn doorsteps at 7am in the morning, searching petrol stations for directions and boxes of Mr Kipling almond slices; and always, always, looking out of the window at the skies first thing on Sunday morning. Season by season our squad strengthened, as word of our fame and our convivial ethos spread. Bit by bit we attracted players who liked the cut of our jib, that of competitiveness seasoned with humour. On the rare occasions we played against sides that took it all too seriously, we'd merely suggest that if they were as good as they thought they were, then why were they playing against no-hopers like us? It usually shut them up.

One of the more piquant occasions was when we played the village of Nuthurst on their wondrous old ground near Horsham. With Sunday approaching and the team one short, I recruited the services of a young director I'd worked with called Sam Mendes. I knew he was handy, but not that he'd once opened for England Schools and had played in a village final at Lord's. With the Baldwins marooned, as was our custom, on 55 for five, he rescued our collapse, hitting 80 coming in at number seven before taking five wickets in as many overs as fifth change, with brisk medium fast, rounding it off with a catch at slip that Bobby Simpson would have been proud to have claimed. Afterwards the Nuthurst secretary and his fellow players (quite rightly) had some stern words for me as opposing captain about drafting in players who were palpably far too good for our standard: but, just as he was about to let rip, Mendes' then girlfriend, Kate Winslet, arrived in a sporty open top. I've never seen eleven men change their expressions so quickly.

It's odd how the results have long faded from memory, while individual moments are still burned on the brain. I recall going out to face a young tearaway fast-bowling teenager on a dodgy track at Petworth House to the sound of a brass band playing *The Dead March* from Handel's *Saul* in an adjoining field. Then there was that game at Ardingly in Sussex in which our leading bowler (a paramedic) interrupted his over in order to attend to a drowning child in a nearby swimming pool (the child survived but our batting didn't).

In short, my memories are of endless summer days, each one rounded off with a visit to the pub where we'd sit round like old gits and discuss the game afresh, while our long-suffering wives sat in mute horror, trying to understand the endless fascination exerted by

the best-loved game. It was my long-suffering wife Julia who once described the matches involving the Baldwins, and indeed social cricket in general, as "meaningless encounters between groups of pathetic middle-aged sexually inadequate no-hopers". I've yet to find a more apt description.

And now, 25 years on, we're about to mark the equivalent of our jubilee. Nearly 300 players have appeared for the Baldwins – we've played at innumerable venues from council recreation grounds to Hove and the main strip at Arundel Castle. Our opponents have ranged from ten-year-old boys to Alvin Kallicharran (now playing for South Hampstead CC) to the actor currently playing Carson in *Downton Abbey*. My 2007 book, *Fatty Batter*, chronicling (in part) the fortunes of the team, has given us a degree of (utterly unjustified) profile, with the result that we now get beaten by better teams than we once did.

The years have, of course, changed things. Embrocation and liniment have replaced snazzy aftershave as the aroma of choice in the dressing room. Many of the club's most venerable players have moved away, retired or even died (a sure sign of a club's venerability), while I have now given up the captaincy, which has passed on through Britain's leading expert on the poems of Wordsworth, via an actor now carving a name for himself in *Desperate Housewives*, to the director of the hit show *War Horse*. Our fate currently rests on the shoulders of the author William Fiennes, whose approach to the game is so pitch perfect to the club's needs that I wouldn't have been all surprised to hear he'd been revealed as a distant descendant of the great Harry Baldwin himself.

As we approach our 30th anniversary, I look back (albeit with the aid of bifocals) at some great days spent in the company of great blokes. There's even talk of us celebrating our anniversary with that most venerable of badges of true middle-aged opulence – a dinner-dance. I can see us now, all spreading waistlines within straining cummerbunds, prawn cocktails, and a little gentle jiving to some old Abba hits played by a three-piece combo on a tiny stage in front of a glitter curtain.

And you know what? I wouldn't have it any other way…

Journeymen

Founded: 1988

by Stephen Chalke

"How did you lot get together?" the opposing captain asked in the side bar of a Devon pub. It was 1989, our second summer, and we had just embarked, rather anxiously, on our first tour of the West Country. As the team's founder I was all set to explain our convoluted origins – the unsatisfactory cricket some of us had been playing in London parks, the hours of debate about who to invite, the adoption of strict rules about on-field behaviour – when Geoff, a freer spirit, leapt in.

"These two," he said, pointing to our bald-headed seam bowler and the bearded off-spinner at his side, "met in Wormwood Scrubs prison." Around the room he went, itemising our various crimes: armed robbery, GBH, petty fraud. Then there was Peter, with his distinguished grey hair and his 1950s blazer and flannels, he was the governor who had set the team up, as part of the prison's rehabilitation programme. "And, of course, this man," he went on, pointing at me, "was the chaplain."

At the time we were a pretty ropy bunch of cricketers, oscillating between good-humoured despair and earnest discussion about how to improve the team. In the end, the earnestness won out. If we were going to play at nice village grounds, enjoy their well-prepared pitches and delicious teas, the least we could do was give our opponents a decent game.

We had some bowlers. In his youth Anthony Douglas had led the attack for Middlesex second eleven. Andrew, my brother, had mixed his leg breaks and googlies in good club cricket, and Marlon Hayes, our Barbadian all-rounder, was fast enough to frighten a few village batsmen. But the batting just wasn't good enough. We had all the disadvantages of an away team – playing on unfamiliar tracks, driving long distances to the games – and we lacked the technique to adapt. If we batted first, we were happy to reach 130.

Anthony's 40th birthday party was a turning point. He was a rising star in the world of social work management, and a woman in his department turned up with a newish partner, a lawyer who in conversation revealed himself to be a cricketer. A batsman, too. Anthony and I spent the afternoon circling round him and comparing notes. He'd played for the first eleven at Marlborough … his current team were packing up … he was thinking of retiring. Back home I found him in *Wisden*: J.Goodrich, top of the Marlborough batting averages in 1970. Furthermore, two of those below him had played for the Public Schools XI at Lord's. But then John's father was only a Church of England vicar; their fathers were Freddie Brown and Denis Compton.

All we had to do was convince him he wanted to play for us – without conveying any sense of our desperation. Luckily he took the bait as, two years later, did Nigel Bloch, a refugee from apartheid South Africa who after each game would ring his wife to tell her how many runs he had scored and what his season's average now was, always to two decimal places. He also had a disconcerting habit at the start of every over of pointing at each fielder, counting aloud to eleven, as if he half-suspected the opposition were trying to sneak on an extra man when he wasn't looking.

With Nigel and John at the top of the order, we became a good side. One time in Essex a newcomer was told to bat at number six. "That's nice," he said to somebody, only to get the reply: "Forget it, you won't get in at six." And he didn't.

First and foremost we were a team of friends, often bringing our families to games. As several of us moved out of London, we took to bunching up the fixtures: a week in the West Country, four days over the late May bank holiday in Norfolk, a long weekend in Derbyshire – and, best of all, three consecutive all-day games at Fenner's.

It was in Derbyshire that I made my highest ever score, 84 not out. At one point their fast bowler sent down a fiery over, full of short-pitched deliveries, which he accompanied with a fair amount of grunting and bad language. At the end of it he ran into the pavilion, emerged with his bag and drove out of the ground at high speed. "It's nothing personal," their keeper reassured me. "He's gone to conduct choral evensong."

By the mid-1990s our fixture card had mushroomed to 30 games, and several of us, travelling from here, there and everywhere, were playing almost all of them. One week we would be beside the lake in front of Holkham Hall, the Earl of Leicester's Palladian home in Norfolk; three weeks later we would be in *Last of the Summer Wine* country in south Yorkshire; then we would be on the waterfront at Instow in north Devon. We could have been sponsored by Esso.

We even had a no-nonsense motivator, Chris, the son of a career soldier. "Come on, guys, get out here," he'd bellow as we lurked pre-match in the changing room. Then he would hit up great steepling catches that match after match left us taking the field with bruised fingers and thumbs. But somehow we let him do it; it was all part of our mad enthusiasm. Chris was a fitness fanatic, with a rowing machine at home. "I'm the second fastest in the world for my age," he told us one day.

Some opponents said we were their favourite fixture. We were from far away, not part of their niggling local rivalries, and we were a happy bunch. We played the game keenly and competitively – but not at the expense of friendliness. In those years we preferred clubs who did not play league cricket. They tended to treat the games more seriously, and mostly they played the declaration format. To get the best out of such afternoons, we insisted that each new Journeymen captain read EM Rose's *How To Win At Cricket*, a superb primer for positive captaincy in such contests.

In the early years we talked about which of us had turned forty, speculating how long we could carry on. The talk was much the same when we were turning fifty. The bonds of friendship were strong, that was the essence of the team. However, when eventually we needed fresh recruits, it was hard to persuade younger players that they wanted to spend twenty days a summer with a bunch of 60-year-olds.

One by one our opponents have joined leagues, and their games with us have become only a light diversion from the main action of their summer. But perhaps, as we have grown old and less capable, the contests matter less to us as well.

The Journeymen at an autumnal Kew Green, by Susanna Kendall

In the late 1990s I passed the organisation to Humphrey Keenlyside. Unlike his ancestor, the arresting officer in the Gunpowder Plot, he always sees the best in everybody, and that's kept us going in our declining years. In 2001, to breathe fresh life into the venture, he set up a trip to Oporto, and the success of that led to further sorties into Europe: to Paris, Amsterdam and Sofia; Malta, Menorca and Milan.

John Goodrich has returned to squash, winning a place in the England Over-55 team. My brother Andrew, late to have children, can no longer spare the time. But the rest of us keep going one way and another. Marlon battles on despite major surgery on his bowling shoulder. Anthony finds time despite holding down a high-profile government job in childcare. And Chris, though he is now swimming 180 lengths three evenings a week, is starting to become more tolerant of our "rubbish fitness".

Some things haven't changed, though. At the end of each afternoon Nigel still updates his batting average, for season and for career, though I did notice that he's only doing it to one decimal place now. One evening after a couple of drinks I confidently challenged him to a game of chess, only to discover rather rapidly, to much background laughter, that he'd twice represented South Africa in Chess Olympiads in the early 1970s. For the record he's now scored 12,346 runs for us at an average of 46.41. With 16 hundreds and 92 fifties.

We are now entering our 26th summer, approaching our 500th fixture. Marlon has played almost 400 of them, and several more of us are close to 365. A whole year out of our lives. But then, as Anthony says, why not? There are many worse ways to spend a year of one's life. And it won't last much longer.

Website: *www.thejourneymen.co.uk*

Rain Men

Founded: 1998

by Marcus Berkmann

It all started with Robert Falcon Scott, CVO, as so many things do. Back in the late 1970s, when Mike Gatting was still young and promising, I was an undergraduate at Oxford, heading inexorably for a double third in maths. To distract ourselves from the work we weren't doing anyway, a group of us formed a cricket team, which we named the Captain Scott Invitation XI. We were inspired by the legendary polar explorer, who, though resolutely stiff of upper lip, had a merely average record in his core activity of polar exploring. Roald Amundsen, who beat him to the South Pole, had taken huskies, as recommended in all the books. Scott eschewed these hardy little dogs and took horses, which all died, as did he and his men on the way back home. We could sympathise. As cricketers, we played hard and we never gave of anything less than our best, but our best simply wasn't any good. In our first couple of seasons we lost game after game after game in villages around Oxford, but my, did we enjoy it. And when we graduated with our BAs and our sharp new forward defensives, we took the team with us, and started all over again in London.

Wandering cricket teams, especially new ones, tend to acquire their characters from the monomaniacs who run them, and the Scotts had two: me, and Harry Thompson, who had been my best friend since the age of ten. Harry went on to be a successful TV producer, biographer, novelist and renaissance man before dying dreadfully young in 2005 at the age of 45. I mourn him still. But we had a tempestuous friendship, I think it's best to say. We fell out appallingly several times over the years, but carried on writing together and running a cricket team together, although as the years passed we came to disagree even on that. I saw the Scotts essentially as a social construct, as a group of friends who liked driving around the home counties at weekends playing a modest standard of cricket on beautiful village greens. Harry was more single-minded. Having started as the team's worst cricketer – quite an achievement in itself – he had transformed himself into an obdurate opening batsman and a nifty medium-pace bowler, with more variations than batsmen tended to realise. He captained the team on Saturdays, I captained it on Sundays. Yes, we played twice a weekend. Why not? We were in our twenties and there was nothing else to do. But while the Sunday team remained the same faintly shambolic outfit it had always been, the Saturday team gradually became sharper, fiercer and more interested in crushing the opposition underfoot like an ant.

By 1994, when I came to write *Rain Men*, we effectively had two different teams playing every weekend, neither of whom much liked each other. This may account for the book's deeply cynical tone, although I would still say that it was written more in sorrow than in anger. As it is, the success of the book probably accelerated the process of dissolution. After the 1997 season I and my friends had had enough, and we seceded, on an amicable basis, we hoped, given that the players who remained were probably just as happy to see the back of us as we were of them. It took me some years to realise that the resentments on their side were deep and lingering, and probably exacerbated by the fact that on our side, we barely gave them a second thought. After all, we had a new team to run.

And so came into being Rain Men CC, blatantly named after my book because we thought we would get better fixtures that way. (This turned out to be true.) Harry had retained the rump of the talent base, but I had the bald and the fat, the partially sighted, the unco-ordinated and the enthusiastic but useless, which number naturally included myself. I should emphasise here that I am a genuinely poor cricketer by any possible definition of the term. I am a stodgy, strikingly limited batsmen, who used to open from time to time but never scored any runs, by dint of not having any shots. I'm a moderate fielder, in that I can catch the ball, or dive over it rather stylishly if it's going very fast, but I can't throw it back to save my life. And I haven't bowled since 1985 in Finchingfield in Essex, when my first (and only) over lasted 15 balls. I have often felt that I have the right temperament to be a decent bowler. It's only the ability to get the ball down to the other end that I seem to lack.

From the first, Rain Men had an open door policy. I believe strongly that a wandering side needs to be in a state of permanent recruitment. You never know where players are going to come from; you just know that the ones you already have might not stay. In their twenties or thirties, players are apt to find girlfriends or wives, and if those girlfriends don't like cricket, that's it: they're off. In their thirties or forties, it's children; in their forties or fifties, it's golf; in their fifties or sixties it's simple decrepitude. There are countless reasons not to play cricket, and I hear most of them in the course of a season. But a wandering team that starts with a clique and won't expand from it will not survive in the long term. So new players turn up, often by the most circuitous of routes. Once I put an alert out on Facebook with a day's notice and the husband of a friend of a friend of an ex-girlfriend of mine said he was free. In 2012 he was our player of the year.

Gradually, then, we have built up a squad of around 25 to 30 players, some of whom play all the time, some of whom manage half a dozen games a year, some of whom play barely at all but like to be part of the gang. We play one game a weekend every weekend, all but a handful outside the M25. There's still a healthy base of fixtures in Oxfordshire, a couple of which we inherited from Scotts. One or two of us have been braving the sub-arctic squalls at Charlton-on-Otmoor since 1980, and trying to remember the combination to the electronic gates at Tusmore Park since 1981. We also play in Essex, Kent, Cambridgeshire, Suffolk, Berkshire, West Sussex and Hampshire: wherever people will have us, in short. Wandering sides can still flourish because the people who play on beautiful village grounds would rather play there than anywhere else. They don't want a return fixture on some godforsaken council pitch with crabgrass on a good length and syringes at mid-on. We have no home ground and we will not be getting one in a hurry. Our job is to turn up, play to the best standard we can and get on with everybody. I'd like to win a few more games than we have been managing – in 2012 we played 13, drew three and lost ten – but the opposition don't seem to worry too much if we lose. In fact, I get the distinct impression that many of them prefer it.

The Rain Men at Stonor Park, in the Chilterns

The real enemy, of course, is age. Most of us are now in our 50s, and time suddenly seems short. Each of us knows that at any time the injury could strike that ends it all, just like that. And so, curiously, some of us are playing more often than ever. They always say you should live in the moment, and that's much easier to do after a certain age, when tomorrow ceases to be a foregone conclusion and next year seems an infinite distance away. Cricket being the most dynastic of sports, we have also introduced a few keen sons to the mix, aged from 10 to 17. They do all the running, while some of us stand in the field like Easter Island statues. My ten-year-old son gets very frustrated that the slip catches he is bowling for are not being taken, but I have to explain that slip and gully are only fielding in those positions because they are too infirm to go anywhere else, and not because they have a cat's chance in hell of catching anything. At the same time I quite relish the sight of a bowler giving serious eyeball to a fielder 46 years his senior. Deference to age has no place in the modern game.

So we keep going. One or two of the villages now put out seniors sides against us, which is kind. We no longer play many games in London, because most of the travelling sides we used to play are now younger than us and very much more aggressive: there's not much fun being sledged by some 25-year-old Australian bartender with perfectly balanced chips on each shoulder. (We'll take it from our team-mates, but not the opposition as well.) Because, in the end, that's what we're playing for: fun. 'For God's sake look after our people,' wrote Robert Falcon Scott on his deathbed, doubtless thinking of a village green far away.

Wandering cricket in Scotland

by Anthony Gibson

The Scots have been playing host to wandering cricket clubs since 1852, when I Zingari, 'batting with more gaiety than sense', lost to a local Perth XI by 33 runs in a one-off game. Free Foresters made the long trip north not long afterwards, for the first of many tours, and clubs like the Yorkshire Gentlemen, the Northern Nomads and the Borderers have been regular visitors over the years.

But home-grown Scottish wanderers have been conspicuous largely by their absence. No doubt there were various colourful assemblages of cricketing gentry playing country-house matches in the 19th century, but apart from all of that, and one or two more recent ephemera, like the Bats and the 62 Club, there have really been only three Scottish nomadic clubs of note: the Gnomes, the Capercailzies and the Wayfarers.

The geography hasn't helped, of course. Cricket clubs – and cricketers – are much thinner on the ground in Scotland than they are in, say, Sussex, and the distances to be travelled and the difficulties of raising a side are inevitably that much greater. Besides which, 'amateur' cricket in Scotland has always been mainly the preserve of the old boys' sides, or 'Former Pupils' as they're known in those parts, and for most of their existence, those have been firmly connected to their parent schools.

There was, however, a period when that did not apply, and it was that which accounted for the formation of the Gnomes. This was in the late '50s, when the schools which had previously hosted former pupils' friendly matches on a Sunday decided that this was more trouble than it was worth and withdrew their facilities. Alternatives were few. The only grounds in Edinburgh were Carlton and Grange, and they were fully occupied.

So towards the end of 1960, a prominent cricketer called George Goddard sent a letter to 30 of his cricketing friends and acquaintances, inquiring if there was sufficient interest to make it worthwhile forming a nomadic club, consisting of good cricketers, which would play its matches on a Sunday. The response was encouraging, and the Gnomes, as they became known, played their first match on 14 May 1961.

Why the 'Gnomes'? With typical Scottish whimsy, they adopted the name on account of the tendency of one of the earliest and keenest members, Michael Killey – a man of considerable stature – to dismiss anyone of lesser proportions with the put-down "Och, ye'r just a wee gnome!" The club tie naturally features a garden gnome, wearing a club cap of yellow, green and red which is in the finest jazz-hat tradition.

But in cricketing terms, there was certainly nothing gnomish about the ability of the members of the new club. George Goddard had already been capped for Scotland when the Gnomes played their first game, and he would go on to become one of the country's most distinguished cricketers, making 78 appearances (22 of them first-class) and being awarded the MBE for services to Scottish cricket in 1982. His finest hour was unquestionably the 1973 match against the MCC, when Goddard took eight for 134 with his off-breaks and then followed that with an unbeaten 113, after Scotland had been reduced to 82 for seven.

His great friend and fellow Heriot's FP, Hamish More, was almost equally prominent in both the Gnomes and Scottish cricket. He kept wicket for Scotland in 45 matches, scored almost 2,000 runs for his country and signed off his first-class career with a flourish, when he was selected for TN Pearce's XI against the great West Indian touring side of 1976. Between them, George and Hamish not only pretty much ran the Gnomes, as Hon Sec and Fixtures Sec respectively, but also made them a match for any opposition. Nor were they on their own. The Gnomes fairly bristled with good cricketers, like Ronnie Scotland (brother of the rugby international Ken) and Sandy Stark. "When we turned out our best players, we were a very strong side, and we certainly won a lot more than we lost," Hamish recalls.

At their peak, the Gnomes played around 20 matches a season, against the strongest Scottish club sides, like Kilmarnock, Stirling, Melrose and West of Scotland, and on tour to Yorkshire, where they would take on and beat the best that the leagues had to offer. But if this was a glorious Scottish flowering of wandering cricket, it was also a fairly brief one. In the early '70s, the schools began to relent in their no-cricket-on-Sunday embargoes, and the Gnomes gradually returned to their FP clubs. Now only one fixture remains, against St Boswell's, and Hamish More has every intention of playing in it, 52 years on from his first appearance when the Gnomes were formed.

'If the Flamingoes, the Penguins, the Sparrowhawks and the Seagulls have graced the cricket field, why not the Capercailzies? They are simply a bunch of cricketers from Scotland who, in their convivial after-match moments, have dreamed of spreading their wings and flying to other parts of the globe.'

Archie Bell, President, 1978

If the Gnomes were a strong wandering side, then the Capercailzies were supercharged. Once again, Goddard and More were among the prime movers, although it was another Gnome, Jim Fiddes, who was the first to suggest the idea of forming a Scottish touring side. The spur was a decision by the Scottish cricket authorities not to authorise an overseas tour, on the grounds that, in the eyes of the TCCB in those days, Scotland was the equivalent of a county, and counties didn't play international cricket. So Fiddes, Goddard, More and Ian Stevenson put together what was effectively an unofficial Scottish side, raised the necessary funding and, in 1978, set off to tour Hong Kong and Malaysia.

The touring party, which was led by the President, Sheriff Archie Bell QC, comprised the core of the current Scottish XI, augmented with a clutch of good young players, most of whom would eventually play for their country.

The tour was a roaring success. The Capercailzies were as popular off the field as they were successful on it. They finished the tour unbeaten and rounded off what their captain, George Goddard, describes as "an experience which will remain with the tourists for the rest of their lives" in style, when Archie Bell was given the honour of firing the Noonday Gun in Hong Kong.

Further hugely enjoyable tours followed, this time under the captaincy of Hamish More, to Barbados in 1981, Vancouver and West Canada in 1984 and a return to Hong Kong in 1987. It must have been almost a disappointment when Scotland's status changed and the national side could go on official tours.

The Wayfarers seem to have been cast more in the traditional mould of a wandering club. Rather like the Butterflies in England, they drew their members from the six principal public schools in Scotland: Fettes, Merchiston, Strathallan, Glenalmond, Loretto and Edinburgh Academy. The Wayfarers played each school once a year, not just at cricket, but also at rugby and sometimes golf. The school fixtures gradually fell away in the 1960s, and the club has now to all intents and purposes disappeared, although a 'Scottish Wayfarers' side does still sometimes play a match against Scotland under-19s, as a trial game.

So, if the history of wandering cricket north of the border may not be long, it is unquestionably distinguished, and it can surely be only a matter of time before other Scottish cricketers follow in the nomadic footsteps of the Gnomes, the Capercailzies and the Wayfarers.

Cricket at Strathallan School in Perthshire

Old Boys and The Cricketer Cup

by Steve Pittard

Although old boys sides aren't necessarily wandering teams – almost all play at their former school grounds – the early XIs shared a similar ethos to their nomadic peers, and the links between these two strands of English cricket have always been strong.

Old boys cricket is one of the longest traditions in the game. It pre dates by more than half a century even the earliest wandering teams of county gentlemen. The first encounter between representatives (past or present) of public schools occurred in 1760 between Old Etonians and Old Wykehamists at Oxford. In the 1800s Old Etonians and Old Harrovians regularly locked horns and also played their respective schools. Arthur Haygarth, in his original 1862 *Scores and Biographies*, noted that Eton and Harrow accounted for around half of all the amateur cricketers involved in great matches. Winchester, Westminster and Rugby also featured prominently, with Cheltenham, Marlborough and Charterhouse each chipping in with a handful of players.

Wandering cricket was just becoming fashionable when Alfred Lubbock, along with a nucleus of the 1862 Eton XI, formed the Eton Ramblers. The idea was to arrange a tour in August, to play opponents within easy reach of London. The original intention was to select only former first XI cricketers, although in the event they had to resort to including all past pupils in order to muster a side. Over 100 players appeared most seasons. Even so, their vast squad took a very lackadaisical approach towards attendance and strangers frequently had to be roped in. Between 1881 and 1890 only 41 matches were played and, amid talk of winding up, the Honorary Secretary resigned. 'It is difficult to maintain an organisation in a flourishing condition when there is such an astonishing absence of internal energy and interest. ... *Vale! Floreat Etona!*'

It was a quite different story with the Uppingham Rovers, who were founded in 1863, a year after the Eton Ramblers. In 1872 the school employed a professional coach, the inspirational 'HH' Stephenson, who ten years earlier had captained the first England tour of Australia. So great was his influence that by 1877 five of the Cambridge side in the Varsity match were proteges of his at Uppingham. The benefit was inevitably felt by the Rovers who, between 1879 and 1906, played 191 matches, many of them against county sides, and only lost 11 times. Unlike the disorganised Eton Ramblers the club kept a record of all its matches, which duly appeared in handsome, leather-bound volumes. Such was their reputation that their matches were regularly featured in the national press.

Their star player was AP 'Bunny' Lucas who, during an 1890 game against United Services at Portsmouth, bowled one of the most celebrated deliveries in the history of cricket. He propelled the ball like a quoit so that it soared some thirty feet in the air before plummeting down onto the batsman's stumps. His victim? Sir Arthur Conan Doyle, who called it 'the most singular ball that I have ever received. I tried to cut it off my stumps with the result that I knocked down my wicket and broke my bat.' So inspired was the writer by his dismissal that he penned *The Story of Spedegue's Dropper*, about an asthmatic schoolteacher whose perfection of such a delivery won England the Ashes.

The Harrow Wanderers were not formed till 1870, their pioneering spirit being Isaac Walker, the most accomplished of the famous seven Walker brothers from Southgate. In his pomp, ID Walker was regarded by *Wisden* as being second only to WG Grace among the batsmen of his time. He, more than anyone, was responsible for the advent of a golden age in Harrow cricket, through his coaching at the school and the creation of the Wanderers. By the 1890s, the Wanderers could boast the cream of amateur cricketers: AN 'Monkey' Hornby, FS Jackson and Archie MacLaren were all England regulars, AJ Webbe had also represented his country, whilst HT Hewitt and MC Kemp had played for the Gentlemen.

An XI of 'Old Harrovian Captains' existed in the mid-1860s whilst another off-shoot was Harrow Blues. Arthur Haygarth, an ex-Harrovian himself, initially refused to countenance them in his definitive *Scores and Biographies* as they admitted non-Harrovians and 'their performances in consequence have no record in these pages.' This was somewhat harsh, given that Haygarth was happy enough to detail the exploits of a team which went by the name of Fourteen Clowns. In reality many old boy sides contained ringers, or 'emergencies' as they were known at the time. Old Wellingtonian Lt Colonel Gerald French cheerfully admits in his book *The Corner Stone of English Cricket* to having at various times posed as an Old Carthusian, an Old Felstedian and an Eton Rambler. The keener old boy cricketers often belonged to several different wandering clubs. It wasn't unusual in the world of public school and wandering cricket for Eton Ramblers to find that five or six of the team they were playing were fellow Etonians.

The choice of club tie was an important one, with the Eton Ramblers giving much consideration to the matter. A 'beastly' white with narrow pink stripes affair got short shrift and eventually a bold combination of fuchsia, purple, leaf green and copper gained approval. The club jealously guarded their colours and passed a motion that anyone not having paid their subs would be barred from wearing them. This principle applied even in fictional circles. Edgar Wallace's colonial commissioner 'Sanders of the River' balked at the prospect of an African prince being crowned in a straw hat adorned in Ramblers' ribbons: 'It is not right that you should wear upon your head the ju-ju of a tribe which you can never rule.' Middle-Eastern dictators have also attempted to use the famous colours to bolster their status. Decades before Saddam Hussein was toppled, Sir Alec Douglas-Home had his measure: "Rum fellow, that Saddam ... he's wearing an Eton Ramblers tie."

Eton Ramblers cricket was a sociable affair. Extended lunches were the order of the day and the sheer amount of drinking involved often scuppered adversaries. Colonel McColmont's XI allowed one bottle of wine per player and in the afternoon session collapsed to 31 all out. One addled visiting skipper crawled out from the pavilion, crooning in a husky baritone "I would I were a bird." After much discussion he repaired to the dressing room for a siesta.

Partly because the games gained a reputation for conviviality, but also as a result of the organisational influence of Arthur Dunn, the England footballer, the Ramblers recovered from their crisis of the 1880s. In 1891 they played 30 matches; two years later they had 480 members. Country-house cricket was in full swing, and Rambler Weeks, all over England, were full of fun.

Among the stalwarts of the years leading up to the First World War was Henry Wright, who played for Derbyshire but is now perhaps better known as the great-grandfather of Sarah Ferguson. Whilst fielding against Haileybury College he was on fire, literally. In his pocket some matches had ignited, but removing his smouldering flannels was out of the question – not with ladies among the spectators! So he hot-footed it to the distant pavilion, flames and smoke by now belching from his lower port-holes and, more alarmingly, the galley. Oil was applied and wine partaken to remedy his 'misdirected self-consciousness'. Another unusual incident occurred when the Ramblers had their wallets fleeced. A bounder, sporting a bogus (one hopes) Incogniti blazer, strolled into the dressing room, with both sides naturally presuming him to be a gentleman.

Lord Harris, aged 68, waiting to bat for the Eton Ramblers 2nd XI, on Upper Club, June 1919
Leaning over him is Dr Cyril Alington, the headmaster

The Ramblers went from strength to strength between the wars. At its peak the fixture card sported more than fifty games, and membership rose to 1,400. On one memorable day five different matches were played, one as far away as Gezira, and all five were won. Brian Johnston, as enthusiastic an Eton Rambler as he was a practical joker, was in his element. The butt of much of his humour was the Ramblers' long-standing Secretary and President, Colonel 'Buns' Cartwright. At one country house, Johnners somehow persuaded his host to inform Buns that a previous guest had only just departed and the maid hadn't had the chance to clean his room. Buns found a disgusting-looking chamber pot beside his bed. On closer inspection he discovered its true contents (lime cordial, sausages and lavatory paper) and launched said concoction over Johnners.

Not all old boy sides ran as extensive a fixture card. The Old Westminsters' season was focused primarily on a fortnight of cricket in August, and it was much the same story for the Lancing Rovers and the Charterhouse Friars. But the years between the wars saw a growth in old boys cricket, with the formal establishment of such sides as the Repton Pilgrims, the Downside Wanderers, the Old Hurst Johnians and the Sherborne Pilgrims.

Many old boys sides shut up shop completely for World War Two, while those that did attempt to carry on, for the sake of the collective morale, struggled to raise teams. The Old Cranleighans sent out one invitation to a player that eventually received a reply from a prisoner-of-war camp in Germany. He was indeed keen to play, but he feared that his guards at Oflag 1287G might have something to say about the matter. He added that there were several other OCs in captivity there, and they were hoping over the Whitsun weekend to play a match between England and the Rest of the World. The Eton Ramblers found it particularly difficult to soldier on, given the sheer number of officers that they supplied to the armed forces. There were more than 80 majors alone on their 1939 active members' list.

Old boys cricket, like its wandering equivalent, has always been determinedly amateur in outlook. In 1915 the influential London Club Cricket Conference, which acted as a fixture bureau for many old boys' clubs, decreed that its members 'shall neither recognise, approve of, nor promote any cup or league system.' They even declined to endorse campaigns for better timekeeping or professional coaching, as not really in keeping with the Corinthian spirit. In 1952 the CCC tested the water by holding a vote on competitive cricket but the status quo was upheld by a comfortable majority. Lt Colonel AT Burlton summed up the prevailing attitude in his 1956 book on the etiquette of the game, *Cricketing Courtesy*. He acknowledged that whilst league cricket was all well and good for Northerners, it could turn the game into a grim business. 'It is liable to make more enemies than friends. If you can influence your committee to ban "cup" cricket, you might be well advised to do so.'

In the 1960s the *Evening Standard* organised a cup competition. This consisted of superimposing a merit table on the existing fixture list, with the winners of the North and South London sections going head to head in the final. The old boys sides initially declined to take part, but in 1964 Old Whitgiftians broke ranks and entered, reaching the final. Afterwards they felt rather grubby about their dalliance with the world of competitive cricket. 'It is a matter of some doubt whether the league table is in the best interest of the club, and the committee will shortly be reconsidering whether the club should take part.'

But competitive old boys cricket was, in fact, just around the corner. It was in 1966, during an I Zingari / South Wales Hunts match, that over a glass of port Old Harrovian Tony Winlaw and Shrewsbury Saracen Henry Lewis mooted the idea of an old boys limited-overs knockout tournament. On their return to London they chanced upon Ben Brocklehurst in the bar of the Bath Club and, after a few more drinks, during which the idea was kicked around, the competition was born. Brocklehurst, the former Somerset captain and proprietor of the *Cricketer* magazine, put the wheels in motion and turned the dream into a reality. Christened *The Cricketer Cup*, and sponsored by *Champagne Pol Roger*, it ran on the lines of the Gillette Cup, albeit with only 55 overs a side to avoid ridiculously early starts.

No strict criteria applied to the 16 schools invited to take part, though it would have been unthinkable to snub the six Butterflies schools (Charterhouse Friars, Eton Ramblers, Harrow Wanderers, Rugby Meteors, Old Westminsters, and Old Wykehamists). Lewis and Brocklehurst brought on board their respective alma maters, Shrewsbury Saracens and Bradfield Waifs. Repton Pilgrims warranted a place, as the establishment had then provided more county regulars (those with a minimum of 100 appearances) than any other school. Marlborough Blues, Radley Rangers, Sherborne Pilgrims, Old Malvernians, Old Tonbridgians, Old Wellingtonians and Uppingham Rovers filled the remaining berths. Repton Pilgrims, with ex-England skipper Donald Carr at the helm, started the competition 5/2 favourites.

Cup cricket has arrived.
Ted Dexter, bowling for
Radley Rangers against
Uppingham Rovers.
First round, June 1967

The standard of cricket was high. The Ramblers' skipper was bon-vivant Colin Ingleby-Mackenzie, who had led Hampshire to the county championship in 1961, whilst the Charterhouse Friars felt able to pass over the captaincy claims of Peter May in favour of Oliver Popplewell QC, later an eminent high court judge. Repton and Charterhouse clashed in the semi-final. May had compiled a century in an earlier round, but on this occasion Richard Hutton castled him for a duck as the Friars folded. In the final at Burton's Court, Chelsea, Repton posted 240. The lordly Ted Dexter led the charge for Radley Rangers but, with wickets tumbling around him, was left stranded on 80 as his side capitulated to 144 all out. The victorious Donald Carr received a case of champagne on behalf of his team, a moment made memorable by the former MCC President Lord Nugent introducing Madame Pol Roger as Madame Bollinger. The defeated Dexter was left to reflect on the absence of much of his middle-order batting – one in Canada with MCC, one with an injured hand and one with mumps – but he conceded the undoubted star quality of the opposition.

The day had been a resounding social success, certainly if judged by the depleted picnic hampers and discharged Gordon's bottles in evidence. Two champagne marquees flanked the boundaries, there was Watney's Red Barrel for the less discerning, and the sun shone down on the intimate Chelsea ground. It all made for the perfect summer's cricketing day, given added piquancy by the recent demise of the Gentlemen versus Players match and the downgrading of Eton versus Harrow to a midweek fixture. *The Cricketer* thoroughly approved, not least of the bevy of pretty girls which the occasion had attracted. It was amateur cricket in the finest traditions of the Golden Age – even the entry fee was quoted in guineas – and, as the cricketers packed their bags and the caterers folded their tents, no one was in any doubt that a new cricketing tradition had been founded.

So well received was the new competition that, by 1969, the CCC had given it their blessing and the entry was expanded to 32 clubs. The newcomers were Old Amplefordians, Old Blundellians, Old Brightonians, Old Cheltonians, Old Cliftonians, Downside Wanderers, Old Alleynians, Felsted Robins, Haileybury Hermits, Old Cholmeleians (Highgate), Lancing Rovers, Old Merchant Taylors, Oundle Rovers, St Edward's Martyrs, Stowe Templars and Old Whitgiftians.

Felsted Robins immediately made their presence felt by beating Charterhouse Friars, though perished shortly after when somehow six of their batsmen managed to run themselves out. It was the Robins' bowlers who were in the firing line when they came up against the Eton Ramblers' Henry Blofeld a few years later. Even after the cycling accident which almost killed him, Blofeld was a formidable cricketer, and he scattered the Robins' opening attack to the four winds, cracking boundaries galore – like a kicking horse, one imagines – to reach his fifty in the first four overs of the innings.

Part of the charm of the competition, especially in the early years, was that mere mortals could rub shoulders with their childhood sporting idols. Veteran Ashes hero Trevor Bailey was on parade for Old Alleynians in the 1974 final and, despite being over 50, pulled off an excellent slip catch. The 'Barnacle' was an obdurate customer, even in his Dulwich days. 'Bailey awoke from an apparent coma to strike a boundary,' wrote PG Wodehouse in his report of one Dulwich match, having himself once taken nine for 14 for the school, and turned out for the old boys' side.

Andrew Strauss (Radley Rangers) is perhaps somewhat in the image of the old-fashioned gentleman cricketer, though one chap who defies the stereotype of an ex-public school player is PCR Tufnell ... yes, that's right: Tuffers! He briefly attended Highgate before leaving under a cloud (of smoke perhaps) having allegedly tried to burn down the school gymnasium. Tuffers insists this scurrilous story is an urban myth. Genuine or not, the Old Cholmelians forgave him his misdemeanour sufficiently to pick him for their team, though he failed to set the match alight. In fact, the batsmen tucked into his bowling with such relish that he was not called upon to bowl his full quota of overs.

Another England performer Roger Tolchard gave stout service for Old Malvernians, appearing in three victorious campaigns over three decades (1975, 1986 & 1990). Having a championship pro can make all the difference. Sussex's John Barclay took four for 19 to secure victory for Eton Ramblers in 1992. Nick Pocock highlighted the gulf between professional and casual cricketers in 1977. The Hampshire trundler (first-class bowling average 99) destroyed Oundle Rovers' top order, taking four for 16. Then for good measure he raced to 96 not out out of 118 for one as the Shrewsbury Saracens romped home with 30 overs to spare.

*John Wilcox of the Old Malvernians receives the Cup from Gubby Allen, 1975
Jim Swanton, with glass of champagne, looks on*

One of the most sensational knocks happened in the 1973 final. Rugby Meteors had seemed to be out of the reckoning when their number seven batsman DAC Marshall arrived at the crease with 78 runs still required from 8.4 overs. Such run chases are now commonplace but back then, with no fielding restrictions, a Rugby defeat looked all Lombard Street to a China orange. Marshall had other ideas, clubbing four sixes en route to a half century which carried his team to an appropriately meteoric victory.

Eyebrows were raised in 1982 when Old Malvernians declared! It wasn't as if they had a mountain of runs on the board, at 104 for 8 after 52 overs. But their wily captain, Jeff Tolchard, reasoned that, with rain looming, Old Wykehamists were always going to be ahead of the run rate, and the only sniff of victory lay in bowling them out pronto. Wykehamists looked to be on track at 48 for 2 but almost committed hari-kari as they slumped to 79 for 9. Before the last man could reach the crease, the heavens opened to save Wykehamists' bacon.

The 1983 tournament was hotly contested, rather too much so for the sensibilities of *Wisden* editor John Woodcock. His notes in the *Almanack* acknowledged the good spirit in which cricket that season had generally been played, but highlighted one lamentable exception. This occurred 'in the Cricketer Cup when the old boys of two great schools, Malvern and Repton, allowed themselves to be carried away by an inordinate desire to win'.

The charged atmosphere which marred the semi-final arose because of confusion over the rules. In a 55-over match Repton Pilgrims had been bowled out for 194 in 47 overs and, when rain arrived, the Old Malvernians were on 94 for eight off 25. The Pilgrims claimed the superior run rate, but the Malvernians insisted that Repton's 194 was to be divided not by 47 but by 55, making them the winners. The *Cricketer* magazine wrote that 'the game reached Cricket's Wonderland in that both sides won. Unfortunately, it weren't so much 'armonious as acrimonious.' The Cup Committee finally declared the Pilgrims winners, but it was not the competition's finest hour.

Stowe Templars may not have the most glittering track record in the Cricketer Cup – won 22, lost 43 – but their appearances have certainly not been without incident. In 2007 they were on the receiving end of a whopping 415 opening partnership by James Wood (207*) and James Hamblin (235) for Charterhouse Friars, which dwarfed the previous highest stand, 239 by JLP Meadows and WM (Bill) Lawry (no relation) for Old Cliftonians against Old Tonbridgians in the 1993 final. Then there was the incident in the Templars' game at Clifton in 1986 when a dead mackerel mysteriously landed next to Old Cliftonian batsman Simon Hazlitt. It wasn't courtesy of a Stowe Templars' bowler – for starters, the mackerel had pitched on a decent length. It transpired that a passing seagull must have dropped the weighty fish, almost a foot long, having liberated it from the sealion pen at nearby Bristol zoo.

The 1991 Final
The bowler is Charlie Ellison of 14 times winners Old Tonbridgians. The batsman is the Charterhouse Friar Chris Bidwell, with 2,615 runs the competition's leading run-scorer.

The team ethos being so important to old boys cricket, the Cricketer Cup has never gone in for 'man of the match' awards, or similar. In the early years, the winning team was rewarded with a weekend in Epernay and an inscribed teak bench to take pride of place on their old school cricket ground. The only trouble was that Tonbridge amassed so many benches that they were in danger of having to apply for planning consent.

In contemplating individual achievements in the Cricketer Cup, the prolific Chris Walsh stands proudly at the head of the batting averages with 2,410 runs at 54.77 for Old Tonbridgians. But spare a thought for the ever-reliable opening batsman Andrew Bernard, who amassed over 2,000 cup runs between 1985 until 2001 at an average of over 50 for Downside Wanderers, without ever lifting the trophy, his endeavours mainly serving to ensure that the Gregorians from Downside didn't get a complete pasting. Bernard also holds the record for centuries in the competition, with seven, although that would have been equalled by Chris Walsh in the 2003 final at Sir Paul Getty's Wormsley ground, had he not showed commendable self-restraint by scoring the winning runs with a gentle push for two through the covers, when a boundary would have carried him to 100.

Amongst the bowlers, Old Alleynian Simon Dyson takes the honours. Between 1969 and 1997 his spitting cobras snaffled 96 victims at a miserly 11.48 runs apiece, showing just why many experienced observers – including Trevor Bailey who advocated England taking him on tour – regard him as the best bowler never to have played first-class cricket. In keeping with the tradition of gentlemen preferring to bowl leisurely spin, à la AJ Raffles, slow bowlers have always featured strongly. Tonbridge's dominance in the noughties owed much to their spinning all-rounders Jamie Ford (1,822 runs at 45.55 and 90 wickets at 16.63) and Alistair Owen-Browne (1,712 runs at 50.35 and 83 wickets at 21.26).

It wasn't until 2006 that there was any change in the line-up of the 32 Cricketer Cup schools, when Old Blundellians withdrew, having twice been unable to raise a side. Their place was taken by Old Cranleighians, who had three times won the Brewers Cup for old boys sides unable to break into the magic circle. That competition came to an end in 2006, but not before some controversy in its penultimate season. This was in the match between Old Leightonians and Old Tauntonians, for whom a batsman called Chris Gange hit a big hundred in rapid time. The Leightonians smelt a rat and, sure enough, a trawl through the 158-year-old Taunton register revealed only one pupil with that surname, and she was a girl. The male Gange turned out to be a former captain of Somerset under-19s! Under the circumstances, the Old Leightonians' skipper, John Acland-Hood, was remarkably restrained in his comments on the affair: "I wouldn't have minded them playing a ringer, but when he scores 171 off 111 balls, you really have to take offence!"

At least one genuine lady cricketer has, however, taken the field in the Cricketer Cup. She was Clare Connor, who played for Old Brightonians in 2002, having qualified by virtue of being capped for the school first XI a few years earlier. As Robin Marlar pointed out at the time, it placed her opponents in a deuced awkward position. What was a fast bowler to do? If he'd been brought up properly then "he shouldn't want to hurt a lady at any cost." Fortunately Lancing Rovers chivalry wasn't put to the test as Clare didn't get to bat. Lancing, though woefully behind the clock, treated her left-arm spinners with exaggerated respect. In their desperation to avoid the ignominy of getting out to a girl, they garnered only 14 runs from her eight wicketless overs and lost emphatically.

There has been no shortage of incident and change in the most recent years. At the 2011 final the paparazzi turned out in force, not to capture Alex Loudon's captain's knock of 48 for Eton but to photograph his squeeze, Pippa Middleton, promenading in a vibrant red polka-dot dress. That year there was some ill-feeling when the Cricketer Cup committee decided to remove founder members and perennial whipping boys Old Westminsters (won 7, lost 44) from the competition, along with fellow strugglers Lancing Rovers. Eastbourne and Bedford filled their shoes.

Shrewsbury Saracens were winners in 2012 despite James Taylor being unavailable for the final, although the Notts batsman – *Wisden* Young Cricketer of the Year in 2008 – showed just how much this competition means to its participants when he announced that it was only being called up by England which had prevented him from taking part.

2011 saw the launch of the Cricketer Trophy as a belated successor to the Brewers Cup. The competing schools are currently Denstone, Hurstpierpoint, King's Canterbury, Lancing, Monmouth, Warwick, Westminster and St George's, Weybridge, the intention being that the most successful of them should be elevated to the Cricketer Cup should any further vacancies occur.

One of the oddities of old boys cricket is that potentially the strongest side of all doesn't feature in either competition. This is Old Millfieldians who could put out a strong XI of current first-class players, namely Rory Hamilton-Brown, Daniel Bell-Drummond, James Hildreth, Craig Kieswetter, Keiron Powell, Arul Suppiah, Adam Wheater, Wes Durston, Simon Jones, Dean Cosker and Max Waller. But until fairly recently, Millfield didn't have an old boys side at all, mainly – according to one former master at the school – because their old boys were far too busy playing the first-class game!

Unusually there are no Tonbridge alumni on the county scene at present, although there is plenty of time yet for Fabian Cowdrey to break into Kent's first XI. The Cowdreys and Tonbridge have been synonymous with the Cricketer Cup throughout its history, and who better to offer a final word on the competition than Colin Cowdrey, who played for the winning Tonbridge sides of 1972 and 1976?

> The Cricketer Cup gave me as much pleasure as any cricket I played. It reawakened the old schoolboy's boost of playing in a famous setting for the first time ... best of all it brings together so many talented cricketers, their appetites whetted by the friendly but competitive spirit. What a pity it was not thought of at the turn of the century by those brilliant amateurs of the golden years of English cricket. How they would have loved the Cricketer Cup.

Cricketer Cup Finals

	Winners	Losing finalists
1967	Repton Pilgrims	Radley Rangers
1968	Old Malvernians	Harrow Wanderers
1969	Old Brightonians	Stowe Templars
1970	Old Wykehamists	Old Tonbridgians
1971	Old Tonbridgians	Charterhouse Friars
1972	Old Tonbridgians	Old Malvernians
1973	Rugby Meteors	Old Tonbridgians
1974	Old Wykehamists	Old Alleynians
1975	Old Malvernians	Harrow Wanderers
1976	Old Tonbridgians	Old Blundellians
1977	Shrewsbury Saracens	Oundle Rovers
1978	Charterhouse Friars	Oundle Rovers
1979	Old Tonbridgians	Uppingham Rovers
1980	Marlborough Blues	Old Wellingtonians
1981	Charterhouse Friars	Old Wykehamists
1982	Old Wykehamists	Old Malvernians
1983	Repton Pilgrims	Haileybury Hermits
1984	Old Tonbridgians	Old Malvernians
1985	Oundle Rovers	Repton Pilgrims
1986	Old Malvernians	Downside Wanderers
1987	Shrewsbury Saracens	Old Cliftonians
1988	Oundle Rovers	Shrewsbury Saracens
1989	Oundle Rovers	Shrewsbury Saracens
1990	Old Malvernians	Harrow Wanderers
1991	Old Tonbridgians	Charterhouse Friars
1992	Eton Ramblers	Repton Pilgrims
1993	Old Cliftonians	Old Tonbridgians
1994	Old Tonbridgians	Old Cliftonians
1995	Old Wellingtonians	Old Malvernians
1996	Bradfield Waifs	Uppingham Rovers
1997	Bradfield Waifs	Old Tonbridgians
1998	Old Tonbridgians	Rugby Meteors
1999	Old Tonbridgians	Bradfield Waifs
2000	Charterhouse Friars	Old Tonbridgians
2001	Eton Ramblers	Oundle Rovers
2002	Old Tonbridgians	Bradfield Waifs
2003	Old Tonbridgians	Harrow Wanderers
2004	Old Tonbridgians	Old Malvernians
2005	Bradfield Waifs	Charterhouse Friars
2006	Old Malvernians	Old Tonbridgians
2007	Old Tonbridgians	Oundle Rovers
2008	Old Malvernians	Old Cranleighans
2009	Old Tonbridgians	Repton Pilgrims
2010	Old Malvernians	Oundle Rovers
2011	Old Malvernians	Eton Ramblers
2012	Shrewsbury Saracens	Harrow Wanderers

Further wandering clubs in brief

by Stephen Chalke

Hetairoi

In ancient Greece the hetairoi were travelling companions, notably of Odysseus in *The Odyssey*. They were wanderers and fellow drinkers, the perfect name for a nomadic team formed by a trio of classicists, who upon graduation in 1980 decided to maintain their friendship by organising occasional games of cricket.

The core of the side came from Oriel College, Oxford, though they soon recruited from New College, and there were three from Trinity Hall, Cambridge. In the first year they arranged two fixtures, both of which were cancelled due to torrential rain. The next year they played six and lost them all.

Breakthrough came in 1982, with a century by John White, grandson of Jack 'Farmer' White of Somerset and England, taking them to victory over St John's College, Cambridge. The following year they ventured on their first tour: August Bank Holiday weekend in Suffolk, staying in a Southwold prep school for two pounds each a night. The beds were too small for the six-footers among them, and they were woken early each morning by the reveille at a scout camp on the common outside. But they loved it, and thirty years on they are still going, albeit in more comfortable accommodation. In 1984 they added a Yorkshire tour.

The fixture list grew and grew till it passed 40 games a summer. Only occasionally was there a mismatch, such as their first encounter with Australia House who, hearing that they were an Oxford side, assumed they were all former Blues and put out an especially strong eleven.

Their first Patron was Hugh Lloyd-Jones, Regius Professor of Greek at Oxford, a man who had a great memory for old *Wisdens* and who spoke each year at their annual dinner. He would entertain them with tales of professional cricketers in years gone by, often ending with the line: "He turned to running a pub and became his own best customer."

In 1999 the club toured the Eastern Cape in South Africa. One of their number, Chris Megone, had spent time at Rhodes University and had coached in the townships, helping to break down the racial barriers in the local cricket. He developed a close link with the Swallows Club, based in a poor district in Grahamstown, and used their players to strengthen the Hetairoi tourists.

The trip was a great success so the following year, when the *Cricketer* magazine advertised their Oxford-based Millennium Festival for wandering clubs, Hetairoi entered a team supplemented by six Swallows. He can still recall the sense of marvel when he conducted the visitors about Oxford on the day of their arrival. Then, against the Butterflies, the union reached its full glory, Tim Greenwood, an Armenian specialist, putting on 150 in partnership with Simphiwe Nzundzu of the Swallows.

That summer of 2000, back in Oxford twenty years on from their wet beginnings, was the zenith of the Hetairoi. The South Africans stayed for three weeks, taking in the Festival, the tour of Yorkshire and a week of fixtures in the south: 15 games in all – as well as a trip to the Test match at Headingley where, to their great joy, they got themselves photographed with Viv Richards. In 2001 Hetairoi returned to South Africa.

The years pass. The friendships that they wanted so much to preserve back in 1980 are still there, stronger than ever, and for many years the Southwold trip has been a great family outing. Not prep school beds any more but mornings on the beach and trips to the circus on the common. Many of the original team are still playing, though they are in their fifties and mostly holding down high-powered jobs. No longer managing to play four or five days of cricket in a row, they are supplemented by sons and by younger players attracted to the ambience of a well-established, well-organised and happy side.

Paddington

Founded in 1920, Paddington was initially a local team, full of traditional, down-to-earth West Londoners. They played on the Paddington Recreation Ground but, after the war, wanting to improve the quality of their cricket, they turned themselves into a nomadic side, building up an impressive list of Sunday fixtures, many of which survive to this day.

The heart of the team in the post-war era has been its family feel. Ron Bunning played in five decades starting in 1947, and he brought along his four sons, two of whom still play. Chris, who made his debut in 1965, is in his sixth decade, and his son Matthew is now the club captain. Others – John Cox, Eric Shepperd, George Jones – also introduced their sons.

In the 1950s and '60s, before the arrival of leagues to Middlesex and Surrey, the general standard of Sunday cricket was very high, and

Paddington played good clubs – as far north as Hoddesdon, as far south as Horsham. They were always popular opponents: competitive on the field and sociable off it.

Those were the golden years, when the club could sell 120 tickets for a dinner-dance. Nevertheless they are still in fair shape, still good enough to be invited to play the powerful Ealing club during its cricket week.

Their connection with Paddington is long in the past. Today's recruits are from far and wide, usually friends of current players, and the closest the club ever comes to a game on their old home patch is the biennial match against Cross Arrows at Lord's.

Yet they remain true to the spirit of the club's forefathers, and Chris Bunning is already looking ahead to their centenary in 2020. "If it's my life's work to keep the club going," he says with pride, "I'll do it."

Ipswich Greyhound Regiment

Founded in 1965, the Ipswich Greyhound Regiment draws the majority of its members from leading clubs in the Ipswich area. They play a handful of games each year, including a week-long tour of Kent and Sussex. The Regiment has also toured overseas to Kenya, Australia, Sri Lanka, Argentina, Barbados and the USA. Among those who have represented them are the former Essex left-armer Ray East, the Ipswich Town footballer Russell Osman and the Deep Purple frontman Ian Gillan.

It is not entirely clear whether the Regiment has any genuine military connections though the founder and Colonel, Paul 'Digger' Crane, is reputed to have been involved in special services operations. This has led to rumours that their matches are a front for covert activities, a theory given especial credence as a result of their tour of Argentina during the troubles.

It is certainly true that the team operates on strict regimental grounds: an officers' mess

of wealthier, round-buying South Suffolk and North Essex cricketers augmented by a rank-and-file of toiling stalwarts and a clutch of latrine orderlies. Two travelling padres oversee the moral wellbeing of tourists and supervise the gambling pool. Field promotions are made for centuries and five-wicket hauls; demotions are rather more subjective, though the relegation of 2nd Lt Thew to the ranks in the early 1990s drew a cheer that raised the rafters and warms young privates to this day.

If the club's military origins remain obscure, the reason for the moniker 'Greyhound' is more straightforward. On an early tour the Colonel was so moved by the sight of his team warming up that he recalled the words of Henry V before Agincourt:

I see you stand like greyhounds in the slips,
Straining upon the start. The game's afoot:
Follow your spirit, and upon this charge
Cry 'God for Harry, England, and Saint George!'

While the team may not be quite so limber these days, their spirit glows as brightly as ever.

Further wandering clubs in brief

by Stephen Chalke

Cornish Choughs

The Cornish Choughs began life in 1906, not long after the Somerset Stragglers and the Devon Dumplings. In the early years they played just a few matches, mostly in August, mostly two-day affairs at country houses. Their first fixture, won by an innings, was against Lord Eliot's XI in the grounds of Port Eliot.

Club colours were estanlished as green, white and blue, and the annual subscription was five shillings, a rate that was maintained till 1963. By 1910 they had 110 members. Harry Tresawna, captain of Cornwall from 1905 to 1934, was their leading player.

In August 1913 they defeated the Duke of Cornwall's Light Infantry in a two-day match at Lanhydrock House, but by the following August the country was at war. In the words of the Choughs' history, 'The multi-coloured club and regimental blazers, the be-ribboned straw hats and public-school caps, were put away, in many cases never to reappear. The great days of country-house cricket were over.'

The Choughs reformed in 1921, and gradually a different fixture card emerged, with games against schools, local clubs and occasional touring sides. In the late 1950s they were at their zenith, with 240 members and almost 30 fixtures a summer. By the 1960s they were venturing overseas: to the Isles of Scilly, then to Jersey.

They went into decline in the 1980s, victims of the rise of league cricket and the increasing difficulty of raising sides for midweek games. In 2002 there was the real prospect of disbandment but Tim Meneer, the President, worked hard to regenerate the club. In 2006 their centenary was celebrated with a match at Falmouth, and they are now in better health.

Spasmodics

The Spasmodics started out in north Liverpool as the Blundellsand Boozers, recruiting from Formby and from the Liverpool Cotton Market. They became the Spasmodics in 1935 and, with the opening of the Mersey Tunnel, started to venture into Cheshire where they played at such delightful venues as Tattenhall, Tarporley, Malpas Cholmondley and Eaton Hall.

In those early days they were a team of modest means, travelling with a collective kitbag. At one point, owning only one club cap, they called a special meeting to agree the purchase of a second. However, as befitted a team who played for fun, there was always money for post-match refreshments, with a tradition developing that whenever they won they put £5 in a kitty to entertain the opposition.

By the 1950s they were travelling further. A trip to the Bank of England ground at Roehampton was a highlight, and in time there were tours to the Lake District, Hampshire and the Cotswolds. They could put out a strong side, though not always. At Lower Slaughter in the Cotswolds one year, agreeing to play a 12-a-side match, they were bowled out for 66 and lost by eleven wickets. Some older members also recall a game when they turned up with nine and the opposition allowed their last man, upon dismissal, to stay in and bat for ten, then eleven. Each time he was out first ball, giving the bowler a bizarre hat-trick.

Their spiritual home for many years has been the Royal Liverpool Golf Club where they hold their annual dinner. Since 1992, thanks to the initiative of Spasmodics stalwart Joe Pinnington, they have played an annual cricket match against the Royal Liverpool on the practice ground at Hoylake.

The Royal Liverpool and the Formby Golf Clubs are sources for fresh recruits, as is the Liverpool Ramblers Football Club, a Corinthian bunch who share the Spasmodics' spirit of fun. They have adapted to changing times, now playing only eight to ten fixtures each year, all in high summer, but the friendships and the enthusiasm remain strong.

Nondescripts

The original Nondescripts were members of Hampstead Cricket Club many of whom, in its golden age in the 1870s, were not being selected as often as they wished. Formed in 1876 they arranged matches on the Lawn ground in the village and called themselves Lawn CC. Three years later they transferred to the Heath and, after a short spell as Heath Nondescripts, they became simply the Nondescripts.

Their membership flourished, and they settled for a wandering life, building up a strong fixture list against London club sides and, from 1887, undertaking a tour to Devon that in its heyday lasted a fortnight.

Their London matches declined with the rise of league cricket in the 1970s, but the annual tour, where they set up base in Sidmouth, still takes place – as it has, with the exception of wartime, in all but three years since 1887.

As with all wandering clubs, they rely heavily on hard-working stalwarts. Roger Oakley, Carl Openshaw and Tony Lousada, all tourists as long ago as 1962, have given great service as, more recently, have the Marchant family – Derek, Miles and Nick – and William Dean. The tour is popular enough to attract new, young recruits but also to see the return year after year of familiar faces.

Their mascot is a wooden pelican with a cricket ball in its beak; it sits outside the pavilion whenever they play. No longer, however, do they end the evening with a rousing rendition of their song:

A most wonderful bird is the Pelican;
His beak can hold twice what his Belican;
We're told he can catch,
Bat, bowl – win a match,
But we can't understand how the Helican!

The Nondescripts, with their ever-present mascot, 1964
back: P Shott, WJ Smith, PA Raven, A Lousada, R Oakley, C Openshaw,
R Craske, P Langdon   front: MR Fellows, CTA Wilkenson,
JA Baker-Harber, CB Franks, JA MacDonald, JH Williams, J Houghton

Further wandering clubs in brief

by Stephen Chalke

West Norfolk

West Norfolk was formed in 1900 by a group of farmers and landowners in the north and west of the county. There was already a well-established Gentlemen of Norfolk Club, but they were based in the south and east, most of their games 50 or 60 miles away.

In the event it was the newer West Norfolk Club which turned out to be the more durable, the farming founders providing offspring to replenish the team amply through four generations. Walter Hammond, a prolific run-scorer for many years now, is one such descendant. Then there are the four Stanton brothers, great-grandsons of Dersingham's RR Stanton – and other names, too, which have recurred in the scorebook pages down the years: Mason, Thompson and Thorne. Indeed, so close-knit were they in the 1960s that one summer they required only 12 players to fulfil a fixture card of 24 games.

Their seasons followed a pattern. They played midweek games: mainly school and Cambridge college sides in May, followed by several Gentlemen fixtures, then in late June and early July hosting touring sides, often at Hunstanton where they held the ground lease till 2000. As July drew towards a close, they packed away their cricket bags, staying on their farms to bring in the harvest.

The highlight of the summer was the two-day Whitsun visit of the Gentlemen of Leicestershire. One of them would erect a marquee on his lawn, and on the eve of the first day's cricket they would stage their celebrated West Norfolk Ball, with as many as 250 guests in attendance.

Those days have gone now. Even the Gents of Leicestershire fixture has gone. But West Norfolk remains a thriving club, playing 16 to 18 games a year, including fixtures against I Zingari and Free Foresters.

They cast the net a little wider for players than they once did, recruiting effectively from Gresham's School in Holt, and also tapping into Norfolk's holiday-home population. They even play in August, ending their summer at two of the area's most attractive venues: the amphitheatre at Castle Rising and the lakeside ground in front of the Earl of Leicester's Palladian Hall at Holkham.

Thames Valley Gentlemen

Thames Valley Gentlemen CC was established in 1968, initially for the purpose of running a tour of Kent and Sussex which two years earlier the Teddington club had taken over from Maidenhead & Bray. With fixtures against Hastings, Rye and The Mote, it was proving too great a challenge for the midweek side of any one club.

The new team proved popular with one and all, and in time they added midweek games in the London area. With access to Teddington's picturesque Bushy Park ground, they had no difficulty attracting such opponents as the Stoics as well as touring Australian teams. Then they undertook a second tour, to South Devon, where again they played at superb grounds: Sidmouth, Seaton and Budleigh Salterton.

Twice they have ventured overseas: in 1976 to Jamaica and in 1985 to Barbados, when their party included a 19-year-old Angus Fraser, who is now their President.

The names of a fair roll-call of Test cricketers can be found among their past teams, among them Majid Khan, Steve Waugh, Devon Smith and James Tredwell. It was certainly no gentle afternoon in the park for Waugh when he played against his fellow countrymen, the Australian Old Collegians. Veterans of that day still tell of the seeming eternity that passed between Waugh edging a fast bowler into the hands of third slip and the umpire realising he was going to have to raise his finger.

The club remains healthy, still playing the two tours plus half a dozen London matches.

Butler XI

The Butler XI takes its name from Gareth Butler, the moving force behind the club's founding in 1988. They were a group of Cambridge graduates, starting out on careers in the media in London, and their early games were casual affairs, against such media teams as ITN, the New Statesman and Channel 4. The games were, in the words of one veteran, "of a shockingly poor standard", taking place mostly at the cramped and far-from-salubrious Islington council ground at Wray Crescent.

As a boy Butler had captained the Abingdon School second eleven, but at university he neglected his teasing off-breaks, giving greater attention to Jim Beam than Jim Laker. Now, with a first-class degree in history and a demanding job as a rising star in the BBC World Service, he threw himself back into cricket. In the words of the club website, 'Memories of his fleeting cricketing triumphs welled up again, like a Proustian biscuit – or, in Gareth's case, like last night's curry.'

He organised the fixtures, captained the team, looked after the kit and, at the end of each summer, produced highly detailed and witty end-of-season reports.

With time the Butlers became better players, and they attracted better players, too, so that their horizons were soon extending beyond the rudimentary pitches on Hampstead Heath. They undertook a tour – or, more accurately, a lads' weekend – to Bristol. Then they ventured overseas, first to Saumur in the Loire Valley, then to Brittany.

They combined forces with the struggling Radio News team, taking their name and going from strength to strength. Such was Butler's obsession with it that he paid for an Australian to come to England, with the promise of a job, if he would play for the side. That summer the club won almost every one of their games.

Other brief recruits included a man who had fielded as a substitute for New Zealand and a Cambridge Blue whose boast was that he had once survived six overs from Glenn McGrath.

Then in early 2008, at the age of 42 and with his career reaching fresh heights, Gareth Butler had a massive heart attack and died. The club, stunned, resolved to revert to its original name, the Butler XI, and established an annual memorial match with Captain Scott's Invitation XI, whose own passionate master of ceremonies, Harry Thompson, another Oxbridge graduate with a glittering career in radio and television production, had died three years earlier.

The Butler XI continues in good health, playing at venues very different from Wray Crescent. At Eton College they play a team of masters; at Arundel Castle they take on Private Eye.

The club is organised now by another of its founders, David Nicholson, and they have no difficulty finding fresh recruits, often from within the BBC but also among their offspring, notably Nicholson's own son Samuel who, at the age of 15, took a hat-trick.

In August 2013 they will be in Slovenia.

Civilised cricket at Arundel

*Ian Hislop of Private Eye,
bowled by the Butlers'
James Weymes, stops
to shake his triumphant
adversary's hand.*

Further wandering clubs in brief

by Stephen Chalke

Moose

The Moose started in East Sussex – in the Star Inn in Waldron, to be precise. Three young blokes fed up with the negative mindset of the local leagues, wanting – in the words of one of them, Nick Ogden – "to play cricket for cricket's sake". There were to be no defensive field settings, no playing out time for dull draws. "We wanted a more free-flowing form of the game. More gung-ho. More attacking."

That was 1979, and for a year or two their fine talk amounted to no more than occasional matches against the Star Inn and the Blackboys Inn near Uckfield. Yet the seed of something more had been sown and by the summer of 1981, the year of Botham's Ashes, they had turned themselves into the Moose and were playing on Sundays at the Waldron ground.

For two or three years they set up base at the nearby Hellingly psychiatric hospital, which some reckoned was their perfect spiritual home. Founder-member Robert Stewart's father was a psychiatrist there, and it was a lovely setting, with rhododendrons around the field, but the institution fell victim to the Care in the Community policy so they decided to become a wandering team.

Through the 1980s they grew in strength and ambition, and by the end of the decade they were undertaking overseas tours: first to Paris, then for a long fortnight to Jamaica, a monumental trip organised by club member Jeremy Burke, a lawyer with family in Kingston. Their new-ball attack on this tour sported an average weight of 18 stone, but against the Ocho Rios Police, in front of a fair-sized gathering, they found themselves facing a young and very rapid Franklyn Rose. They also played at the remote Chalky Hill, Rose's home village, where they had to share the outfield with wandering goats and wild pigs. "On two or three occasions," Nick Ogden recalls, "the pigs helped us out."

It was a wonderful trip, and there followed further tours to Menorca, Rome, Oporto, Majorca and Jersey. The team was in its pomp.

By the early 2000s, however, the club was on the wane, the first generation of pioneers all retiring, but more recently there has been an infusion of younger talent. Nick Ogden's son Tom is one, fellow founder Robert Howie's nephew James another.

The enthusiasm of the '80s and '90s has been passed to a new generation, and the fixture list is growing again. They play an all-day game in Bluemantle's' cricket week at the Nevill Ground in Tunbridge Wells, and there are fixtures against fellow free spirits such as the Chelsea Arts Club, Harry Baldwin's Occasionals and the Oxford-based Goblins.

And why the Moose? According to Nick Ogden, it was a name dreamt up when the alcohol was flowing after an abandoned match, and it happened to stick. "We wanted a large animal with a set of horns. There was already a team called the Stags, and the Deers didn't seem quite right. So we became the Moose."

A team member brought back a large rack from Canada, and over the years it has done the rounds of various pubs in East Sussex and Kent. The horns were last seen in the George and Dragon in Speldhurst.

Law Society

The Law Society XI was established in 1929, quickly developing a fixture list of matches against such other professions as Doctors, Architects, Chartered Accountants and Consulting Engineers – as well as Lords and Commons and two Oxbridge colleges.

The needle match of each summer was with the Articled Clerks, and they also played the Bar, an all-day game of sufficient standing that by the 1950s it was held on a Saturday in June at The Oval, with proper Surrey County Cricket Club scorecards, regularly updated, on sale for three pence throughout the day.

Before the war they made an annual tour, first to Kent, then for several years to Sussex, but in the late 1950s they visited Holland, playing a team of Dutch lawyers as well as several club sides. This led to a succession of further tours – to Denmark, Switzerland, France, Ireland and Portugal – as a result of which a 1969 history of continental cricket referred to them as 'modern missionaries'.

Most of the club's fixtures took place on weekdays, and firms were happy to release their solicitors to play them, considering it a great honour to have a member of staff selected for the XI. But by the 1980s that culture was changing, and the club now finds it harder to raise sides for their games. Anthony Fincham, a leading employment lawyer, does his best at his firm Cameron McKenna, and his latest recruit – Andrew James, a former Australian Under-19 – has added class. But it is not unusual now to find non-lawyers, even cricket writers, turning out for the Law Society XI.

In their heyday they played 25 matches in a summer; now it is more like 12, though that still includes an annual trip to Oporto. Of the ancient fixtures the Chartered Accountants and Lords and Commons survive, and they are supplemented with days out at Richmond, Maidenhead & Bray, Middleton Stoney and St Catherine's College, Cambridge.

The annual contest with the Bar, now a weekend side called the Refreshers, has been revived this year as an evening game, at Dulwich Cricket Club.

So what qualities do solicitors bring to the cricket field? Are they a disputatious bunch? "We've had one or two like that," their secretary Richard O'Hagan admits, "but on the whole I'd say we're far more inclined to be fair."

Bill Owen's XI

For 42 years Bill Owen's XI have been popular visitors at clubs around the West Country.

Back at the beginning Bill Owen was a young solicitor, starting his working life in Bristol and looking to enjoy some cricket at the Portishead Club. But, as a player of limited ability, he never seemed to get much of a game.

Then one evening in 1971 he and some friends organised their own match, and out of the success of that there emerged more matches, then a team, a fixture list and a club. Fellow cricket-loving lawyers were recruited, plus kindred spirits from Portishead and others who liked the happy atmosphere. They opted to play every second Sunday, which suited the men with young families, plus a few evening games.

They travel around North Somerset and West Wiltshire, also venturing into Devon.

For some fixtures, such as their annual match against the Forty Club, they hire a ground: either Abbots Leigh or Chew Stoke.

Bill Owen's XI have now completed well over 700 games, and Bill himself has missed barely 30 of them. He is, and always has been, the hub of it all: secretary, treasurer, kitman, selector, captain, record-keeper and, crucially, a wise and sympathetic listener whenever a team member has troubles. The assumption is that the club will stop when Bill stops but, though he is 68 now, there is no sign of that yet.

He has only ever made one fifty – against the Exeter Geriatrics in the grounds of Devon's County Hall – but, as he says, looking back on all the lovely venues, the thrilling finishes and the lifelong friendships, "I really have had the best career ever of any talentless cricketer."

Further wandering clubs in brief
by Stephen Chalke

Min

It all began, in 1982, with a group of Bristol University students who liked the idea of getting up their own cricket team. In that first year they managed to arrange 11 matches, ranging from an evening game at Clifton College against a team of masters called the Lobsters (they had a rule that in every game one of them had to bowl an over of lobs) to a never-forgotten trip to Leyhill Open Prison near Wotton-under-Edge. The warders acted as umpires, and several times play was interrupted in mid-over as one of them broke off to admonish a passing inmate: "You horrible little man, what do you think you're doing?" At the end of the game the students' kit went missing, only to be discovered after much searching in the prison team's bag.

Three of the founders had been on holiday to Egypt, where they had encountered Min, a god of fertility with a flail which one of them thought bore a passing resemblance to a cricket bat. So, with what Richard Beswick now calls "the underdeveloped humour of teenagers", they decided to call themselves Min and to elect Rameses II as their Club President and Spiritual Leader.

Thirty years on, Richard Beswick is the publishing director of Little, Brown and Abacus. "It seemed funny at the time," he reflects, "but over the years it's become slightly embarrassing. But it's too late now to discard it."

Upon graduation most of them moved to London, and they resolved to keep the team going, initially picking up games through the Club Cricket Conference fixture bureau. It was all a bit haphazard. Sometimes they would end up on council recreation grounds, other times on idyllic village greens. Yet several fixtures from those early years survive: Reigate Pilgrims, Stowting near Ashford and Watton-at-Stone in Hertfordshire. In 1990 they added a tour to Somerset, which for many years has included a magical afternoon playing in the beautifully laid out park of Stourhead House.

Five of them from Bristol days, now into their fifties, are still going, and they have recently recruited a couple of young Indians, discovered in the nets in East London's Victoria Park. Through the years they have stayed on a remarkably even keel: always playing around 15 matches and generally winning a few more than they lose – though that is never the club's main aim. A better idea of priorities can perhaps be obtained from their website where the match report takes second place to photographs of the teatime spread.

Did Richard Beswick think the team that journeyed out to Leyhill Prison would still be going thirty years on? "I think we'd have been quietly optimistic. Several of us were obsessive enough to keep it going. And I would never have joined another team. We were friends first and foremost. We still are."

Tea at Middleton Stoney

Privateers

The Privateers were created by two Old Haileyburians, Ian Bland and Michael Meacock who, after school, had joined Richmond Cricket Club and all too often were not getting selected. When they did play, the venues were not inspiring – so they resolved to set up their own side and to arrange fixtures in attractive places.

They invited friends, mostly from Haileybury and Eastbourne College. In the first season, 1958, there were just eight games: two near London, the other six on a tour of Devon.

The first club rule established their name, the second their ethos:

The club shall provide social and sporting entertainment to members, guests and opponents and endeavour to tour once a year.

They quickly gained a reputation for being a 'fun club', recruiting good cricketers from their fellow young workers in the City of London. Eight games in 1958 became 16 in 1959, 32 in 1960. Travelling four to a car, they would take on opponents anywhere from college sides in Cambridge to the Trojans in Southampton. Then in 1962, as their ambition grew, they undertook their first overseas tour, to Holland.

According to Kit Peake, an early recruit and now President, they quickly became "a damn good side, with Minor County cricketers, as good as the Incogs and the Free Foresters." For all that, they stayed loyal to the ethos of their founders, never becoming too grand to find places in the team for the lesser lights among them.

By the late '60s they had 44 fixtures on their card, sometimes putting out two teams on the same day. Then came league cricket and the breathalyser, and slowly they retracted till now they play only six or seven games a year.

Nevertheless, since the turn of the century, they have been to Holland, where they have a strong relationship with De Flamingos, to South Africa, playing at the magnificent Oppenheimer Ground in Randjesfontein, and to Philadephia, where they took part in a tournament involving six wandering clubs.

Most importantly the lifelong friendships remain strong, as can be witnessed by the attendance at their meetings.

London Erratics

The Erratics were formed in 1974 by a group of Balliol College graduates living in London. They wanted to play cricket but did not fancy the "training, dedication and competition" of an established club – nor, in the words of Richard Heller, "the prospect of shame and condemnation at the blind swipe, the dropped catch, the slow legside full toss which would inevitably accompany our efforts".

Through contacts they found fixtures in pleasant villages in the south-east, and the team grew as friends introduced friends: 'Evans begat Walker ... Walker begat Bush ... Bush begat Scudamore.' Bush – Bill Bush, now the Premier League's Director of Communications – also begat a young research assistant called David Miliband, a free-scoring, front-foot batsman who stayed with them long enough to score 2,086 runs at an average of 34. He also bowled fast-medium swing and held some astonishing slip catches.

Heller's own statistics are less impressive – he attributes his long career only to availability – but he did come second in the 1996 final of *Mastermind*, answering questions on Garry Sobers. He has also been Denis Healey's chief of staff, written a regular column for the *Mail on Sunday* and contributed additional dialogue to the film *Cycle Sluts Versus The Zombie Ghouls*.

The Erratics are still going strong, playing once a weekend through summer, the village games mixed among fixtures against the Bank of England, Chelsea Arts Club, the V&A Museum and The Times.

Further wandering clubs in brief
by Stephen Chalke

London Theatres

It was the summer of 1957. Brian Rix was starring in the farce *Dry Rot* at the Whitehall Theatre while Dougie Blackwell was appearing in *No Time for Sergeants* at Her Majesty's. Rix was a cricket fanatic, Blackwell was in a cast of twenty young men, and the outcome was a challenge match at Parliament Hill Fields.

Other teams soon joined in: the Arts Theatre, the BBC (calling themselves Shepherd's Bush Empire) and the Black and White Minstrels. The matches were all on midweek afternoons, on matinee-free days, and in 1958 this little world spawned the London Theatres XI.

The driving force in the early years was Dougie Blackwell. "Do you play cricket?" he would ask fellow actors such as Roger Mutton, the current chairman, whom he met on the set of *Z Cars*. That was in 1966, by which time the club had become a Sunday side playing a good standard of cricket, mostly around north and west London.

They had their share of familiar faces – from The Master in *Doctor Who* to the gamekeeper Mellors in the film of *Lady Chatterley's Lover* –

and that gave their opponents a buzz when they turned up. But they also had good cricketers, not least the Master himself Anthony Ainley, the opera singer Tim Evans-Jones and the Gambian-born actor Louis Mahoney. Then there was Peter Hughes, an actor and cricket coach whose son Simon turned out for them occasionally before he joined Middlesex.

In the early 1980s, captained by Philip Stone, they were a strong side. As an actor his specialism was unpleasant authority figures. As a skipper he was true to his Yorkshire roots, playing at all times with gritty determination.

They are strong again now. Michael Vivian, who directs theatre school productions, keeps his eye open for young cricketers, and captain Dean Chisnall is an outstanding all-rounder. Unfortunately last summer he was playing the leading role in *Shrek – The Musical*, and this involved Sunday performances, a West End trend not welcome to the London Theatres XI.

They play 30 fixtures a summer. The club logo features the masks of Comedy and Tragedy over a set of stumps.

Old Sawbuttkeane

Old Sawbuttkeane is the baby of this book, created in 2007 by BBC producer and cricket writer Simon Lister who, after 20 years behind the stumps in league cricket, had grown tired of the grim and formulaic nature of it all. "Nothing mattered other than the result. My mindless stream of 'encouragement' for the bowlers and fielders delivered nothing but self-loathing. Worst of all, no one ever told a joke."

With friends he created Old Sawbuttkeane, as a mythical English village, and it has saved him. Old, sore but keen, and overweight, they would have been a decent side twenty years ago, but now they are happy to settle for the camaraderie and the 'craic' – with just four fixtures each summer, four breaks from their weekend routines driving children to swimming

galas and drama productions. "They are my four favourite days of the year," Simon says.

Each match, in the minutes before they take the field, they open a bottle of champagne, and the toast is always the same: "For the fun of it."

At the start of his tenth game, a player is awarded a club cap – a navy blue baggy bearing the motif of a rampant Galapagos tortoise, its front foot raised over a submissive cricket ball. "It exemplifies us perfectly – venerable, wise, wrinkled, dreadfully slow over the first ten yards and possessing tiny reproductive organs."

They have even started to convince people that they really are rural cricketers from afar. "Ah yes, Old Sawbuttkeane," one elderly spectator nodded recently. "I'm fairly certain my wife's sister lives in the next village."

Woozlers

They started in the year 2000 as the Genitals, a group of Cambridge graduates looking to keep in touch by playing occasional cricket. Genitals soon became Genials. Then, following the trend of many such clubs to take the name of an animal, and with several members working in law, banking and management consultancy, they opted for the Weasels. But that didn't quite fit the ambience of their cricket so one of the team, who was reading *Winnie the Pooh* to his child, suggested the Woozles – and from that they turned into the Woozlers. It was a long journey to a name, and every AGM their President, Anthony Hyde, proposes in vain that they go back to being the Genitals.

They play about a dozen games a year, mostly in Cambridge: in term time against college sides, in vacation on college grounds against other nomadic teams, such as the Free Foresters and the Quidnuncs. For a strong fixture they can put out a good side, with former Blues and Crusaders, but they make sure there are also games of an appropriate standard for the club's lesser lights.

They are now starting to travel further afield for fixtures. They play at Stansted Park in Hampshire, on the beautifully kept lawn in front of the imposing stately home, and they end each summer at Arundel Castle where in 2012 a 58-year-old John Barclay, making up numbers for the Castle XI in his only game of the summer, snatched victory from the Woozlers with a six-wicket spell.

So happy was the spirit of the game, and so triumphant his own part in it, that back home John told his wife he was thinking of playing rather more often in 2013. "Those six wickets," she told him several days later, "were just about the worst thing that could have happened to you."

New Woozlers are drawn from all walks of life, anybody who shares the values that underpin their cricket. Some also play for league sides, though it is important that they "don't bring the ways of league cricket to the Woozlers".

Newcomers, once they have played, are offered life membership. After 13 years there are now more than 100 of them. Twenty live overseas, returning from time to time to renew old friendships. The club has even made its membership hereditary, no doubt hoping that, as the founding generation grows old, their children will take over.

The ethos is best summed up by Anthony Hyde: "We take our cricket very seriously, but we don't take ourselves too seriously."

Warwickshire Imps

The Imps, named after their 1925 founder Norman Impey, have strong links with the Warwickshire county club. For many years they played at least one fixture a summer at Edgbaston, and their teams have often featured ex-county players, notably Jamie McDowell who captained the Imps for several years in the 1990s.

The current fixture list runs to 15 games, mostly against fellow wanderers and school sides but also containing a three-day Devon tour.

Gentlemen of Herefordshire

The Gentlemen of Herefordshire began in the middle of the 19th century. Back in the 1960s the team was made up of farmers and businessmen, a dentist and an auctioneer, men who could take time off in the week, even for a leisurely two-day match against the Eton Ramblers. Now they are mostly club cricketers, some of them county players, and they have six or eight midweek fixtures, against such sides as the Gloucestershire Gipsies.

Further wandering clubs in brief

by Stephen Chalke

Brighton Brunswick

The Brighton Brunswick club was formally established in 1870, when developers gave Sussex County Cricket Club two years' notice to leave their seafront Brunswick Ground. The developers' plan was to build houses on what is now Fourth Avenue so the county set up a new base at Eaton Road, taking much of the turf with them. Meanwhile the local gentry vowed to keep alive the name of Brunswick in the world of Brighton cricket.

The new Brunswick club arranged to play some of its games at Eaton Road, becoming an informal nursery side for the county and having its own pavilion in the south-west corner. But effectively it was now a wandering side, a Brighton-based gentleman's club playing midweek fixtures.

Among their number in those early years was Walter Humphreys, an under-arm lob bowler who in 1893, at the age of 43, took an extraordinary 150 first-class wickets. He was taught to bowl in this way by Brunswick's Joseph Herbert, whose grandson Percy Fender played many times for the club before becoming an inspirational captain for Surrey. Fender, still holder of the record for the fastest ever first-class hundred (35 minutes), was a great Brunswicker, becoming President in later life.

Between the wars and into the post-war years the club continued to have a close relationship with the county. Arthur Gilligan played for them, as did the Langridges and, later, Les Lenham and John Snow. But in 1959 Sussex entered a side into the newly formed Second Eleven Championship and, with Club and Ground games as well, the role of Brighton Brunswick was reduced. Now they play only one or two days a year at Eaton Road.

Their fixture list runs to 25 or 30 games a year, almost all of them midweek, including a six-day tour of Devon, which has been running since 1934. They cannot call on up-and-coming county players as readily as they once could, though some have turned out, including Joe Gatting playing alongside his father Steve, the former Brighton footballer. For all that, it remains a good standard of cricket – and there is also a good standard of banter and camaraderie.

Fleet Street Wanderers

The Wanderers began life in 1989, the creation of Chris 'Crash' Lander, Ian Botham's ghostwriter and for many years the cricket correspondent of the *Daily Mirror*.

The idea was a simple one. The cricket correspondents spent several months each year covering tours. Why should they not have a tour of their own?

Like so many wandering sides, they make an annual pilgrimage to the West Country, usually playing three games in midsummer and staying at Lynton, near the spectacular 'Valley of the Rocks' ground – though for a while they changed the routine by booking into Butlins in Minehead. The idea of the move was that they would spend the mornings playing golf on the adjoining course. The plan, however, had omitted to take account of the nights before.

In 1999, to celebrate their tenth anniversary, they travelled to Monaco where they played Monte Carlo on their first (and so far only) overseas tour. Sadly the following spring Lander died, but the tour goes on.

Derek Pringle, Simon Hughes and Vic Marks have all taken part, Marks claiming that a slip catch at Lynton was the best of his career, but they do now embrace others beyond cricket writing, even occasionally beyond journalism. One such was the former Exeter City goalkeeper Len Bond who, fielding down by the stream at Bridgeford, held a spectacular, one-handed, leaping catch on the boundary, a real goalie's special, only to tip over the fence and fall helplessly into the water. They say that when he eventually emerged, dripping wet, he was triumphantly holding the ball aloft.

Gaieties

Gaieties Cricket Club was started in 1937 by Lupino Lane, a Hackney-born music hall entertainer who was about to become a very wealthy man as a result of his role in the musical *Me and My Girl*, the show that introduced the *Lambeth Walk*.

Contrary to the club's long-held belief, Lane was not at the time performing at the Gaiety Theatre in the Aldwych, but he clearly had a great affection for the decaying, old building which he bought in 1946 in an unsuccessful attempt to restore it after wartime damage.

During the 1960s, by which time Lane's son Laurie was captain, another Hackney-born theatre man, Harold Pinter, joined the club. He had taken his son Daniel for a net at the Alf Gover School and been recruited by the coach Fred Paolozzi, a flyman at the Palladium.

Pinter was never a great player – a batsman with a highest score of 39 – but he had a lifelong passion for the game, once famously calling it "the greatest thing that God created on earth, certainly greater than sex – though sex isn't too bad, either."

Gaieties Cricket Club became a passion that remained with him through the last forty years of his life. He became captain in 1972 and, after retirement, was chairman. Even in his last months, when he was too ill to attend regularly, he always wanted to know the full details of the latest game.

Another who started playing for Gaieties around that time was the former Somerset and England all-rounder Arthur Wellard, who was lured from Sutton Cricket Club by the Gaieties' sense of fun. The actor Robert East recalls his first encounter with him, at a rained-off match when, playing cards, he lost half his week's wages to Wellard, then found himself appointed the old man's chauffeur for the summer. One Sunday, after a particularly boozy night, he left Wellard to lurch his way up his crazily paved front path: "I'm all right, son. See you next week."

Next week Wellard reported that he had fallen into the hedge. "Woke up soaking wet and the missus standing there in her nightie. She wasn't best pleased. I'll have to go a bit easy tonight." He didn't.

In later years new members of Gaieties would receive from Pinter a signed monograph about Wellard. The piece began by describing the closing overs of a game at Banstead when the 72-year-old Wellard, his rheumatism killing him after 18 overs of bowling, found himself having to go out to bat at number eleven. He lumbered out to the middle, cursing the wretched batting performance of most of the team. Having declined several easy singles, he found himself on strike at the start of the last over with one run wanted for victory:

> The Gaieties side to a man stood, smoked, walked in circles outside the pavilion, peering out to the pitch through the gloom. It appeared to be night, but we could discern Arthur standing erect, waiting for the ball.
>
> The quickie raced in and bowled. We saw Arthur's left leg go down the wicket, the bat sweep, and were suddenly aware that the ball had gone miles in the long-on area over the boundary for four. We had won.
>
> In the bar he pronounced himself well pleased: "No trouble. 'E tried to get me with a yorker. ... Where's the boy who made the ton? 'E did well. Tell 'im 'e can buy me a pint."

The club continues in good health, playing fixtures around the Home Counties and occasionally touring overseas, notably to India in 1996 when the first match in New Delhi was won with a lofted six off a turbanned spinner by the film director Sam Mendes. In no time a match report was arriving by fax at Pinter's home.

Among others who have appeared for Gaieties are Denis Compton, the author Sebastian Faulks and the New Zealand Test cricketer Jeremy Coney.

Further wandering clubs in brief

by Stephen Chalke

Sydenhurst Ramblers

Chiddingfold, a pretty village in the heart of the Weald, has an association with cricket which goes back to the early 19th century when Tom Walker, a leading member of the famous Hambledon Club, lived there. Records suggest that the village had a team as far back as 1881, and in the years before the last war they were playing in splendour on the estate of Sydenhurst, an 18th-century country house.

The conflict put an end to their happy idyll. The ground was dug up to plant potatoes and never restored, with the house sold in 1949 to the Association of Ukrainians who converted it into a residential care home for their wounded countrymen.

Chiddingfold Cricket Club's response was to turn themselves into a nomadic side, the Sydenhurst Ramblers, and on Sunday 7 July 1946 they played their first match – against Farncombe at Broadwater.

A fortnight later they were at Brook and Sandhills, where the Surrey batsman Jack Parker turned out for them. The previous day at Blackheath he had hit the Kent attack for 82, and he returned to the county game on Monday to take five for 46 and score a second-innings century. His 'rest day' was spent hitting 84 for the Ramblers.

Over the years many famous cricketers have appeared in the ranks of the Ramblers, notably Jack Hobbs (who scored a century) and Ken Barrington. More recently, on their 2002 tour of Trinidad and Tobago, they had the West Indian bowler Mervyn Dillon open their bowling, though the advantage of his guest appearance was more than wiped out by the presence in the home side's eleven of Brian Lara.

Mike Gauntlett was the club's prime mover in its early years, and it was he who introduced the emblem which adorns its flag. His inspiration was a pub sign by the River Thames near Standlake, a rambling rose standing revived in a tankard of ale. What better image could there be for the Ramblers from Sydenhurst?

In their heyday, before league cricket held sway, they played 30 or 40 games a summer, but now the list is more modest. They have a close connection with Brook Cricket Club, often using their ground for fixtures against such wandering sides as Stoics, Nomads and Emeriti. And most years they maintain the tradition, started in 1990, of an overseas tour.

Gentlemen of Shropshire

There was a team called the Gentlemen of Shropshire who played the Gentlemen of Cheshire as far back as 1805, but the present club did not have its first match, against the Leeds Grasshoppers, till 1906.

Since then, they have played between 12 and 20 matches each year, mostly midweek, all-day games with a declaration format and players expected to walk when they are out. The highlight remains, as it has always been, the cricket week which is held at Shrewsbury

School and includes an annual dinner and a drinks reception.

They play against schools, other county-based gentlemen sides and, until its recent contraction, an Army side from the Copthorne Barracks in Shrewsbury.

The club has not quite got the status it had in the 1960s, when players had to apply early to be considered for selection during cricket week, but, in the words of one stalwart, "it is still thriving, if only with a small t."

Wandering Clubs 1855 - 1875

Arthur Haygarth, in volume 6 of his *Scores and Biographies*, covering the years from 1855 to 1875, wrote the following:

> It may here be mentioned that a great number of gentlemen's clubs sprang into existence about this time. Nearly all had no fixed ground, and the members generally paid no subscriptions, playing anywhere, after the manner of the I Z. The following are the names of some of them:-

Incogniti	Desperadoes	Fenians
Knickerbockers	Hic et Ubique	Fly-by-Nights
Accidentals	Gryphons	Essex Calves
Inexpressibles	Crusaders	United Shepherds
Dingle Wanderers	Blue Mantles	Cotswold Magpies
Suppositions	Nonentities	Pelicans
Anomalies	Grasshoppers	Medlars
Gnats	Casuals	Eton Gitanos
Perfect Cures	Cricket Company	South Coast Wanderers
Active Fleas	Cicadae	Argonauts
Perambulators	Oxford Cardinals	Don Quixotes
Limits	Utopians	Cochin-Chinas
Free Foresters	I Lazironi	Bohemians
Na Shuler	Harum Scarum	Welsh Wanderers
Midland Counties Diamonds	I Vagabondi	Wiltshire Wanderers
X Y Z	Staffordshire Rangers	Uppingham Rovers
Owls	Kentish Stars	Eton Stars
Cambridge Quidnuncs	Idle Boys	Middlesex Rangers
Oxford Harlequins	Variegated Annuals	Will-o'-the-Wisps
Rouge-et-Noir	Pilgrims	Lavender Kids
Etceteras	Peripatetics	Anythingarians
Jolly Dogs	Rose of Denmark	Spiders
I Zingari	Unmitigated Duffers	South Yorkshire Wanderers
Odds and Ends	Eton Ramblers	Surrey Grasshoppers
Caterpillars	Harrow Blues	Lancashire Witches
I O U	Harrow Wanderers	Devonshire Wanderers
Waifs and Strays	Anonymous	Omnium Gatherums
Butterflies	Needwood Forresters	Incapables
Dingle Dale	Fossils	Revellers
Eccentrics	Cock-a-doodle-doo	Ravens

They are with us no more

by Stephen Chalke

Friars

The Friars, in Derbyshire, were one of the earliest county-based nomadic sides. Founded in 1878, the club was named after the house, The Friary, where over dinner the idea was hatched. Colours of black, red and white were agreed, and a committee of five appointed. The moving force in those early years was Arthur Wilson, who fifteen years earlier had begun the Butterflies.

In 1881, in a two-day match against the Gentlemen of Nottinghamshire at the County Ground, Derby, the Friars batsmen had the time of their lives. With the option of declaring an innings not allowed till eight years later, they set a new record for all cricket with a total of 742.

They were still going strong in the 1960s, each summer playing 15 to 20 midweek matches, many of them all day. One, against the Gentlemen of Lincolnshire at Woodhall Spa, was a two-day affair. It was a good standard of cricket, perhaps less competitive than the local leagues, and it attracted accountants, schoolmasters, businessmen and several solicitors.

For many years, from the '30s to the '90s, the great moving spirit of the Friars was Harold Pepper, an accountant who was captain, secretary, treasurer and finally the club's Grand Old Man.

He was a left-handed opener of great fortitude, still taking the field occasionally in his 80s, and he was also an umpire whom you questioned at your peril. On one occasion, already suspicious about the amount of tape on the blade of an opponent's bat, he turned up armed with a six-inch ruler, holding the game up while the poor man was forced to pull away layers of binding till he was down to the requisite 4¼ inches. The next ball Pepper gave him out lbw.

His fellow umpire was Alf Pope, the former Derbyshire all-rounder, whose son Tony played for many years, witnessing the gradual decline of the club. They toured New Zealand in the early 1990s but, by the 21st century, younger men – living in a world in which work and family had become more demanding – were not coming forward.

In 2010, amidst much anguish, the club decided to wind up. They played a last, emotional match against Repton School, then disposed of their remaining kit.

A younger man, David Jepson, has formed the Derbyshire Casuals, playing two or three fixtures a summer in the spirit of the Friars, but the club formed over dinner at the Friary, the team who scored that record 742, is no more.

Musketeers

The 'Muskets' were founded in 1926 and, for some years before and after the war, were a leading wandering side in the south-east, able to call on top-class cricketers such as Donald Knight, 'Father' Marriott, Hugh Bartlett, Billy Griffith and Freddie Brown.

Brown, an England captain, called his autobiography *Cricket Musketeer*, movingly describing the matches he and fellow Musketeer Tim Toppin improvised in Italian prisoner-of-war camps. Toppin, who eccentrically batted without a box, was a true amateur:

He once turned up for a match at Halton without a pair of flannels and without a bat. He promptly bought a bat off John

Human for one and sixpence, borrowed a filthy pair of trousers from the bottom of Hugh Bartlett's bag and went out to make 146 of some of the best runs I've ever seen. Bartlett made him a present of the trousers as a reminder of the occasion.

The team was still going strong in the 1960s, playing all-day games on eight or ten Sundays each summer – from Rankin's near Southend to Middleton-on-Sea in Sussex. Freddie Brown played frequently, as did Denis Moore (the pre-war Gloucesttershire amateur), 'Tolly' Burnett (the Eton schoolmaster who briefly captained Glamorgan) and a young Ian MacLaurin.

Vic Lewis Charity XI

Vic Lewis was a cricket-mad bandleader who in the 1950s organised his gigs around the first-class fixture list. He was also an impresario, and this ability led to his setting up his own team for Sunday charity matches.

A keen collector of cricketana, Lewis was a player of extremely modest talent. Brian Johnston described him as 'in musical terms the equivalent of the second trumpet player in a local village band'. But he had such an infectious enthusiasm that he was able to assemble sides which mixed star cricketers with household names from the world of entertainment. Photos show Wes Hall sitting next to David Frost; Jim Laker beside Harry Secombe; Garry Sobers, Hanif Mohammad and Ray Lindwall with Peter Cook, Oliver Reed and Johnny Dankworth. Their President was Lord Montagu of Beaulieu.

At The Oval in 1972, in a match played for Micky Stewart's testimonial, the star attraction was the American singer Andy Williams who, walking out to bat to strains of *Moon River*, was greeted by an excited stampede of middle-aged ladies. Alas, despite coaching from Stewart and Barrington on the previous Friday evening, the American, a baseball player, could not get the hang of the ball bouncing in front of him.

Lewis himself yearned to make a fifty, and on Kew Green he finally achieved his dream. He had only one effective shot, a pull to leg off a long hop, and on that famous day the opposition conspired to serve him up overs full of such balls, leaving the square leg area vacant. With his mother watching, he came off in seventh heaven, only to find himself ignored completely in the dressing room, a practical joke set up by his team-mate Elton John.

In another match, for the benefit of Rohan Kanhai at Edgbaston, Lewis's attempt to catch a high swirler ended in the ball landing painfully on his head. Lying on the ground, with a bump fast swelling on his pate, he uttered the never-forgotten words: "I don't know what everyone's laughing at. I was nowhere near it."

He collected cricket ties, reputedly owning 12,500 and writing a guide book about them. The Vic Lewis XI tie was green for the cricket field, blue for jazz and purple his favourite colour.

He was a true lover of the game.

Vic Lewis XI at Hove, 1974
Back: Geoff Greenidge, Paul Phillipson, Oliver Reed, Tom Adams, Dick Richardson, Robert Powell
Front: Alan Mansell, John Alderton, Vic Lewis, Denis Cox, Malcolm McFee, Phil Everly

They are with us no more

Seniles

Founded in 1933, the Seniles were perhaps light-hearted forerunners of the Forty Club. Their primary aims, agreed at the inaugural meeting at Simpson's in the Strand, were 'to fan the embers of expiring youth' and 'to prove that "too old at forty" is a base libel'.

The constitution set out the qualifications required to be a Senile:

> (a) that he must have passed his fortieth birthday
> (b) that he must bear all the signs by which a Senile recognises a Senile
> (c) that as regards his Cricket ability, so long as his heart is in the right place, it really doesn't matter where his bat is. (It usually isn't.)

A bound record survives of their first five seasons, during which they played between six and eleven games a year, mostly against villages in Surrey. The impression given by the notes is of a very poor standard of cricket: 'Gordon suggested that we should have "L"s

on our bats ... Arnold tried the new bat and scored a valuable run – a glorious off-drive over slip's head.' Yet one suspects that there was talent beneath the self-mockery. Among their number was Chris Hurst, once of Oxford University (captain, 1909) and Kent (top of the county's batting averages, 1922).

Late in the book the members are each assigned a suitable quotation. For Senile Six, 'Meg' Megginson, it is Shakespeare: 'I have a good eye, Uncle. I can see a church by daylight.' For Senile Ten, Chris Hurst, it is Pope:

> The ruins of himself! now worn away
> With age, yet still majestic in decay.

It is not known how much longer they lasted, but the brief minute of their 1936 spring meeting, at Simpson's, suggests that they had plenty of fun along the way:

> Truth compels us to record that no business was done at this meeting; it was simply an orgy.

Pessimists

A Bristol club, founded in 1941 after the more august Optimists had closed down for the duration of the war, the Pessimists were a Saturday side, several of whose members were old boys of Bristol Grammar School. Some of them also played on a Sunday for the Filton Wayfarers, another Bristol-based wandering club.

For many years the Pessimists were captained by a man with the somewhat inappropriate name of John Jolly. He was an outstanding batsman/keeper and, with the all-rounder Gren Loxton, the Pessimists were a formidable side, with a fixture card which included visits to such leading local clubs as Clifton and Stapleton.

Among those who played for the club were the brothers David and Jonathan Smith, the latter the father of England cricketer Ed. David captained the team for three years in the 1960s while Jonathan has written about the side in his book *The Following Game*:

It may be a geographical thing or just fate, I don't know, but when it comes to the dead sea of pessimism most Bristolians are out and out naturals. And for those of us with a sceptical cast of mind cricket is the best game in the world. It tends to pessimism.

If you asked a fellow Pessimist fielder how things were going when you passed him between overs he would never say: 'Really well, we've got them on the run.' He would say: 'Early days. Remember last year, it could still go tits up from here.'

When leagues took over Saturday cricket in the 1970s, the Pessimists struggled to retain good fixtures, also finding it hard to recruit young players. As a result, they withered away during the 1980s.

By contrast, the Filton Wayfarers, as a Sunday side, have kept going. In 2005 they took the momentous step of establishing a home base and joining the North Somerset League.

Ravers

The Ravers began life in the summer of 1954, a bunch of jazz musicians playing occasional cricket games on the Paddington Recreation Ground. It was the brainchild of Wally Fawkes, clarinettist in Humphrey Lyttelton's band and cartoonist Trog in the *Daily Mail*. He had no trouble recruiting other cricket nuts from the jazz community, among them fellow clarinettist Monty Sunshine, Ray Smith of Collet's Record Shop, writer Jim Godbolt and bandleader Mick Mulligan and his drummer Pete Appleby.

Then came Frank Parr, the man who came to be the beating heart of the Ravers, skippering the side for more than 30 years – from those early days on the Rec through to the summers when they fulfilled a fixture card of 35 matches at attractive out-of-London grounds.

Parr was Mulligan's trombonist, but in a previous life he had kept wicket for Lancashire – come close, in fact, to playing for England – till his scruffy jazzer's lifestyle fell foul of the county's narrow-minded captain, Cyril Washbrook. He found solace in whisky, and he threw his cricketing soul into the Ravers.

"We're just piss artists," he liked to say, and enjoyment of a drink was certainly an important qualification for membership. But it was about much more than that. Parr, with a few shots of whisky in him, was the Brian Close of keepers, fearlessly standing up to all the bowling. Even at the age of 60 he was effecting leg-side stumpings that were too quick for the village umpires. He hated losing, but at all times he was true to his lifelong love of the game, ensuring it was fun and upholding the highest standards of fair play.

The team broadened out from its jazz base, though with Parr at the helm it was never going to become a sober side – and that helped with fixtures. Even on the bad days, the bar takings would secure an invitation back.

After 34 years Parr handed on the captaincy to Rupert Harris, one of three brothers who in the early 1980s injected some fresh talent into the side. Gradually, however, the team wound down, playing its last season in 1995 – though the memory of it all lives on. "Ravers cricket was always competitive," Rupert says, "and always filled with laughter."

back: Eddy Bishop, Martin Ash, Tom Murphy, Gordon Burns, Adam Harris, Toby Harris, Peter Greenwood front: Rupert Harris, Carey D'Arcy, Frank Parr, Tim Prowse, John Robinson

They are with us no more

by Stephen Chalke

Thespids

Founded by C. Aubrey Smith, one-time England captain and later Hollywood film star, the Thespids were a theatrical team who played Sunday cricket in the London area in the '20s and '30s.

They included Basil Rathbone and Nigel Bruce, cinema's definitive Holmes and Watson, music hall's O'Gorman brothers (who would often travel overnight by train from a show in the far north), the actor-manager Gerald du Maurier and the overweight entertainer Davy Burnaby who popularised the Ogopogo Song: '*His mother was an earwig, his father was a snail.*'

Joe O'Gorman was good enough to play for Surrey, and the team was often reinforced by cricketers with more tenuous connections to the stage: 'Gub' Roose of Richmond on the basis that he was Peggy Ashcroft's uncle; Donald Knight (of Surrey and England), Henry Grierson (founder of the Forty Club) and EW Swanton (of the *Evening Standard*) simply because they added talent.

They played a good standard of fixture, too. On one occasion their opponents included seven who had represented the Gentlemen against the Players that summer at Lord's. Their matches often attracted a good crowd of spectators.

'They were a capital lot, and deadly keen,' Grierson wrote. 'Brian Egerton ran the show for them, and the standard of the cricket was remarkably high. The thing that used to excite my admiration was the splendid way in which they'd go for "impossible" catches that no self-respecting pro would even have attempted – and bring them off. '

Not all of them were star cricketers, though. Basil Rathbone, an opening bat, 'doesn't make many runs, but he looks very good, and as this is more than half the battle

it really doesn't matter. Moreover, he adds to the gaiety of female notions by reason of his general appearance and get-up and is therefore good value.'

Then there was the Ogopogo man himself:

Dave Burnaby came to awful grief one day at Wimbledon. He was going all out after a ball when suddenly he slipped and fell. He had twisted his ankle, and as he couldn't rise and was far too heavy to lift, he had to be rolled off the field. A most disturbing performance, but he bore up wonderfully.

Swanton caught the flavour of the Thespids when describing a match at Woodford Wells:

I rang Brian Egerton to say I was afraid I'd be late. 'It doesn't matter, old boy,' he said. 'I've got a marvellous batting side.' When I got there, the first seven were out for 35. I scrambled in at about 50-odd for eight to join a red-faced major on leave from the east. He lasted a while, and then made way for our No.11, an actor with small pretensions. However, by this time the ball was looking very big, and 'Egie' ultimately declared at 250-odd for nine, E.W.S. not out 143. We then bowled out the opposition for not very many and returned to London for a celebratory dinner.

They were still playing fixtures in 1949, but they do not seem to have lasted much beyond that, as Swanton records:

All sporting institutions, if they are to prosper, must have at least one tireless, selfless person to do the work, and in the case of the Thespids it was, to give him his full name, B. Egerton Todd. When in the fullness of time dear old 'Egie' passed on so did the Thespids.

Pioneers

The Pioneers were formed in 1966 by Major Norman Butler, a career soldier, and the former Derbyshire cricketer Alf Pope. They had met the previous year on a Salamanders tour to Paris, during which Butler expressed an ambition to play cricket in the capital city of every European country.

Each September they ventured abroad, their party fortified in the early years by several county cricketers. Ray East, a natural comedian, and Rodney Cass were regulars; others included Glenn Turner, John Lever, Harold Rhodes and Mike Hendrick. Paris was their first venture, then followed Brussels, Berlin, Amsterdam, Geneva, Gibraltar and Dublin.

There was much good cricket, and there was much off-the-field, end-of-season fun – though their trip to Dublin started unpropitiously when they found themselves booked into a dry hotel. In Southern Ireland, it turned out, a Pioneer was one who had signed a pledge renouncing all alcohol.

In Switzerland Glenn Turner hit a six that cleared a railway line and landed in France. In Gibraltar those wearing MCC sweaters had to remove them, the colours too similar to those of Spain. And in Berlin they ended up one evening in a brothel, being entertained by a sexual exhibition by two girls. Much raucous noise accompanied the performance. Then in a brief lull the voice of Alf Pope, from the back, could be heard: "I remember getting four for 26 at Old Trafford on a day when it was doing a bit."

Alas, this was the tour when a coach crash badly injured many of the party, ending the career of the Hampshire batsman Mike Barnard.

By 1980 Norman Butler had left the Army, going to work in Saudi Arabia, and Alf Pope's son Tony took on the organisation, venturing first to the United States, where they played on Bob Hope's ranch in Santa Barbara. Then, for their last tour in 1982/83, they travelled to Australia and Fiji.

Dragonflies

Before the First World War there was very little Sunday cricket in and around London. There were a few theatrical teams, but somehow it was not quite the done thing to play on the Sabbath. 'We were keen enough,' HE Powell-Jones recalled in his book *Famous Cricket Clubs*, 'but had the feeling that we were rather under a cloud.' For all-day games there also seemed to be a problem about lunch, 'which we used to get over by the expedient of packing some bread and cheese in our cricket bags. It used to taste of bat-oil and our batting gloves used to smell of gorgonzola.'

In the early 1920s, in a railway carriage between Beckenham and London, a group of young men, frustrated that they could not get off work in time to play whole-day matches on Saturdays, resolved to form their own club with a special mission to develop cricket on Sundays.

They called themselves the Dragonflies, establishing colours of dark green and yellow with a white stripe, and they were an immediate sucess. An initial membership of a dozen or so was soon a couple of hundred, and they attracted not just those who could only play on a Sunday. As Powell-Jones put it, 'A Butterfly of Saturday often emerges into the Dragon Fly of Sunday.'

They could put out a strong side, having among their members several who had played first-class county cricket. In September 1925 they undertook a four-match tour of Holland, and by 1929 Powell-Jones was writing of them:

Nowadays there aren't enough Sundays in the season to accommodate all those who want to play with or against the Dragon Flies and the programme includes regular Saturday fixtures as well as some midweek games and a South Coast tour.

Records suggest that they were still playing in the 1950s.

They are with us no more

by Stephen Chalke

Allahakbarries

The Allahakbarries were the creation of JM Barrie. A team of writers, they played for some years before the First World War. Among their number were Conan Doyle, Jerome K Jerome, AA Milne, PG Wodehouse and EW Hornung.

Conan Doyle was a good cricketer. Barrie was not. He once said that, after bowling the ball, he liked to sit down at mid-off and wait for it to reach the other end, "which it sometimes did."

They called themselves the Allahakbarries under the mistaken notion that *allah akbar* was Arabic for 'God help us'. Their annual highlight was a match in the Cotswold village of Broadway against a team of artists assembled by Madame de Navarro, a beautiful American actress who famously bowled Barrie in one encounter.

Barrie produced a delightfully whimsical monograph about the 1899 Broadway match. It ends with a set of seven hints to the team, the last of which reads:

> *If bowled first ball, pretend that you only came out for the fun of the thing, and then go away and sit yourself behind the hedge.*

Barrie, bowled by Mary de Navarro

Gloucester Nondescripts

'Bomber' Wells, the old Gloucestershire off-spinner who bowled off one pace, often before the batsman was ready, used to tell this story:

(to be read in a broad 'Glorster' accent)

> *Back in the '40s I played for a couple of years for the Gloucester Nondescripts. The Nondies. We only played away matches. Went out by charabanc. Had a sing-song:* Ghost Riders In The Sky, She Wore Red Feathers. *All the families used to come.*
>
> *Anyway, we played at Witney one day, and they had this chap Len Hemming who played for Oxfordshire. Wonderful player. Well, I came off my*

> *one-pace run, and I bowled him. And as he was going off, Bill Hook said to our skipper Jack Stevens, 'I don't think he was looking when Bomber bowled him. I'll get him to come back.' We played all away matches, you see. We didn't like to offend anyone.*
>
> *So he came back rather sheepishly, and I bowled him next ball as well. And everyone started laughing. Well, Bill turned to Jack Stevens again. But before he could say a word, Len Hemming swung round. 'If you think I'm staying here for him to get his bloody hat-trick, you've got another think coming.' And off he went.*

Devon and Somerset Wanderers

It could be argued that, of all the clubs in this book, the Devon and Somerset Wanderers are the most distinguished.

Their story began in 1894 at Castle Cary Cricket Club in Somerset when the Secretary William Stephens Donne organised a week-long club tour of the Isle of Wight. They won only one game but, with their appetites whetted, they ventured next year to the Isle of Man where, strengthened by some players from other clubs, they won all six matches.

Donne was a large man, almost twenty stone, and his contribution on the field was minimal. But, my word, he was a great organiser. One recruit recalled meeting him for the first time on the train at the start of the Channel Islands tour of 1896:

> He handed us a 'book of the words'. This consisted of a time-table for each day – what time we got up – had breakfast – started for match, and how; by rail or charabanc – time of starting match – lunch – tea – drawing of stumps – dinner and bed. His remark when handing it over was: "Keep this in your pocket. Ask no more ruddy questions, and you'll get no abusive answers."

The tours grew longer and more ambitious, each year to a different place. In 1897 they played ten games in the Lake District. In 1898 they sailed to Holland, playing eight times in 12 days and still finding the energy for plenty of night-time activity. It was on that tour that the first century was hit against them – by a Dutch student let out on licence from jail where he was serving time for firing a revolver at a girl's window.

When the Wanderers reformed after the First World War they became less adventurous, going for a fortnight each year to Hampshire where they always stayed at the Royal Beach Hotel in Southsea.

Curiously the tour for which they are now remembered, to Paris in 1900, was the shortest and least well organised. They played only three games, with the scores from two of them uncharacteristically lost. But the third was a 12-a-side, two-day affair at the Velodrome de Vincennes which they were shocked on arrival to discover was advertised on billboards as 'MATCH DE CRICKET: FRANCE CONTRE ANGLETERRE'.

They won easily, with their two Somerset county players starring. Alf Bowerman hit the game's only fifty and, when the French team were bowled out for 26 in their second innings, Montagu Toller took seven for 9. Donne himself was run out for 0.

It turned out that the match was part of a World Exhibition being staged in Paris, and the West Countrymen left with commemorative winners' medals from the Exhibition Committee. But what they did not know was that the World Fair also incorporated the second Olympic Games of the modern era, a loose set of events spanning six months with no opening or closing ceremony. Years later the Olympic committee deemed that the cricket match was one of the events.

As cricket has not yet returned to the Games, the men of Castle Cary and beyond, including the indefatigible William Stephens Donne, remain the reigning Olympic champions.

Devon and Somerset Wanderers, 1922
WS Donne is in the middle of the back row

The Millennium Festival at Oxford 2000

In August 2000 the *Cricketer* magazine, in aid of the Lord's Taverners, staged an International Millenium Festival for Wandering Clubs. In four days, across Oxford's school and college grounds, 56 matches were played between 28 clubs, including the Gentlemen of Philadephia from the USA, De Flamingos from Holland and Stanley from South Africa.

The clubs participating were:

Band of Brothers	Gentlemen of Philadelphia	I Zingari
Butterflies	Gentlemen of Staffordshire	Romany
Cryptics	Gloucestershire Gipsies	South Oxfordshire Amateurs
De Flamingos	Grannies	South Wales Hunts
Flycatchers	Grasshoppers	Stage
Free Foresters	Hampshire Hogs	Stanley
Frogs	Hetairoi	Stragglers of Asia
Gentlemen of Cheshire	Incogniti	Sunday Barbarians
Gentlemen of Leicestershire	Invalids	Wiltshire Queries
		Yorkshire Gentlemen

I Zingari and Free Foresters met for the first time since 1878, playing out an exhilarating 565-run draw which ended with IZ's last pair at the wicket. For the Foresters Robin Jones hit a double cenury while Nick Harrop enlivened the run chase with a whirlwind 76. Each received a jeroboam of Champagne Duval-Leroy.

The Cryptics took the field with an 82-year-old, David Money, behind the stumps while on Wednesday evening the Stage XI entertained the teams with a sparkling revue which included an energetic rendition of *Wides, Sixes and Fours*, an umpires' version of Village People's *YMCA*.

Results were not the sine qua non of the week, with no club winning all their matches, but among those who lost all four were the Invalids, whose Geoffrey Hartley had dreamt up the whole idea. In *The Cricketer* fellow Invalid Jeremy Paul contributed a witty diary of the week:

> At breakfast I'm greeted by a face that is vaguely familiar but I can't place it. We go through the cheery routine:
>
>> 'Hello, how are you?'
>> 'Fine, you?'
>> 'Yes, in good shape.'
>> 'Good day yesterday?'
>> 'Yes, very enjoyable.'
>> 'Did you win?'
>> 'We did actually.'
>> 'Who were you playing?'
>> 'You,' he says, strolling off.

The report in *The Cricketer* ended as follows:

> The week's social activity reached its climax with a black-tie dinner at Keble on the Thursday evening. After dinner, Christopher Martin-Jenkins and Lord MacLaurin delivered speeches to 300 players and club members, who had expressed such enthusiasm for the festival that MacLaurin pledged to find a sponsor if the organisers were prepared to stage another festival in five years' time. Ben Brocklehurst, the proprietor of The Cricketer, confessed that he was thinking more in terms of the next millennium, but it is not impossible that he will be swayed.

Bibliography

The following books have been consulted:

E Keith Alcoe, *A Potted History of the Gentlemen of Essex Cricket Club 1907-2007*

RL Arrowsmith & BJW Hill, *The History of I Zingari* (1982, updated 2006)

PJ Barnicott, *Devon and Somerset Wanderers 1894-1933*

Clifford Bax, *The Buccaneers Cricket Club 1930-1951*

Bill Blackshaw, *100 Not Out – Chronicles of the Cryptics Cricket Club* (2009)

Freddie Brown, *Cricket Musketeer* (1954)

Eric E Bullus, *A History of Lords and Commons Cricket* (1958)

Stephen Chalke, with Bryan 'Bomber' Wells, *One More Run* (2000)

Stephen Chalke, *Guess My Story – The Life and Opinions of Keith Andrew* (2003)

Gerald French, *The Corner Stone of English Cricket* (1948)

Leslie Frewin, *The Boundary Book – A Lord's Taverners Miscellany of Cricket* (1962)

David Gibbs, *Summers by the Sea – The Sussex Martlets Cricket Club 1905-2005*

Henry Grierson, *The Ramblings of a Rabbit* (1924)

Lord Harris, *A Few Short Runs* (1921)

Maurice Latey & Peter Hill, *The Quest for the Bushmen* (2009)

PC Lennard-Payne, *The History of the Somerset Stragglers Cricket Club 1900-2000*

Roderick MacDonald, *Reminiscences of a Flycatcher* (2000)

AG Macdonell, *England, Their England* (1933)

Michael Meyer, *A History of the Jesters Cricket Club 1928-1975*

David Money & Tony Lurcock, *75 Years of the SOA*

Martin Moseling & Tony Quarrington, *A Half Forgotten Triumph* (2013)

Ian Orr-Ewing (ed), *A Celebration of Lords and Commons Cricket 1850-1988*

Eric Parker, *The History of Cricket* (1950)

Jeremy Paul, *Sing Willow – The True Story of the Invalids* (2002)

Tony Pope, *How's Frank Getting On?* (2010)

HE Powell-Jones, *Famous Cricket Clubs* (1929)

JE Prothero, *The Cornish Choughs Cricket Club 1906-1976*

Brian Scovell, *Our Beloved Cricket – from Village Green to Lord's* (2013)

Jonathan Smith, *The Following Game* (2011)

EE Snow, *A History of Leicestershire Cricket* (1949)

Howard Spencer, *Moore Cricket – A History of the Buccaneers Cricket Club* (2002)

Peter Spencer, *Three Shades of Green – The First Century of the Devon Dumplings Cricket Club* (2001)

EW Swanton, *Arabs in Aspic 1935-1993*

EW Swanton, *Sort of a Cricket Person* (1972)

EW Swanton, George Plumptre & John Woodcock (eds), *Barclays World of Cricket (1986)*

Harry Thompson, *The Captain Scott Invitation XI Cricketers' Almanack 1979-1999*

Robert Wallers, *Oxford 2000 – Flycatchers CC at the International Millennium Cricket Festival*

Claire Whickman, *Wanderings of the Unknown – 150 years of the Incogniti Cricket Club* (2010)

Philip Whitcombe & Michael Parsons, *The Free Foresters 1856-2006*

Benefactors and Patrons

This book would not have existed but for the generosity of a small number of people who were prepared to make significant personal donations having seen the sketchiest of plans. The money raised was sufficient to cover the overheads associated with researching, writing, publishing and printing the book. Thus the Cricket Foundation was relieved of all financial risk, and all proceeds from book sales (less distribution costs) will flow directly to the *Chance to Shine* project.

Our sincere thanks go to the following individuals for their belief in the project and for their generosity:

Adrian Beecroft	Christopher Coley	Michael Estorick
Jeremy Caplan	Simon Dyson	Lord MacLaurin

We would also like to thank the following clubs who, as a result of this book, have made generous donations to *Chance to Shine*:

Craven Gentlemen	Northern Nomads
Devon Dumplings	Romany

Many thanks are due to all the featured clubs for the efforts they have made to promote this book among their members. It was our intention originally to list pre-publication subscribers by club, but in the event there have been far more orders than we anticipated and space has not allowed us to do that.

Special thanks are due to those clubs which drummed up large numbers of orders. Appropriately I Zingari were in first place, followed by Free Foresters, but a strong third place was achieved by the Gloucestershire Gipsies, thanks to the tireless efforts of Chris Coley. Sussex Martlets, Invalids, Incogniti and Butterflies also did particularly well and, among the smaller clubs, several punched well above their weight, notably the Captain Scott Invitation XI, Grannies, Journeymen, Weekenders, Jack Frost XI and Fleet Street Strollers.

Starting on the next page is the list of those who have bought the book in advance and become patrons of *Chance to Shine*. We thank them all. Their generosity will help to keep this wonderful game of ours alive in state schools.

Chance to Shine

Before the Cricket Foundation launched *Chance to Shine* in 2005, fewer than 10 per cent of state schools played any form of meaningful cricket. Now in 2013, in its eighth year, the campaign has brought the educational benefits of cricket to two million children in 7,000 schools.

Anyone who would like to send their own additional personal donation to the Cricket Foundation can do so in one of two ways:

1. Send a cheque made out to The Cricket Foundation at Lord's Ground, NW8 8QZ
2. Visit the *Chance to Shine* website at www.chancetoshine.org and click "DONATE"

Nick Abell
Jono Addis
Jonathan Agar
Barry Aitken
Philip Albery
Anthony Alexander
David Alexander
Patrick Allen
Richard Allen
Arthur Anderson
Nigel Anderson
Jonathan Andrews
Peter Andrews
Stuart Annan
Warwick Armstrong
John Arthur
Lt Col John Arthur
Patricia Arthur
Richard Arthur
John Ashworth
Paul Askew
Thomas Askew
Sir Robert Atkins
Edward Atkinson
Jon Ayres
Martin Baber
John Bailey
Kimball Bailey
Patrick Bailey
Dr STR Bailey
Charles Baillie-Hamilton
Simon Baillie-Hamilton
Rupert Bairamian
Richard Baker
John Ball
Andrew Banks
DS Banner
GWP Barber
Richard Barber
Mike Barford
Paul Barford
Tom Barford
Andrew Barker
Geoffrey Barker
Derek Barnard
Don Barnes
Stuart Barnett

Anthony Bartlett
Jonathan Bartlett
Peter Bartlett
William Barton
Peter Bateman
David Batten
James Battersby
MW Bawden
Richard Beasley
MJ Beaver
James Beckett
Robert Beeney
Tim Begg
Guy Beresford
Grahame Berkeley
RJ Berkeley
Andrew Bernard
James Berry
Gordon Bickley
Andrew Birch
Ted Birch
Andrew Bishop
D Bishop
Hugh Blackett
Ron Blackman
WS Blackshaw
Christopher Blair
Julian Blake
Sir Michael Blake
Nicholas Blake
Sam Blake
Tim Blatt
George Blewitt
Nigel Bloch
JDJ Bluett
Michael Blumberg
John Boden
John E Bodie
Geoff Bond
Peter Boreham
Willy Boulter
Mark Boulton
JB Bourke
Peta Bouverie
Robin Boycott
Charles Brain
Steve Brandes

JN Brankin-Frisby
Ronald Branscombe
David Braulik
Giles Brealy
Lawrence Brennan
Tim Bridge
Mark Briers
John Bristow
Peter Bristowe
Tom Bristowe
Nick Brittain
Ronnie Brock
Sam Brodbeck
Simon Brodbeck
Robin Brodhurst
Nick Bromwich
Lord Brooke
    of Sutton Mandeville
Michael Brooks
MM Brooks
Richard Brooks
George Brooksbank
Pendrick Brown
Dominic Bryan
KMA Buchan-Smith
Chris Bunning
Hugo Burge
Oliver Burge
Patrick Burgess
Robin Burns
John Burmester
Michael Burrell
John Bushell
Richard Butler
Allan Butt
Ashley Butterworth
Joshua Byrne
Charlie Campbell
Peter Canney
Matt Cannon
Tom Carmichael
Christopher Carruthers
Jeremy Cartland
Andrew Casstles
Peter Cattrall
Philip Cayford
Freddie Chalk

John Chalk
Leo Chalk
Oscar Chalk
Richard Chalk
Andrew Chalke
Stephen Chalke
Bill Champion
Martin Chandler
Nigel Chapman
Roy Chapman
Michael Chase
AAJ Chaudry
John Chawner
Leslie Cheeseman
Brian Chetwynd
Harry Chichester
Graham Chidgey
Tom Christopherson
Richard Clark
Chris Clarke
David Clarke
Graham Clarke
Bill Clay
Christopher Clayton
David Close
Patrick Cobb
Michael Cockerell
Oliver Coddington
Antonia Cohen
Chris Coley
Simon Collins
David Colthorpe
Bob Combes
Richard Compton
Clare Connor
James Cook
Leo Cooper
Mark & Karen Cooper
Martin Cooper
Stephen Cooper
Richard Coote
Nick Cosh
Paul Cosh
Duncan Cox
Stephen Cox
Denis Crapnell
Mark Crawley

Warren Crocker
P Croker
Oliver Croom-Johnson
Michael Croton
EAC Crump
Mark Cullinan
George Curtis
Dougie Dalrymple
Tim Daniel
Tom Davenport
Janet Davies
Adam Dean
James Dean
Oliver Dean
Tony Debenham
Christopher Dean
Ron Deaton
Anthony de Grey
Sir Jack Deverell
Desmond Devitt
Peter Dibb
Alexander Dickinson
Robert Dick
Charlie Dickins
Chris Dickson
David Dickson
Mark d'Inverno
Charles Dinwiddy
John Divett
Hubert Doggart
Andrew Don
Chris Dorman
Paul Dorrans
Peter Douch
Anthony Dougall
Anthony Douglas
Christopher Douglas
AM Douglass
Nigel Draffan
Paul Drew
Nigel Drury
Charles Duffell
Isabelle Duncan
James Dunkerley
Neil Durden Smith
Simon Dyson
Derek Ebbage

Stephen Edlmann
Ian Edward
DG Edwards
Paul Edwards
GF Elgey
Mrs J Ellis
Anthony Ellison
Hugh Elphick
Richard Endacott
Andrew Evans
DJ Evans
Nick Evans
Peter Evelyn
James Everton-Wallach
Giles Falconer
Ian Farrell
Sir Henry Farrington Bt
David Farrow
Sebastian Faulks
Charles Fellows-Smith
Mark Fenn
Ian Ferris
Chris Finch
David Fischel
Colin Fleetwood
Neil Fletcher
David Forcey
Adrian Ford
Roger Ford
Peter Forrest
Charles Forward
C Foss
Neil Foster
Nigel Fowler
Anthony Fowles
Simon Fox
Adam Frankowski
Michael Freeman
Terry Freeman
Peter French
Anthony Fry
Dominic Fry
AW Fuller
Steve Gardner
John Garland
Michael Gauntlett
Philip George

Nick Gibbs
John Giffard
Edward Gillespie
Ewen Gilmour
David Gluckman
Grant Goldie
James Goodhew
John Goodrich
Roger Goodwin
Tom Goodwin
Edward Gordon Lennox
Richard Gracey
James Grant
Jim Grant
Charlie Grave
Chris Gray
Norman Green
Roger Greenslade
Bill Greenwood
Andrew Gregory
Michael Gretton
Anthony Grice
Michael Groves
Richard Grubb
Matthew Gullick
Richard Gwynn
William Haggas
Bill Hall
David Hall
John Hall
Jonathan Hall
Michael Hall
Tim Halstead
Anthony Ham
Bryan Hamblin
Ian Hamilton
John Hamilton
Mike Hamilton
Edward Handley
John Harnack
Bob Harragan
Adam Harris
Rupert Harris
Toby Harris
Charles Hartley
Geoffrey Hartley
T Hartley

John Hawkins
C Hayden
Marlon Hayes
Richard Head
Jim Heaton
Miles Hedges
Douglas Henderson
Dennis Henn
Thomas Henry
Nicholas Heroys
Paul Hewett
James Heywood
Richard Hiam
Patricia Hillman
Nick Hills
Charles Hiram
Joe Hiram
Alexander Hoare
David Hoare
John Hoare
James Hodgson
Jim Hodgson
Keith Hodgson
Richard Hodson
RP Hodson
Graham Hogben
Bill Holland
Tim Holloway
MD Holmes
Chris Horner
John Horsfall
Keir Hounsome
Philip Housden
Nicholas Hove
Michael Howarth
Gilly Howell
Alan Howick
Peter Howland
Gerald Hudd
AA Hughes
Gwyn Hughes
Paul Hughes
Peter Hughes
Anthony Hughes-Onslow
Matthew Humphrey
Oliver Humphrey
Toby Humphrey

Richard Hutchinson
Jack Hyde-Blake
Harry Ingham
Piers Inkin
Joe Ireland
Austen Issard-Davies
Brian Jackson
Cosmo Jackson
Mike Jackson
Andy James
Donald James-Griffiths
Peter Jarman
Damon Jarrett
Clyde Jeavons
Richard Jefferson
Adrian Jeffrey
Nick Jelley
Charles Jenkins
Bill Jenkinson
Bernard Jepson
Howard Johnson
Mark Johnson
Alan Victor Jones
Dylan Jones
Ian Jones
John F Jones
John L Jones
Chris Joyner
Bill Jung
Mervyn Jupe
Digvijay Kathiwada
Christopher Keenan
Humphrey Keenlyside
NSA Keess
David Kelly
Richard Kemp
Tom Kemp
Jonathan Kennedy
CM Kenyon
Chris Kiernan
Jonathan King
Dr John Kirkaldy
Sam Kirkaldy
Mike Kirkman
Matthew Knight
Alastair Lack
Paul Lack

Simon Lainé
George Lamb
Roger Lambert
Stephen Lambert
Simon Landale
Oliver Langdon
Peter Langdon
Rowland Langdon
Ronnie Langdon-Grey
HB Langlands
Peter Lapping
Tim Lardner
Chris Larlham
GR Last
Bill Latey
Jane Lawrence
Martin Lawrence
Richard Lawrence
Robert Leachman
Jezz Leckenby
PR Le Cras
Tim Ledsham
Alan Lee
Peter Lee
Robert Lee
Simon Lee
Tony Leek
David Leppington
Robert Levy
Andrew Lewis
Roy Lincoln
David Lipop
BO Little
Barrie Lloyd
Charles Lloyd
Robert Lo
Michael Lock
Chris Locke
Simon Loup
Geoff Lovell
John Low
Mark Low
Andrew Lowe
Robert Lowe
James Lubbock
RS Luddington
Tim Lynch-Staunton

Julian Lyons
James Macartney
Alastair Macaulay
Patrick McCanlis
Richard McCullagh
John McCutcheon
Joseph McDonald
Roderick Macdonald
Tony McDonald-Barker
Hamish McDougall
J McEntyre
Terry Macfarlane
Barry McGahan
Colin MacGregor
Peter Mackinnon
Clive Mackintosh
Alisdair Maclay
NO Macleay
Duncan McLeish
Patrick Maclure
David Maddocks
Edward Maidment
Miles Mallinson
Peter Marno
Ben Marsh
John Marsh
Simon Marsh
Patric Marshall
Andrew Martin Smith
Tim Martin
Brian Mason
James Mason
Philip Masters
Paul Mathieu
Eyre Maunsell
Allan Maxwell
James Meacock
Michael Meacock
Christopher Megone
David Meilton
George Menzies
Richard Merricks
James Middleton
Bob Miller
RF Mills
Colin Mitchell
Tony Monteuuis

Howard Moore
Michael Moore
Richard Moore
David Mordaunt
Andy Morgan
Michael Morgan
Mike Morgan
Nick Morgan
TW Morkill
Johnny Morris
Andrew Moss
Roger Moulding
Roger Moulton
Bill Moyle
Charles Moyle
Nick Mumby
Anthony Murley
Roger Mutton
Tim Mynott
Peter Nathan
Michael Nelmes-Crocker
Charles Nevinson
Roy New
David Newall
Quinton Newcomb
Alan Newman
Tony Newman
John Newton
Charles Nicholl
William Nicholl
Mark Nicholls
Peter Nicholson
Richard Norman
Andrew Oakes
Roger Oakley
Susan O'Brien
Michael O'Connor
Bill Oddie
Nick Ogden
Brian O'Gorman
Warwick Okines
Martin Oliver
David Osborne
Piers Ovenden
Peter Over
Bill and Sue Owen
Peter Paget

Clive Paish
Sir Geoffrey Palmer
Nicholas Palmer
Roger Parker
Simon Parker Bowles
Vic Parkes
Andrew Paterson
RFW Paterson
David Patient
Maggie Patston
Peter Patston
Mark Pearson
James Pease-Watkin
Edward Peck
Stewart Peet Lord Penrhyn
DR Peppiatt
Robert Percival
Mike Peregrine
William Petch
Joe Phelan
Nigel Philp
James Philpott
Anthony Pilkington
Rajesh Pillai
Steve Pitts
Martin Pluck
PCB Pockney
Nigel Popham
Alex Potts
JD Potts
Mark Pougatch
William A Powell
Graham Prain
Dennis Pridmore
Nick Priestnall
Charlie Pritchard
Ted Pritchard
Peter Probyn
David Pugh
Tony Pulham
Paul Ramage
Geoff Ramsey
Sam Ramsey
John Rawlinson
Thomas Rawlinson
John Raybould
Nick Read

Simon Redfern
TH Reed
Simon Rees
Sean Reilly
Charlie Rice
Michael Rice
Nigel Rice
Tim Rice
Neil Richards
Jeremy Richardson *(G of Suffolk)*
Jeremy Richardson *(Incogniti)*
Michael Richardson
Jim Ridge
James Ritchie
Anthony Roberts
David Roberts
BD Robinson
John Robinson
Bill Rodwell
Tom Rodwell
Murray Ross
Peter Ross
James Roundell
J Rowe
Rupert Rowland-Clark
Douglas Roxburgh
Gavin Roynon
Nick Rundle
Nigel Russell
W Rutter
Rob Rydon
Jonathan Sale
Lt Col PA Salisbury
Evan Samuel
Tony Sanford
Julian Sayers
AP Scarlett
Nigel Schooler
Andrew Scoley
Mike Scott
Brian Scovell
Robert Sears
John Seaton
Keith Shannon
Stuart Sharpe
Marian Sheard
John Sheldon

Edward Shellard
David Sibree
Matt Siebert
Peter Silcock
David Simons
Michael Simpson
John Singleton
David Sitch
Stanley Slaughter
David Sleight
Edward Slinger
Chris Small
Alastair Smellie
David FJ Smith
David T Smith
Edward Smith
HD Smith
Jeff Smith
Kit Smith
Patrick Smith
Christopher Snell
Anthony Snook
Robert Spaight
Roger Squire
Donald Steel
Harry Steel
Kirk Steel
Patrick Stephenson
Chris Stevens
Mike Stevens
Gordon Stevenson
Robert Stewart
Anthony Stodart
Bryan Stone
CMR Stoneham
Kenelm Storey
Victoria Stott
Andy Stovold
Kyle Stovold
Patrick Strachan
Jonathan Strange
Colin Strang Steel
James Stringer
Patrick Sumner
Mark Surridge
Michael Swabey
Christopher Swan

Alastair Sword
Will Sykes
Nick Syrett
Brian Taylor
Gerald Taylor
John Taylor
Mark Taylor
RCC Taylor
CR Terras
Mike Terrington
Duncan Thomas
EJStJ Thomas
Ian Thomas
Martin Thomas
Richard Thomas
RN Thomas
Ian Thompson
Paul Thompson
Richard Thomson
Robin Thorne
John Thornley
BD Thornycroft
Bryan Thubron
David Tickner
James Timperley
Sandy Tittershill
William Tod
Trevor Tollerfield
David Tompkins
Robin Topham
Chris Townsend
JLH Townsend
Geoff Trett
John Trumper
Tony Tudor
John Turnbull
Hon. Nigel Turner

Julian Vallance
Grant van der Horst
Michael Vandome
Dale Vargas
Richard Venables
Sam Vestey
Andrew Vickery
James Virgin
Rev Michael Vockins
James Wakefield
George Wakeley
Steve Walford
Chris Walker
Ian Walker
John Walker
Ashley Wallace-Cook
David Walsh
Terry Walsh
Mike Ward
Jamie Warner
Roddy Warren
Jon Warrick
DJ Wasley
John Waterman
Nigel Watling
Chris Watson
JMC Watson
Malcolm Watson
Michael Webb
Michael Webster
Richard West
Mark Wheeler
John White
Richard White
Rob White
Peter Whyte
Robin Wight

Roland Wild
William Wild
Peter Wildsmith
Michael Wilkins
Hugh Wilkinson
Nick Wilkinson
James William-Bulkeley
Clive Williams
John Williams
Mark Williams
Michael Williams
Stuart Williamson
D Willis
Geoffrey Wills
Julian Wilson
NJW Wilson
Richard Wilson
Steve Wilson
ASR Winlaw
John Winn
John Winnifrith
Charles Winter
PN Wiseman
Francis Witts
Charles Womersley
Howard Woodbridge
John Woodcock
Charles Woodhouse
James Woods
Michael Wooldridge
Simon Woolfries
Ian Wootton
Anthony Wreford
Walter Wright
Russell Wyatt
Henry Wyndham
David Yorath

and the following from the Captain Scott Invitation XI:

Sean Reilly
Jamo 'Love' Reilly
Riaan Botes
Paul 'Magic' Daniels
Tone Brennan
Gary West
Mike Stepney
Dan 'Jockey' Vale

'Uncle' James Weymes
Jimmy Slatter
Jim Hunt
Brett Hawson
'Monty' Dan Montefusco
Stephen Baxter
Cliff 'The Cat' Allen
Graham 'Sideways' Crabb

Ketan 'Doc' Patel
Aymon Nackvi
Stuart Parmenter
Sunny 'Golden Arm' Sandhu
Bobby 'Mohali Missile' Vrik
Aiden Naude
and
Harry and Lisa Thompson